The Goba
of the
Zambezi

University of
Oklahoma
Press:
Norman

The Goba of the Zambezi

Sex Roles,
Economics,
and Change

by
Chet S. Lancaster

Library of Congress Cataloging in Publication Data

Lancaster, Chet S   1932–
   The Goba of the Zambezi.

   Bibliography: p. 333
   Includes index.
   1. Gova (Shona-speaking people)
   2. Matriarchy. I. Title.
DT963.42.L36   968.9   80–24220

Contents

Illustrations

Maps and Figures

Tables

Preface

This book fills an important ethnographic gap in the cultural anthropology of sub-Saharan Africa. This record of the Zambezi Goba is the first full account of a relatively remote, reasonably intact group of the historically important Shona-speaking peoples centered in present-day Zimbabwe-Rhodesia. As this book goes to press, the region is still the scene of prolonged guerrilla fighting and political unrest.

The Zimbabwe people of the fourteenth to sixteenth centuries possessed the most powerful political system in all of Bantu Africa. In the fifteenth century the center of power shifted to the floor of the rugged, isolated Middle Zambezi Valley. Earlier anthropological studies have focused on highland groups more acculturated to the European presence. This book is the first attempt to portray the traditional history, political organization, social life, and subsistence activities of a remote group in the middle Zambezi Valley, a group that still exhibits connections to its rich past. Important new perspectives emerge on the sociopolitical and subsistence adaptations of these people. The record is particularly valuable now that most of the Goba's ancient Zambezi Valley homeland has been destroyed by major hydroelectric projects at the Cabora Bassa Rapids in Mozambique and the Kariba Gorge on the border of Zambia and Zimbabwe-Rhodesia, which have created large man-made lakes, flooded the best lands, upset flood-farming techniques, and rendered countless thousands of people homeless and forever unable to return to their former way of life.

When the early Portuguese attempted to dislodge Swahili coast traders from the fabled medieval gold trade of Zimbabwe, their valuable reports describing the middle Zambezi Valley Goba of the Mwene Mutapa Confederacy made known a people unique for the formal authority, rather than mere influence, exercised by high-ranking women. Similar female authority patterns were observed during my period of field research from 1967 to 1969. I believe that it is fair to say that this book comes closer to a firsthand description of a matriarchal system than any other study carried out to date under modern research techniques. Matriarchy was a favorite early stage in the fanciful "evolutionary" systems imagined by nineteenth-century theorists interested in social change and development. Modern cultural and social anthropology, however, has denied such a possibility for women, as illustrated in Fox's study of kinship and marriage (1967) and Schlegel's study of authority in matrilineal social systems (1972). It is my hope that this report of a field study planned and carried out well before current feminist interests in anthropology will help open fresh lines of inquiry in the traditionally male-biased study of kinship and social organization.

It is well known that nineteenth-century theorists linked matriarchy with female control of early kitchen gardening— incipient agriculture, or horticulture, as it has often been called. It would be unpardonable in modern times to discover a surprisingly matriarchal village system without carefully looking for its causes and analyzing the agricultural system just as carefully, especially if it is obviously woman-centered. I believe that this book contains the most thoroughly documented study available of woman-centered shifting cultivation and its connection to sociopolitical life, including material that ecological specialists often document less fully if at all: calculation of man-land ratios; work patterns and labor inputs; per capita acreages and yields; consumption patterns; and marketing. This kind of original low-input organic farming was once worldwide. Precisely this kind of farming has supported Bantu peoples in subequatorial Africa since 300 B.C. In view of the declining returns being experienced in modern mechanized agribusiness, the worldwide energy shortage, and the sharply increasing food needs of developing nations everywhere, it is important to understand the advantages and limits of this kind of farming. Too much Western-inspired thinking still disparages "native" agriculture; too little has been done to improve it by providing appropriate technology for the people.

If it is a mistake to ignore the ethnography of subsistence life, it is also amiss to ignore twentieth-century developments in the cash economy, political organization, and court system that enhance the positions of husbands and fathers as against the rights of wives and mothers. In a classic 1950 paper Audrey Richards showed how changing fortunes in the eternal battle of the sexes lay at the heart of variations in social organization in the famous central African matrilineal belt. The last parts of this book document the rise of the local cash economy and social changes that undermine the role of Goba women, who, when I left the field, were in danger of falling behind their men in the battle of the sexes that has long determined the pattern of social organization on Africa's savannas. Among Goba north of the Zambezi in Zambia, who have been separated by artificial political boundaries from the main body of Shona-speaking peoples on the south, these twentieth-century changes have been accompanied by a change in ethnic identity as they assimilate with their geographic neighbors, the Tonga.

Zambia and Zimbabwe-Rhodesia were sister British colonies known as Northern and Southern Rhodesia until Zambian independence was finally won in 1964. Southern Rhodesia unilaterally declared its own independence the following year, without making concessions to the vast African majority within its borders. Difficulties arising from that policy made it impossible for me to engage in prolonged work south of the Zambezi during my field study from March, 1967, to March, 1969. My entry to central Africa was through the auspices of the Zambian government, and Zambia did not encourage frequent trips to the south for economic and political reasons. South-bank Goba populations had been resettled in any case, and the sites I would have chosen to visit were already engulfed in guerrilla warfare by 1966. Two Goba populations straddling the Zambezi-Kafue confluence under Chiefs Sikaongo and Chiava were in Zambia, however, and these were my targets from the beginning. Because my anthropologist wife, Jane Lancaster, and my four-year-old son, Thomas, were with me, I chose the westernmost group as my main area of study after a general reconnaissance and thereafter made only day trips across the Kafue to draw comparisons and check for variations in important topics as the work unfolded. Chiava chiefdom on the east was less acculturated and thus more appealing, but there was no reliably passable road in case of family illness, and guerrilla activity against the white settlers in the south prompted the police to warn us away from the area.

The western group, known as the Banamainga, in the territory of Namainga under Chief Sikaongo occupied an area of 535 square miles. I made an initial survey of the entire area on the valley floor, visiting all the villages. I found them on the fine

1:50,000–scale maps available from the government printer and checked them against aerial photographs to note settlement and land-use patterns. Because the Banamainga were a homogeneous Goba population speaking a northern Shona dialect and not a heterogeneous mixture as I had expected, I spent my two years in a single central location. This was the Njami District, the capital of Namainga where the chief had his seat and much the largest population was gathered. Political, social, and religious activities centering on the chief and his counselors, together with a number of attractions—the government courthouse, an agricultural demonstrator, a grade school, several dry-goods stores, and a commercial beer hall—drew people from all corners of the territory and brought them into my area of study. We spent the first four months in a strategically located tent, and then, when it was clear that we were harmless and useful, we accepted an invitation to build an adobe hut in the center of a large village close to the chief's own village.

Participant observation is the social-cultural anthropologist's main stock in trade in the field. After the initial surveys this activity took me in widening circles from scene to scene, family to family, and village to village as I followed groups of friends through their normal repertory of activities as unobtrusively as possible in such a situation. Social events, curing dances, spirit offerings, coming-of-age ceremonies, death mournings, succession ceremonies, beer "drinks," serious village council meetings of various kinds, quarrels, court cases, and trips to stores, distant towns, jobs, clinics, and friends took me almost everywhere except the small neighborhood of Ibwe Munyama, high in the escarpment hills overlooking the valley. When nothing exceptional was happening, I augmented this peripatetic kind of general participant observation with tactics aimed at specific points of inquiry rather than general background. I appeared at court cases or sent an assistant; mapped and collected genealogies in a selected sample of nine settlements; ran partial studies in many others; measured fields, gardens, and granaries; checked store inventories; elicited oral traditions; visited historic sites; and asked questions as my program of research dictated. Once the people in my village were convinced that I was determined to understand their history, social and political system, family relations, and economy, they held Friday-evening review sessions for me at my hut, drinking and nibbling whatever European delicacies I could offer from my monthly supply runs to town. Passersby were welcome too. We went over what I had tried to learn that week. The sessions were always instructive to me and kept the people informed of my motives and activities.

This activity was augmented by two additional techniques. I used a comprehensive individual census form developed by highly experienced Rhodes-Livingstone Institute anthropologists (Colson 1967). Filling out this form carefully in informal interview sessions gave me more or less complete personal information on 161 men and 80 women, as well as information on their descent-group leaders, parents, siblings, spouses, children, and villages. To this information I added a large number of categories especially relevant to my particular interests.

Everything—all my notes from seemingly casual participant observation, deliberate questioning, census data, maps, sketches, village layouts, genealogies, diagrams of seating arrangements, measurements, and so on—was edited, checked, and typed onto blank 10½-by-8-inch edge-sort analysis cards, as suggested by Mitchell (1967). The cards can be coded and cross-coded for quick retrieval of almost anything desired. The things one needs to know are not always immediately apparent. As clues and new information emerge about the career of a village, variations in behavior throughout the annual cycle, the career of a particular dynastic title, inheritance practices, descent-group organization, variations on an oral tradition, the manner in which certain kin terms are used, or the activities of a particular person at different times and places, edge-sort cards offer two great advantages. The first is that the researcher can repair to his hut, say, once a week, after everyone is asleep, and run a needle through the stacked cards to review quickly everything recorded on the topic. Inconsistencies, patterns, and gaps are quickly detected. And when a topic is exhausted and a test sample is large enough, he can move to other tasks quickly and safely. The number of possible analytic categories he can handle is large. Anyone who has filed even a year's worth of notes in an index file under a necessarily limited number of categories knows how time-consuming it is to search for elusive bits of information. Expensive field time should not be wasted that way. The second advantage is that confidence in that data-retrieval system encourages the recording of more information, particularly prices, measurements, statistics, odd bits of this and that, and variations that a first-time field worker cannot afford to ignore, especially one whose language skills are limited.

At the beginning of the field project, while surveying, mapping, and concentrating on census work, I spoke through two local interpreters who had good-to-excellent command of English, working with one in the morning and the other after lunch. After about a year I could complete a census alone, but I always found it useful to have an interpreter available when difficulty arose.

Many good friends have helped me develop my thinking and conduct my work. Sherry Washburn, the late Ted McCown, Phyllis Dolhinow, and Irv DeVore, who were on the staff, and Ted Grand, the late Judy Shirek-Ellefson, John Ellefson, Richard Lee, and my wife, Jane Lancaster, who were then graduate students, were the encouraging people whose exciting ideas and careers drew me into graduate work in anthropology at the University of California at Berkeley. Gerry Berreman and John Rowe, along with McCown and Washburn, eventually sponsored me for the National Institutes of Mental Health predoctoral fellowship (number 5 FO1 MH28688–05), which helped me through the graduate years, along with some part-time work, family donations, and a hard-working wife. Nelson Graburn, Gerry Berreman, James Anderson, Laura Nader, Carl Rosberg, Martin Klein, George Dalton, and many others on the faculty, in the office, libraries, and Gifford Room helped me as I went along. Virginia Raphel and Gerry Moos must be singled out for special praise. Near the end of my graduate course work Elizabeth Colson patiently introduced me to African studies in the Manchester tradition. When I asked her for an optimally exciting field site where I could try to build on the work of others and work with history, social change, and economic development, she told me about the Goba and sponsored my National Institutes of Mental Health predoctoral supplements for language study at Berkeley and a two-year trip to Zambia. Ted Scudder, who had already spent two years among the neighboring Valley Tonga on the Zambezi, also helped me plan the field work and, like Professor Colson, generously made his field notes available. Desmond and Betty Clark, whose experience already included twenty-five years in Africa, mostly in Zambia, also kindly helped me prepare for this exciting experience.

Once I was in Africa, Scudder visited me twice, and his help has been important, as is attested to by my frequent references to his work. I am also gratefully indebted to the Office of President of the Republic of Zambia and the Institute for Social Research in the University of Zambia, formerly the Rhodes-Livingstone Institute, which cleared my project for a visa. The institute let me use its guest house, Africana library, and field gear and gave my family a place to stay whenever we spent the night in Lusaka, the capital of Zambia. Jaap and Ruth van Velsen gave us hospitality while my wife recovered from a serious automobile accident. Ronald Frankenberg, Dorothea Lehman, Norman Long, Jan and Eva Deregowski, Harry Langworthy, and Robin Fielder were good friends at the institute. The staff members of the National Archives in Lusaka also made their valuable services available, and I thank them too.

Down in the Zambezi Valley itself, Chief Chali Sikaongo of the Banamainga was a friend, guide, and companion until his death in October, 1968. Special thanks must also go to Chief Chiava, John Chadukwa, Melek Katobolo, Smart Makumbiro, Johnny Mwanja, Amos Mweemba, and White Manyama and his late wife, Noria. The late Ngoro Nyambekhwa and Siayumbu Mututa were two of my closest friends. I must also thank my research staff, who never failed me when I needed them: Timothy Hakalle, Penias Chirimbwa, Anderson Mukuna, Alec Kanyungu, Langson Dzikamunenga, Anderson Nyambekhwa, Masoondo Siachifupa, Mangras Makosa, Christof Luwaili, Kapaso Limbembe, Peirson Madzongwe, and Tommy Lancaster. Both Jane and Tommy provided perspectives and data I would never have thought of, and their many friends helped make our house a popular one.

The Reverend McCarthy of the Catholic Mission at Chirundu always helped us in times of trouble, as did the kindly sisters and the Reverend Emilio. Thanks must also go to Mr. Mazeko, the assistant district secretary at Siavonga; Lance Gardener, for rest and recuperation at Siavonga; the Vlahakis family; all the local government and United National Independence Party people at Chirundu, Lusitu, and Siavonga townships; and all the schoolteachers, local police, and storekeepers who helped. We might not have survived had not Frank Buckingham of the Zambia Mobile Police Unit saved us from trouble with the Zimbabwe Freedom Fighters as he patrolled the Zambia border and found us there, unaware of the situation. Both in the valley and on the Zambian plateau Brian Fagan, David Phillipson, Laurel Lofgren Phillipson, and Joseph Vogel gave us hospitality, nursed us through *bilharzia*, and stimulated my research through their interest in local history and archaeology.

CHET S. LANCASTER

Norman, Oklahoma

The Goba
of the
Zambezi

1
The Goba: A Historical Introduction

The prehistoric origins and spread of farming peoples in the region with which this book is concerned are still the subject of important scholarly research and debate. The same is true of the more recent origins and migrations of ethnic groups or "tribes" in the ethnographic records compiled by anthropologists. The records on many large areas about which we need to know a great deal are totally blank. Others are known only at certain time periods. Only a tentative outline can be suggested here. It is only fair to warn the reader that to provide even that I will have to use broad strokes and consider developments throughout very large portions of sub-Saharan Africa. That should satisfy the introductory needs of this chapter nicely enough, but it cannot eliminate the likelihood that the picture presented below will seem outdated ten years from now as fresh information and new interpretations continue to appear.

The Early Iron Age

From about 300 B.C. to A.D. 600 a major change took place throughout central and southern Africa in the region lying roughly between the equator and the Vaal River in what is today the Republic of South Africa. This change was marked by the appearance of a characteristic type of pottery that seems to belong to a single great stylistic tradition, though regional variations are readily apparent to specialists. The pottery is found in association with evidence for the working of metal: iron and in some places copper. This is the earliest known evidence of metallurgy in subequatorial Africa, and the cultural complex to which the pottery and other artifacts belong is known as the Early Iron Age (Phillipson 1968; Huffman 1970, 1971; Soper 1971).

3

The Early Iron Age peoples were settled village dwellers who practiced a mixed farming economy, including both crop raising and animal husbandry. In east Africa, in the Great Rift Valley and adjacent highlands of northern Tanzania and southern Kenya, roughly similar communities were established at least as early as 1000 B.C. They had apparently derived from an even earlier food-producing economy that had become established by the second millennium B.C. at the latest, throughout most of the Sudanic belt, the broad savanna region stretching across Africa between the southern fringes of the Sahara and the northern limits of the equatorial rain forest. Most of the cereal grains later cultivated by Early Iron Age farmers south of the rain forest were species known and perhaps originally domesticated in this vast Sudanic belt, including the sorghum that today is still very important to the Goba. The animals that accompanied Early Iron Age farmers—goats, sheep, and cattle—although not originally domesticated in the region, were in all probability herded there two thousand years before the Christian Era. In addition, the two best-known early centers of ironworking in sub-Saharan Africa are Nok, in Nigeria, and Meroë, in Nubia. Both are adjacent to the great east–west Sudanic belt, and knowledge of metallurgy doubtless diffused very rapidly throughout the region, though the direction of diffusion remains uncertain.

South of this early east African complex derived from the northern savannas of the Sudan, on the southern savannas that concern us more directly, it appears that Early Iron Age food-production techniques were introduced to a vast region where the indigenous population lived almost exclusively by hunting and gathering. Many aspects of Early Iron Age culture therefore represented major innovations on the plains south of the rain forest, and the culture was introduced in full-fledged form almost everywhere. Earlier, ancestral forms of pottery have yet to be found in the region, with the possible exception of the extreme south. Metallurgy also appears for the first time, and in an efficient, fully developed form. The domesticated animals and several of the domesticated plants were species unknown in subequatorial Africa even in wild forms. And the most striking contrast to earlier Stone Age sites is in the size of settlements. Early Iron Age villages often extended over an acre or more. Abandoned deposits tend to show several inches of darker midden soil, containing potsherds, bone fragments, and traces of houses. From the beginning, houses resembled those of modern rural Africans, with hardened floors, walls of upright poles or slender logs covered with clay, and thatched roofs. It is from the size and siting of these villages and towns that the practice of agriculture can most often be safely inferred, rather than from carbonized seed or surviving tools. The population of these settlements could not have been fed any other way. The siting of settlements usually reflects skillful selection of favorable soils. This Early Iron Age culture evidently was introduced by means of a rapid and coherent movement of people who brought a full-fledged life-style that had undergone its formative processes elsewhere (Phillipson 1978).

The Late Stone Age Hunter-Gatherers

It is difficult to assess the scale of human migration involved in this dispersal of Early Iron Age culture to the plains south of the equatorial rain forest. The people probably came in sufficient numbers to support a technology that was largely independent of the stone-tool-using culture of the previous inhabitants. In fact, in some areas descendants of the older population continued a hunting-gathering way of life into the nineteenth and twentieth centuries.

Human remains are sparse but consistent in showing that almost all the Late Stone Age peoples south of the equator were of Khoisan type while the new people coming from the north were of Bantu type. The Khoisan type was yellowish rather than black in complexion. The hair grew in separate whorls rather than as a woolly mat. The skull was broad at the forehead and narrow at the jaw. Modern representatives of the group are short, though archaeology shows that in former times the stock was taller. Dwarfing changes began about ten thousand years ago, though larger individuals occur in sites from periods as recent as the third and second millennia B.C.

On the eve of the Early Iron Age south of the equator, most of the subcontinent was still inhabited by Khoisan types practicing what is known as a Late Stone Age subsistence stance, hunting and gathering their food rather than producing it. Toward the end of the Late Stone Age, almost certainly within the first millennium B.C., in a few areas subequatorial Stone Age peoples apparently became farmers, but these late developments affected only the moist southern fringes of the Congo forests. In at least three-quarters of the subcontinent the people continued to live by hunting and gathering.

The reason for this apparent conservatism south of the rain forest may be that the climatic changes that were so severe in Saharan latitudes were more marginal in their effects. The climate began to become markedly drier from about 2500 B.C. onward. The change was most critical in areas already tending to aridity, which here ran not in a lateral zone corresponding to the Sahara and Sudan but in a diagonal line from northeast to southwest, from the deserts of Somalia and northeastern Kenya, across central Tanzania and Zambia to the Kalahari and Namib deserts of Botswana and Namibia.

It was only at the extreme ends of the drier zone that any substantial areas became uninhabitable. Rather than turning to agriculture hunting-gathering peoples were evidently able to survive in this region by adapting to larger territories with sparser food resources and by taking up smaller and lighter tools and weapons. Their microlithic Late Stone Age tool and weapon industries show a general similarity all the way down the eastern side of Africa from Ethiopia to the Cape of Good Hope, and are collectively known as Wilton, after a rock shelter in South Africa where such implements were first found.

All indications are that most of the Wilton toolmakers were of Khoisan stock. Small remnants of these peoples survive today in the southwest corner of Africa, speaking very distinctive clicking languages call Khoikhoi (Hottentot) and San (Bushman) or, collectively, Khoisan. Khoisan skeletal remains have been recovered by archaeologists from all over the Republic of South Africa, Namibia, Botswana, Zimbabwe-Rhodesia, Zambia, Tanzania, Uganda, the southern Sudan, Somalia, and Ethiopia.

Throughout much of this region a common tradition of rock art depicts a common mode of Late Stone Age existence. The hunter-gatherers of the savanna regions of eastern and southern Africa could draw their meat supplies from a rich and varied fauna. In more thickly wooded areas they clearly placed more emphasis on food-gathering. Those who lived nearer the southern edges of the rain forest appear to have practiced simple vegecultural techniques, even if they did not grow vegetable foods deliberately (Hiernaux 1974; Oliver and Fagan 1975).

The Bantu Expansion

Recent research has defined two major Early Iron Age traditions in subequatorial Africa. As of this writing, these traditions have been provisionally termed the "eastern stream" and the "western stream." In this brief review I will refer mainly to the eastern stream. Archaeological sites attributed to the eastern stream are found mainly in the coastal hinterlands of east Africa, which is to say Kenya and Tanzania, and farther south in Malawi, eastern and southern Zambia, most of Zimbabwe-Rhodesia, and in the Transvaal, Natal, and Swaziland. The eastern stream is distinct from the western in pottery style, economic practices, relative chronology, and geography (Phillipson 1978).

The two-stream phenomenon is most clearly recognized in the southward spread of Early Iron Age culture from an important early settlement area in the Great Lakes region of east Africa, where its earliest known manifestations are characterized by a pottery known as Urewe ware. The producers of this pottery were probably settled around the western and southern shores of Lake Victoria by 500 B.C. The eastern stream is clearly derived from these Great Lakes Urewe settlements. The western stream may be derived from them or share an earlier common ancestry. The eastern stream reached the coastal hinterland of southern Kenya, adjacent parts of Tanzania, and perhaps Somalia in about the second century A.D. Between A.D. 300 and 400 there was a rapid movement of Early Iron Age culture southward through Malawi and eastern Zambia to Zimbabwe-Rhodesia and on into the Transvaal and Swaziland. This well-documented process apparently took place with amazing speed. The Early Iron Age south of the Limpopo River started about A.D. 400.

In contrast to the Khoisan-speaking hunter-gatherers of the Late Stone Age south of the rain forest, the bearers of the new Early Iron Age culture spoke Bantu languages and dialects, and their migrations have been known as the "Bantu expansion." Evidence in favor of a linkage between the spread of Early Iron Age culture and the dispersal of Negro populations speaking Bantu languages is almost entirely circumstantial and convincing. Regions occupied by Bantu speakers today are those where evidence of Early Iron Age settlement is found. Earlier archaeological horizons in these areas rarely show adoption of an Iron Age culture. There is a close linguistic similarity between the Bantu dialects now spread so widely throughout subequatorial Africa; this similarity suggests derivation from a common ancestral tongue within relatively recent times. A correspondingly brief history and common ancestry are attributed to Early Iron Age culture on archaeological grounds. A final piece of circumstantial evidence comes from linguistic reconstruction of proto-Bantu languages, and this work generally supports the theory that a Bantu-speaking expansion of Negro peoples was indeed responsible for the dispersal of Early Iron Age culture throughout Africa south of the equator (Hiernaux 1974; Phillipson 1975, 1978; Oliver and Fagan 1975).

The Zimbabwe Culture and the Later Iron Age

It was only in the 1960s that Iron Age sites in Zimbabwe-Rhodesia were first explored systematically and subjected to radiocarbon dating. The information that emerged revealed a widespread Early Iron Age culture belonging to the eastern stream of the Bantu expansion, with a time span from the second or third century A.D. until the ninth. The newcomers were probably few, and during the period agriculture and stock raising gradually superseded the hunting-gathering way of life.

Then in the tenth and eleventh centuries there was a rapid eclipse of Early Iron Age culture over almost all of the eastern half of subequatorial Africa. Nearly all the later Iron Age pottery traditions appear to be markedly distinct from those of the preceding era (Sutton 1972). This sharp discontinuity has been particularly well documented in Zambia, where it has been attributed "to the arrival of a new population element ancestral to most of the peoples who inhabit northern and eastern Zambia today." There is a precisely similar break in Malawi and Zimbabwe-Rhodesia (Phillipson 1974; Garlake 1973). Although the evidence is incomplete, a comparable sequence seems to be emerging for areas farther south. The spread of the Later Iron Age, brought from the north by a second wave of Bantu-speaking migrants, seems to have taken place with a rapidity at least comparable with that of the Early Iron Age itself (Phillipson 1975).

Around the tenth century more specialized pastoralism seems to have spread across central Zambia and down both sides of the Kalahari Desert. At the same time in eastern Zambia and Zimbabwe-Rhodesia a growing population lived in greater concentrations and engaged in more extensive exploitation of copper, gold, and other natural resources than did the Early Iron Age people who preceded them. The main developments in south-central Africa at this time, in the area between the Congo-Zambezi watershed and the Limpopo, took place on the western part of the Zimbabwe-Rhodesia plateau, where a culture known as Leopard's Kopje II developed. It was characterized by walled villages, the earliest dated mining shafts, and evidence of international contacts in the form of glass beads typical of Indian Ocean trade routes.

Sometime around the twelfth or thirteenth century, simultaneous with the rise of stone-built Arab-Swahili settlements on the Kenya and Tanzania coast, the archaeological horizons of the Zimbabwe culture show a great enrichment in material wealth. Known as Zimbabwe III, this period saw the emergence of radically new architectural styles that included more substantial sleeping huts with larger dimensions and thicker walls. The people began using stone for platforms, enclosures, and free-standing walls to encircle and divide living quarters, just as reed fences serve elsewhere in Bantu Africa. While basically continuous with earlier horizons, the material culture of Zimbabwe III shows a general enrichment in numbers of metal objects and imported glass beads. One major innovation is spindle whorls, indicating the presence of a weaving industry.

It is clear that period III at Zimbabwe reflects commerce based on the export of gold and ivory to the Indian Ocean markets of the medieval world. It is interesting that in Marco Polo's time thirteenth-century east Africa was known as Middle India (Skelton 1958). The political and religious center of the culture was evidently the site known as Great Zimbabwe, and in period IV, dating perhaps from the fourteenth to the mid-fifteenth century, the culture reached its height in wealth and power. This stage shows a new and much superior style of masonry, with dressed stones and regular coursing, epitomized in the royal palace with its conical tower and great girdle wall more than thirty feet high (Garlake 1973). This period saw the arrival of nearly all the valuable foreign imports of Chinese porcelain. Imported glass beads became common, and luxuries of African manufacture became apparent in gold and copper ornaments and jewelry.

The wealth exported from precolonial Zimbabwe-Rhodesia is best indicated by the ancient workings scattered thickly over the gold-bearing areas of the granitic plateau. Miners usually worked open pits, exploiting the many surface outcrops and following the reefs underground to considerable depths. In places these open shafts were up to a thousand feet long and two hundred feet wide. Underground mines were also dug. Roger Summers, who collected evidence of more than three thousand ancient workings, estimates that between twenty and twenty-five million fine ounces of gold were extracted, mainly in medieval times (Summers 1969). During the early colonial period the Ancient Ruins Company was formed to rifle the stone buildings dotting the Zimbabwe highlands, and great quantities of golden objects are known to have been taken. The two richest sites excavated scientifically in more recent times are at Mapungubwe, in the Limpopo Valley, and at Ingombe Ilede, in the Zambezi Valley. The latter lies beside the precolonial capitol of the people to be described in this book. At both places impressive quantities of gold ornaments were found in the graves of a few important individuals who lived during the fourteenth and fifteenth centuries.

Great Zimbabwe was probably abandoned around 1450. By the time the Portuguese arrived on the scene around 1500 to sack the Arab-Swahili cities along the east coast and capture the much-fabled gold trade for themselves, the center of political power was situated three hundred miles on the north at the edge of the Zimbabwe plateau overlooking the Zambezi Valley. According to traditions collected by the early Portuguese, the new center had been there for two generations. The "empire" they described extended from the Zambezi to the Limpopo and from the Indian Ocean to the Kalahari. Its social and political organization was typically African. The king, known as the *mwene mutapa*, was a divine king. Women played an unusually important role, and the king was supported by a queen sister and queen mother, who completed the trio of high royalty. Eight other titled "great" wives had their own compounds, or apartments, within the palace complex, which housed about three thousand lesser wives, women-in-waiting, and page boys. The *mwene mutapa's* capitol, or *zimbabwe*, included titled officers of the king's court and representatives of tributary kings and provincial chiefs. The main symbol of authority was the royal fire, from which burning brands were taken once a year to rekindle the fires of subordinate leaders. Once a year, before the annual rains, the king visited the royal graves, where a spirit medium would become possessed by the spirit of the king's father, imitating the late king's speech and mannerisms. Except on ceremonial occasions, the king was seldom seen in public; within his compound he was approached crawling, a tribute still rendered to Goba chiefs, and his person was usually concealed behind a curtain. Until its eventual decline under Portuguese contact, the *mwene mutapa* was probably the most powerful ruler in all Bantu Africa, just as his predecessors at Great Zimbabwe had been uniquely preeminent in the fourteenth and fifteenth centuries (Oliver and Fagan 1975).

The Zambezi Goba of chiGoba (or chiCova)

Like all the other Bantu-speaking peoples of present-day Zimbabwe-Rhodesia, the Goba speak a dialect of the Shona language group. This is a major group of Bantu languages closely related to those spoken by kindred African peoples south of the Zambezi. It is also the language of the ancestral later Iron Age peoples of Zimbabwe.

The name Goba has been a locational term of reference for those living in relatively low lying areas. The name is known to have been applied to various groups scattered throughout the Shona-speaking world once allegedly controlled from Great Zimbabwe. They include groups in lowland southern Mozambique, the Limpopo Valley, the lowlands of Lake Ngami, the Makarikari depression, and the Caprivi strip west of the Zimbabwe highlands, and the Zambezi lowlands southeast of Victoria Falls. In addition to groups on the edges of the Zimbabwe plateau, the name has been applied to highland groups occupying comparatively low lying areas, such as the Goba of the upper Mazoe Valley south of Mount Darwin and the Goba south of Gwelo (Lancaster 1974b). This locational term of reference has probably never been exclusively attached to a specific ethnic group, "tribe," or political unit in the history of the Shona-speaking peoples. Nonetheless it is the name commonly used by the group I lived with and describe in this book. Their home on the floor of the great Zambezi Valley is a well-known major landmark to all those who live on the neighboring high plains of the interior. A section of this valley roughly three hundred miles long has traditionally been known as chiGoba or chiCova, depending on local variations. The name literally means "place of the Goba," and in their thinking it also refers to their very cultural essence, their customs, language, and spirit as a people. This portion of the valley extends roughly from the mouth of the Sanyati River tributary near the Kariba Gorge downstream to the Cabora Bassa Rapids above the old Portuguese town Tete, which stands at the head of the lower Zambezi Valley in former Portuguese East Africa.

This section of the valley was especially well known to the Portuguese almost from the beginning of their quest to control the gold flowing from Zimbabwe, which they learned about from the Arabs and which they romantically associated with Ophir, the queen of Sheba, and King Solomon's mines. The impressive chain of Arab-Swahili city-states on the east African coast, which the Portuguese unexpectedly "discovered" after their heroic rounding of the Cape of Good Hope, had been founded as trade depots based on the gold of Zimbabwe. After attempting to destroy these settlements, the Portuguese, like the Arabs before them, were drawn to chiGoba in their attempts to find and come to terms with the fabled ruler of the mineral-rich highland interior occupied by the Shona-speaking peoples of Zimbabwe.

A comprehensive historical account of this culture as the early Portuguese saw it is yet to be written in English, though Axelson (1960) and Garlake (1973) have provided a great deal of interesting information, and many Portuguese works can be consulted (Barros 1552; Santos 1609; Barreto 1667; Faria y Sousa 1674; Boccaro 1876). Though others were sent on intelligence missions, the first Portuguese to journey to the far interior, in 1514–15, and return with news of the great leader in the interior was Antonio Fernandes, a prisoner, or *degredado*, from the mother country (Gomes 1644). The leader he visited was the *mwene mutapa*, who divided his time between the highlands overlooking the Zambezi Valley, where he could graze his large cattle herds, and the floor of the valley at the foot of the steep escarpment, where year-round springs and streams permitted permanent rather than shifting cultivation. The *mwene mutapa* soon lost political control of his mineral-rich highland territories. But in the seventeenth century his seat in chiGoba continued to attract Portuguese officials, missionaries, and adventurers, and the *mwene mutapa* and his successors used the Portuguese to their political and military advantage whenever they could in frequent civil wars.

One reason for the continued Portuguese interest was their zeal to find incredibly rich silver mines that they were led to believe existed on the valley floor a short distance above the Cabora Bassa Rapids. This area remained within the *mwene mutapa's* shrinking sphere of influence, and the Portuguese eventually built a fort near the alleged mines, thinking, as they still do, that chiGoba was a specific place rather than a large geographical region. There can be no doubt that silver mines existed. Pure chunks of silver weighing as much as six hundred pounds were produced from the mines, and some were actually shipped to Lisbon for analysis. It is unlikely from a geological point of view that hard-rock silver or gold mines could exist on the valley floor, and despite enormous efforts the mines have never been found (see Guerreiro 1944 for the fullest account available). It seems likely that the mines would have been on the mineralized highlands rather than the valley floor, and according to one early report the silver mines were on the Urungwe highlands across the Zambezi from my field site, though more than one silver mine may have existed (Lancaster and Pohorilenko 1977, pp. 8–10).

Before 1967 none of the Goba peoples on the floor of the middle Zambezi Valley had been the subject of a full-scale ethnographic study. For reasons discussed in the Preface, I concentrated my field research on a single group, the Banamainga, who have inhabited the territory they know as Namainga since well before the recent colonial era. Unlike many other current hereditary leaders of rural African populations whose line began by colonial appointment, the Banamainga chief I knew in the years 1967 to 1969 was a successor in a long line of indigenous kings occupying roughly the same territory. This territory lies on the left, or north, bank of the Zambezi above its confluence with the Kafue River (see fig. 1). It seems appropriate to conclude this historical introduction with a brief review of the oral traditions describing the founding of the Banamainga kingdom. Experience has led me to believe that other middle Zambezi Valley Goba groups have shared roughly similar backgrounds featuring northward migration from politically and economically important territories on the Zimbabwe highlands.

The Founding of the Banamainga Kingdom

The first inhabitants are said to have been small-statured hunter-gatherers who roamed widely and had no fields or villages. Similar tales are common throughout the region, and Khoisan peoples may well have been encountered by early Bantu migrants to the area (Clark 1950; Lancaster and Pohorilenko 1977, pp. 19–23). Some traditions suggest that the hunters were killed off or chased away, though most imply voluntary withdrawal to less-well-inhabited areas of the valley. Study of genetic traits of the blood suggests substantial assimilation (Hiernaux 1974, pp. 108–109) but local traditions give no hint that the Khoisan comprised a politically important element to be absorbed and given a role in the organization developed by later arrivals.

The first significant populations are said to have been Shona-speaking farming people known as Tonga, or rebels against Shona kings who "crossed long ago from wars and troubles with Mambo" in the southwesterly portion of the Zimbabwe highlands. The original Banamainga were Tonga who came as part of this earliest-remembered influx from the south. While small numbers of Tonga immigrants continued to move out of the south, the Banamainga stress the difference between early arrivals who crossed the Zambezi from wars with *mambo*, the Shona word for "king," or "paramount," and those who mostly came "much later" from more easterly directions dominated by the Korekore. The Korekore group is today the major northern division of the Shona-speaking peoples. The original Korekore have been identified as a band of invaders from the south who entered the middle Zambezi Valley in the mid-fifteenth century and established the Mwene Mutapa Confederacy

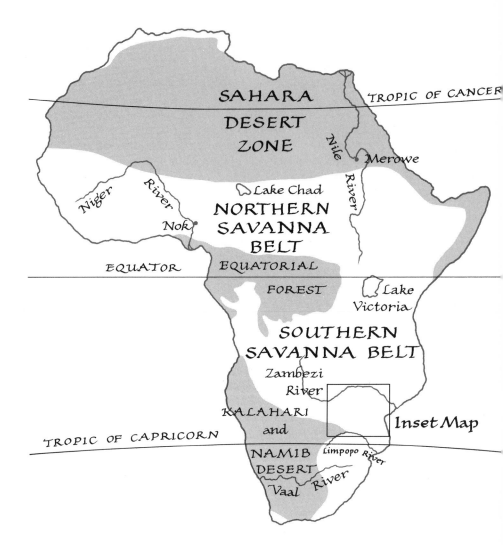

Fig. 1. The Goba Area in Africa. Inset map on opposite page.

(Abraham 1962; Garbett 1966). Like the southerners, these east-erners came in small groups over long periods of time and were associated with trade and political problems south of the Zambezi. Though they came from Korekore country, they too were Tonga, rebels against Shona kings.

These movements from the south and east may have started as early as the fifteenth century, after the fall of Great Zimbabwe. Oral traditions make it appear that small groups continued arriving in later times, and it is known that population dislocations to the south and east were caused by civil wars and Portuguese activities in the sixteenth to early eighteenth centuries, Ngoni and Matabele migrations and raids in the nineteenth century, the closing stages of the Portuguese-English scramble for colonial territories in the later nineteenth century, the Matabele War, the Shona Uprising of 1896, the imposition of colonial head taxes in 1898, and the revolt in Portuguese East Africa in 1917 (Lancaster 1974b). In fact, migrants fleeing from the White Settlers south of the Zambezi were still entering the area during the years 1967 to 1969. This background of migration is reflected in a sample of 209 Banamainga respondents who were asked to name the homeland of their ancestors: 26 percent named more easterly portions of the Zambezi Valley, and 67 percent named areas south of the Zambezi, with 41 percent of the latter from southern portions of the valley and 26 percent from the Zimbabwe highlands. When asked to name still earlier, ultimate ancestral homelands, 60 of the respondents gave the following information: 80 percent named the Zimbabwe highlands and 20 percent named the eastern valley and Mozambique.

Near the confluence of the Zambezi and Kafue rivers, where the Zambezi is said to be easily forded in several places, the Banamainga claim to have been the first of the early Tonga from the south to cross over. In fact, some say that Banamainga means "those who crossed the river or boundary." As the name Tonga implies, they originally came without a king, though many descent-group heads, warrior leaders, and magicians established small followings and land shrines first on the south bank and then, "much later," on the north.

As groups continued crossing over and filling the land, some Tonga finally spilled over onto the northern highlands east and west of the Kafue River and settled in the present homelands of the Soli Manyika and Plateau Tonga. The crowded valley floor nearer the fording places became a place of warring as new groups arrived and competing strong men "tried to build ladders to the sky" in various parts of the country to establish their fame. Then Kasamba, a powerful woman shaman, was called back from Soli Manyika to unite the Banamainga. Any earlier leaders or epochs have been forgotten, and the remembered past begins with her.

Kasamba succeeded in making peace and established herself as the land-shrine medium at Njami Hill, the oldest shrine in the country. It is not known which spirits she served. The Njami people under Kasamba were a mixture of original Banamainga plus some Balumbila (an early name for inhabitants of Plateau Tonga country) who had come back to the valley with her from the northern highlands. This early Njami period of conquest and unified rule is impossible to date. Pottery discovered at the foot of Njami

Hill near a spring and sacred grove has been identified as Dambwa-style Early Iron Age ware introduced from the southern highlands (Phillipson 1968, p. 204; 1975, p. 335). This would suggest a fifth- or sixth-century date, well beyond the possible recall of oral tradition, though at the time the material was found, Phillipson equated it chronologically with Ingombe Ilede pottery, which has subsequently been redated at about 1400 (Phillipson, personal communication; Lancaster and Pohorilenko 1977, p. 15). After her death Kasamba's powerful immigrant spirit became the main land-shrine spirit at Njami Hill. Subsequent rulers have had to have the approval of her *basangu* spirit; it is believed that those who have not won her approval have died.

As fresh refugees continued to fight for a place, some territory was lost, and the Banamainga eventually took up arms to bar further immigration. Many claim that this event rather than the first river crossing is the origin of their collective name and that its essential meaning is "those who bar the way." The increasing need for defense is said to have led to role specialization. Kasamba's shamanistic successors at Njami Hill continued to tend the land shrines and to legitimize succeeding rulers, but a male relative was chosen for the lesser job of enforcing court decisions and conducting military skirmishes. The only male war leader remembered in this line is Ntambo. At a time when some territorial subchiefs had seceded and the country was torn by internal struggles, pressure from immigrants, and the presence of alien trading groups, Ntambo became jealous of his "queen sister" and finally killed her with medicine. He then tried to act as both war leader and shrine priest and moved his capitol closer to the Zambezi. It is impossible to distinguish the real as opposed to legendary situation at this time, or indeed at any other time much before the present, but Ntambo's usurpation is generally taken to have signaled the increasing influence of eastern ethnic and trading groups, particularly the Korekore.

Ntambo's warriors turned increasingly to elephant hunting and ivory trade with the Portuguese, largely through visits by their African agents from the lower Zambezi. The Portuguese called these agents *mussambazes*, and the Banamainga refer to them as Vazambi (Lancaster and Pohorilenko 1977, pp. 23–28). Ntambo's Banamainga headquartered near the Zambezi were well situated to practice fairly large scale flood farming along the lower Lusitu River tributary to supplement their regular cultivation of sorghum. They had large fixed villages swollen by captives and visiting trade groups. But sometime after the split from the old guard at Njami,

Ntambo's followers realized that they had made a mistake, for they had no rain and were forced to seek aid and to come to terms with the Njami shrine people. So the ancestral Banamainga remained "owners of the spirits and the land" and were respected. They lived in smaller settlements and relied mainly on shifting cultivation among the foothills below the northern valley escarpments. The warriors, traders, and foreigners a few miles away near the Zambezi were also respected as "owners of the people" because of their trade goods, Portuguese connections, and military power.

In the era of Ntambo, it is said, the south-bank Korekore kings across from the Banamainga lived along Zambezi tributaries not far upstream from the main river, where the kings had their main towns, armies, trade centers, and land-shrine groves. The senior south-bank king, Nyamhunga and his successors are said to have crowned Banamainga kings for a long time. Nyamhunga is the only king in the immediate area consistently referred to as *mambo*. That may be a practice of some duration; a hand-drawn map attributed to David Livingstone, dated "1855 or 1856" (housed at the Livingstone Museum at Victoria Falls) clearly shows "Mambo" where Nyamhunga's realm is located. The word Banyai, meaning "vassals," is written across the territories of the other south-bank kings in the vicinity. But Nyamhunga's seniority appears to predate Livingstone by a long time. The most powerful land spirit in Nyamhunga's realm was the famous Nyanehwe Matope, nicknamed "Nebedza." He is the spirit the allied Banamainga would turn to in times of severe drought. In life Nyanehwe was the most important son of Mutota, the original *mwene mutapa*. At one time Nyanehwe controlled the Zambezi Valley as far west as the Sanyati River tributary, the western terminus of the chiGoba, and he eventually succeeded his father as *mambo* over the northern Zimbabwe confederacy (Abraham 1962, p. 65). After his death his land spirit was paramount in the region. It seems possible that the remarkably rich trade that flourished at the archeological site known as Ingombe Ilede, and dated about 1400, situated in the traditional Banamainga capitol near the Zambezi, is somehow connected with the era of Ntambo, Nyanehwe, or one of his successors, and the fabled long-distance trade of the *mwene mutapa*'s segmentary state (Fagan 1969, 1972; Lancaster and Pohorilenko 1977).

Eventually the Vazambi traders took control of the Banamainga. Some came to be recognized as territorial subchiefs or petty kings, who are still known as Vazambi. Along the lower Lusitu River tributary to the Zambezi, where particularly good floodland farming helped support the largest population, the strongest became head of a relatively powerful central kingdom, or statelet, surrounded by tributary subkingdoms settled by allied elephant hunters, traders, and raiders. The first *muzambi* to accomplish this kind of trade-oriented centralization backed by local warriors and Portuguese connections was Munenga. In reciting their king list, the Banamainga typically mention Kasamba, Ntambo, Munenga, and so on, as if Munenga had been a direct lineal descendant. But Munenga was a stranger who had previously been active in Plateau Tonga country before becoming king of the Banamainga. We can assume that, like Kasamba and Ntambo, he represents an era rather than an ordinary successor. A typical statement about him is as follows: "When Munenga was king, the land was covered by fallen animals, and there was much wealth. He was a strong man and gave us the law that the ivory belonged to the king. The Portuguese wanted the ivory, and so he made our kingdom strong." Munenga made the Banamainga strong through trade, though his enemies also remembered him as a castrate and a *mwana mambo*, another word for "slave," or an agent of the Portuguese on the east. Succeeding where Ntambo had failed, he established what is still the main land shrine for the territory as a whole, and he appointed a male follower as shaman-priest, leaving Kasamba's followers at Njami to function as keepers of a local shrine.

If the Kasamba founding tradition can be said to represent the fifteenth century, the Ntambo tradition of, perhaps, the sixteenth century marks the time when Banamainga political organization was brought in line with that of related south-bank kingdoms in the Mwene Mutapa Confederacy. The Munenga tradition can perhaps be assigned to the seventeenth or early eighteenth century, an era when frontier Portuguese freebooters, *canarins* or Goanese, and African merchants established private dominions in the Zimbabwe gold fields, raised stockades and armies, and waged fairly constant warfare against each other and against local African groups whom they displaced (Lancaster and Pohorilenko 1977, pp. 23–28).

According to tradition, Sikaongo has been the dynastic title for Banamainga rulers since Munenga's first, or first-remembered, major successor, Sikutangatanga, literally "the first in the line." He was a stranger brought upstream by the Portuguese or Vazambi in a flat-bottomed boat and installed as king. That probably occurred in the nineteenth century. Many subsequent kings were installed the same way, and many, including Sikutangatanga, were eventually driven away by local forces. The last precolonial king of the Banamainga was Sikaongo Ngoma Mwanachangu, who became a great hero. He was brought upstream by the Portuguese and installed in time to lead a successful defense against the last Matabele raid into the area in the 1890s. He lived to a ripe old age, ruling until the 1930s as a salty anti-British figure who led a prolonged taxpayers' revolt and never accepted government famine relief.

Although the original Banamainga were rebels (Tonga) from Shona kings who sought refuge and independence north of the Zambezi, later alliances with Shona kings in the era of Ntambo and his successors made the Banamainga vassals (Banyai) in the Mwene Mutapa's Korekore hierarchy of northern Shona speakers. The people of Namainga were then known as Banyai or Korekore, rather than Tonga. Under the impetus of Portuguese trading interests and Vazambi merchants similar alliances were subsequently formed in the eras of Munenga and Sikutangatanga and their successors. Others who had originally fled north of the Zambezi and retained their independence apparently continued to style themselves Tonga. Because of their long-term contact with northern peoples from the Congo, these Tonga inhabitants of present-day Zambia in many important respects, including language and culture, resemble people of Congolese origin rather than their former Shona-speaking allies (Ohannessian and Kashoki 1978, p. 12). At the start of the colonial era around the turn of the present century, the incumbent Banamainga king became an appointed "government chief" as far as the British were concerned and along with his peers he was forced to serve, most unwillingly, as the bottom rung in the colonial administrative hierarchy. By 1967 when I went to live among the Banamainga, they had come to resemble their Zambian Tonga neighbors in many respects. In Elizabeth Colson's excellent study of the Gwembe, or Valley Tonga, they generally were considered to be Lower River Tonga (Colson 1960).

2

Environment and Population Movements

Africa is the only continent cut almost in half by the equator. The equatorial climate is characterized by heavy rainfall and constantly high temperatures and humidity, corresponding with the distribution of humid closed rain forest. North and south of this equatorial belt a tropical climate extends over a very broad zone (see fig. 1). This zone has a marked dry season during the cooler half of the year, and, in general, the length of the dry winter season increases as one moves away from the equator. Africa's tropical climate corresponds with various forms of savanna vegetation, which cover an enormous area comprising 60 to 80 percent of the continent south of the Sahara. All the savannas are characterized by the dominance of annual grasses, with trees occurring sporadically, either scattered or in clumps in the wetter areas, especially along watercourses. The savanna zone south of the equatorial rain-forest belt, known as the South Central African Zone, is ecologically similar to its northern counterpart, the western and eastern Sudan. These vast southern savannas extend almost to the tip of South Africa in the southeast, and in the northeast they merge with the savannas and grasslands east of the rift-valley systems of East Africa.

Students of Africa usually divide the continent into four main areas: North Africa, including the Sahara; East Africa, lying east of the Great Rift Valley; West Africa, including the equatorial rain forest and the humid Congo Basin; and South (or Southern) Africa. There also exists a more vaguely defined Central section that overlaps the other main divisions. As the foregoing summary of climate and vegetation indicates, Central Africa is largely covered with savanna woodlands and provides a link between the rain forest on the north, the grasslands of the east, and the more varied vegetation patterns farther south (Phillips 1959; Carlson 1967).

All of this vaguely defined central section is part of an extended interior plateau three to six thousand feet in average elevation. Most writers compare it with a huge inverted dish, tilted slightly upward toward the east and south. Except for those of southern Mozambique, the coastal plains forming the rim of the dish are rarely more than a few miles wide. Beyond them lies the plateau, the central part of the dish, approached by a short but often steep escarpment that forms an effective barrier between the coastal rim and the interior, The interior is like a vast plain bent into gently undulating depressions and uplands. Streams rise on the uplands and collect as rivers or form lakes and permanent swamps in the depressions. The major river systems, such as the Zambezi and its tributaries, cut large valleys across the open savanna and eventually find their way to the coasts by working across the rims of the plateaus and plunging down the escarpments, following courses generally marked by deeply incised valleys, gorges, waterfalls, and rapids.

To speak in very broad terms, the savannas of Central and Southern Africa have mainly supported shifting cultivators or mixed farmers who grow grain or root crops as their food staples and also keep some small and large stock. Nomadic pastoralists and cultivators more interested in cattle have also been found in the area, particularly in the sparsely inhabited arid southwest and in the far south, beyond the Limpopo River. In precolonial times the entire region was rich in natural food resources, such as big game and wild-food produce, so that in general there has never been as great a dependence on cultivation or stock raising as has been found in other regions. Trypanosomiasis (sleeping sickness in human beings), transmitted by the tsetse fly, and other diseases that attack human beings and livestock, combined with uncertain rainfall and low population densities, have generally made specialized and intensive farming methods unnecessary and even impracticable, though certain areas have been exceptional in this respect (Fagan 1965, pp. 23–30; Allan 1965). Today most Africans on the southern savannas still live off the land under some system of shifting cultivation. Most of them will continue to do so into the foreseeable future. It has been estimated that 73 percent of Africa's population makes its living this way. In Zambia and Zimbabwe-Rhodesia, the areas we are most interested in here, the figure has been as high as 89 percent in recent years (Phillips 1959).

Zambia lies astride the upper reaches of the Congo and Zambezi drainage systems, and large areas of the country are high, undissected plateaus with gently undulating surfaces lying between three thousand and five thousand feet above sea level. Some areas

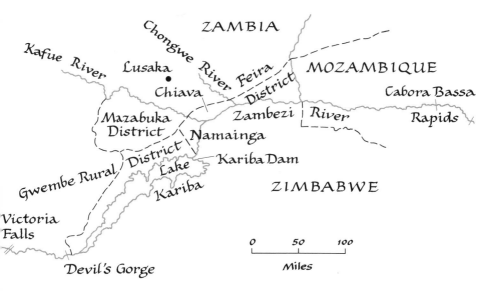

Fig. 2. The Middle Zambezi Valley

have been affected by trough faulting, however, and they provide an extreme contrast to the plateau. One of these spectacular rift formations is the middle Zambezi Valley. The low-lying, almost flat-floored rift valley is enclosed by steep escarpments of rugged, much-dissected country. The terrain proved to be a major obstacle to communications during the colonial era, and until recent times the valley was one of the most isolated parts of the country. From a geological point of view the middle Zambezi begins about 75 miles below Victoria Falls, where the river finally emerges from the narrow, twisting Devil's Gorge leading down from the falls (see fig. 2). The upper Zambezi runs above the falls to its source in Angola. The middle Zambezi extends from Devil's Gorge down to the Cabora Bassa Rapids in Mozambique (formerly Portuguese East Africa), a distance of some 480 miles, while the lower Zambezi runs another 265 miles to the Indian Ocean.

This book focuses on the portion of the middle Zambezi Valley that extends from the wall of the Kariba Dam downstream past the mouth of the Kafue to the Chongwe River tributary, a distance of

about eighty river miles. This part of the river is sometimes called
Gwembe by both Shona and Tonga speakers, though many say that
the Gwembe comes to a downstream terminus at the Kafue, while
others say that it ends even farther downstream. The valley here is
relatively narrow and steep-sided. The valley floor ranges from ten
to thirty miles wide, and the escarpments rise to a height of four
thousand feet. At the midpoint of this section of the valley, where
the Kafue River joins the Zambezi, the elevation is only twelve
hundred feet above sea level. At this low elevation the newcomer
from higher elevations and latitudes finds the tropical climate un-
comfortably hot and sultry most of the year, and the inaccessible
valley was considered unfit for European habitation during the colonial era. To reach the valley floor from the north, one must de-
scend the escarpment through fifteen or more miles of deeply dis-
sected, broken country. In places the escarpment is even steeper.
Approaching from the south, one finds about the same terrain,
though there the plateau margin is sometimes less well defined,
and a wider belt of less steeply inclined broken country may have
to be traversed before one reaches the valley floor.

Most of the streams flowing into the valley drain only the escarpment zones. They are not major rivers, and while they cascade
from the hills and flow in torrents across the plains below during
the rains, the fierce heat and sandy soils of the valley cause them
to sink into their channels and dry up fairly quickly when the rains
cease. Some form shallow ponds in depressions (pans) and last a
little longer. But even during the annual summer rains that comprise the growing season, most of these short streams never reach
the Zambezi, though they are perennial in the escarpment. Consequently, permanent sources of surface water are scarce on the
valley floor, apart from the Zambezi and its major tributary, the
Kafue. Other significant tributaries in this section of the valley,
such as the Lusitu, the Musaya, the Chipongwe, the Lesser
Chongwe, the Musandya, the Greater Chongwe, and their feeder
streams, leave standing pools of water through much of the year if
the rains have been good. In poorer years the useful life of these
pools is extended by digging.

The scarcity of year-round water means that, in regions where
soil exhaustion, river-bank configuration, or some other factor has
led to abandonment of vegetable gardens along the muddy banks
of the Zambezi or Kafue, the population is likely to retrace the
course of tributaries and shift inland along their middle and upper
reaches toward the foot of the escarpment. There escarpment
seeping water, springs, and streams that have not yet dried into

the hot valley floor still support small streamside gardens for tasty vegetable relishes and the traditional trading crop, tobacco. These small, naturally irrigated gardens are not large enough to provide the basic food supply. Though maize is commonly grown there, much of it is eaten green off the cob as a vegetable. The remainder is dried, and the kernels are eaten parched as snack throughout the year. The basic food supply must come from very much larger slash-and-burn fields, whose crops are dependent on the light and uncertain annual summer rainfall, which averages twenty to twenty-eight inches a year. It is the location of soils favorable for such staple fields of cereal grain, together with sources of drinking water, that determines the settlement pattern.

Because of the irregular annual rise and fall of the Kafue and Zambezi and the potential destructiveness of their swift currents, riverside gardening has always been uncertain along these major watercourses and, to a lesser extent, along smaller streams and escarpment floodplains. Plants must always be close enough to the natural water flow to receive sufficient moisture, but untimely high floods commonly wash them away. Sometimes an entire garden is eroded away or buried under a deep layer of sterile sand and grit. Despite these problems the pattern of movement toward the valley uplands at the foot of the escarpment is a well-established one, according to local traditions. This is supported by a 1914 tour report filed by the colonial district officer, which is preserved in the Zambian National Archives in Lusaka. The uplands back from the Zambezi, being slightly higher, often enjoy welcome cooling breezes. Because they are drier, they have fewer mosquitoes and fewer outbreaks of malaria after the rains. There is also less danger to the streamside gardens from the maurauding nocturnal hippos that still live in the big rivers. In some upland locations there is even less danger of tsetse infestation, and it is possible for the farmers to keep cattle for prestige purposes, for the making of alliances through cattle loans, for use as an emergency store of value, and for use in plowing.

Soils and Vegetation

Several authors have noted that the main valley soils in this region are relatively infertile. For the most part, however, the Zambezi and its larger tributaries wind through deep beds of fertile alluvial loam, whose riverside vegetation stands in striking green contrast to the valley floor, which is dry much of the year (Jackson 1961). Undue attention has been focused on the riverside vegetable gar-

dens because most observers in the days before roads found it convenient to travel in boats or along the banks of the big rivers. Some
earlier descriptions of this section of the valley are worth noting:

A map showing the distribution of native villages bears out the importance of permanent water supply, as it will be seen that most villagers are
situated on the banks of those rivers from which water may be obtained
throughout the year, although in the wet season a nearby pan may be
used in preference to the muddy river. Through this combination of soil
and water-supply the bulk of the population lies along the Zambezi, some
villages are placed on the banks just above the reach of normal floods,
while others are several miles inland, very often on or near a stream that
flows into the Zambezi and from which water is obtained for most of the
year. The Zambezi is the only river in this area which has a permanent
and visible supply of water, although there are several where water can
usually be found by digging in the sand.

Throughout Rhodesia [in the highlands of present-day Zambia and
Zimbabwe-Rhodesia, where there is greater rainfall] maize is usually
planted in the fields in November with the first rains, but in the valley
an additional planting takes place in February and March at the end of
the rainy season, which is not possible elsewhere. The seed is planted in
the silt brought down by the floods, which provide a fresh supply each
year, and the plant is able to obtain moisture by capillary action from the
river during the dry months. A continuous supply of food throughout the
year is obtained by sowing the seed in successive rows as the flood dimin-
ishes. It is not unusual to see a river garden where maize at the highest
point is fully ripe while near the water-level the plants are only a few
inches high. Small lagoons are sown with maize as the water evaporates,
and islands, which only appear when the river is low, are also utilized.
[Keigwin 1935, p. 258]

The river scenery is exquisite. At the time of my writing [1900], some
twenty miles east of the Kariba gorge (now the site of the dam), either
bank is lined with small patches of thriving mealies [green maize] running down to the water's edge at various intervals. Each little kraal
(homestead) has its own garden, where the women, armed with native
hoes, perform their daily duty, either in weeding or hoeing, whilst at
night, accompanied by their spouses, they rest in a kind of a pigeon-loft
or sentry-box, built on four long poles, and ascended by the most rickety
of ladders, keeping guard over their gardens against the depredations of
serenading hippos, who, in the witching hours of midnight, land for
meals. These patches of garden are extended as the river declines, their
crops quickly vegetate and arrive at maturity before the river overflows
its banks at the appointed season, replenishing and manuring the gardens
for the succeeding crop. The Umsigile, with its black foliferous branches
and papilionaceous fruit, line the river's edge, affording a striking contrast

to the parched grass and stunted mimosa that forms the principal shrub in this district. [Harding 1905, p. 285]

Similar conditions were reported by Garbett (1967), who worked among Shona-speaking Valley Korekore in the Musengezi area. Conditions appear to be roughly similar throughout much of the middle Zambezi Valley (for corroboration see Trapnell and Clothier 1937; Floyd 1959). The Musengezi is a southern tributary of the Zambezi, about 145 miles downstream from the mouth of the Kafue. Garbett noted that much of the land away from rivers is agriculturally useless, consisting of soils with a high sodium content under *mopani* forest. The best soils are narrow bands of alluvium along the major rivers and streams. Wet gardens, known as *dimba*, are prepared on broad, flat beds of alluvial silt alongside these water courses. They average about half an acre and are mainly planted in maize. These streamside gardens dry out rapidly as the rivers fall and require labor to dig down to the moisture level. Sometimes pits as much as two feet are dug for the seedlings. Properly managed winter gardens can give green maize for almost nine full months of the dry season, from April to December. In addition to those living beside the rivers, and especially the year-round tributaries, many other Valley Korekore live along the foot of the southern escarpment to take advantage of the more reliable water supplies there. But most of the staple grain harvest comes from dry slash-and-burn fields (*munda*) averaging three to six acres. These wet-season summer fields are planted in millet and sorghum on uplands away from the river system, and new fields are cut every four to five years when the soil is exhausted. Garbett also noted that rainfall is marginal and heat excessive and that there are very few cattle because of the tsetse fly. Extensive crop failures are not infrequent, and then the people rely on hunting, fishing, gathering, and cash remittances from male migrant wage laborers. The same description could well be applied to the Goba at the Kafue confluence.

Garbett's description of conditions in the Musengezi area is doubly interesting because the area lies in what was the *mwene mutapa's* home territory (the Dande) after the Korekore people moved north from Great Zimbabwe in the fifteenth century (Abraham 1962; Garlake 1973). Much of what I have to say about Goba subsistence life will thus be broadly applicable to the center of the historically important Mwene Mutapa Confederacy, a point to keep in mind when in Chapter Six I discuss the relationship of subsistence life to precolonial political organization.

Fortunately, more detailed analyses of the local soils and vegetation are available. I summarize them briefly below, following Trapnell and Clothier's important study (1937) and Scudder's more recent work (1962). Scudder's detailed analysis of the human ecology of the Gwembe, or Valley, Tonga, as they were before the creation of Lake Kariba is a major contribution. In attempting a summary here, I am relying on his work to satisfy the reader wishing to know more about the natural environment and human ecology of the Zambezi Valley near the Kafue confluence. In Scudder's work the easternmost Gwembe down to the Kafue is known as the "Lower River" section. His coverage of the Gwembe's natural environment, population and settlement patterns, subsistence economy, and famine problems includes the Lower River section and is recommended reading for additional background. His viewpoint often reflects his focus on the Tonga-speaking peoples of the Upper and Middle River sections, however, and some of their practices differ from those of the Shona-speaking Goba living east and west of the Kafue. Another valuable document is Bainbridge and Edmonds's unpublished "Northern Rhodesia Forest Department Management Book for Gwembe, South Choma, and South Mazabuka Districts" (n.d.). I will also draw on this clear, descriptive account, which was based on many years' cumulative field experience.

Broadly speaking, there are three main soil types in this section of the valley: escarpment soils, soils developed on karroo sediments, and alluvial soils. The broken, hilly escarpment country is characterized by skeletal soils, surface rock, rubble, and laterite crust. Other soils derived from limestones are fertile but are usually eroded from all but the gentlest of slopes. Erosion in the escarpment and hill zones usually outpaces the processes of soil formation, with the result that most soils are thin, stony, and immature. The escarpment zones and outlying hill ranges associated with them generally carry Brachystegia woodlands similar to those found on the savannas of surrounding higher plateau country, though they are less well developed on these thin soils.

On the valley floor by far the commonest soils are those derived from mudstones, siltstones, coarse-grained sandstones, and other underlying rocks of the karroo geological formation, largely by colluvial and alluvial processes. Generally known as karroo soils by specialists, they are mainly fine-textured, dark-gray-to-brown, clay-type or mudstone soils overlying shale. Most of these very poor soils are poorly drained, heavy, alkaline clays containing large amounts of calcite. Because of their fine texture, the absence of

Mopane gives little shade, and the short trees are spaced by bushes and a thin covering of poor grasses.

slope, and the high water table during the heavy rains, the clays frequently become waterlogged and impassable when wet. They harden into a dense, compacted mass when dry. The Goba consider these soils much too hard to work and leave them alone, though villages are sometimes sited on them if they are near good field locations.

Also included in this category of karroo soils are deep, loose, sandy soils derived from escarpment grit and sandstone, as well as certain fine red marly soils. This range of soils is characterized by low, poor-scrub woodland, often with a very thick understory. Staple slash-and-burn fields are sometimes found on these fertile soils, but they contain relatively little humus, tend to dry out quickly, and like most other local soils are severly susceptible to the valley's recurrent droughts.

The dominant vegetation on the valley floor is the characteristic *Colophospermum mopane* subarid wooded savanna that flourishes on the karroo soils, especially on the vast, poorly drained gray-brown alkaline flats. Mopane gives little shade, and the short trees are spaced with bushes and a thin covering of poor grasses. The valley is largely covered with extensive stands of these well-spaced trees, though in drier places they give way to a denser scrub-thicket subarid vegetation known as mopane bush. Notable and distinctive associates of the mopane bush are the towering, grotesque baobab or cream-of-tartar tree (*Adansonia digitata*) and the large, cactus-like Euphorbia, or candelabrum tree. Along with escarpment vegetation and occasional springs, these subarid savanna woodlands still support impala herds, warthogs, large groups of elephants, and other animals that largely forage from leafy growth. The mopane forests also supply marginal grazing for livestock. Mopane is relatively impervious to termites, which abound in great mounds, and is therefore the preferred timber for all kinds of construction, though I found its heavy, dense wood extremely tiring to chop and transport. It also has a low moisture content and burns slowly and evenly and is therefore the favorite local firewood. Along the edges of pure stands of mopane and elsewhere grow many edible and medicinal plants (Fanshawe 1962; Scudder 1962; F. White 1962; Reynolds 1968).

In contrast to mopane soils, pockets and strips of alluvial soils are particularly valuable and, while they vary a good deal in quality, they are by far the most popular sites for staple-grain cultivation and river gardens. The soils range from loose, coarse, loamy sands to finer, silty soils. Younger deposits of riverside alluvium with high clay content are the most fertile soils. They are generally found in narrow strips along the Zambezi and its major tributaries, most notably in the alluvial fans at their outlets. Those nearest the water are flooded annually, and in places where the riverbanks are suitable, these soils can be cropped continuously. The construction of Kariba Dam has eliminated most of the riverine farming along the Zambezi, though some attempt is made to open the floodgates at appropriate times. Gray-to-brown alluviums on older floodplains no longer flooded annually can also support permanent to semipermanent cultivation in localities watered by good rains. There are extensive deposits of fertile older alluviums back from the Zambezi, and they merge in places with the sometimes equally fertile karroo sands.

The dominant vegetation associated with these fertile alluviums includes tall acacia trees, dense combretum and kirkia thickets, and grasses excellent for grazing (Scudder 1962, p. 16). The larger rivers, streams, and alluvial floodplains evidently were once marked by dense fringes of this acacia-combretum riverine vegetation, supported by groundwater. It was formerly the highest and most striking vegetation in the valley, because extreme temper-

Alluvial soils are associated with tall, flat-topped acacia trees and fine grasses for grazing.

atures, generally low groundwater-retention characteristics, and low seasonal rainfall mean that large trees will be found only near riverine groundwater.

These dense gallery forests were apparently already partly cut out by Livingstone's time. While it seems clear from Livingstone's accounts that stands of riverine vegetation with both thickets and many big trees were considerably lusher in his time than they are now (Livingstone 1858, pp. 614–16), large winter-garden clearings were already to be seen along the banks of the Zambezi and on islands (Livingstone and Livingstone 1865, p. 239; Livingstone 1858, p. 615). Now, after repeated river-garden exploitation along

Now, after repeated river-garden exploitation along the Zambezi, only a few large trees have been left standing here and there to provide fruit and shade.

the Zambezi, only a few larger trees have been left standing here and there to provide fruit and shade. A relict patch of very large trees was still to be seen along the Zambezi in 1967 at the downstream terminus of the Kariba Gorge. The broad Zambezi is compressed at this point into a very narrow, deep channel, and the land along the north bank seems never to have been cleared for cultivation. The high banks are very steep and perhaps unsuitable for gardening. Just behind the riverbank the land surface is thickly covered with rock talus from the towering Kariba Hills, which rise abruptly over a thousand feet above the river.

The large, thick trees surviving along the river at this point, (notably *Tamarindus indica*, known locally as *MuSika*), probably were once part of the climax riverine vegetation throughout the middle Zambezi region. Across the river, along the south bank, there has been no riverine cultivation; people there were resettled to higher ground in 1958 as part of the Kariba development program. There the natural regrowth was very marked in the years 1967 to 1969 compared with that on the Zambian side, aside from the tall trees just mentioned, and gave a good idea how things must have looked when populations were less dense. Since the uninhabited south bank was over run with game and tsetse flies, north bank vegetation between Kariba Gorge and the Kafue has been further eliminated since the later 1950s by government tree-felling operations designed to eliminate tsetse habitat. That has not affected riverine growth east of the Kafue, however, where recurrent riverside gardening must account for the absence of all but a few large trees.

Population Movements

It seems reasonable to conclude that population patterns have been changing. After Livingstone's time there seems to have been a marked increase in the cultivation of winter gardens along the Zambezi. That would account for the almost total disappearance of dense climax riverine vegetation along the Zambezi since his time. Of course, it is hazardous to extract too much from his observations, since he always traveled on foot in the area and was therefore less likely to be overly impressed by the winter gardens so vividly described by later travelers moving along the river. Even today, in many places where vegetation is thinner, winter gardens are almost impossible to see when one is traveling by land until he steps right into one.

Livingstone was aware of their existence, however, though he made very little of them, just as he might today, after Kariba. While at one point he referred to a large human population on the left, or north, bank of the Zambezi and on islands between Kariba Gorge and the Kafue, these people evidently were taking refuge from Matabele raids mentioned by the doctor and recorded in local traditions. Livingstone did note that the over-all population was not large. Rather than river gardens, the fields he referred to in some detail were planted with "immense" crops of tall sorghum, which has always been planted in large rain-fed slash-and-burn fields some distance from the river system (Livingstone and Livingstone 1865, pp. 221–40). Because later travelers made very much more of the winter gardens and because riverine growth along the Zambezi noted by Livingstone has in fact been largely eradicated, it seems fairly certain that Zambezi winter-garden clearing became more popular in the years *after* Livingstone.

We can postulate two different kinds of population movement to account for this change. First, valley people may have moved down to the banks of the Zambezi from inland locations along tributaries and seep water at the base of the escarpment. In his work elsewhere in the valley Scudder reported examples of fairly long term shifts of this nature between the foot of the escarpment and the banks of the Zambezi, and there is no reason why that should not have happened among the Goba in the nineteenth century as well (Scudder 1962, pp. 131, 136–37, 140, 142). Second, there may have been an over-all increase in population after Livingstone's observations, caused by net immigration into the area from colonial-era disturbances in Zimbabwe-Rhodesia and Mozambique. There is quite a bit of support for this possibility. According to Trapnell and Clothier:

> The Tonga of the Lower Zambezi Valley [below Victoria Falls in their context], known in part as the We, and including alien Gowa and Kalanga elements towards the Kafue confluence, may be collectively regarded as a people of eastern origin, racially akin to the Tonga of the plateau but culturally distinct. [Trapnell and Clothier 1937, p. 44]

"Gowa" is a variant pronunciation of Goba, and "Kalanga" is simply a general term for Shona-speaking people such as the Goba. Similar statements are found in administrative records left by various district officers and travelers in the earlier years of the colonial era. After a reconnaissance for the British South Africa Company in 1898, Gibbons had this to say about the people immediately downstream of the Kariba Gorge:

> During the afternoon local natives put in an appearance. These people were not Batongas, but were distinctly of the South African type. Their language was incomprehensible to the Zambezi boys, but Machin, who was a Zulu, could make himself understood. They are undoubtedly refugees from the south, and had possibly receded before the Matabele oppression, or more probably were a section of that heterogeneous community which had preferred to place space between themselves and their white conquerors rather than settle down under civilized rule. Police hats from Bulawayo, old coats, a brilliantly striped jersey, showed that these alone of the tribes we had hitherto encountered were in communication with the mining districts [to the south]; but when they spoke of the "steamer which runs along the ground which the Great Englishman is bringing up the Zambezi," we required no further confirmation of the opinion we had formed. . . . From the high country through which the Lushito [Lusitu] flows, the great mountains surrounding the Kariba gorge were easily discernible. Twenty-eight degrees east longitude roughly marks the eastern border of the Mashikolumbwe country [Ila peoples on the northern highlands]. Their neighbors, who are of the Makalanga [Shona] tribe, are very distinct from the Mashikolumbwe. . . . The Makalanga are essentially a river [or valley, in this case] tribe and are quite distinct from their Matoka as from their Mashikolumbwe neigh-

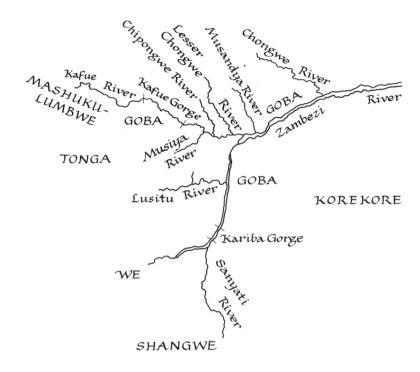

Fig. 3. The Study Area

bors. They seemed to Captain Hamilton to bear more resemblance both in type and language to the tribes dwelling lower down the Zambezi. [Gibbons 1904, 1, p. 68; 2, p. 210; and see Fig. 3].

Read corroborated these comments, adding that people fled to the valley early in the nineteenth century, during the occupation of the south by the Matabele and other Zulu offshoots, and later, during the fighting with white settlers. Read added: "Traits peculiar to the old Portuguese and the natives they brought with them are still noticeable amongst these people" (Read 1932).

David and Charles Livingstone noted that east of the Kariba Gorge "the people, though Batoka, are called BaWe and Ba Selea" (Livingstone and Livingstone 1865, p. 225). "Batoka" is a variant pronunciation for "Batonga" in Barotseland on the upper Zambezi, where the Livingstones recruited their interpreters. Solea, or Selea, is shown on the north bank of the Zambezi in Lacerda (1867). That placement may have been copied from Livingstone. In local tradition BaWe means "people of the east," in reference both to their more easterly location within the Gwembe portion of the valley and to their places of origin. BaSelea was similarly used in reference to subgroups of local Tonga or Goba people who had come from the east.

In Livingstone's time Shona-speaking political confederacies were still intact in some places, and situational use of the Tonga (or Toka) label indicated nonmembership, among other meanings presumably lost to us now (Lancaster 1974b). The Shona-speaking BaShangwe peoples southeast of the Gwembe Tonga, or BaWe, as they are alternately known, were a leading group in the Shona confederacies, and Shangwe chiefs were sometimes regarded as political paramounts over some of the We. With regard to the BaSelea (or BaSerero, as they are known locally), my sources indicate that they were migrants from eastern sections of the valley in Mozambique. Cabral called them *sereros* or *shereros*, noting that they are natives of the Zambezi above Tete, in western Mozambique "so named because they eat the fruit of a tree named sherero" (Cabral 1925, p. 25). Many Goba recount traditions of eastern origin and also trace important southern connections to and migrations from the BaShangwe and Korekore areas in the south (Livingstone and Livingstone 1865, pp. 224, 231).

The disappearance of the formerly dense riverine growth along the Zambezi can thus be accounted for by two different kinds of population movement. One would have involved temporary shifts to the river while upland cultivation areas were rested. The other would have involved a net increase in total population through immigration, which might have increased land pressure throughout the valley. Certainly no one has maintained that the valley experienced expanding populations through natural increase alone. On the contrary, its harshness for farming and its role as a refuge area have always been stressed (Bond and Clark 1954; Scudder 1962).

Oral traditions suggest that both kinds of population movement did in fact occur in the later nineteenth century, after Livingstone's time. As in earlier times, valley populations were still attracted to the banks of the Zambezi for long-distance trade (Lancaster and Pohorilenko 1977). This commerce actually experienced a local resurgence late in the nineteenth century as the Portuguese made their last efforts to claim the interior between Angola and Mozambique. In addition to the trade itself, the large, prestigious villages of trading leaders along the Zambezi attracted residents. Since local slave raiding increased in the late nineteenth century, residence in the large fortified villages of the Zambezi trading leaders also served as a measure of protection from the slave trade. When politically united, the Goba in the Kafue confluence area were strong enough to bully Portuguese slavers whom they disliked (Livingstone and Livingstone 1865, p. 230; Lancaster 1979, p. 73). Traditions tell of large fortified villages and almost continuous settlement along much of the Zambezi frontage at that time, and several late-nineteenth-century sites associated with appropriate archaeological surface material have been found (Phillipson 1969, 1972). Too, as in earlier times, immigrants from beyond the valley were still coming in flight from areas of colonial settlement and disruption, as Livingstone himself noted (Livingstone and Livingstone 1865; p. 214; Lancaster 1974b).

Since the Pax Britannica these trends have been reversed. Throughout the present century, as acculturation to colonialism gradually became possible, many Goba were attracted to higher-rainfall and tsetse-free areas on the plateau north of the valley, where European settlement was never as great as it was south of the Zambezi. Many of the more conservative groups choosing to remain in the valley have found it better to move to the foot of the escarpment for ecological reasons now that the old river trade is a thing of the past (Trapnell and Clothier 1937, p. 44; Lancaster 1971). Temporary soil exhaustion and declining yields in sorghum fields near the Zambezi seem to have been a further contributing factor.

Increased land pressure along the Zambezi in the century since Livingstone's day has been such that the fertile alluviums once associated with tall acacia trees and dense combretum and kirkia thickets are now associated with handsome open acacia parklands and pure grasslands, with thickets regenerating on some fallowing lands. The same holds true for alluviums along tributaries. When fresh fields must be cut today on good soils not far from water, the people usually cut into the regenerating acacia-combretum or kirkia thickets, if they feel energetic, rather than felling tall trees. With so many men gone so much of the time on tours as migrant wage laborers, it is often easier to use the grasslands instead. In fact, we shall see that many people simply continue to use their old fields and accept lower yields. Gathering wild foods has never been much of a problem when the rains fail, because so much agriculturally useless mopane woodland and brush must be left uncultivated. That will undoubtedly continue inasmuch as development plans being made in the years 1967 to 1969 were concentrating on irrigation schemes for the alluviums. A growing local cash economy also helps support the people when their crops fail.

An *ngozi* spirit host surrounded by singers.

3

The Annual Round
of Life and Work

The Goba year begins with *mainza*, known as the wet season, which corresponds roughly with the months November through March in the United States. November finds people living in the village rather than among their fields and gardens, and it normally is the last important month of social life before the onset of heavy rains and pressing agricultural work. Most clear, moonlit nights are devoted to social activities centering on spirit possession, curing, antiwitchcraft behavior, dancing, singing, and drumming by the *ngozi* and *mashave* cults. These spectacular events last until dawn and are attended by everyone in the host village. The *ngozi* dances in particular usually draw relatives and friends from nearby villages, and religious specialists often travel from farther afield. In the years 1967 to 1969, many people working and visiting in the towns journeyed sixty miles or more, timing vacation trips and time off from work to attend these events. In addition to the herbal remedies administered, the dances play an important role as dramatic faith-healing performances. The manner in which these affairs are conducted may also substantially affect the social status of the afflicted, as well as the status of the relative who plays the role of host, the host village, and the various musical and medical specialists called in to attend. In fact, large, enthusiastic dances are important in attracting potential residents to a village.

The dance complex is thought capable of effecting real cures by countering the sometimes subconscious forces of witchcraft and sorcery. The emphasis is on performance. Among the Goba there is no clear line between witchcraft and sorcery, and both are believed to represent natural forces stemming from normal human jealousies. The solidarity that the exciting dance performances both strongly encourage and require for their efficacy tends to make the outcaste unenthusiastic performer self-aware, clearly visible, and relatively easy to handle, especially when the dance is believed to be dealing with matters of life and death. Socially and politically, the valued opportunity to participate in a flourishing dance cult associated with village residents strongly validates membership in the village, even for newcomers unrelated to the core descent group. The booming drums can be heard for miles around, and well-attended dances act as an effective advertisement, encouraging recruitment by intensifying solidarity through cooperation in the dance and bringing into the village dance arena scattered relatives and friends who share a concern for the afflicted and the reputation of the village as a good, safe place to live. Villages that hold frequent large dances attended by well-known persons with reputations for curing enhance their drawing power as cultural focal points. Because social organization heavily depends on religious intermediaries and spiritual sanctions in the ancestral cult, there is a very fundamental appeal in possession dance cults stressing the moral purity of persons in a position to tinker adversely with the spirit world. In addition, the bureaucracy of flourishing dance cults provides vehicles for personal enhancement lacking in smaller, more isolated villages. That is especially appealing to adult women, who are more tied to their villages and children than the men are. For individuals less centrally involved in these activities, the dances still provide welcome occasions to gossip, drink beer, meet friends and lovers, and stay up in the hot, uncomfortable nights before the rains.

The Wet Season

Some rain begins falling in November, and some people begin planting their staple grain crops then. Most of the rain falls from December through February, however. Throughout this wet period the mean relative humidity hovers around 80 percent, while mean daily temperatures range from 80° to 85°F. Mean daily maximums are rather higher than that; carefully recorded daily highs inside my grass-covered, tree-shaded hut usually reached the high 90s or low 100s in October and November. The weather is very hot and uncomfortable unless it showers. November rains also bring the annual cycle of mosquitoes and malaria, which attack most people fairly severely. As Colbourne noted (1966), malaria is a serious killer of children one to two years old, and it renders the entire population susceptible to anemia, diarrhea, dysentery, worm infections, pneumonia, and other illnesses. While convulsive malaria attacks cluster prominently in the rains when work

Boys watch as a man breaks up the carcass of a kudu.

Table 1
Game Mammals in the Goba Region, 1967–69

English Name	African Name	English Name	African Name
Elephant	*Nzou*	Serval	*Ndzundza*
Lion	*Shumba*	Wildcat	*Nhiriri*
Buffalo	*Nyati*	Leopard	*Mbada*
Night ape, or			
galago	*Gonga*	Dassie	*Mbira*
Bush baby	*Dahwila*	Black rhinoceros	*Nhema* or
			chipembere
Vervet monkey	*Tsoko*	Zebra	*Mbizi*
Chacma baboon	*Vene*	Warthog	*Njile*
Striped weasel	*Rukoo*	Bush pig	*Nguluve*
Striped polecat	*Nyaore*	Hippopotamus	*Mvuu*
Honey badger	*Chimbule*	Common duiker	*Mhembwe*
Wild dog	*Haba*	Sharpe's grysbok	*Timba*
Side-striped			
jackal	*Haba*	Reedbuck	*Gowo*
Pangolin	*Haka*	Waterbuck	*Ngwarati*
Antbear	*Gwiba*	Sable	*Noro*
Clawless otter	*Chema*	Roan	*Noro*
Spotted-necked			
otter	*Tsenzi*	Bushbuck	*Goho*
Civet	*Ditigwe*	Kudu	*Ndzirawao*
Rusty-spotted			
genet	*Nyungo*	Eland	*Change*
Slender			
mongoose	*Rukoo*	Hedgehog	*Tsese*
Dwarf			
mongoose	*Mutundiri*	Porcupine	*Mhungu*
Large gray			
mongoose	*Jelenyenje*	Scrub hare	*Tsuro*
Water mongoose	*Biti*	Greater cane rat	*Tsedzi*
Meller's			
mongoose	*Rukoo*	Giant rat	*Bende*
Banded			
mongoose	*Simuandilwabana*	Spring hare	*Mudoro*
Spotted hyena	*Mbere*	Red squirrel	*Kamutundili*
Aardwolf	*Mhumi*	Flying squirrel	*Janga*
Caracal	*Nhebera*	Bush squirrel	*Tsindi*

Note: Game was still surprisingly plentiful in the years 1967 to 1969. The supply had been commented on by Robbins and Legge in *Animal Dunkirk* (1959), where they described the remarkable animal-rescue operations connected with the flooding of the Zambezi and the creation of Lake Kariba. Some species of game may have increased in the Kafue confluence area since so much of the valley has been flooded upstream. Only a few storekeepers and government agents had accurate modern long-range weapons in 1967 to 1969. Game was also saved by the relative inaccessibility of the area to most European hunters, as well as by the relatively low population density. The Goba were still hunting many varieties of mammals, of which those listed above could be identified. Smithers (1966) was used in making identifications.

demands are at their peak, it is less well known that infected mosquito bites received even in a short wet weason in the subarid wooded savanna of Zambia cause as much year-round malaria and general weakness as is found in badly infested rain-forest zones. Malaria is found throughout Zambia, and it is particularly severe along the Zambezi.

In November and December there is a good deal of hunting for many varieties of mammals. That is true of all the months until the main harvests because the greenery ensuing from the first showers and then the continuing rains bring game out to the valley floor from permanent pools and springs in the uninhabited escarpment zones. Later, tender garden shoots and ripening crops attract animals, and the men's and boys' hunting sometimes becomes a desperate measure to save the agricultural food supply. In hunger months when last year's crops run out before the next harvest, the people respond by hunting even more. In November and December most hunting is done at night by adult men using muzzle-loading flintlocks dating from precolonial times and freezing the game with the bright lights on their hard hats from the Zimbabwe-Rhodesia mines. Unless a close approach can be made, the low muzzle velocity and inaccuracy of their antique smoothbore weapons renders them fairly harmless against the big game, especially elephants. The charge often only lodges in the animal's skin, where it causes irritating infections. The presence of wounded elephants makes traveling in the bush dangerous, and each year one or more deaths can be attributed to them. Leopards and other game are tracked to trees or dens by packs of dogs, where they are finished off with spears and guns (see table 1 for a list of mammals hunted.) In hunger months some men turn to hunting almost exclusively, and they barter their excess meat for vegetable food or cash. In most areas where government representatives are likely to be found, hunting is conducted secretly with modern weapons. It is unlawful to kill game without a license, unless the animal is actually within a field or garden. This awkward law has been a major source of local controversy.

Though there are often sporadic light rains in November and early December, when the people decide that the real rains have begun both men and women leave the villages before dawn to spend their mornings in the fields planting and weeding. This daily exodus normally begins in December. If the rains have been falling, the weather tends to be cool and overcast, even drizzling slightly, in the early mornings. Even the afternoons and evenings tend to be dark and cool if it has been raining, and often there is much thunder. Everyone turns out to work the gardens if the soil is wet and easily worked from a good rain the previous evening. The workforce includes flocks of small children with their own little hoes, who help in the serious work of cutting down the rapidly-growing weeds that appear with the first showers of November. Illness, old age, and other problems cause great variation in household work schedules, but by December 20 most people have finished their first round of planting. Inside my hut it was as hot as 100° or more each day in December, with the temperature falling somewhat if there were showers. Just before dawn the temperature would fall to the daily low—in the upper 70s or low 80s—but it was always very humid. Like late November, December and January are a time of hard work and little food, and many are ill and weak.

If the year is one of normal rain and crop growth, by early January if not before, most of the adult women have moved out of the village to live in their fields, though most of the boys and some of the older men prefer to continue sleeping in the villages a little longer, if there is a woman to cook for them. At least one family member sleeps in the fields each night from January on to protect shoots from the nocturnal predations of elephants, ungulates, and other game, especially if the rains have been light and the dry bush stands in sharp contrast to the lush green crops. Most families keep their dogs and weapons at their field shelters during the growing season. In the daytime monkeys are particularly bold and destructive raiders. Old men and women with no children are at a particular disadvantage because, when they go for water, the monkeys move into their field shelters to take food. Except for those instances each field and garden always has a human sentinel stationed on the spot. During this early part of the growing season people normally rise for work at 5:00 A.M. Weeding and guarding are the main activities, though bare spots are filled in by transplanting and replanting. By 3:00 P.M. the workers are resting in their field shelters, still on guard round the clock against animals.

On mornings when it is raining hard, the people stay in bed, and no one can be seen in the fields or villages until about seven, when in tsetse-free upland villages people must unpen the cattle. One of the male householders removes the gate poles and gingerly uses a stick to poke the cattle out among the huts and granaries. The cattle slowly file out and stand about in the rain with no herd boys to watch them. By now one or two people still sleeping in the village can be seen huddling in their doorways, chatting and happily raising their faces to the sky. Meanwhile, calves romp and play, and the cattle lock horns, mount, rub against huts, and tear bunches of grass from the roofs.

About 7:30 about ten lads appear with switches in their hands and slowly start the cattle out to pasture. The herd boys, ranging up to the age of about twelve, are ragged in their worn khaki-colored schoolboy shorts.

No smoke is yet rising from the village roofs, anything eaten in the early morning is cold. A boy pushing through his mother's doorway can be seen chewing on a chunk of cold porridge. Later a woman emerges and walks about drowsily in the rain, still topless from the night's sleep. No one else is stirring. She makes several trips to the grassy verge of her hut clearing and brings back tiny sections of sorghum stalk from the ruins of an old granary to kindle a fire from the embers in her sleeping hut, where a smoky little night fire has kept mosquitoes away from the sleepers. Later steam rises from her roof as she begins cooking. It is likely to be 8:30 by this time, late by normal standards. Rain changes things, and people do not follow the usual patterns.

An old woman comes outside and slowly begins scrubbing an old fire-blackened cooking pot in a puddle of brown water beside the hearth. Her married daughter comes out of the hut next door and stands watching for a while. Now a few other women begin appearing in the neighboring compounds. They silently unpen their goats, fat-tailed sheep, chickens, and pigs, while the older boys begin emerging from their huts and try to scrounge a meal from their mothers, knocking at their closed doors and waiting quietly in the rain until the women stir.

The village slowly comes alive as mothers come out and retreat back inside with their heavy mortars. Some younger women can be seen trudging sleepily to their usual stamping places outdoors; there are no leftovers from last night's meal. The mortars are lying on their sides on the wet earth, and the pestles too must be cleaned by rubbing with handfuls of yesterday's chaff. It is all very slow going. Soon pairs of women—mothers and daughters or sisters—are stamping in turns under the tree cover at their workplaces. Half an hour later there are heavy thuds from the other workplaces in the village, while those residing in the field shelters are going through a similar process. None work in the fields while it is raining heavily, and even the animals seem to lie low.

Spirits soar when the heavy rains begin in earnest, especially if the rains have been late or the previous year was drought-stricken. Temperatures fall momentarily and bring relief. Women drop whatever they are doing and ululate for joy the first time they hear the seasonal streams begin gushing and running, moistening the riverside gardens. Tree frogs and insects can be heard for the first time in months, and birds are common once again. Yet the rains are always uncertain in the Zambezi Valley, and by January the people are usually worried about their food supplies, which by then may be running low. Most people eat sparingly and use their cash reserves to buy grain whenever they can as insurance against the coming months. Beer parties slacken off when there is planting to be done, but once most of the sowing is over, there is again more beer brewing and partying, though never as much as in the dry season immediately following the main harvests. It is probably accurate to say that grain consumed as beer in January is merely a substitute for porridge, rather than an improvident extravagance. In January people feel that they can afford to spend more time at home in the villages, even though bare spots can still be seen in most of the gardens.

Of course, the older men are the most noticeable figures at the January beer parties, and they are the ones most likely to be in the village. They make most of their contribution to agricultural subsistence in the early clearing and plowing stages of the annual cycle. At this stage the men are absorbed in discussing such issues as the future succession to the headmanship or chiefship, the illness of a child, the many deaths in the village, the extent of the rains, the chief's lax attitude toward the land shrines and the traditional rain ceremonies, the various oracles aspiring to be heard on matters pertaining to the rain, the bride-service remittances of their sons-in-law off working in the towns, and the prospects for a good harvest. Some of the men take the time to repair or sharpen tools. Others do bits of sewing, or drinking and smoking with their men friends. There may be some friendly visiting as older, more established, popular service husbands come home for a week or so and show off their new clothes and bicycles.

In addition to beer socials, people also make time for some small parties and beer offerings to the ancestors in connection with life-crisis ceremonies, and on clear moonlit nights when visibility is good there again are a few possession dances in the villages. Generally, however, it is very quiet in the fields and villages in January. It is still very hot and humid, with indoor temperatures reaching the 90s and 100s daily. Everyone feels uncomfortable, and tempers sometimes flare. The mosquitoes are terrible, and it is hard to sleep. Elephants and game threaten the crops nightly, requiring wakefulness. Many exhausted people try to nap in smoke-filled huts in the afternoons. Most people's teeth are stained from eating gathered wild foods, and they laugh about their hunger and empty granaries. Some of the older women, especially, are exhausted from the heat, the work, and the lack of food and sleep. But some older men have access to cash from the remittances of their sons-in-law, and, being comparatively idle at this time, they spend more of their time at village beer drinks and commercial beerhalls.

February is also a difficult month. Daily temperatures still climb to the low 90s at least. Even in normal years many people are hungry, weak, and idle by this time of year. Many of them suffer from malaria, infections, and disease because of their weakened condition. Deaths of old people and children seem to occur in clusters about this time. Most nights are very quiet, though sometimes young village boys take out their fathers' drums and play until about 9:00 P.M., when they are finally shouted into silence. In poorer years, such as 1967–68, schools close as parents with younger children disperse to find work in distant towns or to stay with relatives in areas fortunate enough to have had better rainfall. Those who stayed behind in the 1967–68 drought season were very disheartened and deserted their fields, letting the weeding go, scoffing that there was insufficient moisture even for weeds. By late February bush pigs and warthogs were making serious inroads on what little had survived, especially in somewhat moister gardens along streams. The staple sorghum crops of the large wet-season fields had completely dried up, but corn in the river gardens was yielding some stunted ears. There was not enough corn to carry home or warrant a harvest, but enough for some pleasant family eating as it ripened. It was only the marauding animals that belatedly prompted some villagers to return to the fields each day to protect their withered crops, and we began getting tusk wounds for treatment at our compound as sad, dusty men and dogs came home in the evenings.

Even in normally good years February and March are the time when competing oracles are busiest explaining vagaries in the rainfall and drumming up business for themselves. By March, 1968, the worst year in forty seasons according to the *Times of Zambia*, all the ablebodied men under fifty had left to seek wage work, and most women young enough to have only one or two children had gone off with them. Only those too old to travel far and some of the excess youngsters remained. Surprisingly, they were in good enough shape to do quite a bit of work salvaging what corn and vegetables they could, even undertaking a final round of weeding in the process. Though it was very dry, a surprising amount of food could be gathered from the abandoned gardens and dry bush. And

A *mhondoro* oracle wearing traditional wrap-round skirt, shawl, and beads of black and carrying an impressive walking stick.

in the larger villages there was still a reasonably good social calendar in March, aided by purchases from local stores. In one large village I recorded an event for each afternoon and evening, including one or two dance-cult performances, death discussions, mournings, coming-of-age ceremonies for girls, small beer brewings attended by large gatherings, and a Watchtower Assembly meeting.

The Cold Season

The months of April through July correspond with *mupeyo*, which the Goba describe as the cold, dry, windy season. It is no longer humid, and the early months are very comfortable until it becomes too dry and dusty. Daily temperatures still reach the high 90s or more in early April. But daily mean temperatures quickly fall from a monthly average in the high 70s in early April to the high 60s in July, when it commonly dips down to the 40s at night. The Goba huddling around their fires consider this temperature bitterly cold. In good wet years whole families may continue to reside in their fields from January through April and May, sleeping there to protect the fields against elephants and other nocturnal crop predators and spending the day there cultivating and guarding against birds, monkeys, and other daytime pests. But while the main sorghum harvests still lie ahead, only a skeleton protective presence is usually required in the fields after weed growth ceases with the end of the rains, and April and May witness the beginning of a number of behavioral changes in the annual regime.

People are more in evidence in the villages and are freer to move about during the cold season. Both men and women now have time to make trips to see well-known herbalists and curers, and they begin a series of brief visits to other villages. Gathering and foraging increase substantially, and small groups of women and children go out on expeditions to collect medicines, roots, and other foods in moist, uninhabited places near rivers, streams, and permanent water in the escarpment hills. They also collect reeds for making sleeping mats and large winnowing baskets. A few older women also travel to collect clay, ocher, graphite, bark, and other materials used in potting. Men commonly forage in the bush for medicines and lay snares for various kinds of birds, especially large guinea fowl. Daylight hunting with dog packs also increases. Upland boys continue herding cattle in the dry deciduous bush after school, and now they spend their spare time fishing and swimming in the waterholes, whereas they mainly hunt birds while herding in the wet months. Girls and younger women also do quite a bit of fishing in the isolated pans and ponds that remain as smaller tributary water-courses begin drying up and sinking into their sandy beds. Some of the men are still building dugout canoes and fishing the larger rivers with nets; others may buy the catch, split and smoke the fish, and sell them throughout the villages on bicycles. Most school boys over fifteen years old usually leave the valley altogether for adventures and odd jobs in the highland towns during these months, and some of them never return. Most of the old men who remain go on a beer diet. Women do a good deal of brewing in large metal drums, using either their own supplies of grain or mealie meal purchased at local stores. They are often able to turn a small profit for themselves by selling the brew to the men, who always choose beer over porridge.

There is usually at least one such "money beer" (*hwahwa ye mari*) a day in each subchieftaincy during the cold months. Drinking begins in the mornings, often by 9:00 A.M., with knots of men buying their own pots of beer and dispersing to drink it slowly in favorite shady places throughout the host village. The noisy parties often last all day. Some make music with drums, thumb pianos, and leg rattles and dance and party well into the next morning in these slack, easy months. If the sky is clear and the barefoot people can see in the moonlight that the sandy paths are clear of snakes and other obstructions, they will travel at night to attend parties in other villages. There is always something special to do each night in a large subchieftaincy, ranging from crowded money beers and a renewal of the dance cults to smaller, quieter social beers dedicated to ancestral descent-group guardian spirits at life-crisis ceremonies postponed from earlier, busier times. Meanwhile the younger people flock to distinctive "concerts" of their own in frank imitation of the Europeanized nightclub life they enjoy so much in the towns.

But in early May there are still some people taking turns in the fields, often high up in tree platforms in the broad daylight of mid-afternoon as they watch their crops. Many elaborate scarecrow devices against birds crisscross the fields, and along the larger rivers similar noisemakers are placed at the gullies worn down by hippos when they haul out of the water to begin their nightly browsing in the gardens. As the dry season gets under way and the people gradually withdraw to their villages, the timid elephants fan out over the entire valley floor clear to the Zambezi and often do considerable last-minute damage to any remaining unharvested crops. Elephant-scaring activity is particularly intense around midnight and again just before dawn in April, May, and early June. Some-

A freshly hewn dugout canoe.

Untangling a fishing net.

times a mile or more of scaring fires are lit to keep elephants out of the fields as the people scream, beat loudly on fallen trees, hammer on their large wooden stamping blocks, and beat noisy gongs from tree platforms. Men run waving great burning fifteen-foot stalks of sorghum, setting fires where dry stalks and weeds have been piled for easier harvesting, sometimes approaching within thirty yards of the animals. This can go on for hours if the panicky animals become trapped in the fields within the ring of fires; they go back and forth, trampling the fields as they seek a way out amid loud explosions from the old muzzle-loaders. Because many men are sleeping in the villages or are away at this time, the booming voices yelling, "Where are they now?" "Who has them?" "Which way are they going?" are often the voices of the older, bolder women who can bellow as loudly as the men. They find comfort in this bellowing back and forth in the darkness because each watcher is desperately territorial and tied by necessity to her own field of sorghum or patch of tobacco. Although they dislike the taste of tobacco, frightened elephants can easily wipe out a year's crop as they mill about. Monkeys and huge flocks of tiny birds can also make large last-minute inroads on the ripening stands of small-grained sorghum, which is still highly vulnerable to loss even after harvesting, because it must dry fully, stacked up on exposed platforms where the seed tassels are neatly arranged in pyramidal displays among the field shelters. Only when it is dry will it be head-carried back to the safety of the enclosed village granaries.

By late May to mid-June most villagers have managed to complete their harvests and have abandoned their field shelters to reconvene in the villages for another year, though the small streamside winter gardens will require some attention. Now as they carefully refill their granaries, handful by handful, the people try to assess how much staple sorghum there will be for the coming year. They also carefully preserve tall, clean, unbroken sorghum stalks for myriad uses in making repairs to their huts and granaries and for new construction. These are carried to the villages in huge head loads. The villagers begin cutting and storing bundles of thatching grass to spruce up their neglected villages as time permits. Men spend many hours in the dry mopane forests searching for tall, straight, slender trees, and one begins to see piles of straight poles cut, trimmed, stacked, and waiting along paths leading to the villages. In addition to repairs and village renewal, this is also the prime time for residence shifts. People now have the opportunity to move away from neighbors they quarreled with during the exi-

Old men would much rather take their sorghum in the form of beer than porridge.

Freshly brewed sorghum beer in 55-gallon drums prepared for a succession ceremony. The stockade of sorghum stalks will be destroyed in mock battle to celebrate the end of the important deliberations.

gencies of the crop year, while others find that they need to build new or additional granaries for their crops, new huts for the older children, or perhaps a new kitchen for the wife or a new sleeping hut for a second wife who is finally coming to join her husband's village. Most of the annual building, however, is the result of quarrels and subsequent moves, though some of the activity reflects positional succession and other political factors favoring some territorial regrouping, Whenever an established household moves, its followers usually move with it, necessitating the construction of fresh sleeping huts, granaries, and animal pens. Old timbers and thatched roofs may be carried away for reuse at the new site, if it is no more than a mile or so away. Even so, much woodcutting is required, for the walls and roof of each sleeping hut require an average of 158 trees and saplings.

Soon the broad valley is hazy from the smoke of runaway bush fires set by big-game hunters and foragers for field mice and smaller quarry as they seek to start game, increase visibility, or make it easier to follow tracks. Some fires are set to encourage fresh grass growth for grazing livestock. By June even the older men remaining in the villages begin to leave their beer drinks, and disperse, some traveling to sell their traditional "cash crop" of tobacco and others turning increasingly to fishing. Younger men are selling fish and fresh vegetables from the winter gardens. Men and boys are also forced to spend more time herding cattle to more distant waterholes as the valley continues to dry up. Especially in a hunger year, this is usually the time when small stock is bartered, slaughtered, and converted into food. While people are thus freer, in a sense, in April, May, and June and activity patterns begin to vary, it must be remembered that it is the women and children who look after the fields and bear the very heavy brunt of the final guarding, harvesting, and head-carrying home of tons of food as the crop year winds down to its weary conclusion. They also work in the small winter gardens, though generally the men have always harvested and processed the tobacco and seen to its sale on the distant highlands. Even after most people have left the fields in April, May, and June, it is the women who go back to sleep there at night until all the work is done.

In July the case load at the government court in the chief's village hits its low point for the year. As usual many of the likely defendants, younger men with cash money, are away in the towns. The older village-dwelling men who initiate legal action in connection with marriage payments and most other disputes are dispersed and extra busy at this time of year—in the forests hunting

A new rectangular sleeping hut with roof thatching in progress. When mosquitoes become a nuisance at the onset of the rains, the walls will be sealed with clay.

and looking for timber for the annual round of village renewal, constructing fresh buildings as families shift residence, herding cattle to more distant water, fishing, making long trips to sell tobacco, and attending to a host of other cold season activities. In calendar year 1967, for example, of the total of seventy-three cases heard at the government court only nineteen percent were heard in the six months from April to August, when most of the men were busy with other business. Most granaries have been repaired, rebuilt and filled with the new crop, though in early July a few stragglers are still guarding their drying grain in the abandoned fields. Here and there uncontrolled bush fires continue burning from efforts to start game, frighten elephants, and clear away grass and brush preparatory to cutting new fields. Tall brush around villages is also burned back to improve visibility and appearance. The bush is now pretty much drained of people, and as men go about their business they always carry weapons on the shoulders, an ax, a spear, or a muzzle-loader. The women always have sturdy sharp hoes at hand. Game can now be heard just outside the village at night, and in particularly dry areas elephants may try to tip over granaries in isolated villages.

As it gets windier and drier, dust devils twist along automobile tracks, major pathways, and in the clearings of large old settlements where the ground cover has long since worn away. Many people begin suffering from sore eyes. As the days grow noticeably longer, there is less work of a pressing nature, work that cannot be put off or done slowly, especially in families not planning to shift residence. Construction and building repairs and the carving of fresh ax and hoe handles, stools, and other items are stretched out as time permits. There is more time for evening fun, and now the social season really gets underway again, with large beer drinks, impromptu dances, and long-drawn-out meetings (*dihwe*) to settle problems of succession and wife inheritance ensuing from the death of prominent householders in the last year or so. By late July the possession dancing cults become the dominant nighttime activity once again, finally replacing the elephant hunts, and much of the entertainment centers on the chief's especially large village.

The Hot Season

The Goba year ends with *chirimo*, known as the hot, dry season, which lasts from August to early November. Things continue pretty much as they did in July, but now the first heavy round of slack season partying tends to die down, except in the chief's vil-

A goat has been slaughtered for the participants in an *ngozi* curing ceremony.

When the moon is full and people can see well enough to convene in large numbers, curing dances preempt the night. Here, on a dark night, young women and girls dance and sing *chikambekambe* in a corner of the village.

lage, which earns its reputation as the social and political heart of the country. The game presses still closer to the villages, often close enough to be seen in daylight as people go about their business. The air becomes so hazy that the nearby escarpment hills can be seen only faintly from upland villages. By September some of the men are beginning to return from the towns if they are unemployed to help plant and make sure the fields are ready. At the same time the case load at the government court begins to increase, and that is also true in the village moots as men become embroiled in arguments about old scores, unpaid loans, disputed marriage prestations and services, and problems directly involving their wives.

A well-known magician sits with the divining dice (*hakata*) used to fore-see the future and interpret the wishes of ancestor spirits. Note the an-cient marriage hoe in the foreground.

September also sees the start of final clearing and preparatory work in the fields. By now the country is baking hot, dry, and uncomfortable. Much of it is black, charred, and dusty from months of burning and dry winds. But by late September the biggest trees begin budding and flowering, drawing moisture reached by deep tap roots. Now that the trees have anticipated the coming of spring, the older women return to their fields, one per field, while the younger women of each extended family household stay home in the villages cooking, housekeeping, and caring for the children. The old women leave for the fields by 6:30 or 7:00 A.M. The temperature is 80° by 8:00, rises to the mid 90s or more by 9:30, peaks in the high 90s by 2:00 P.M. and is still in the low 90s at 7:00 P.M. Social events are scheduled for the early mornings and late at night, and the old men and others who do not work in the fields by day tend to lie about idly in the shade. Many are ill, especially from the dust, which causes eye, nose, and throat ailments. In October temperatures return to the highs of the previous November, and the women spend most mornings between 6:30 and 10:30 or later preparing their fields, especially when the ground is soft after a shower. As the land turns green with the tender buds, shoots, and flowers of the false spring, to be followed by the first scattered showers of October, the land softens and hides the barren, thorny harshness of July, August, and September. The sudden greenery attracts the game, and now any younger men who happen to be home from the towns do a great deal more daytime hunting, ambushing game near waterholes as visibility becomes poorer with the new foliage.

4

Summer Rains
Fields and Winter
River Gardens

The Goba maintain two types of agricultural plots. Their subsistence staple is planted in large, irregular clearings dependent upon the summer rains. These fields are the focal points of the subsistence farming system and mainly produce sorghum. Very much smaller gardens watered by natural river and streamside flooding are also maintained. Their main purpose is to extend the growing season beyond the short summer rains and to provide the traditional tobacco crop. Both men and women are addicted to a strong local species of tobacco and this crop has long been an important trade item.

Summer Rains Fields

The mainstay of the agricultural system are the summer rains fields planted from November to December and harvested mainly in May. These fields are called *mitemwa* (pl.; *mutemwa*, sing.), from the verb *kutema* ("to cut"). Their name indicates that they are slash-and-burn fields, which, ideally, should be cut from mature forest growth. Strictly speaking, the word *mutemwa* should be used only the first and perhaps the second year after a fresh cutting from mature forest, for the term really refers to freshly cut, extremely productive fields pioneered as a free good from the lands of the realm. Clearing a well-timbered large new field in this way often takes up much of the winter, beginning in July and finishing with the burning in August, when the cuttings are dry. In a good cutting from a well-fallowed plot, the felled timber should cover roughly the entire clearing with some branches reaching ten to fifteen feet high. In subsequent years, no matter how many, the field may simply be called *munda*, a more general term that includes riverine winter gardens as well as older summer rains fields.

61

Fallow rains field are called *chikura*. This terminological distinction between fresh *temwa* and older *munda* fields is significant in two respects. Use of the same general term (*munda*) for both river gardens and old rains fields indicates that the two categories tend to merge under certain circumstances, and that is the case with *temwa* fields near watercourses. The term also indicates that most soils cultivated by the Goba are fertile enough to be used for considerable periods of time if necessary. To avoid confusion, I will simply refer to *temwa* rather than *munda*.

Most sources agree that three years' use will give excellent yields from freshly cut fields cultivated with only the traditional short-handled hoe.[1] Rarely is a field used for such a short period today. Most able-bodied men in their prime working years are absent much of the time. There is no expectation that a man lucky enough to find work should come home to help farm. The older men and women who remain are either too overworked or too infirm to cut well-wooded new fields after only three years use. A careful survey revealed that most people actually expect five good years from a young field. That was the normative pattern revealed in the process of collecting family histories. A separate study of seventy-one fields showed that the average period of use had actually been at least six years, and I know that even this figure is often exceeded. The fields around most well-established villages have generally been used so long that the original tree stumps and roots have died and been eaten by termites. Clear old fields like these tend to be passed along to young married couples, newcomers to the village, and elderly people unable to find or clear fresher ones. An old woman will commonly take over a field cut by a young son-in-law after he has gone off to work in town, has separated from his wife, or has moved away upon termination of his service cycle. Old women like this may complain of empty granaries from a field

---

[1]The short-handled hoe (*mbadza*) used by the Goba is remarkably uniform in appearance. The hoe handle is normally two feet long, and, like the Valley Tonga hoe, the tang of the iron blade is hafted through a hard knot at almost a forty-five degree angle to the handle so that a normal stroke from a straight-legged bent-at-the-waist position grazes the ground only shallowly. A new blade from the store extends seven inches below the haft (Reynolds 1968, pp. 109–12). In precolonial times hoe blades were made in the villages from ores mined in escarpment areas, though finished blades (*mapadza*, pl.) were also a common trade item, along with chunks of iron bloom. Many of the old blades are still preserved for use in marriage exchanges.

they have cultivated only a few years, but with patience its actual history of use can almost always be traced further back in time. Many widows have probably been using fields well over ten years old, and I can vouch for an eighteen-year-old field that is still producing enough grain to make its woman user a well-known beer-party hostess.

Large old fields look as though they had been stumped to facilitate plowing. There is often only a growth of thick grass to mark their margins, where a few scattered, generally smaller trees have been left standing for shade. Because large rocks are seldom found in good alluvial deposits, many upland families with a source of cash income pay neighbors to plow their older fields occasionally to loosen the soil, bring fresh loam to the surface, and extend its life. That is a common practice in fields more than five years old, and in some localities plowing is thought to permit almost continual land use. The very hard labor required to stump and clear a fresh *temwa* field for plowing, rather than light, shallow hoeing, deters the average villager from doing so. I met no one who had deliberately cleared a newly cut field for plowing, and since plowing is largely undertaken to increase yields, it is hardly necessary in freshly cut *temwa*. But especially in upland areas below the escarpment where there are fewer tsetse, men continually try to accumulate cattle. They are used for plowing. Plowing clean old alluvial fields is thought to prolong good yields, and the existence of such old fields in upland areas away from the main rivers has clearly become a favorable factor in settlement patterns today. Since many older men return to the villages with enough money put by to purchase a plow and a pair of oxen, they do a fairly good local cash business plowing their neighbors' fields, while the younger men who once would have been felling fresh forest are gone to work in the towns and help in other ways.

Information on *temwa* field sizes is summarized in table 2. About half the fields (48 percent of my sample) are worked jointly by a married couple, though a younger husband's aid after the initial task of clearing is usually limited to occasional help with heavy weeding during the early rains. If home long enough from their tours of migrant wage labor, husbands may also help protect the crops from birds and game, especially in the latter stages of the growing cycle when late-maturing green crops attract animals from the dry surrounding countryside. Generally, however, only the older men are home enough to help their wives significantly. In many families today in upland locations middle-aged men help only with an occasional plowing, and much of their effort is spent

Table 2
Temwa Field Sizes
(Based on 71 measured fields)

Temwa Field Types	Largest, Acres	Smallest, Acres	Number in Sample and Percentage of Fields	
			Number	Percent
Husband-and-wife fields: largely worked by women, especially in younger households	7.0	0.9	34	48
Average size in 19 young households: 2.2 acres (41.2 total)				
Average size in 15 grandparental households: 4.2 acres (62.4 total)				
Average size all husband-wife fields: 3.1 acres (103.6 total)				
Fields worked by lone women: Widows, divorcees, junior wives in polygynous marriages, and women whose husbands do not help or are on tours of migrant labor or are ill.	4.1	0.4	34	48
Average size worked by 14 lone young women: 1.8 acres (25.8 total)				
Average size worked by 20 lone grandmothers: 1.9 acres (37.5 total)				
Average size all fields worked by lone women: 1.9 acres (63.3 total)				
Fields worked by husbands alone:	6.8	0.4	3	4
Average size: 3.2 acres (9.7 total)				
Total fields			71	100
Average acreage, all temwa: 2.5 acres				
Total *temwa* acreage in sample: 176.6 acres				
Average years used: 6+ years				

on the fields of neighbors in return for cash. Men in their forties and fifties or more who have ceased their tours of migrant wage labor and help their wives in the fields generally contribute to the largest *temwa* acreages. The largest joint husband-wife plot I measured was seven acres. Including their riverside gardens, this particular family cultivated a total of 9.4 acres, indicating the very active role of the husband in this somewhat unusual instance and the importance of unmarried children as mothers' helpers. Younger couples still moving back and forth between wage labor in town and farming in the country naturally have the fewest mouths to feed and the smallest fields and gardens. Most of the time the young wife tends an old plot conveniently situated next to those of her closest matrikin in the village while her husband is away so that she and the children can have good company as they work and rest. Older fields like those assigned to coresident daughters and other mobile or handicapped family dependents tend to suffer most from relatively minor droughts and are likely to be abandoned if there are no dependents at home to cultivate them. This drawback to the user of an older field is more than offset by the practice of grouping fields to conform with uxori-matrilocal residential clusters in the village. Then if drought, illness, trips to see her husband in town, or severe animal inroads decimate the crop, a dependent can help in her mother's field next door. If the losses are severe enough, the daughter and her family may eat from her parent's granary. It is for this reason that able-bodied older parents reserve the best and youngest fields for themselves, especially in families where children and grandchildren requiring support may return unexpectedly from the towns. Table 2 shows that older people in the grandparent generation are the mainstay in *temwa* field cultivation.

Even in family fields shared by a working husband and wife team, slash-and-burn cultivation is clearly very largely the woman's task. In addition, in my sample 48 percent of the *temwa* fields (thirty-four of seventy-one) were worked by women without any help from husbands. Included in this category were ten widows and five older divorcees unlikely to remarry, six attractive younger women who had been abandoned by their young migrant wage-earning husbands, and three junior wives in polygynous marriages who lived as single women in terms of their subsistence. One woman preferred to work a new field by herself, since her husband was planning to take a second wife and give her the older family plot. The other nine women had husbands who were ill, on tours of migrant labor, or unwilling to help.

Table 2 also indicates that a few older men who had "retired" from their life in the towns occasionally tended a separate rains field of their own. The men usually do this if their wife and family can manage the family subsistence acreage without much help. Men like to have a large crop all their own to assure a grain crop for beer. Although beer brewing is always strictly a woman's task, many wives are reluctant to brew if they feel that the family will need the grain in the hunger months that commonly precede the main *temwa* harvests. Since women perform all the work necessary to produce prepared foods and thus, in effect, control the grain dispensed from the granaries filled by collective family labor, her reluctance to brew beer can be an effective lever when a wife wants labor, cash, or attention from her husband. A wise wife will be especially reluctant to convert an unusual amount of porridge grain into beer if there are many dependents living in troubled villages or working at temporary town jobs who might come seeking food in later months. Polygynous wives are especially likely to resist a husband's requests for beer, since his help in the fields is likely to be even more of a rarity. It is for these reasons that the few able-bodied older men who tend their own rains fields (*zunde*) are polygynists. A wife has a legal right to refuse to brew beer if the husband has not contributed work during the crop year.

Fields are basically thought of in terms of the main food crops they produce. While vegetable relishes and side dishes are important, the vegetables can be gathered wild. The most important food crops are sorghum (*mafundi*) and maize (*chibaage*), and fields are classified as either sorghum or maize producers. *Temwa* fields produce sorghum, and river gardens produce maize. This means that the basic difference between river gardens and rains fields is the amount of moisture they receive. Maize does well in wetter soils where local species of sorghum rot out. Many large *temwa* fields border on river gardens, and in wetter years their lower margins may also be flooded. Because flooding sometimes occurs in *temwa*, small amounts of maize may be sown in lower portions. But for the most part maize is restricted to river gardens, where it is the characteristic food crop (I will describe those gardens separately). While in practice there are fine distinctions and subtle gradations to be observed between higher *temwa* (or *munda*) fields and the slightly lower river gardens, the Goba do not bother overmuch with taxonomic distinctions beyond the general difference between river gardens and rains fields.

Temwa fields are basically devoted to sorghum (or "kaffir corn" as the scornful white settlers used to call it), which is ground into flour and cooked into porridge or brewed as a beer. Sorghum, the main crop, takes up most of the planted space. Though several local subvarieties are grown, the staple white sorghum accounts for as much as 95 percent of the planting in some *temwa* fields. While the Goba love green maize, a full granary of sorghum is always preferred. Sorghum provides more food, since much of the stored maize is composed of inedible cob. Stored sorghum thus lasts longer than an equal volume of stored maize. *Mafundi* is therefore considered the main crop, and the large sorghum granaries prominent in the villages are considered signs of security and prosperity. The small amount of stored maize not eaten green is tucked up under the eaves of the men's houses, together with tobacco, where it cannot be seen. It is said that the symbolic rain beer (*hwahwa re madzimambo*) brewed to please the royal land spirits at the land shrines (*madzimbabwe*) has always been made from sorghum.

Sorghum cultivation does appear to be ancient in this part of Africa, having been used by Early Iron Age times in the first millenium A.D. Sorghum is remarkably drought resistant and grows successfully in all of Africa's savannas. It is sensitively adapted to local climates and there are many sub-varieties, whose taxonomic classifications, botanical affinities, and agricultural histories are still being investigated. Many millions of people in Africa, Asia, and recently in South America, depend upon it as a source of food but in the westernized world today sorghum is often grown only as an animal feed. Too little is known about the sorghums of Africa and the Zambezi Valley. Colonial researchers tended to ignore it, much as they disparaged indigenous farming in general, since the tendency was to replace it with something "better" and to focus on development crops such as maize with markets in the Europeanized towns. Yet sorghum is preferable to maize in any low rainfall area in terms of productivity, and it grows on a wide range of well-drained soils. It does best on reasonably deep, well-drained sandy loams as well as on heavier-textured soils, making it perfect for the Zambezi Valley. It has long been the main food crop among Shona-speaking peoples inhabiting lower, drier areas (Alvord 1929; Floyd 1959; Harlan 1976).

Because the rains are short and irregular, sorghum must be planted (*kunjara*) early in the first rains, when the ground is soft and wet, though it ripens in the dry season. A moist seedbed is required for satisfactory germination, and the seedbed must stay moist long enough for the seedling to establish itself. It is therefore important to be ready to plant quickly upon the onset of the first rains. This calls for winter activity in clearing the seedbed, cleaning it, and working it to a fine tilth (*kundwura*). It is largely the problem of late rains or the onset of false early rains that causes so many of the valley's renowned famines. Delay in planting reduces the yield, and when the rains are really late, the Goba turn to dry planting (*kuparira*), although that gamble normally has mixed results unless the rains come quickly afterward. Continued dry replanting will be attempted until it becomes clear that there will be no concentrated rainfall and therefore no sorghum crop this year. Sorghum tends to adapt to crowding. When plants are close together, they tend to produce less inedible infrastructure in the form of stalk and leaves for roughly the same amount of seed. But the Goba like to leave enough room between plants for easy cultivation (*kurima*), since weed control is so essential in the early stages of growth before the weeds are shaded out.

The Goba women like to plant early in the morning when the soil is moist after a good rain, even while it is drizzling. In planting, the woman first uses four or five easy, shallow overlapping hoe strokes to form a small circle of loosened soil perhaps a foot in diameter. The fifth or sixth stroke is scarcely any work, and it goes into the center of the loosened circle of soil. She then lifts the hoe blade, holding up a slice of earth usually no more than two to three inches thick. Under the slice the gardener drops four or five seeds (a great many more if borers have been at the seed) and presses the little hill of earth gently back into place. All this is done in one fluid motion. The seeds to be planted are often carried in a large land-snail shell. Then, without straightening up, she takes one good stride and works the next little hill, so that the entire field is covered with little circles two or three feet apart. I have watched women planting this way for hours, taking no more than five seconds for each hill and not even breaking a sweat in the cool early mornings from the earliest dawn to 9:00 or 9:30. Throughout most of the morning they maintain a steady, easy work pace, bent almost ninety degrees at the waist. An expert older gardener usually begins planting in a corner of the field nearest a meandering streamlet to take advantage of any moisture available before the rains have clearly established themselves. Most gardeners working in well-established older fields also cut sizable annual extensions to their acreage to replace less productive portions. Because these extensions are likely to be more fertile, they too are selected for relatively early planting. In older villages with large populations most extensions encroach on fields formerly used in the not-too-distant past by individuals who have moved away for social or political reasons, making it a simple matter to remove the grass cover

A mother, a divorced daughter with her baby, and a younger unmarried daughter work together in the dry season using short-handled hoes to remove grass from a briefly fallowed field on which they will depend for sorghum.

even without the help of adult males. This likelihood is increased by the fact that in most areas pockets of superior soils near water have been fairly thoroughly exploited.

Few of the *temwa* fields surrounding most large old settlements have been freshly cut from mature forest growth in recent years. This normally happens only when a village picks up and moves to a new location some distance away. Where a stand of big trees is still to be found today on good soils near a large old village site, investigation commonly reveals that it has been deliberately left standing to serve as a village cemetery grove, a ritual land-shrine grove, or a shady "outhouse" area. Even then the grove is likely to stand on less fertile soil or on eroded areas. This often means that, when extensions are cut, only low, immature brush or grass must be removed. Even so, the fresher annual extensions are likely to retain moisture better and support greener, more luxuriant growth than the rest of the old field, and that is why they are planted earlier.

This practice often results in nice early growth that may be two or three feet tall before the rest of the field has sprouted. As the rains commence, seed accidentally dropped during the previous season also sprouts and gives the field an irregular appearance. In some fields half or more of the acreage may be fairly well planted in this way by means of natural growth that has sprung up in the rains even before fresh seed has been sown. This is most likely to happen in older plots where seeds have been spilled during previous harvesting operations and dropped during meals and food preparation in the fields and around nearby field shelters, since various subsidiary crops are either interplanted with the sorghum or planted along field margins. These crops include cucumbers and sesame, interplanted with the sorghum; okra, various leafy vegetables, cowpeas, watermelons, and gourds, often planted along field margins; and peanuts, pumpkins, squash, and sweet potatoes, sown either in field margins near the field shelters or next to the sleeping huts in the village. While more open expanses of the valley's savanna may offer relatively little for the plant gatherer, old fields provide a varied ecosystem. It is common to see a young girl gathering naturally sprouting domesticated plants such as those listed above while a few feet away in the same field her mother and older sister are bent over planting sorghum. Volunteer crops of both domesticated and wild species gathered in this way around abandoned old cultivation sites often yield a rich harvest that the people depend on, if it is not too dry, and permission is needed before gathering in someone else's field.

If she works steadily for five straight mornings, a woman can plant an entire large *temwa* field. But since she must plant whenever she has time and whenver the ground moisture and rain seem propitious, growth in most fields takes on a stepped appearance. This, of course, is accentuated by the practice of selectively planting more productive annual extensions first. Because small, irregular annual extensions replace lower-yielding older portions in most fields, the over-all age of any field must be computed on the basis of a "moving average." This system complicates accurate computation of various man-land ratios and fertility estimates, since at any one moment in time a "unitary" field is a patchwork of varying ages and productivity. The adaptive value of the system becomes ob-

A *temwa* field showing a typically irregular, or stepped, growth pattern caused by volunteer sprouts which benefit from chance early showers and the earlier planting of fresher field extensions. Part of Njami Hill can be seen in the background. Note the old logs and branches commonly left by uneven burning in younger fields.

vious, however, in poorer years, when fresher additions support growth while older segments lie bare.

When the whole field has germinated, each tiny hill is thinned to two or three sprouts, and bare spots are either filled with transplants (*mahoko*) or replanted. Transplants are taken from stronger volunteer regrowth. The hoe-planting system that everyone uses often has the effect of creating small, shallow water troughs around each plant. The little circle of lightly hoed soil around each set of sprouts soon settles under a rain, since the best soils tend to be light, fine-grained sandy loams. The little hill formed in planting settles slightly below the surface of the field and tends to collect small pools of water. These pools, reflecting blue skies under the bright-green sprouts, make the fields look lush after a rain, and while the pools soon dry out, the water has been used efficiently. After even a light shower the porous soil of most *temwa* is moist to a foot or more below the surface.

In weeding (*kurima*), a woman grasps a swath of weeds in her left hand, hoes them up with her right, and in one continuing motion shakes the loose earth back into place while turning the freed bundle of weeds so that its roots will die in the sun. The weeds are left to fertilize the field, retain moisture, and hold back weed growth. Weeding is also part of cultivation inasmuch as it loosens the soil to facilitate penetration of the rain. A gardener hoes even where there are no weeds, using the same easy motions and bent-at-the-waist posture that are likely to cripple an unwary anthropologist. Since the Goba woman is accustomed to low, backless sitting stools and habitual bending at the waist for farming, cooking, sweeping, washing, and sitting, she can spend hours at a time in that position. When the soil is moist, the light sandy loam is easy to work in the shallow way the woman uses her short-handled hoe. As she weeds and cultivates, the careful gardener remakes the little water troughs around each stalk of sorghum.

The sorghum cycle usually begins with the rains in November and December, when the crop is planted. The small seedlings begin appearing in February and March, attracting great flocks of birds. Like maize, sorghum can also be eaten green from the stalk, beginning in March and continuing in April. Green sorghum has a sweet, creamy, nutty taste and is such a great favorite that parents tell scare stories to keep children from eating too much. Mature sorghum stalks are thinned to three to four feet apart and average fourteen to fifteen feet high, with some even taller. The heavy seed tassels at the top may be up to a foot long when mature, causing the long stalks to bend at odd angles. The stalks are normally hoed

Freshly cultivated young sorghum stalks, still unthinned, showing the light shallow strokes of the short-handled hoe.

down in May, and the detached seed tassels are dried and taken home to the villages in June. In addition to the standard white-seeded sorghum (*mafundi*), most people grow small amounts of various local subvarieties, often to provide special flavorings for beer and porridge. One of these is *musare* (sometimes known as *mugundi*), another tall sorghum whose mildly sweet stalk is chewed in season like a sugarcane. Small amounts of the brown seeds are also used as a flavoring additive for beer. Some shorter brown-seeded sorghums known as *nswonswo* and *kalenge* are also used for beer flavoring. The people also grow small quantities of millet (*mhunga*) to stagger the harvests and vary the diet somewhat.

In earlier times chiefs and their henchmen sometimes resorted to armed threats to collect food from their followers. This practice was especially common in poor crop years. For that reason individuals who identify with the chiefs and their traditions, or perhaps oppose them, sometimes claim that the Goba of past times were raiders and only indifferent farmers. Indeed, there is reason to think that relatively little farming was done during some of the raiding years of precolonial times, when many of the people hid in the escarpment zones. But for the most part the Goba say that they have always been sorghum eaters. And when they talk about their food crops, *temwa*-field sorghum is certainly by far the most important. Even those with large river gardens say that there is nothing to match their sorghum mainstay (*mafundi chete*); the maize from their river gardens is only a distant second.

Good sites for the staple *temwa* fields are therefore the main factor in determining where populations will locate. If the soil is superior for *temwa*, villages and perhaps an entire subchiefdom will come to use it. Of course, additional factors come into play to affect the value of potential *temwa* sites. The availability of drinking water is the foremost of these qualifying factors. In chapter 5, where I review settlement patterns, it will be seen that large, potentially fertile parts of the Namainga chiefdom have never been settled because they lack drinking water.

Potential damage from game is the second major limiting factor that the people must consider. As mentioned earlier, nocturnal hippos cause severe damage to river gardens along the Zambezi and Kafue rivers, and they also like to graze on inland *temwa* crops. Households near big rivers and pools must spend the nights in their fields and gardens as soon as the plants begin to sprout, keeping a round-the-clock vigil. Elephants are also attracted to any riverine vegetation that may be left standing, and a small herd can wipe out a household's *temwa* or riverside garden in a single unguarded night. In areas where threats from game are particularly severe, people must concede inevitable losses and retaliate by watchful guarding and planting larger acreages than they might normally need. Threats from game were severe everywhere in the years 1967 to 1969; areas well back from the rivers are beset by ungulates of various species, monkeys, a host of smaller mammals, and flocks of birds, as well as the wide-ranging elephants. For the most part the best protection against animal pests lies in joining a dense population cluster that is able to scare off most of the game through hunting and other protective actions during the crop year. When elephants attack stands of ripening sorghum, large villages are able to repel them by setting fires around their tightly clus-

Nyamutapwe pan is a large, shallow depression that fills briefly with water during the rains. Its fertile soil makes it an excellent farm site, but it is unlikely to be used unless a large population offers protection from game.

tered fields and gardens, whereas the plots of small, isolated villages are sometimes overrun, at great cost to their owners.

Even where excellent *temwa* soils and good water supplies are to be found, the abundance of game and tsetse in the Zambezi Valley usually means that an area must be populated in reasonably large numbers if it is to be inhabited at all. This need always injects social and political factors into settlement patterns. Like the absence of water, this factor has also eliminated settlement in certain areas at certain times. The "tipping" phenomenon that periodically attracts relatively large populations to previously unused areas eventually takes care of the animal and tsetse factors, but such largely political population movement and redistribution always depend on ample supplies of good *temwa* soils and the availability of sufficient year-round drinking water.

Winter River Gardens

Even more water is required for river gardens (*matoro*) than is required for drinking. These gardens are supposed to be covered with water when the rivers and streams rise during the rainy-season floods. Because the *matoro* are placed on annually flooded riverbanks, terraces, islands, washes, and floodplains, they are conceived as essentially different from the rain-fed *temwa* fields. The word *matoro* carries the secondary implication that renewal by annual inundation maintains the high fertility of the gardens indefinitely, in contrast to fresh forest *temwa*, whose initial high fertility declines after the first few years.

River gardens are also a factor in determining settlement patterns, and every fully constituted household has always had access to some kind of river garden. Only newcomers to a village or temporary returnees from the towns allow many months to pass without establishing their own *matoro*. River gardens provide much of the vegetable spice of life in a dietary sense. They are also used to grow a very strong local species of tobacco. Fired-clay smoking pipes were once fashionable, but young men are now habitual users of home-rolled cigarettes, while older men and women take large amounts of snuff. Most of the women grow a few tobacco plants in their gardens, though large plantings of this fairly demanding crop often take more time than most women care to given them in their busy schedules. In former times tobacco was a major trading item, along with local salt and fish, and in households where older men grow appreciable quantities of tobacco, this trade still brings in most of the family's annual cash income. River gardens also come to the fore in the traditional hunger months. In most households there is usually some variable period from the time the previous year's crop runs out and the next main sorghum harvest. When drought and the likelihood of hunger months begin making themselves evident, people try to step up their "insurance" activity in the *matoro* to eke their way through the year—another reason why villagers feel that they must always have *matoro* gardens.

Wherever they are located, these small supplementary gardens are always subject to the great risks inherent in streamside gardening. In arid years seasonal streambeds may stay dry, and gardens planted in washes, floodplains, and higher terraces along all the watercourses, large and small, may dry up along with the *temwa* fields; in wet years they may be washed away or permanently covered with a deep layer of sterile sand. Wherever they are planted, the *matoro* are by no means as perennial or reliable as their name may imply. In addition, animal inroads are always a major threat to these sometimes tiny plots, and land pressures and riverbank configurations in defensive garden clusterings usually make it impossible to sow larger acreages to make up for this loss, as can be done more easily in the *temwa*. So while all households seek to maintain these unreliable little gardens, they are not as critical to survival as the large *temwa* fields. Moreover, all the benefits these gardens provide in good years can be obtained from alternate sources. The people can provide the vegetables and food relishes by gathering the many wild edible species of plant food available in the valley (Scudder 1971), as well as by foraging for volunteer growth in old fields and gardens. Hunting also supplements the diet, especially in hunger years, and the growing local cash economy allows households to purchase supplies from nearby stores and more fortunate neighbors. Similarly, the loss of tobacco cash crops can be offset to a degree by increased migrant labor, the emergency sale of livestock, the sale of game meat and fish for cash, and the sale of crafts. Finally, in poor years when *matoro* gardens fail, many people temporarily move to old village sites near permanent water sources in the escarpment zones or along the large rivers, where they hastily attempt to reclaim former *matoro* gardens or pioneer "new" ones before their former users make an appearance.

That drought-stricken Goba sometimes flee to make *matoro* gardens on the steep muddy banks of the Kafue and Zambezi rivers has sometimes given the false impression that these gardens are used only in disaster years. The fact is that, although all their benefits can be enjoyed from alternate sources, the Goba show no signs of abandoning their traditional *matoro* gardens, even though they are only a secondary factor in determining settlement patterns. Once ample *temwa* soils, good drinking water, and a large enough population have been assembled together, the people always turn to their *matoro*, and they guard them from animals as tenaciously as they do their *temwa*. Yet because *matoro* are only a secondary factor in settlement patterns and because suitable sites are fairly easy to find along the many small seasonal streams and year-round tributaries that cross the valley floor, more obvious and equally unreliable sites along larger rivers are often abandoned to thicket growth.

Since 1958, when the Zambezi was dammed at Kariba Gorge, the number and quality of *matoro* garden sites have been much reduced along the Zambezi below the dam in the Namainga and Chiava chiefdoms. Before it was dammed, the Zambezi was a sandbank river, rising to enormous heights during the floods and then dwindling rapidly in its deep, sandy bed until it was little more than a connecting flow meandering among series of pools. The great annual floods briefly inundated the grassy floodplains along the river and in some places cut well-defined steep banks of rich alluvium in the main channel, which, like the narrow floodplains, were also exposed for planting as the river fell. After the Zambezi was dammed, the characteristics favorable for *matoro* gardening largely disappeared, and the Zambezi has become a reservoir river. Such rivers seldom rise and fall to an appreciable extent, the banks are less well defined, and, rather than exposed banks and moist, grassy floodplains, there is always a margin of dense aquatic vegetation to hinder effective *matoro* cultivation (Jackson 1961, pp. 2–3). Efforts to imitate the old floods by deliberately opening the Kariba floodgates at appropriate times did little to improve the situation during the period of my field work from 1967 to 1969. Only nine Goba villages in Namainga were still regularly exploiting the Zambezi *matoro* to a significant extent; most of the rest were further inland, where gardens were taken up along streams. Many more villages had used Zambezi *matoro* at various times in the past and some probably would have done so again in due course if the river had not been dammed. Flooding along the lower Kafue has also been impaired, since the flooded Zambezi no longer backs up the mouth of the Kafue as it did in the past. East of the Kafue, *matoro* on the north bank of the Zambezi still benefited from the Kafue floods in the late 1960s, because that river had not yet been dammed, but the floods still could not match those of pre–Kariba Dam days.

Despite the impairment caused by the dam, extensive *matoro* gardens were still to be seen along both banks of the Kafue and the north bank of the Zambezi east of the Kafue in the years 1967 to 1969, and inland villagers in Namainga still resorted to Zambezi and Kafue *matoro* in times of severe drought. That happened during my stay in the valley. The 1967–68 summer growing season was marked by only 13.03 inches of rainfall, as measured by the south-bank meteorological service at Chirundu Township, near the bridge. The rainfall compared with more than 27 inches in each of the two previous, normal crop years. According to newspapers in Zambia and Zimbabwe-Rhodesia, this widespread drought was the worst in forty years, and farmers throughout the region were warned to prepare for total crop failure. But with the loss of formerly major opportunities for *matoro* on the Zambezi, plus impairment of the Kafue *matoro*, it seems likely that the future will see the Goba turning increasingly to large ox-plowed *temwa* fields as the government continues to eradicate pockets of tsetse flies. The Goba know that plowing facilitates increased acreages, and they also know that plowing generally increases the yield per acre. They believe that plowed fields often do better in drought years. Plowing fits the new image the upland Goba have of themselves as a modern, developing people who grow cash crops and involve themselves in the cash economy.

Technically the Goba have recognized two kinds of riverside gardens. Small gardens known as *hombe* may be planted here and there on bare riverbanks exposed by seasonally falling waters. They have most commonly been found along the Kafue and, especially in pre-Kariba days, along the Zambezi. Small *hombe* patches are also to be seen in favorable spots along the larger tributaries. On the flat floodplains behind the riverbanks lies the *matoro* proper, and this arrangement characterizes most river-garden acreage today. Villages are usually sited on higher ground behind the floodplains, seldom more than a mile from the main, usually riverine, source of drinking water. The *temwa* fields are cut on the higher, less frequently flooded portions of the *matoro*, as well as on unflooded older alluviums and fertile karroo soils on ground farther back from the rivers and streams. The steep little *hombe* patches on the riverbank itself are usually part of a larger *matoro* garden, but the Goba rarely bother to distinguish *hombe* patches from *matoro*-at-large, and neither shall I.

The cycle of plantings associated with *matoro* gardening is more complicated than that for the *temwa*, which focuses only on the erratic rainfall. *Matoro* gardening is doubly complicated and vul-

A *Matoro* garden on the steep fertile bank of the Kafue River, as seen from a dugout canoe. The crop seen is maize interplanted with various vegetables.

nerable because it depends on both the rainfall and the annual rise and fall of the watercourses. The interconnection between the *matoro* and *temwa* cycles and the logic behind their timing is based on hunger and the seasons. To describe this complex pattern accurately and take its principal variations into account, I will first describe the pattern found on major rivers, exemplified in the late 1960s only by the Kafue, and then note differences found on major tributaries and finally those on minor seasonal feeder streams.

It is convenient to take the onset of the annual rains as the starting point. *Matoro* acreage is always planted first, usually in November and December, and the crop sown is maize (*chibaage*). In this rains planting the *matoro* is treated like an ordinary older rains field. As in a rains field, the first planting often includes small

A view of the same *matoro* garden looking down from the bank. The more recently sown maize sprouts near the waterline, invisible in the previous photograph, have been placed in individual pits for moisture.

amounts of faster-maturing sorghum, as well as a wide variety of secondary crops. The first rains planting of the year is mainly devoted to maize because by November the people are usually a little hungry for their staple, and filling, cereal porridge. Even if the previous year has been good, some families have run out of grain, others have only a little left, and in the valley all are unsure of the coming harvest. In the best of circumstances the people do not begin eating green sorghum in quantity from the *temwa* until April, and the main harvest does not occur until May, six to seven months after the usual November and December rains. Maize is therefore planted first and in quantity on the *matoro* because the local four-month variety matures in February and March rather than in May, and green maize can be eaten as early as February while green sorghum begins to be available only a month later. Because the inundated *matoro* soils generally have a higher clay content than the *temwa* soils, the little rain that sometimes falls in October is often enough to get a good maize crop started. This further advances the timetable for edible green maize to December and the first larger-scale harvest to January.

If the annual floods are on time, the early rain-fed maize harvest of January is followed by an inundation of the *matoro* in January and February. Good floods on the lower Kafue below its gorge in the escarpment depend nowadays on the opening of three floodgates at the Kariba Dam. After the floods the Kafue (and to a lesser extent the Zambezi) recedes so much that one can cross its gorge on foot in October. If everything goes well, the recession of the floodwaters is associated with the second cropping of the *matoro*. As described earlier, planting occurs in small stages as the water recedes, beginning as early as January, in some localities and continuing into May in others. As the rains begin tapering off in March, *matoro* gardeners usually plant their seed in pits from March onward, reaching down to a level where the ground is still soft and moist. From May through July the Kafue *matoro* is drier than it was before the river was dammed, since the floods are now less extensive and of shorter duration, and the water table sinks faster along the rivers. The last major *matoro* planting now generally takes place in April, and September is usually, the last month in which fresh vegetables are eaten from that source. May plantings are usually minor, which means that the *matoro* presently produces nothing from, say, late September at the latest until December at the earliest.

There are two planting seasons on the Kafue *matoro*. The first is the rain-fed planting of October through December, which yields its main harvests from January through March. The second season, watered by the receding floodwaters, occurs in small stages from January to May, with minor harvests occurring as late as September. The Goba say that it is this multiple cropping characteristic that gives the *matoro* its name: *toro* (or *doro*, as it is sometimes pronounced) means "one"; *matoro* means "many plantings" or "continuous plantings," as was the case before the construction of Kariba Dam. The meaning of multiple cropping and continuous use is extended to convey the notion that the gardens can be used in this fashion indefinitely through the years. It has already been noted, however, that riverside erosion and deposition continually destroys individual small holdings of these "perennial" gardens, just as early or high floods (combined with late rains) commonly destroy much of the early rains planting and late or prolonged floods commonly curtail the second series of plantings.

Compared with that on the Kafue, the optimal *matoro* cycle is abbreviated on minor year-round tributary rivers. The rains planting of October through December is even less likely to produce a good crop before the floods, because the drainage areas served by the lesser, shorter tributaries are nearer to hand, and their floods come earlier, often washing out most of the rain-fed first sowing. *Matoro* along the smaller tributaries are therefore often more valuable for their postflood sowings in February and March. Since the flooded areas are more restricted and the water table is generally lower along the middle and upper reaches of most smaller tributaries, they produce small amounts of food only until July and August. On still smaller seasonal feeder streams, the October and November rains sowings are similarly threatened by early flooding during the rains. Moreover, the second cropping is even less reliable than that on the bigger watercourses since the volume of water and extent of the flooding, while never so damaging in terms of erosion, is more variable on a year-to-year basis. If sizable floods occur, the second planting takes place in January and February, and the last food crops are taken from the gardens in April.

Work methods in *matoro* gardens closely resemble those previously described for *temwa* fields. Indeed in most villages that exploit sites inland from the major rivers, *matoro* gardens are often little more than continuations of *temwa* fields, with only a slight difference in land-surface elevation to account for the greater likelihood of annual flooding. In the late 1960s that was more or less the case in thirty-six of the fifty villages in Namainga chiefdom, where most *matoro* acreage in use at that time was taken up along seasonal feeder streams and tributaries. No more than fourteen of the fifty villages were regularly using Zambezi or Kafue *matoro* to any significant extent, and only nine of the fourteen were really dependent on the Zambezi or Kafue rivers for their *matoro*. Most of the *matoro* gardens on smaller watercourses were thus simply continuations of neighboring *temwa* plots and had much the same soil characteristics, with perhaps a higher clay content in regularly inundated areas.

The *matoro* often centered around a little swale or dip in the ground, which filled with water in the floods. That characteristic was particularly noticeable in flatter upland areas near the base of the plateau escarpment. In such areas rainwater from low-lying foothills and ridges is gently carried away by a network of innumerable, almost imperceptible shallow streambeds, miniature floodplains, and seasonal washes draining the higher ground between the more deeply incised larger arroyos. When these areas coincide with extensive deposits of fertile alluvium or karroo soils, the shallow dendritic drainage pattern etched into the flat land surface provides a system of natural, nonerosive irrigation following minor changes in elevation. In such areas the many armlets in the shallow drainage system disperse the runoff water over a relatively wide area usable for cultivation. That is best appreciated in September and October, when the land is burned off and the fields are cleaned and readied for the rains.

As noted previously, the *matoro* are composed of *hombe* gardens on the steeper banks and sloping sides of watercourses, together with larger plots on the annually flooded alluviums bordering them. In many cases at least parts of these narrow seasonal floodplains had originally been cleared from gallery forest and thicket growth, and they may correctly be called *miunda* (*munda*, sing.), meaning old *temwa* clearings, rather than *matoro*. One therefore often finds an apparently complex sequence of field types as one moves out from the streambed: *hombe* on the banks (and sometimes on the bottoms of the streambed or depressions if they are not too sandy), *matoro* (or *miunda*) on the adjacent flooded areas, and old *miunda* on less frequently flooded margins originally cleared for use as *temwa*, followed perhaps by fresher *temwa* fields a bit farther back. Along small streams this merging continuum of terms might correctly be applied to a single strip of uninterrupted cultivation less than fifty feet wide. In addition, the term *makuti* is sometimes used as a general synonym for old cleared fields, bringing to five the possible number of terms suggesting discrete field types. But, as we have seen, the situation is not as complex as the terminology might seem to suggest.

In upland areas *matoro* often center on almost imperceptible swales and dips forming a shallow pattern of natural irrigation. This little runoff streamlet waters a string of banana plants, and maize has been sown between them.

So far the methods of *temwa* farming have been described in more detail than have those used in the *matoro*. Before concluding this chapter, I shall take a closer look at the *matoro*. In doing so, I focus on the system of tobacco cropping, inasmuch as the use of tobacco to generate substantial cash income will be discussed later. Tobacco farming is of interest for another important reason as well: it represents one of the few customary activities that successfully involve adult men in working the soil daily without degrading their status and violating accepted sex roles. In this it has served as a model for the development of cash cropping by men, certainly the brightest future prospect for the people of the area, if the problem of water shortages can ever be overcome to the advantage of all the people.

Tobacco is customarily sown during the second planting season in the *matoro*, as the floodwaters recede. All of the earlier *matoro* planting is usually devoted to food crops for reasons given earlier, though tobacco volunteers appear at random throughout old gardens throughout the year. In the Kafue and Zambezi *matoro* successful planting may be undertaken as late as April, while *matoro* along the smallest streams must normally be planted to tobacco no later than February. The seed is normally sown in holes 6 to 7 inches wide, about 8 inches deep for moisture, and about 2½ feet apart. Gardeners growing small amounts for their personal use may plant their seed in protected, moist spots before that time and transplant sprouts to the pits in February. As young plants appear in the pits, they are covered with straw to protect them from the sun and retain moisture, especially on feeder streams. Most gardeners hand-water their entire tobacco acreage weekly as long as they can. Bare spots are replanted.

Later, as the plants grow larger, they are hand-pruned, and, depending upon his acreage, a good gardener spends several hours a day tending his crop. Excess small side leaves and flower buds on the crown of the stalk are carefully pinched off without bruising the stem, to prevent rangy growth of tall plants with too many small leaves. This practice also prevents the plant from going to seed too soon. Plants considered ready for picking average about 46 inches high and produce about 22 large leaves. Those at the top and bottom of the stalk average about 1 foot long, while larger ones in the middle grow to some 1½ feet. Harvesting of leaves begins when the full-size lower leaves show signs of turning lighter green or yellow. Harvests are largely completed in June and July along seasonal streams and in August and September on larger rivers.

After the ripe leaves are plucked, the large center veins are removed, and the leaves are stacked to dry slowly in a corner of the garden under a protective covering of neatly stacked sorghum stalks. The stacks are later brought into the family compound in the village for further slow drying on the hard-packed earth floor of the courtyard. When the entire crop has been dried, the leaves are moistened and pulped into a fine thick paste in a large wooden mortar (*ndule*) made specially for this purpose. The finished product is a homogeneous cone (*mbande*) of dried tobacco paste shaped by the carved interior of the wooden stamping block. The cones are various sizes, of course, depending on the shape of the mortar. Among other Zambian peoples tobacco may be prepared in balls or small loaves or braided into thick ropes arranged in a flat spiral. After measuring a large sample, I found that the finished cone in

Table 3
Minor Crops Planted in *Matoro* River Gardens
(In approximate order of importance)
(Goba names and scientific names in parentheses)

Leafy vegetables (*muriywo, suna*): various local plants, plus cabbages, spinach, lettuce more recently introduced

Cucumbers (*makaka; Cucumis,* spp.), the leaves of which are also plucked

Squashes, pumpkins, gourds (*manhanga; Cucurbita,* spp.), with leaves also important

Sweet potato (*mbambaira; Pomoea batatas*), also planted in mounds near/in village

Tobacco (*fodya, kaponda; Nicotiana* spp.)*

Okra (*nderere; Hibiscus esculentus*)

Cowpeas and local beans (*nyemba; Vigna unguiculata; Phaseolus* spp.)

Peanuts (*nzungu; Arachis Hypugaea*)

Peppers (*miripiri; Capsicum annum* vars.)

Onions (*sabola; Allium cepa*)

Tomatoes (*madomasi; Solamum incanum*)

Watermelon (*munuhwa; Citrullus vulgaris*)

Banana (*mabanana; Musa Sapientium*)

Gum tree (*masao; Ziziphus mauritania*)

Papaya (*ipopo; Carica papaya*)

Sugarcane (*musare* [after the sweet sorghum]; *Saccharum officinarum*)

Mango (mango; *Mangifera indica*)

---

*Strictly speaking, *fodya* is the word for smoking tobacco and snuff; *kaponda* is the word for the plant itself.

Note: The crops listed above may be interplanted under maize, sown on margins, in separate beds, or appear as an irregular volunteer in older plots. Not included: maize (*chibaage; zea mays*), sorghum (*mafundi; sorghum* spp.), and wild species. *Matoro* gardeners may also reap a fairly good incidental harvest of fish and land tortoises. Small amounts of early beans (*chilimbangulila*) and dwarf early sorghum (*flamida*) may occasionally be seen. These crops have recently been introduced by government agricultural agents. The Goba say that *matoro* gardening is an old African custom but that many of the crops used were first disseminated throughout the valley from Portuguese estates on the lower Zambezi. I had no way of checking this tradition, though precolonial trade connections may be taken as supporting evidence (Lancaster and Pohorilenko 1977). Crops mentioned include maize, *masao*, mango, peppers, onions, tomatoes, papayas, bananas, and sugarcane. Except for maize, onions, and papayas, all these crops were reported to be in use in the mid-nineteenth century at the Portuguese settlement Zumbo-Feira, at the Luangwa-Zambezi confluence, only about 110 miles below the Kafue (Foskett 1965, p. 227). The Goba frequently traveled there in precolonial times. Many authors have associated the *masao* gum tree with the Portuguese. As its name implies in the Portuguese language, it bears a small fruit resembling an apple or crabapple in taste and appearance. The Goba use it to make a kind of brandy or stew it as a relish for porridge (Jordan 1959).

Table 4
Matoro Garden Sizes
(Based on 60 measured gardens)

Matoro Garden Types	Largest, Acres	Smallest, Acres	Number in Sample and Percentage of Fields	
			Number	Percent
Husband-and-wife gardens: As in *temwa*, wives do most of the work on all crops except tobacco, especially in younger households	2.3 acres	0.1 acres	19	32
Average size in 12 young households: 0.4 acres (5.3 total)				
Average size in 7 grandparental households: 1.2 acres (8.2 total)				
Average size all husband-wife gardens: 0.7 acres (13.5 total)				
Gardens worked by lone women: Widows, divorcees, junior wives and women whose men do not help	1.7	0.05	33	55
Average size worked by 14 young women: 0.6 acres (9 total)				
Average size worked by 19 grandmothers: 0.5 acres (9.75 total)				
Average size all gardens worked by lone women: 0.6 acres (18.75 total)				
Gardens worked by husbands alone:	3.0	0.04	8	13
Average size = 1.2 acres (9.8 total acres)				
Total gardens			60	100
Average acreage all matoro: 0.7 acres. Total *matoro* acreage in sample: 42.05				
Average years used all *matoro*: 6 + years				

Namainga chiefdom had an average height of 8 inches and an average dry weight of 4 3/16 pounds. The cone yielded 78 fluid ounces, or 0.6 gallons, of dry fine-powdered snuff per average cone. In 1967 one tobacco grower working in a three-acre garden on a small seasonal stream produced finished cones weighing a total of 628 pounds. That worked out to a yield of about 209 pounds of final product per acre, probably a fair example of optimal tobacco yields in a year of good flooding and rainfall, when crop protection is optimal. While most plots are unfenced, this man protected his plot with stacked brush, and he spent most of his daylight hours tending the crop. He had the added unusual advantage of having his *matoro* close to his section of the village. The only comparative data available in the literature is a yield of about 200 pounds per acre reported among the related Shona-speaking Shangwe peoples in the southern half of the valley (Kosmin 1974, p. 567). The grower in the example cited above happened to be my next-door neighbor in the village, and he was one of the more successful growers in the chiefdom. Most people grow far smaller acreages of tobacco. In the severe drought of the following year, 1968, there were few rains, no flooding to speak of, and no tobacco planting at all along the seasonal feeder stream that supported my friend's garden.

Most growers finish making their tobacco cones by September and October and keep only one or two large ones for their personal use. When they prepare to use the cones, they break them into pieces and grind them into a consistency suitable for rolling into cigarettes or fatter cigars wrapped in papaya leaves or waste paper from a local country store. Women and some old men prefer to make snuff, which the women may carry in a small gourd tied at their waists. Although I was a habitual smoker in those days, I found the tobacco (*fodya*) far too strong to inhale without dizziness and a burning sensation, unless it was diluted with dry leaves as the Goba mix it when they run short. The Zambezi Valley has long been famous for its tobacco, and traders begin arriving in the villages in October and November to buy the annual crop. As in former times a few local growers still go out on their own to sell their wares at better prices to villagers and farm workers on the distant highlands. The longest such journey I learned of, to the Kafue flats on the northern plateau, covered a straight-line distance of about 110 miles on the map. Nowadays the growers manage these distances by hitching rides on trucks and buses.

Information about subsidiary *matoro* crops is shown in table 3. Tobacco will not grow in most drier *temwa* fields, and peppers,

onions, and tomatoes are found only in the wetter margins of
temwa bordering on *matoro*. Banana trees, gum trees with edible
fruit (*masao*), papayas, sugarcane, and mangoes are planted above
the flood line in the upper margin of the *matoro*. The other subsidiary river-garden crops listed can also be found in smaller quantities in *temwa* fields.

Information on *matoro* sizes is given in table 4. When this information is compared with that for the *temwa* given in table 2, which
was drawn from the same population, it will be seen that fewer
matoro gardens are enumerated. In many young households where
the husband is still working in town and the wife makes occasional
visits to town, only a small *temwa* field is maintained—if possible
next to those of the wife's sisters and mother, who look after it in
her absence. The rest of the discrepancy is accounted for by the
number of older women working alone. Because of their age and
smaller food requirements many of the older women conserve energy by using *temwa* fields near *matoro*, which therefore take on
some of the characteristics of both. Because of their great love for
cigarettes and snuff, older men no longer earning cash in the towns
are forced to grow their own tobacco. That factor increases the
older male's actual work inputs in husband-wife *matoro* and tends
to mask the fact that most younger households have no *matoro*. It
also increases the number of tobacco gardens worked by men exclusively, while their wives handle all the *temwa* plus a small *matoro* for family relishes. It can be seen that *matoro* gardens are
almost always smaller than *temwa* holdings.

It is also noteworthy that the supposedly perennial gardens are
used no longer than the supposedly short-lived slash-and-burn
fields. Several factors account for this. First, the *temwa* are established on highly fertile soils and can be used indefinitely, though
the high yields of early years fall off considerably. Second, *temwa*
life is prolonged by the absence of the younger men who are working in the towns and who, even when they are home, give their
attention to the tobacco gardens or, more recently, the cotton crops
rather than to renewing the *temwa* clearings. Finally, economic
development and tsetse eradication have combined to increase
chances for plow preparation of *temwa* seedbeds, which is believed
to maintain satisfactory yields for longer periods. On the other
hand, several factors reduce the useful life of *matoro* gardens, including erosion and unwanted sedimentation, which is most common on more important watercourses. Another factor is that *matoro* are subjected to more intensive cultivation in the form of
multiple cropping, which clearly takes its toll of drier soils and

eventually may mean the abandonment of those along smaller streams. Finally, the sample of winter gardens used in Table 4 is drawn entirely from plots on small seasonal streams in the upland Njami area (see figure 4). In such areas all the *matoro* are abandoned when the *temwa* are moved some distance away in an effort to keep all plots together in as tight a cluster as possible for defense from animal predation. Along the Kafue, and along the Zambezi in pre-Kariba days, the more valuable *matoro* has reportedly been used somewhat longer and is abandoned only when unusual political factors cause the village population to leave the vicinity or when suitably fresh *temwa* are simply too far away. Even then a family may try, usually with mixed success, to keep an eye on old plots so that they can be reclaimed in the recurrent famine years. All of this reflects the fact that *matoro* have been only secondary factors in the settlement pattern.

This pattern is likely to change in the future. Tsetse eradication along the major rivers, the use of plows in large *temwa* near the *matoro*, and artificial irrigation, which was being introduced as I left the field in 1969, will probably result in denser future populations along the Zambezi and Kafue rivers. As populations are attracted, we may yet see a return to the riverine settlement pattern prevailing in certain earlier, precolonial periods.

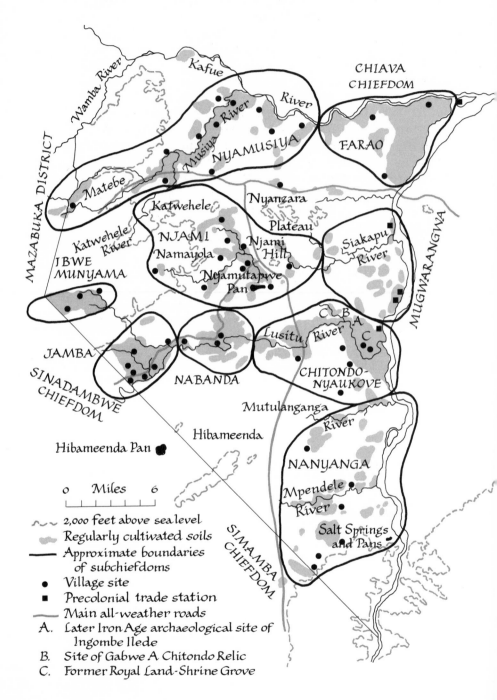

Fig. 4. Village Sites and Areas Cultivated by the Goba (Namainga)

5
Settlement Patterns and Man-Land Ratios

In gathering field material for a definitive study of contemporary man-land ratios and settlement patterns, including time-consuming measurements, detailed information about local practices and conditions, and the impact of government development activity, I found it necessary to concentrate on Namainga chiefdom alone. My general impression was that the situation in Chiava, east of the Kafue, was roughly similar to that in Namainga.[1] Some border changes affecting Namainga were made during the colonial era, though I lack precise information about them. The western border in the escarpment zone was moved east, and the southwestern corner was moved north. These administrative changes eliminated fairly large tracts of country, with the result that many people who

[1] In 1967–69 most of the settlements in Chiava as in Namainga were close to watercourses. Soils along the Kafue below its gorge in the escarpment are less favorable than those lower down at the mouth of the Lesser Chongwe, the Zambezi confluence, and the lower Musandya River, with the result that most villages in the lower Kafue Valley were situated along smaller upland tributaries near the foot of the escarpment rather than along the Kafue (see figure 3). Below the Kafue were scattered villages all along the Zambezi, and there was considerably more emphasis on *matoro* gardening than there was in Namainga. Somewhat more millet (*mhunga*) has traditionally been grown in the *temwa*, though sorghum is also important. Because villagers along the Zambezi eat their *matoro* produce as it ripens, granaries are usually fewer and smaller, reflecting smaller *temwa* acreages. Because the Kariba Dam had impaired flooding of the Zambezi *matoro*, some villages and many people, including Chiava himself, had shifted to the base of the escarpment, where *temwa* fields were much larger than along the river. Others had joined the long-term pattern of migration onto the northern plateau. Tsetse precluded cattle keeping and plowing throughout Chiava. The many small settlements at the foot of the relatively dry northern escarpment suffered from lack of year-round water, and the government had not yet provided wells.

Table 5
Land Use in Namainga

	Square Miles	Percent
Total area	535	100
Escarpment	94	18
Valley floor (below 2,000 feet)	441	82
Area cultivated	118	22
		(27% of floor)
Unutilized valley floor	323	60
		(73% of floor)

call themselves Banamainga now live outside the territory. In the late 1960s, Namainga still occupied about 535 square miles between the Kariba and Kafue gorges. Despite the changes, this represents the bulk of the late-nineteenth-century territory actually controlled by the Banamainga (see fig. 4).

About 18 percent of this 535-square-mile territory is composed of escarpment hills lying above 2,000 feet. With a few exceptions the hilly area, 94 square miles in western Namainga, is uninhabited today. The remaining 441 square miles, 82 percent of the chiefdom, lie in a comparatively flat valley floor less than 2,000 feet above sea level, though the region contains many escarpment spurs and outlying hill ranges capped with rock. About 118 square miles of the valley floor have been cultivated by the Goba. The cultivated area represents 27 percent of the valley floor and 22 percent of the total chiefdom. These figures are shown in table 5.

My estimates of cultivated areas were based on aerial photographs taken in 1954 by the one-time Federal Department of Trigonometrical and Topographical Surveys, Rhodesia and Nyasaland. These photographs were surveyed to produce a series of fine 1:50,000 maps published in 1961 by the Government Printer, at Salisbury, Southern Rhodesia. I used copies of these photographs and maps in making my own surveys of village sites and cultivated areas to corroborate, update, and supplement those shown in the maps and aerials. The basis of this survey work was the assumption that in a limited, well-known sample area inhabited by cooperative people, all land normally regarded as cultivable would have been cultivated recently enough to show in the photographs if not always on the maps prepared by those unable to invest time in careful "ground truthing" (Allan 1965, p. 25). Areas cultivated by the Goba are shown in figure 4. Because of the scale of the map they are of course only gross indications of cultivated areas, including fallow areas, village sites, and other clearings left untilled for various natural and cultural reasons. Nevertheless, they suffice as the best available indications of gross land-use patterns.

Two general features of the settlement pattern emerge from figure 4. The first, noted earlier, is the general movement of villages away from the Zambezi, reversing earlier patterns when the river and its fortified trade depots provided an attractive refuge from nineteenth-century dislocations associated with Portuguese occupation to the east and Matabele, Boer, and British occupation to the south. The location of five nineteenth-century trading stations (*aringa*) is shown in figure 4. Once the Pax Britannica ended raiding and brought villagers out of hiding in the escarpment, many returned to the valley floor. But many more small household and village groups gradually worked their way onto the neighboring northern and western highlands, where good tsetse-free land in higher-rainfall areas was available to Africans for the taking. Thus in referring to the escarpment zone bordering Chiava chiefdom north of the lower Kafue, the Lusaka District Notebook states that the "Shamifwe reserve . . . was once thickly populated in its southern part, though it is hilly, but that part is now pretty empty as people have shifted to the railroad line" on the plateau. It is impossible to assess the numbers involved in this movement with any degree of accuracy, but the *general* order of magnitude can at least be estimated.

The territory that most attracted Banamainga Goba is the homeland of the Plateau Tonga of present-day Mazabuka district (see fig. 4). The railway to the Katanga (now Shaba) Copperbelt mines, a major highway and a string of new towns pass through Mazabuka district, and the area has attracted a large African population throughout the present century (Colson 1958). In the latter part of the nineteenth century the Mazabuka Tonga were bordered by the Mashikolumbwe, or Ila, along the middle Kafue on the north, the Zambezi Valley escarpment on the east and south, and the powerful Lozi kingdom on the west. This territory must be described in tentative terms, since the Plateau Tonga were not unified politically, and along its borders their territory tended to merge with that of their neighbors.

Throughout this ill-defined highland area centering on present-day Mazabuka, the inhabitants have generally been known as Tonga. Southwestern Tonga living within the variable sphere of influence of the Lozi Kings have been known as Toka, after Lozi usage (Holub 1975, pp. x, 283). In 1890, Luiz Ignacio, the Portuguese governor of Zumbo-Feira at the Luangwa-Zambezi confluence, wrote a valuable report detailing Portuguese knowledge of the peoples of this region. While it undoubtedly was written for propaganda in the scramble for colonial territories, the report is accurate in a number of details and can be used to make a rough population estimate for the Plateau Tonga of those times. Ignacio wrote:

To the south of the Securumbues, between those lands and *prazo* Inhacoe (Chief Sicauongo), there is the Batonga race, whose territories on the west border those of Lewanika. They have approximately 4,000 to 5,000 souls and present 800 to 900 armed men for war. [Lancaster 1979a, p. 79]

The "Securumbues" are the Mashikolumbwe, or Ila; Lewanika was king of the Lozi; and "*prazo* Inhacoe" under "Chief Sicauongo" was the nominal Portuguese estate centered at that time in the Goba neighborhood Chitondo-Nyaukove at the delta of the Lusitu River. It was the traditional seat for Banamainga chiefs, who are still known by their dynastic title, Sikaongo. The area between Namainga and the Ila corresponds more or less to present-day Mazabuka district. The Mazabuka area contained about 4,000 to 5,000 people in 1890. It had a population of 157,240 in 1963 (according to Republic of Zambia statistics for 1964) and a population density of 36.7 per square mile as against the Zambian average of 5.6 per square mile (Kay 1976b). Much of this population growth has resulted from natural increase since the Pax Britannica, and a good deal has come from immigration from various directions, though most of the Plateau Tonga of Mazabuka district are said to trace their descent from migrants who left the Zambezi Valley on the east (Colson 1962, p. 174–75).

In a reflection of this significant westerly trend in population movement since the Pax Britannica, only nine of the fifty Banamainga villages were within three miles of the Zambezi in the late 1960s (see fig. 4). The rest had moved inland, and even those nearest the Zambezi took their daily water supplies from inland sources. Two other villages had been established along the important Lusaka–Chirundu–Salisbury all-weather road for various reasons, and another had been established near Chirundu Township for the opportunities the region presented.

The second major characteristic of the settlement pattern is that almost all the villages were exploiting alluvial soils in plots within

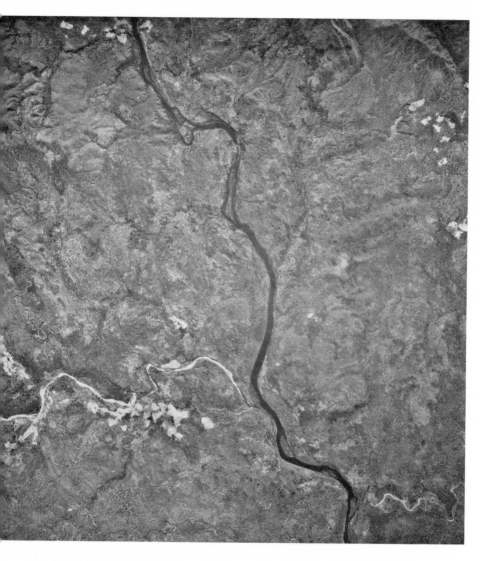

A major feature of the settlement pattern is that almost all the villages exploit alluvial soils within convenient daily walking distances from their sources of water, whether the sources are rivers, streams, or springs. This is illustrated here by the light reflecting from fields and gardens along the lower Musaya River tributary to the Kafue River. The photograph was taken in 1954.

Table 6
Local Trees Indicating Desirable Garden and Field Sites
(Fanshawe 1962; F. White 1962)

For *Matoro* clearing:

Muvurumira, or *musanta* (*Kirkia acuminata*): A key indicator, growing up to 70 feet tall, frequently occuring in unexploited gallery woodland fringing seasonal watercourses, striking readily to form live fences. There is a good deal of oral tradition about this tree: it is planted at house entrances, where it has long been used as a spirit tree and offering place to the ancestors. In former times it was also used to make defensive palisades (*aringa*) for settlements and trading posts along the Zambezi, and circles and rows of *muvurumira* associated with archaeological material can still be found along the Zambezi in uncultivated areas.

Musangu (*Acacia albida*): A tall tree growing up to 80 feet high, often found on riverbanks and alluvial flood plains.

For *Temwa* clearing:

Muzunga (*Acacia tortilis*): A tall tree growing up to 30 feet high, abundant on deep alluviums and fertile karroo soils, especially along watercourses.

Munyenyengwe (*Acacia usambarensis*): A large tree growing to 65 or more feet high on deep alluviums and fertile karroo sands, especially along rivers and small streams.

Mobobo (*Albizia versicolor*): A large tree growing to 50 or more feet high, often on sandy alluviums fringing watercourses.

---

convenient daily walking distance from their sources of water, whether rivers, seasonal streams, or springs. This feature too emerges clearly in figure 4 (though some streams were too small to include in the map), suggesting that the drilling of wells and the construction of small earthern weirs to retain water could free villages from their streamside locations and open up large new areas for cultivation. In many places fertile soils known to the Goba have gone unused for lack of water. In the late 1960s the Goba remaining in Namainga were fortunate in being able to exploit the more conveniently located alluviums. When scanning mature forest growth for signs of potential cultivation sites, they look for key tree species to indicate the presence of deep alluviums along riverbanks, streams, and flood plains (see table 6). The accuracy of this was verified by local surveys.

A Survey of Namainga

Namainga is still divided into locally recognized subchiefdoms that once had greater political significance, and they in turn are further divided into smaller neighborhoods and named localities. It is important to survey these subchiefly areas to facilitate an analysis of the demography and man-land ratios. In addition the survey will highlight ecological problems arising from the resettlement of six thousand Valley Tonga refugees from Lake Kariba and will be useful in assessing nearer-term possibilities of opening up new zones for settlement. Over the longer term a systematic area-by-area review of the Namainga ecosystem as it was in the late 1960s will be a valuable base line for future studies as conditions change and nationally significant plans for economic development are carried out in the territory.

The center of the chiefdom has been known as Chitondo (see fig. 4). There, along a slight rise two to four miles from the Zambezi and not far from extensive garden sites on the lower Lusitu River, is the former seat of the Banamainga chiefs. The place is still marked by a large stone slab (*gabwe a chitondo*), which early chiefs are said to have used as their stool. Two large ritual areas devoted to the spirits of former chiefs, royal relatives, and slaves are situated nearby. Twelve spirit huts were still in use in the late 1960s. Lying on the ground near these sites is a large, hollow baobab tree. It is said to have been the chief's storehouse for ivory and grain in early times. From a certain angle it resembles a reclining cow (*ingombe ilede* in Tonga) and has given its name to an important Iron Age trading site nearby. There used to be thick riverine growth along the Lusitu, including its lower reaches and alluvial delta, and extensive *matoro* gardening was carried out there in pre-Kariba times. The lower Lusitu area nearer its delta is known as Nyaukove, after the fingerling fish that could be caught in baskets during high water. Since much of the area had been preserved for the ritual groves and the population was relatively small, the Chitondo-Nyaukove area was plagued by elephants, hippos, elands, kudus, wild pigs, baboons, monkeys, and tsetse flies. Long ago newly chosen chiefs were allegedly required to survive a night alone in this wilderness to show the people that the ancient spirits of the land (*basangu*) had accepted them.

The banks of the lower Lusitu were once farmed and settled by scattered villages all the way to the delta. Other villages exploited the Zambezi south to the Mutulanganga tributary and north to Mugwarangwa, though the extensive *matoro* on the lower Lusitu are said to have been more reliable than those along the bigger river. Local villages specialized in growing large amounts of corn and tobacco in *matoro*, while treeless river terraces and pockets of alluvial soil a mile or more from the rivers were planted with staple sorghum. Fresh *temwa* acreage for sorghum near drinking water is said to have been relatively scarce, especially in Mugwarangwa, and that led to gradual abandonment of Chitondo and Mugwarangwa by the late 1940s when yields declined after many years' continual use. Animal inroads on more isolated *temwa* fields cut farther from water are also given as a reason for leaving. Most of the villages that left in the late 1940s withdrew to the Jamba and Nyamusaya areas, with some later moving to Ibwe Munyama and Matebe (figure 4). A seventh village is known to have moved south to Nanyanga. Another five villages left the Chitondo in 1951, when a newly installed chief moved his çapitol and close followers to the area west of Njami Hill. The move was made largely for political reasons, for most of the Zambezi frontage was empty by that time. While five villages remained in the Chitondo-Nyaukove area after that population shift, Mugwarangwa was completely empty. It had been an important district in the late nineteenth century. Although it had lacked large *temwa* acreages, three trading stations had been established there by traders who served the Namainga region and ate from *matoro* along the Zambezi.

Like the dry interior of Mugwarangwa, much of the land in from the main rivers in Farao is sterile *mopane* forest, with surface rock, stony ridges, and stunted shortgrass. Farao also suffers from the elephants that come down without hindrance from the uninhabited escarpment between Matebe and Namayora. The elephants also plague the Nyamusaya and Njami districts. In addition much of the alluvium at the confluence of the two major rivers is now covered with sand deposits. Nevertheless, the three villages in Farao district in the late 1960s were reasonably large, scattered settlements whose total population would be easy to underestimate, though much of the old *temwa* acreage was lying fallow. A good deal of *matoro* gardening was carried out there in pre-Kariba days, for the banks are lower and more easily flooded than those in Mugwaranga. Some of the farmland in Farao is being removed from village-level subsistence cultivation. A Catholic mission under the bishop of Monze has opened there, with a clinic, a small hospital, and a government grade school. As I left the field, a planned 25,000-acre experimental farm was being established to teach local people mechanical irrigation of riverine alluviums and other European agricultural techniques. Plans had been made to settle graduates of this course in favorable spots along the lower Kafue, the lower Lu-situ, and the Zambezi. Separate plans were being made to irrigate the banks of the Zambezi near the Kafue in Chiava chiefdom.

Mission operations in Farao district merged with developments associated with Chirundu Township at the Beit Bridge, which spans the Zambezi. On the Zambian side of the river the town consisted of two African country stores, a store run by an Indian merchant, a beer hall, gasoline station, and the regional police headquarters, together with a jail and a fairly large police housing compound, a customs and immigration post and its staff housing, and a depot for the Central African Motor Service. Some of these operations were curtailed or shut down after the former British colony Southern Rhodesia succeeded in making good its "unilateral declaration of independence" in 1965. As a result activity in Chirundu and travel across the bridge were much reduced. By the late 1960s sporadic guerrilla activity had begun against the white regime across the river, including the 1968 bombing of an army barracks in the southern half of Chirundu Township in what was then Southern Rhodesia (Maxey 1975).

The Nyanzara area behind Farao has never supported a recognized subchiefdom, since it has only short seasonal streams and does not benefit from any escarpment drainage. There are only a few scattered pockets of farmable soils near year-round drinking water, and these areas were being exploited in 1967–69 by a large, widely dispersed settlement that had recently been established on the all-weather Lusaka–Salisbury highway. Nyanzara District is named after the imposing mesa rising in its midst. There are small springs around its base, and the mesa ("place of hunger") was occasionally used as a refuge from precolonial raiders.

The Nyamusaya area is still thickly populated. Like the Chitondo-Nyaukove, Nanyanga, Nabanda, Jamba, and Ibwe Munyama districts, it was formerly headed by a chief or subchief. Like Farao and Mugwaranga, which were at times headed by traders, there was at least one precolonial trading station there, near the Kafue. Most of the population exploits alluvial soils bordering the lower Musaya River. The Musaya *matoro* have been considered more reliable than those of the Kafue. After the Musaya and Kafue alluvials, the third-most-favored location in this subchiefdom is the handsome hanging valley known as Matebe, in the escarpment at an elevation of 2,300 feet. Several villages are said to have migrated onto the northern plateau in Mazabuka district by working the soils of Nyamusaya, along the lower reaches of the river, and gradually moving upstream to Matebe and beyond. The Matebe and Namayora neighborhoods were more densly populated in the late nineteenth century and around the turn of the century, when many villages were still in hiding from the population dislocations, hunger, and raiding connected with the final gasps of the local slave trade and the start of the colonial era. That was also true of the upper Katwehele refuge area and several other arable pockets of land farther west in the escarpment hills, which, now uninhabited, were once crowded with heterogeneous immigrant groups and early tax dodgers. The uprising of the Banamainga in 1907 to 1914 was centered there and in the Namayora neighborhood, where the people drank from various upland streams and occasionally sallied forth to attack the touring district officer, who was intent on collecting head taxes and getting on with colonial administration. Some of the Matebe and Katwehele people joined the westward movement to Mazabuka or moved north of the Kafue Gorge to the area of the famous Shaman Sikoswe. Others migrated onto the plains near Lusaka. The Banamainga refugees were joined in these movements by others from Chiava and districts south of the Zambezi.

Like Mugwarangwa and Farao, Nanyanga subchiefdom contains a good deal of land that could be useful if water were more readily available (see fig. 6). The area behind Njami Hill contains large expanses of fertile soil. In areas near water that have long been worked by a series of villages, only a few big trees have been left standing, and the people have been turning to plowing and more fixed settlements. This is also noticeable in Nabanda, Jamba, the western Chitondo district, and in neighboring Sinadambwe chiefdom. There is little need for further tree clearing in most of these areas, except in northern Njami and Katwehele along the foot of the escarpment, where good soils have previously gone unused because of game, tsetse, and inconvenient water conditions. There is also some good unused land in dry game-and tsetse-infested territory between Njami and the westernmost Chitondo, as well as between Njami and the Nabanda and Jamba areas. These fertile areas have not been cultivated in living memory, and my sources were doubtful that they had ever been worked because of lack of water. Most of the rest of Njami, Nabanda, and Jamba is covered with *mopane* and rocky ridges. Njami, Nabanda, and Jamba are plagued by game, especially herds of elephants coming from the escarpments and the empty Hibameenda, but these districts have drawn a large population because cattle can now be kept in open areas. Over the long term the population of Njami, Nabanda, and Jamba has been draining off to the west along the Lusitu to the

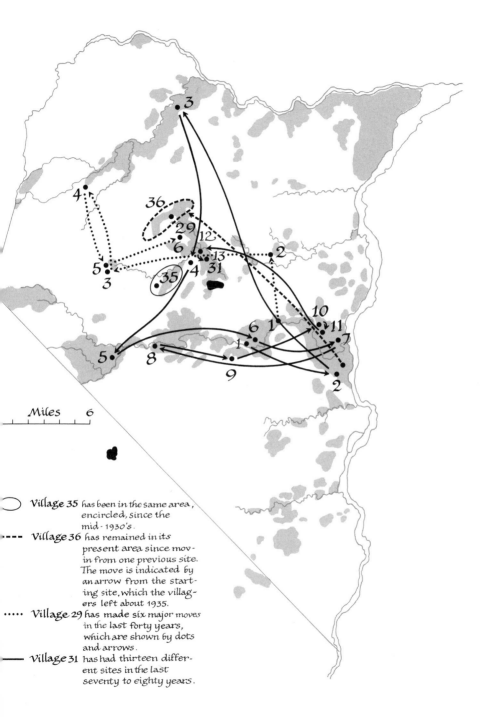

Miles   6

Village 35 has been in the same area, encircled, since the mid-1930's.

Village 36 has remained in its present area since moving in from one previous site. The move is indicated by an arrow from the starting site, which the villagers left about 1935.

Village 29 has made six major moves in the last forty years, which are shown by dots and arrows.

Village 31 has had thirteen different sites in the last seventy to eighty years.

Fig. 5. The Pattern of Village Mobility

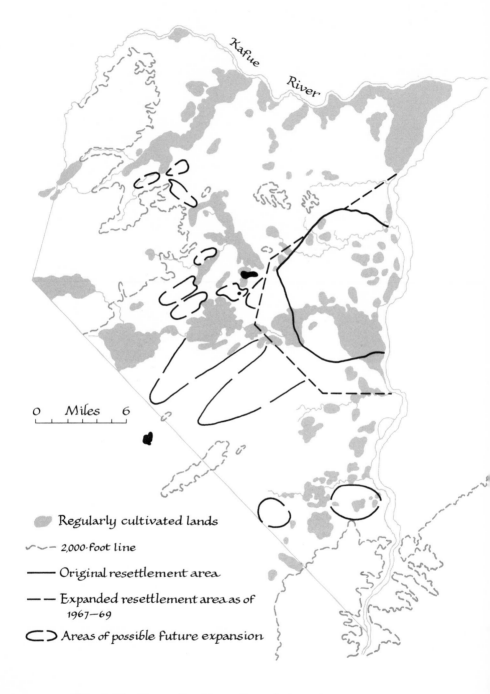

Regularly cultivated lands

2,000-foot line

Original resettlement area

Expanded resettlement area as of
1967–69

Areas of possible future expansion

Fig. 6. The Expanding Tonga Resettlement Area

area of Sinadambwe chiefdom, where cattle have been more numerous. Small groups have also migrated up to Ibwe Munyama subchiefdom and the Mazabuka region behind it.

The Hibameenda area south of the Lusitu and west of the Kariba road is named after a large, swampy depression that has long been a favorite spot for hunters in the dry season. According to tradition, the pan may have been settled long ago, but most of this area is composed of dry mopane forest and rocky ridges frequented only by hunters. Because of the game only a few of the good soils near Lusitu *matoro* sites have been cultivated within memory, though a survey conducted by the former Northern Rhodesia Agriculture Department (1955, p. 7) found that large areas south of the Lusitu could be farmed if water were made available (see fig. 6).

Finally, three Goba villages occupy a fairly large valley in the escarpment, watered by the upper reaches of the Mulolobela and Shindu tributaries of the Lusitu. This hanging valley, at an elevation of 3,400 feet, is known as Ibwe Munyama. While in recent years some families have shifted between Ibwe Munyama and the valley floor, the long-term population trend has been westward into Mazabuka district. Like Namainga, most of the inhabitants of Sinadambwe, south of Ibwe Munyama, are Goba whose ancestors originally came from Zimbabwe-Rhodesia. In fact, Siambezyo subchiefdom immediately west of Jamba along the Lusitu was once under Banamainga control. As Goba gradually migrate west along the alluvial soils bordering the Lusitu, most of them move on into the Changa area of Sinadambwe, where fertile soils at the foot of the escarpment are watered by the upper Lusitu. There are fewer tsetse to infect cattle, and the people have taken to plowing large, squared-off fields along the graded dirt track that connects Changa with the present center of Namainga at Njami Hill. Changa is generally considered to be a more progressive and prosperous area than Namainga.

When they settle in these uplands of Sinadambwe, the erstwhile Zambezi Goba lowlanders call themselves Zambian Tonga, and, indeed, that is the ethnic label indicated for the area in standard ethnographic sources (Colson 1960, 1971). Instead of continuing on to Changa, some migrants have moved up to Ibwe Munyama, also considered to be a Tonga area today, and from there many have continued on to the Mazabuka highland chiefdoms of Mweenda and Naluama. Casual checks in Naluama reveal that many people there still consider themselves Banamainga, though now they are Banamainga Tonga rather than Banamainga Goba. Because of its good defensive position, precolonial Banamainga chiefs sometimes

The valley uplands of Njami, Nabanda, and Jamba have drawn a large population because cattle can be kept in open areas. Cattle are a favorite investment and a great source of pride. Here a cattle owner proudly points to his herd. These are of the long-horned Sanga type found throughout subequatorial Africa.

made their headquarters at Ibwe Munyama, where they kept their cattle and controlled more territory than at present.

The Pattern of Village Mobility

As an individual village shifts from area to area, it develops its own set of local place-names. After it moves away, they are remembered as its old sites (*matongo*), and other villages tend to avoid them. Even if the original village later returns to farm the same soils, the village itself will occupy a slightly different spot and use a different cemetery. Death and sadness are commonly believed to pollute a place, and their occurrence may be taken to mean that

Cattle are so prestigious that those wanting their pictures taken in upland cattle-owning villages commonly pose by the main gate whether the cattle are theirs or not. The men shown are Penias Chirimbwa and Timothy Hakalle, my assistants.

living people have deliberately acted to kill, leaving a residue of aggrieved local spirits. That is another way of saying that people move, and stay away, because of bad memories.

Matongo refers to the places where a particular village has lived and has buried its dead. In the chief's village the word *Chitondo* is used instead. Sometimes people speak in more general terms, referring to their old subchiefdom as their *matongo*, especially if the village has moved about throughout the subchiefdom for a long time. Then the subchief may be referred to honorifically as the symbolic "owner" of the spirit realm (*sikatongo* or *ulanyika*), especially if he is a popular senior relative.

Elders usually have no specific plan to return to a particular site after it has been abandoned, especially if they are determined to join the drift to the uplands. Villages associated with prominent descent groups have been more conservative in this respect, since they have much to lose by leaving an area where they are well known to compete in upland areas that have become increasingly crowded and less attractive. If the *matongo* is remembered as a place with good soil and water, it may be returned to later if it is unoccupied when the village decides to move again at a later date and if the residents agree. But there is no rule that a village should necessarily plan to return to its old sites or that other villages should necessarily avoid them entirely. Questions of convenience, politics, and life-style prevailing at the time of the contemplated move affect such decisions. When a village is considering such a shift today, there are usually elders who remember whether the soils and water are good at former sites. Until recently these major factors have often been taken for granted, since population pressure has not been too great, though several old sites may have to be considered before an unused one is found in an environment most of the villagers favor at the moment.

Social and political factors may rule out all the old sites that are still remembered. Such considerations have kept many villages from returning to their old subchiefdoms along the Zambezi, which had been associated with old-fashioned life-styles, lack of cattle, and unreliable *matoro* gardens long before the Kariba Dam made artificial irrigation a practical, and attractive, necessity in those areas. Now some progressive Goba families have returned to the Zambezi in hopes of becoming vegetable-growing truck farmers, and one or two progressive Tonga households from the Mazabuka district have returned to open stores and take up large acreages for cotton. More of this migration is expected in the future.

But most of the Goba, who were still living in villages in the late 1960s, are mainly interested in avoiding residential isolation. They prefer fairly crowded neighborhoods, provided there is sufficient room for annual field extensions, for food gathering, for building materials, and yet some hunting areas, conveniently at hand. If the fields and gardens can be situated near those of friendly neighbors, much less sleep and food will be lost to animals during the long growing season. Crowded neighborhoods of political allies also assure large gatherings for parties and successful curing ceremonies and increase the likelihood that there is a store nearby. In some places today there are also a well, a school, a beerhall, and perhaps a clinic, an agricultural demonstrator, and bus service on the road to town. These factors are becoming increasingly important and often cause neglect of fine old sites too far from the new conveniences. Relevant ecological factors are changing. But in the final analysis, though a few small groups may still migrate to the uplands, and when all the above factors have been taken into consideration, there is still a general feeling, if not a rule, among conservatives that it is somehow right that a village that has survived through the generations should manage to stay near or return to one of its favored *matongo*.

The extent to which villages actually shift about under a system of "shifting cultivation" is largely if not entirely determined by the character of the soils exploited. As noted earlier, the Goba farm three kinds of soils. They cultivate young alluviums near rivers and streams for winter and summer crops. These fall into the category Allan called "permanent cultivation land" (1965). Throughout Zambia soils of this type can be used without permanent damage for comparatively long cultivation periods, ranging from ten to fourteen years, followed by a short fallow. Only limited amounts of land of this type have been available in Namainga. The average size of upland *matoro* gardens is only 0.7 acres (table 4). In tabulating the number of mouths actually fed from forty-seven of these streamside gardens in the Njami area, I found an average per capita *matoro* acreage of only 0.167. That is probably typical of Namainga as a whole. Since it includes acreage that floods reliably only in rare good years, it can be seen that "permanent cultivation land" of this type does not loom unduly large in the Goba scheme of things.

Most of the acreage depended upon is composed of older alluviums falling into Allan's "semipermanent" to "permanent" land categories. Like permanently cultivatable soils, semipermanent soils also allow a definite, more or less lasting relationship between the cultivating household and a particular parcel of land, approximating the Western concept of the small family farm. These lands can normally be hoe-cultivated for four to six years before falling yields suggest the need for a rest, an appropriate crop rotation, or a thorough plowing. Many *temwa* fields in the relatively tsetse-free upland areas of Njami, Nabanda, Jamba, and Ibwe Munyama are plowed every few years to keep the soil loose and easily tillable with the hoe and to improve or maintain yields. Some of the *temwa* fields exploit fertile karroo soils as well as old alluviums. Some of these karroos fall into Allan's "recurrent cultivation" category, though many may be classified as semipermanent or even permanent soils (Allan 1965, p. 148).

Since the Goba rely almost exclusively on permanent to semipermanent soils, some villages have been fairly permanent settlements, while others have exhibited a range of "voluntary" mobility. For example, in figure 5 village 35 has occupied the same general site since the middle 1930s. There have been considerable rebuilding, expansion, and contraction during the intervening period, but as of 1967–69 there had been no significant shift for some forty years. Some of the original buildings and timbers were still in use. In addition to fine upland-valley soils, there were no termites near village 35. Village 36 has had a similarly stable career. It voluntarily left the Chitondo-Nyaukove area for political reasons around 1935 and has occupied the same general location under the northern Njami foothills ever since, though five short moves have been made within this area because of dilapidation and site fouling caused by termites and other factors. None of these moves exceeded two hundred yards, and they occurred at intervals averaging six or seven years. Village 29 has followed a more volatile pattern, making six major moves in about forty years, for an average of six to seven years per site. Similarly, village 31 has occupied thirteen different sites in the last seventy to eighty years of its remembered history, approximating some six years for each major shift, a span of time that was probably related to *temwa* yields in the days before cattle-drawn plowing was a possibility in most of upland Namainga. In former times most *temwa* fields were abandoned after about six years' use, and contemplated village shifts were likely to occur at the same time. Village 31 exhibits a mixed pattern in figure 5. Like village 29, it has made a number of major moves. Like villages 35 and 36, it has also shown some tendency to linger near its *matongo*.

Man-Land Ratios and the Carrying Capacity of the Land

Most young village residents today favor a stable habitation pattern featuring periodic plowing, permanent fields, some cotton cash cropping, a village site near a road, and such modern necessities as a permanent well, country stores, and motor transportation. The preceding section shows that some villages have in fact been sedentary in the past, but the extent to which the entire population can accomplish this depends, in the final analysis, on the carrying capacity of the land (Allan 1965, pp. 8–9; Brush 1975). To calculate this factor, within broad working limits at least, figure 4 can be used as a soils map, since it is based on time-tested local patterns of land classification and land use. In the preparation of figure 4, it was found that about 118 square miles of the valley floor in Namainga (22 percent of the entire territory) have been available for cultivation under prevailing conditions.

The next task was to estimate the population factor. Earlier population figures compiled by Europeans and their assistants were unreliable for this remote area, and the Goba saw little reason to cooperate. In colonial times taxes and work obligations were imposed upon those enumerated in censuses. In 1933, Thomson (1934) estimated that there were 7,015 Goba on the valley floor below Ibwe Munyama in Namainga and Chiava chiefdoms. In 1961 local tax records showed 5,374 in Namainga alone (Bainbridge and Edmonds n.d.). My own estimate for Namainga in the late 1960s was about 7,800. This figure allows an average population of 150 for each village, including temporarily absent migrant wage earners. While it exceeds the known population of a number of smaller villages, it makes allowance for many of the outlying hamlets that apparently have never been included in local counts and also allows for the growing local populations to be found around the Chirundu and Lusitu townships (see fig. 9). On this basis Namainga has a population density of 14.6 per square mile. This figure rises to an average of 66.1 per square mile of choice cultivated farmlands shown in figure 4. Densities of this magnitude in the region are not unusual. Population is known to have exceeded 300 per square mile in Zambezi River meander zones in upper-river sections of the Gwembe district and at the mouths of larger tributaries, where particularly well disposed alluvial terraces could be exploited for *matoro*-type gardening before Kariba Dam was built (Scudder 1962, p. 130).

This level of population pressure on the prime soils farmed by the Goba makes available a per capita average of 9.7 acres of choice farmland. As compared with this figure, my figures show that the Goba actually keep a per capita average of only 0.83 acres under cultivation at any one time (see table 7).

The veteran agricultural mainstays enumerated in table 7, group 1, are usually older man-wife teams working together on comparatively large acreages. But since their young dependents regularly rely on them for food because of crop failure in their own plots, lesser skills, illness, or most commonly in recent times an inability to find wage work in town, their *net* per capita acreages are actually substantially lower by harvest time even in average crop years. Older couples with many children and grandchildren take this eventuality into consideration when planning their seasonal cycle. The acreages tabulated for veteran mainstay households also in-

Table 7
The Cultivation Factor:
Per Capita Acreage Kept in Cultivation (Allan 1965)

Group 1: Veteran "mainstay" households supporting many dependents
  Sample size: 19 households
  Average *temwa* acreage per mouth: 0.55
  Average *matoro* acreage per mouth: 0.17
  ⟡ 0.72 acres per capita

Group 2: "Partial" households relying on town money
  Sample size: 17 households
  Average *temwa* acreage per mouth: 0.5
  Average *matoro* acreage per mouth: 0.1
  ⟡ 0.6 acres per capita

Group 3: Younger prime-adult households
  Sample size: 9 households
  Average *temwa* acreage per mouth: 0.68
  Average *matoro* acreage per mouth: 0.22
  ⟡ 0.9 acres per capita

Group 4: Old women working alone
  Sample size: 6 households
  Average *temwa* acreage per mouth: 1.61
  Average *matoro* acreage per mouth: 0.16
  ⟡ 1.77 acres per capita

Group 5: Old women or couples with few dependents
  Sample size: 9 households
  Average *temwa* acreage per mouth: 0.59
  Average *matoro* acreage per mouth: 0.18
  ⟡ 0.77 acres per capita

Average per capita, all 60 households
  Temwa acreage: 0.67
  Matoro acreage: 0.16
  ⟡ 0.83 acres per capita

clude any separate fields the father or grandfather may have planted for beer and trading purposes, since these crops are readily diverted to subsistence use in hard times. The elders in group 1 are typically senior, central people with many social ties and many mouths to feed, even in good times. Because of that they are also the most overworked members of the agricultural community. Though their unmarried youngsters help them in the fields, elders do not, and cannot, control the labor or drain off the produce of other adults or other households. On the contrary, they attract children and elders in distress or left behind by those in town, and most of the labor they exploit is their own.

The "partial" households listed in table 7 as group 2 are young married couples who farm only irregularly because the wife visits her husband in town and sometimes fails to return in time to sow a crop or fails to attend it regularly during the crop year. The wage-seeking husband is rarely home to help, and the wife and children must either purchase food with his cash remittances or depend on her parents if her own fields are insufficiently productive. She usually does a little of both. At this stage in the family circle these "partial" families are not self-sufficient agricultural units, and their per capita acreages are the smallest. Both their living compounds in the village and their fields and gardens are likely to be clustered near those of the wife's mother. Because wage-paying jobs are sometimes difficult to find and keep, employed men cannot plan to come home to help at peak labor times in the crop year.

Group 3 households are those in which the husband, slightly older now, has finally come home permanently and is helping in the fields. He is especially likely to work his own plots (zunde) for beer, excess grain that he can barter or sell for petty cash, and tobacco. Combined per capita acreages are larger in these growing families. As their children and friends make their home a center of village activity, these prime-adult households begin forming visibly separate residential clusters within the wife's mother's village. They are normally fully independent subsistence units, though a very bad year can always send them looking for help from relatives and friends. When their bride-service obligations are completed, political and social considerations often motivate the husband and wife to rebuild their miniature village in various spots throughout the settlement or even farther afield.

The older women farmers of group 4 are still great assets to the agricultural community, and the same active good health that makes this possible also makes them senior figures in the social system. Because they are usually widowed and many of their children have already formed independent subsistence units, these older women may have unusually large grain reserves. They represent the final phase of the life cycle, having passed through the vigorous years of prime-adult independence to form large mainstay households when their husbands were still alive. As long as they retain their health, perhaps well into their sixties and seventies, these remarkable women will see their homes and gardens ringed

Table 8

The Cultivation Factor in Zambia:

Average per Capita Acreage Kept in Cultivation in Various Ethnic
Groups (Allan 1965, 57–58)

	Acres
Zambia (Northern Rhodesia) as a whole	1.07
Plateau Tonga	1.11
Swaka (Red loams)	1.09
Chinamora Shona (Zimbabwe-Rhodesia)	1.08
Mzimba Tumbuka	1.08
Ngoni-Chewa	1.08
Ndembu Lunda	1.07
Lamba	1.01
Valley Tonga*	0.97
Goba	0.83

*Scudder 1962, calculated from Appendix B.

by those of descendants and friends. Since they maintain very large fields, their per capita acreage is generally the highest in the community. Their fields tend to be less productive older ones, however.

Older women or couples living more or less alone in their section of the village and in failing health (group 5), have the most difficult time. Their daughters are no longer nearby for help and company, and their sons-in-law are no longer remitting money from town to help with plowing and other needs, nor are they clearing fresh *temwa* fields.

The average per capita acreage, or cultivation factor, of 0.83 (table 7) is the lowest yet recorded for the region (see table 8). According to Scudder's material, a representative group of pre–Kariba Valley Tonga upstream of the Goba have the next-lowest known cultivation factor, an average of 0.97 acres per capita. This figure compares fairly closely with the 1.07 that Allan previously established as subsistence average for rural Zambia. Allan's somewhat higher figure is based on plateau ethnic groups lacking the kind of year-round *matoro* gardening typically found in the Zambezi Valley, and this factor may account for the lower figures reported for the valley-dwelling Tonga and Goba. The *matoro* factor should not be given too much weight, however, since acreages have been small and results unreliable. Unavoidable mechanical errors in accurately measuring actively used acreages and in counting the full number of dependent mouths actually eating from any one plot virtually guarantee that there will be a range of per capita acreage figures in any representative sample. Furthermore, the observed cultivation factor, or active acreage required for life support, normally varies considerably among households and ethnic groups supplementing (as all do) subsistence cultivation with variable amounts of gathering, hunting, fishing, animal husbandry, use of cash, and barter. Individual and life-cycle differences with respect to the intensiveness of labor inputs and varying individual indifference to declining yields on older plots also make it unwise to place undue reliance on a precise figure for the cultivation factor. As Allan has shown, the cultivation factor among the Swaka on the northern plateau varies from 1.09 to 1.67, depending on soil characteristics. Health, age, marital status, number of dependents who unexpectedly return home and seek support, and factors of personal inclination have similar scattering effects in individual cases and thus affect larger statistical samples, as illustrated in table 7.

While such figures obviously must vary, a cultivation factor centering roughly on a figure of one acre per person has generally been taken as the actively cultivated acreage required for normal subsistence support from one major staple harvest to the next. Given the low population densities characteristic of Africa's savannas in areas least affected by cities and the former colonial reserve system, a cultivation factor of this order of magnitude has normally left ample room for gathering wild foods and medicines, grazing, hunting, and collecting other items required by the material culture. The analysis of farming yields in chapter 9 will show why supplementary food-getting activities are so necessary.

Finally, in making a realistic assessment of the carrying capacity of the land under any one system of cultivation, one must consider the relationship between the duration of active land use and the period of subsequent rest considered necessary for restoration and maintenance of acceptable fertility. This land-use factor, as it has been called (Allan 1965), will also vary with local conceptions of adequate "rest" and "fertility." One way of expressing the land-use factor has been to determine the number of "garden areas" required by the average family. This number should include the total subsistence acreage currently in use plus the acreage of all the unused former plots lying in varying stages of fallow and natural regeneration. In theory the total number of garden areas held in inventory by each family should be sufficient to enable every farm family to abandon land temporarily when yields fall below (and necessary work inputs rise above) some locally acceptable standard at the same time that old acreages can be taken up again without shortening the period of fallow required to maintain them in perpetually "undamaged" condition. This idealistic but useful working concept rests on the unproved assumption that human knowledge and population density may remain in such a balance that life can be sustained indefinitely from cultivation of the soil.

In the Goba example each person should have an active "garden area" averaging about 0.83 acres. This is the cultivation factor ascertained by empirical investigation. If this area should happen to be comprised of annually inundated *matoro* that gives a year-round yield, is never covered by sterile layers of sand, and is never eroded away, the land-use factor would be 1, since the same garden area could theoretically be used in perpetuity, if social and political factors permit. That would place it in Allan's "permanent-cultivation" category, though in practice Allan found that in most cases of permanent cultivation land each individual actually requires up to 2 garden areas (Allan 1965, pp. 31–32).

Much of the land cultivated by the Goba falls into the semipermanent category. Before the advent of plowing, Allan calculated, land of this type might typically be farmed for six years, rested for six years, farmed for another six years, and then left alone for twelve years or more. In this cycle each garden area would be used some 40 percent of the time (twelve years out of thirty). To provide the cultivator a supply of suitably fresh acreage each and every year, a 40 percent use factor requires him to maintain a total inventory of 2½ to 3 full garden areas. It is this 2½-to-3 land-use factor that characterizes Allan's semipermanent land category. It is of interest to note that the "recurrent-cultivation" soils of most of Africa's savannas require a land-use factor of 4 to 8 full garden areas.

Relatively low population density (14.6 per square mile) and the presence of ample permanent to semi-permanent land have evidently been enabling the Goba to use their land more selectively and for longer periods than have most other African savanna cultivators. Their land-use factor has probably ranged from, say, 2 to 3 full garden sets per family rather than 4 to 8, though some families and settlements have chosen to be more mobile. If we take the more conservative figure of 3 as the land-use factor, we find that on a per capita basis the average individual *requires* something on the order of 2.49 acres (obtained by multiplying the cultivation factor of 0.83 by the land-use factor of 3). As compared with this per capita land requirement of only 2½ acres, we have already found that the estimated 7,800 Goba in Namainga have actually had available a per capita average of 9.7 acres of the choice cultivated soils shown in figure 4.

The maximum long-term carrying capacity of the soils actually cultivated by the Goba with their current techniques, knowlege, and desires has averaged one person per 2½ acres. On this basis the 75,520 acres (or 118 square miles) of choice land shown in table 5 could support some 30,000 people (or 254 per cultivated square mile), over three times the 1967–69 population of about 7,800 (66 per cultivated square mile). But at that population density, and especially in bad years, there would surely be considerable land pressure resulting from the combined needs of upland cattle grazing, lowland small-stock grazing, vegetable gathering, fuel and building-supplies gathering, and hunting, though there is no way to quantify these important land-use factors with any confidence. Because subsistence cultivation has not been sufficient to feed the people without considerable inputs from gathering, animal husbandry, hunting, fishing, and the cash sector of the economy, it must be kept in mind that the "carrying capacity" of the land is a dangerously incomplete indicator to the extent that it excludes these other life-supporting activities. Yields from subsistence cultivation are analyzed in chapter 9.

The Valley Tonga Resettlement and Future Prospects

All available evidence indicates that the Namainga Goba have not been suffering from land pressure in recent decades. Man-land ratios probably were tighter in the turbulent second half of the nineteenth century, though it is doubtful that this was a refuge area throughout precolonial history. Since the Pax Britannica regional population patterns have changed, leaving the more conservative groups who have remained in Namainga in a situation of considerable slack as measured in terms of man-land ratios. It was this slack, combined with the near desertion of the Zambezi frontage, that made Namainga the home of about six thousand Valley Tonga refugees displaced by the formation of Lake Kariba. Most of these refugees were placed in the old Goba districts of Mugwarangwa, which had been entirely abandoned, and Chitondo-Nyaukove, where only four Goba settlements had remained. The resettlement began in 1956.

The good soils of this underpopulated "Lusitu Resettlement Area," as it has come to be known, had long caught the eye of government planners. In 1952 the Northern Rhodesia colonial government gave financial backing to an attempt by Rhodesian Sugar Refineries, Ltd., to set up a pilot sugarcane operation in Mugwarangwa (Northern Rhodesia Government Reports 1951, 1952, 1953; Federation of Rhodesia and Nyasaland 1962). In the testing for this project most of the area inland from the Zambezi was found unsuitable for irrigation. As Goba land-use patterns suggest, the best soils were found to be alluviums along the lower Lusitu and its delta, though some were being used by the small Goba population still in the vicinity. One hundred trial acres of sugarcane were planted near the banks of the Zambezi north of the Lusitu, largely on old *matoro* soils, but results were mixed on shallower soils back from the river, and the scheme was abandoned (Northern Rhodesia Government Reports 1954).

While the uneven surface area and high sodium content of the soil made large-scale commercial irrigation impractical, the vicinity was resurveyed a few years later in connection with plans to resettle Valley Tonga refugees from the impending formation of Lake Kariba (Northern Rhodesia Government Reports 1956). This second survey earmarked an expanse of 25,000 largely uninhabited acres, some 39 square miles, in Mugwarangwa, Chitondo-Nyaukove, and eastern Njami districts. Figure 6 shows that roughly two-thirds of this area had been uncultivated in the past. Applying our carrying capacity figure of one person for 2.5 to 3 acres of cultivable soil, the approximately 8,300 acres of formerly cultivated soils in the resettlement area could support 2,800 to 3,300 traditional cultivators. This calculation makes no allowance for the impairment of *matoro* gardening since the Kariba Dam. But the resettlement planners did not use African land-use standards in making their calculations. They considered that most of this 25,000-acre zone was arable, though most cultivation sites would be far from water. It was calculated that the carrying capacity of the area was roughly one person per 5 acres, and while even this unrealistic planning should have suggested a figure of 5,000 refugees if water was made available, 6,000 Tonga were moved there in 1956–57.

This is not the place to review the story of the resettlement of the Tonga and their subsequent attempts to come to terms with their new Goba neighbors. Most of the story has already been published, and both the resettlement planning and Tonga reactions to it are well known. For an authoritative discussion of the resettlement see Colson (1960), along with popular accounts by Clements (1959), Robins and Legge (1959), and Howarth (1961). For subsequent Tonga reactions and adjustments see Colson (1971), Scudder and Colson (1972) and Colson and Scudder (1975).

However they may have reacted in earlier years, by the late 1960s most of the Goba felt little resentment that so much of the valley floor in Namainga had been settled and, for all intents and purposes, taken over by foreigners who had formerly lived a hundred miles upstream. Except for migrant laborers meeting by chance in towns or on jobs in the valley, there had been no social, political, religious, or economic contact between these peoples before the resettlement. Now the newcomers, under their own chief and with government backing, occupied about 9 percent of the valley floor, including the former seat of the Banamainga chiefs in Chitondo-Nyaukove. In the process they had obliterated the main land-shrine groves and eliminated any remaining chance the Goba had to use *matoro* on the lower Lusitu and in Muwarangwa in such drought years as 1968. Most of the lingering resentment was kept alive by rival ambitions within the conservative royal clan. The family currently in power had forced most of the remaining villages to vacate the Chitondo after the succession of Chali Sikaongo in 1951. By 1967 dissident royals seeking to replace the aging Banamainga chief with their own candidates were using this activity against the incumbent branch of the chiefly clan. They claimed that the chief's connivance with an unpopular colonial government in withdrawing from the Chitondo had made the fateful Tonga resettlement possible. Just as I left the field, Chali Sikaongo's bitter successor from an opposing branch of the royal clan was planning to return the Banamainga capital to its rightful place in the Chitondo area, this time south of the Lusitu, despite the presence of the intrusive Tonga.

Although the move is designed to be a symbol of change from the policies of the old regime, it will be difficult for the new leader to have much impact unless the court and a sizable village population move with him. Such a move would give easy access to government development agencies in the resettlement area, but is unlikely. The area south of Chitondo is crowded with Tonga and lacks water. The other genuine source of resentment, held mainly by the few Goba still residing in the resettlement area, stemmed from the loss of the *matoro* and its *masao* trees, though the loss was clearly tempered by the fact that Kariba, rather than the refugees, had sealed the fate of the Zambezi and lower Lusitu *matoro*.

Before the coming of the refugee Tonga in 1956–57, the resettlement area had been tsetse-infested. That is verified by the report of a commission of inquiry on this area in 1958, now on file in the Lusaka archives (and see Scudder 1962). As we have seen, most of the Goba had voluntarily left the area for the Namainga uplands and neighboring areas in Sinadambwe and Mazabuka districts, where small streamside *matoro* are still available and cattle could be kept. When Chali Sikaongo led his closest royal followers to Njami in 1951, it was to share these upland benefits and prevent the chiefship from becoming an outmoded, isolated relic in its unpopular old ritual area. Another factor prominent in Chali Sikaongo's succession had been opposition charges of government interference in his selection, since Chali's father had not been patrilineally related to his chiefly predecessors. His opponents therefore called him a "government" chief, a charge Chali unsuccessfully sought to weaken by withdrawing from the budding government center at the nearby Mugwarangwa sugar operation, where game department and administrative headquarters were also situated.

Aside from the stratagems of chiefly aspirants, much of the resentment still voiced by the Goba in the late 1960s was really aimed at diverting government development funds to themselves rather than turning back the clock to enable a mass return of Goba to the Zambezi. As noted many times, the move to the uplands had already been an old, established pattern well before this time and most of the Goba, including the royal clan, had been intent on joining this trend, assuming an upland or Tonga status, and acquiring cattle. Indeed, the most lasting source of friction with the resettled people may well prove to center on this question of ethnic identity (see Lancaster 1971, 1974b), since the refugee Valley Tonga and most of the government agents sent to help them have not fully realized that the Banamainga Goba in upland neighborhoods had already been successfully posing as Tonga for some time.

As the Goba (or Banamainga Tonga) put it, most of the Tonga resettlement area had been "useless" to those seeking cattle before the government launched an ambitious campaign to eliminate game, fell the forest and bush, and thus attempt to control if not eradicate the tsetse fly. Water was also made conveniently available. This program, lavishly expensive in local eyes, took a long time, and in the interim the refugee Tonga suffered and were not envied. As late as 1968 pockets of tsetse were killing stock in the resettlement area, and even in 1969 work was still in progress to provide adequate water supplies. The wells originally drilled to supply water in 1956–57 had had to be abandoned in favor of mineral-free running water pumped in from the Zambezi. When I left the field in March, 1969, the Gwembe Rural Council was still in-

Gwembe Rural Council employees installing a water-storage tank in the Lusitu Resettlement Area.

stalling twenty 10,000-gallon water storage tanks in the resettlement area. Each tank was to have a large concrete cattle trough, water taps, and lines running to outlying settlements. The resettlement area had also been well laid out, with roads, schools, and a clinic. Government funds had been forthcoming to aid in cash cropping, making the Lusitu Resettlement Area one of Zambia's important rural-development showcases. Despite the obvious hardships previously suffered by the newcomers, the resettlement area was seriously overcrowded by the late 1960s, although it had become an object of some envy among Goba who had previously inhabited the area and called it their own but who now felt that they had too little share in these attractive developments.

By 1969 the number of resettled Tonga had grown above their original number of about 6,000. They had numbered 6,437 in 1961 (Bainbridge n.d.), and while no accurate count is available for later years, an estimate of 7,000 may be used for 1969. If we continue to use a per capita cultivation factor of 1 and a land-use factor of 3, Namainga's previously cultivated soils could support a total population of about 25,000, assuming that all the people were free to utilize the entire territory. That is still well above the 1969 combined population of 14,800, comprised of 7,800 original inhabitants and about 7,000 refugees. That the resettlement area was becoming well watered, thus adding acreage to the cultivable category, and that the upland Banamainga are periodically plowing their fields and thereby perhaps shaving their own land-use factor somewhat, though needing additional grazing land for their growing number of cattle, should make us feel even more comfortable with this favorable man-land ratio. Assuming that the Namainga soils map (fig. 4)., Allan's soil classifications and land-use factors, and the population estimates and land-use factors are all reasonably near their intended marks, there is still no desperate population pressure in Namainga as a whole. But the validity of the analysis rests on several important provisos.

The resettlement area is very tightly packed with people. This area, only 7.3 percent of Namainga, now supports a population nearly equal to that of the original inhabitants of the entire territory before resettlement. No environmental degradation was noted in Namainga before the construction of the Kariba Dam. Now the denuded Lusitu Resettlement Area is desperately overcrowded with people and stock, even with the provision of water to make large tracts habitable for the first time. In addition, this violation of the Valley Tonga's normally dispersed settlement pattern along watercourses creates unusual hardships. In the late 1960s the resettlement area had a population of 180 per square mile. The people living in the center of this large, roughly circular area six to seven miles wide (see fig. 6), were far from the grazing, gathering, and hunting grounds that comparably dense populations strung out along rivers had enjoyed in their old middle-river homes before the dam was built. The crowding is made worse by the loss of old-time Zambezi *matoro* and hostile relations with Zimbabwe-Rhodesia across the river. In former times dense riverine populations commonly used the environment of both banks of the Zambezi for gathering and intensive *matoro* cultivation. Now that is impossible. In the regions immediately north, southwest, and south of the resettlement area the grazing is poor, tsetse are still present, and household water supplies are inadequate. Those living in the center of the resettlement area and nearer the Zambezi are thus caught in a particularly severe situation.

A 1972 photographic image of the Lusitu Resettlement Area taken by the National Aeronautics and Space Administration's Landsat experimental satellite program for monitoring the earth's resources. The denuded resettlement area reflecting light on the left bank of the Zambezi is midway between Lake Kariba and the Kafue River. The heavily farmed Tonga highlands are west of the darker valley escarpment zone. The right bank of the Zambezi had apparently been cleared of vegetation for military reasons.

The serious overcrowding could be alleviated by expanding the artificially improved environment of the resettlement area, by moving the newcomers elsewhere altogether, or by allowing the people to move freely throughout the natural environment of the remaining portions of Namainga. Although rumors of further removals were upsetting some of the refugees in 1967–69, there is no reason that the refugees should be moved again, after all their hardships and the government's efforts. If the man-land calculations presented in this chapter are at all useful, they indicate that Namainga can in fact support its presently doubled population if people are allowed to leave the resettlement area to exploit the natural environment of the entire territory on their own. But in the late 1960s the government had evidently decided not to permit the refugees to redistribute themselves freely in this manner.

Two factors seemed to underlie this decision. First, there may still be cultural and political factors favoring differential treatment of the two populations now sharing Namainga territory. Cultural differences would probably become negligible in time if refugees were allowed to leave the resettlement area gradually to mingle with the Banamainga, especially if government services were equally accessible and available to all the people. While it would be uneconomic to disperse government facilities presently head-quartered in the Lusitu area, greater attention to Banamainga settlements throughout the territory would improve the situation, especially if benefits meant for the refugees were maintained or stepped up. Many Banamainga already take advantage of opportunities in the Lusitu, especially agricultural advice and government loans. A few intergroup marriages have been initiated, though in the late 1960s none had yet stabilized into lasting marriages.

The significant political factor associated with differential treatment is that the refugee Tonga in their new showcase home have been supporting the political party in power at the national level, UNIP. Like most other inhabitants of Zambia's Southern Province, the older inhabitants have continued to support the rival African National Congress (ANC), the parent group of UNIP, which had been officially banned by 1967. Government representatives visiting Namainga have declared that only UNIP members will receive government help. An additional factor is the irrigation school in the Farao area. At the time I left the field, it was scheduled to occupy another tract of about 25,000 acres, equal in size to the original Lusitu resettlement zone. If the irrigation plans materialize, this lightly inhabited region would no longer be available for village-level subsistence purposes, and it would soon be extremely difficult for the expanding population of UNIP-supporting refugees—to say nothing of the Banamainga—to find suitable soil, grazing, gathering, and hunting areas, if the government was impolitic enough to leave them to their own devices.

Since it seems both humanely and politically unwise to leave the Kariba refugees crowded as they are, to resettle them, or even to leave them alone to pioneer an increasingly crowded environment, the only solution to the problem of extreme land pressure and environmental degradation in the original Lusitu resettlement area is obviously to expand it, making provision for water supplies and tsetse clearance, as before. Planning for such expansion was already well under way in 1969. In fact, figure 6 shows, the original resettlement area had already been expanded, its borders extended, at least on paper, though rank-and-file Goba were unaware of it, and few resettled Tonga villages had had time to take advantage of it. Additional areas were already being earmarked for further development, pending availability of funds for water development and tsetse clearance. What happens next will have to be the concern of future field study.[2]

---

[2] According to Scudder (personal communication, October, 1978), today the original Lusitu Resettlement Area is a dust bowl and population pressures are desperate in places. Some refugee villages had actually moved out of the resettlement area by 1967. It was common knowledge among the Banamainga, who were watching the situation closely. To the best of my knowledge government officials had persuaded all but one of these villages to return, though I occasionally encountered refugee men and women hunting or gathering beyond the limits. More recent information from Scudder and others suggests that refugee villages have now had time to occupy the additional areas allotted to them in the expansion I learned of before leaving the field. One village may have moved farther, into uninhabited portions of Nanyanga.

The Zambezi Valley's exposed military position plus national economic hardships stemming from Zambia's economic boycott of the breakaway British colony of Southern Rhodesia, now Zimbabwe-Rhodesia, have greatly curtailed development plans. Because of that the large additional areas earmarked for refugee expansion (see fig. 6) have not been developed. The plight of the refugees is therefore still severe inasmuch as the first-round expansion opened up poor areas for cultivation, except for the soils on the west along the Lusitu River.

On the bright side for the Banamainga, the Zambezi training farm at the Kafue confluence occupies only 250 acres rather than the 25,000 originally called for.

6
The Traditional Chiefdom and its Wider World

The senior descent group in a chiefdom in Central and Southern Africa has typically been the royal or chiefly line. Other descent groups radiate from this line in a fairly irregular fashion, which has been called the "drift method of segmentation." Links among descent groups are always political in nature, since the groups' relationships to one another, their relative seniority in the ancestral cult, their ability to attract and retain adherents, and their claims to chiefly and subchiefly stools all rest to a significant extent on their alleged seniority of segmentation and connection to the chiefly line. The result is a merging segmentary series of descent groups, each of which traces some real or fictive connection to the main chiefly line or organizational spinal cord of the chiefdom (Middleton and Tait 1958; Fox 1967, pp. 125–26).

The image of a main line of chiefly descent has been a political fiction among the Goba, since most precolonial successions were ultimately based on force and sometimes were accompanied by secession of dissident factions, shifts to other territories, the arrival of new groups forging new links and claims to the chiefly line, and outright usurpation by groups of warriors and traders. Yet through all the changes some image of a worthwhile if fictive and imprecise chiefly line has nonetheless been maintained for its symbolic value. Even after the colonial era, when violent self-help was outlawed, successful accession to the chiefship has always been a matter of live political force rather than simple precedent or cut-and-dried genealogical seniority, as the term "chiefly line" might seem to suggest. While commoners are clearly distinguished from chiefs and important councilors, a great deal of overlap has occurred between royal and commoner descent groups since the political units within which all must live (villages, subchieftaincies, and chiefdoms) have been relatively small, largely endogamous, and crosscut by patron-client ties expressed in the unifying idiom of kinship. Cognatic descent groups are never clearly bounded, and at all levels of the segmentary-descent-group system, from village cores to competing chiefly lines, there has been a lack of indisputable precision in ordering the seniority of component groupings. The political scene was even more opportunistic in the precolonial era, when groups of traders, raiders, elephant hunters, shifting cultivators, immigrants, and political and religious emissaries were on the move.

Today as yesterday each descent group in the chiefdom has a different vision of the common fictive chiefly spinal cord and the group's relation to it, and the many traditions surrounding the chiefly line constitute the political history of the country. These commonly include elements of myth combined with selectively remembered bits of history. The historical element is likely to be preserved in a tightly compressed allegorical form designed to serve the current interests of opposing factions. Taken together, myth and fact approximate what Malinowski had in mind when he coined the term "historical charter." For whether they tell of heroic migrations and founding efforts, of rightful conquest, of primal occupation dating from some unchallengeable zeropoint in time, or of some fictive line of ancient descent, the myths associated with ruling groups and high office are always designed to support political claims to prerogatives of various kinds. That is why Goba elders have maintained their fiction of a chiefly line in the face of a very different reality, and Goba traditions repeat all these legitimizing themes.

Since the stock of free-form traditions embellishing a chiefly line obviously contains many elements in a segmentary society, each descent group competing for influence highlights those traditions that pertain to its own position in the political arena, and descent-group elders stress the relationship of their own apical ancestors to the chiefly line. For groups not currently in power this competition is usually expressed in allegiance to the memory and shrine of a particular chief of the past from whom they trace their best current claim to seniority, and the order and manner in which the names and deeds of past chiefs are recited—or omitted—usually reflect on the incumbent group and contain an implicit suggestion for the next succession. Once in power the effective descent group of the incumbent usually grows large, since it is essentially an unbounded political faction, and an attempt is made to limit future successions to its branches only and thus to exclude rival groups.

The "king lists" collected from elders in rival descent groups tend to have common characteristics. The names of a few early, possibly mythical figures are given at the top of the list, as if to ensure a sense of ancient legitimacy, and one has the impression that considerable unrepresented time has been telescoped between them. The inventory of names used in this connection in Namainga chiefdom contains the following: Kasamba, a queen from the Zimbabwe highlands, representing the influence of women and the establishment of the first major land shrine; Ntambo, an early warrior-king, who brought Namainga into the Mwene Mutapa Confederacy; Munenga, the first great trade leader, with early Portuguese connections; and Sikutangatanga, the founder of the present chiefly line of men using the dynastic title Sikaongo. Kasamba is still a particularly popular descent name for women, paralleled by the use of Munenga for men. The names of the first group have by now apparently come to represent more or less stereotyped views of major eras of the past: early migrations, rightful claims to the land, political control of the territory, establishment of regularized relations with neighboring groups, the beginnings of remembered long-distance trade, and the start of a recognizable modern era. A second category of names associated with the chiefly line represents what Evans-Pritchard called ideological history (1940, pp. 199–200). Here real people and events of major local importance are remembered in more detail, though still, it appears, in a highly telescoped and selective fashion. In Namainga the names Siasuntwe, Siagunku Mukuru, Munenga, Siazumina, and Simonje usually appear in this part of the list. Munenga's name, having become a dynastic title, may appear in this portion of the list more than once. It is usually this part of the king list, apparently representing the nineteenth century, that competing groups manipulate most to achieve desired political effects (Richards 1960). The last part of the list tends to represent "real historical" time and may include in their proper chronological order the names of chiefs of the last hundred years or so. Here the Banamainga use such names as Siamusungwe, Siagunku Mwana Changu, Kanyenye, Mwanakarombe, Malumisa, and Muropa. But even here the order is likely to be altered and "unimportant" names omitted, depending on the speaker's standpoint.

The chiefly line principally pertains to the political center of the country (*Chitondo*). This realm should include the village of the current chief and those of his closest councilors and followers, together with the spirit huts (*mazimbabwe*) and the ritual grove devoted to former chiefs and their influential mothers or wives. In addition, subsidiary realms similar to the core chiefdom were established by alliance, conquest, or grants to favorite followers, who might be kinsmen, former slaves, or trade associates. These sub-chiefs were known as *vazambi* (pl.; *muzambi*, sing.). While it is not clear how permanent the subsidiary realms were in view of the checkered careers of the chiefly lines themselves, the nineteenth-century ideal was to build up the territorial size, manpower, and reputation of the chiefdom by surrounding it with a protective ring of loyal subsidiary realms (*nyika re vazambi*). The realms acted as buffers between neighboring chiefdoms and were allies in times of war. Like the central realm, each subrealm established its own land shrine dedicated to the ancestral spirits (*basangu*) of its ruling descent group, and the linked land shrines provided a hierarchy of appeal through which the inhabitants of allied spirit realms could seek ritual protection (see fig. 7).

The Basangu are a beneficial class of spirits who can help the community through the intermediacy of a shaman emerging from the general populace. Just as individual family members, and, in the past, adopted slaves, can seek spiritual protection and guid-ance in personal matters from the ancestral guardian spirits of their compound elders, the inhabitants of a chiefdom or subchieftaincy could turn to the spirits of the ruling family of the land in which they worked the soil with respect to matters concerning the gen-eral public welfare. This assistance is generally sought in connec-tion with rainfall, supervision of the agricultural cycle, epidemics, and periodic strife brought on by contested successions to the chiefly stools. It is a common pattern in Africa (for this region see Colson 1948; Abraham 1966; Garbett 1966). Banamainga land shrines are little used today, but each of the chiefdoms and sub-chieftaincies has in the past been a land-spirit realm or cult district as well as a political unit under a secular leader, and allied realms in any one political confederacy were graded hierarchically on the basis of their ritual and political seniority. Because a leader sur-rounded himself with many service husbands courting the cap-tured "slave" daughters and free women of his prestigious matrilo-cal descent group, and because he could also call other men of the realm to arms, the fundamental connection between realms was probably military.

A network of trade was associated with the political system. In the nineteenth century as today there was minor local traffic within and between settlements in such items as foodstuffs, small stock, fish, tobacco, crafts, and medical and spiritual services. The trad-ing appears to have been relatively casual, for most family com-pounds have normally been fairly self-sufficient in these matters. Some local exchange, such as trade in salt from local springs,

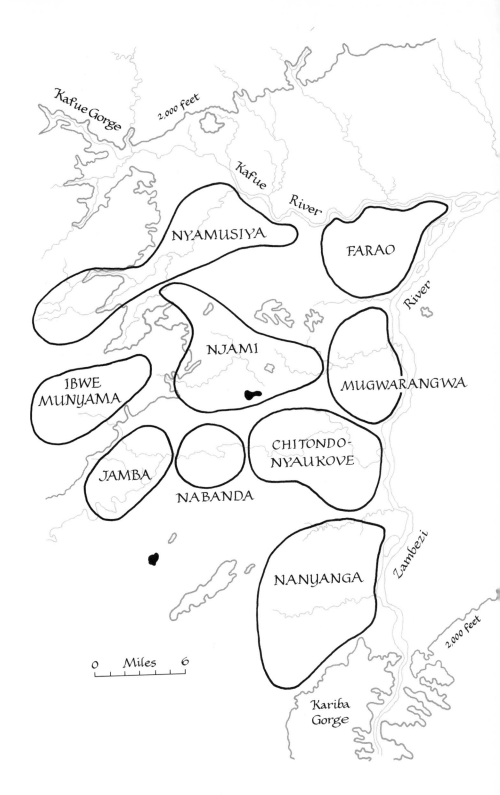

Fig. 7. The Realms of Sikaongo

tended to offset differences in local environments. Even in the dry months of the year people living near permanent water could grow vegetables, fruit, and tobacco that could be exchanged along with smoked fish for game meat, skins, ivory, thatching grass, small stock, and pottery and other crafts products sometimes available from settlements in drier areas.

In addition to local trade, some realms along the Zambezi and Kafue rivers had access to imported trade goods brought in by African, Portuguese, and Indian traders using the Zambezi as a route to the interior. They brought in muzzle-loading flintlock rifles, fathoms of cloth, large quantities of beads, earrings, iron hoes acquired in other chiefdoms, seashells, porcelain, brass and iron wire, and gunshot. These they exchanged for local copper bars, wire, bangles, armlets, and globules; for local iron pipe tongs, knives, hoes, spears, arrows, axes, bangles, armlets, and globules; and also for bark cloth, fired-clay pipe heads, and ivory bangles. The major export was ivory tusks, in which the area was long known to be rich. Hippo ivory was also traded out of the area, and even in the late nineteenth century there were still small amounts of gold dust to be bargained for. In hunger years the children of debtors, slaves, and other clients could also be obtained to work on plantations in the lower Zambezi Valley, and a few of them may have found their way into the world slave traffic (Livingstone 1858, p. 628, Tabler 1963, pp. 111n.1, 117n.2, 134, 149–51, 171n.2; Lancaster 1979a; Lancaster and Pohorilenko 1977).

Much of this external trade was funneled through the political structure of subchief and chief. Most chieftains organized elephant-hunting expeditions in the nineteenth century and stored the ivory at their compounds, where it could be collected once or twice a year by itinerant traders. Major Zambezi chiefs, such as Sikaongo, had permanent trade centers (aringa) near their headquarters, and these helped orient valley populations toward the banks of the Zambezi (Conceicao 1696, p. 66; Lobato 1962, p. 88).

Long-distance trade in this area can be traced back to the fourteenth to sixteenth centuries. During that period the political confederacy centered at the monumental stone ruins at Great Zimbabwe, on the southern edge of the Zimbabwe highlands, broke up into three main segments. The group that moved north to straddle Zambezi Valley trade routes to the east African coast is the one best known to us today because of its long contact with the Portuguese, who chose to operate along the Zambezi after 1500 in attempting to dislodge Swahili trade with the interior. This early trade is known not only through Portuguese documents but also from archaeological investigation of the Ingombe Ilede culture, first discovered at the Chitondo seat of the Banamainga chiefs. Some oral traditions have also been collected (Chaplin 1960; J. D. White 1970; Fagan 1969, 1972; Garlake 1973; Lancaster and Pohorilenke 1977).

Swahili traders from the Indian Ocean trading system had probably been operating in the region since at least the fourteenth century, and the Zimbabwe area of present-day southern Mozambique and Zimbabwe-Rhodesia was probably a significant source of world gold from at least the tenth to perhaps the early seventeenth centuries. This focal point for mining and trade in the far interior was apparently the only region in all of eastern sub-Saharan Africa where coastal elements are known to have established long-term settlements more than a few miles inland. From the tenth century on, mining in the Zimbabwe goldfields was the main trade support for the coastal Swahili city-states, towns, and ports that flourished along the east coast as far south as Sofala (see fig. 8).

Centuries later the Portuguese assault on the Swahili coast helped precipitate the fall of Great Zimbabwe as a trading center and split the confederacy of Shona-speaking peoples into three main groups. The northern Shona block came to be known as the Mwene Mutapa Confederacy, after the name of its leader. His Shona-speaking followers in the move north from Great Zimbabwe, together with those they assimilated, became known as Korekore; that group still comprises the major northern division of the Shona-speaking peoples of Zimbabwe-Rhodesia. Korekore occupying the floor of the Zambezi Valley have also been known as Goba, or lowlanders. Technically the Goba are simply Valley Korekore, but I have used the former term to distinguish them from a distant group of Valley Korekore in Zimbabwe-Rhodesia and Mozambique previously studied by G. K. Garbett (1966, 1967, 1969).

Despite its sometimes dramatic stone enclosures and its long-distance export trade in gold, ivory, and copper, Great Zimbabwe, like its northern successor, the kingdom of Mwene Mutapa, and its Goba descendants today, depended on subsistence farming in a subarid wooded savanna bioclimatic regime. In keeping with this subsistence base, Garlake has estimated that at its height the total population at Great Zimbabwe numbered between 1,000 and 2,-500 adults, including the 100 to 200 adults living inside the stone walls. Under the circumstances it was surely an impressive settlement, comparable to the famed military towns established in the same region by the Ndebele in the nineteenth century. It has been claimed that in the fourteenth to sixteenth centuries Great Zimbabwe and the successor Mwene Mutapa Confederacy were among the most powerful polities in all of central and southern Africa. But neither Great Zimbabwe nor the Ndebele capital approached the concentration of population found in more urbanized portions of precolonial West and East Africa, supported by systems of labor and capital-intensive cultivation and permanent cropping. Even with an abundance of permanent to semipermanent soils such as the Banamainga have enjoyed, none of the large settlements on the Zimbabwe highlands could hope to last very long before dispersal and migration became necessary (Garlake 1973, pp. 184–98; Lancaster 1976).

What the Zimbabwe culture and its northern offshoot, the kingdom of Mwene Mutapa, represented was not a state, a nuclear state, or an empire, as most authors have tended to assume—apparently on the basis of the stone buildings, the trade, and the palace courts and dignitaries (Abraham 1964; Fagan 1965; Oliver 1966; Gann 1971; Oliver and Fagan 1975). Instead it seems to have been an alliance of comparatively low-density descent group systems, probably much like that of the Banamainga (see Lewis 1959; Alpers 1970). The many ruins of stone enclosures shown in figure 8 probably represent the relatively short lived village sites of chiefs and subchiefs, along with their land shrines and ritual areas. Like the internal organization of precolonial Goba chiefdoms, the loose and situational confederacy was probably held together by an intermittent traffic in tribute (or trade), diplomatic and military missions, and religious congregations coming to the shrines (mazimbabwe) at the various confederacy headquarters (Barros 1552, p. 271; Gomes 1644, p. 204; Conceicao 1696, p. 66; Bocarro 1876, p. 357; Theal 1901, pp. 398–99; 1901a, pp. 484–85; Andrade 1955, p. 310; Abraham 1966).

Rather than a "centralized empire" or "state," as it has been called by historians and archaeologists, this society should simply be called a "segmentary society" like those found in many other regions dependent on long-fallow, low-density shifting cultivation. The availability of exposed parallel-sided tabular slabs of granite throughout much of the Zimbabwe highlands—though not in the Zambezi Valley or the eastern lowlands of southern Mozambique— has left us some impressive archaeology, which in turn has focused attention on the trade goods and material culture found at these sites. Most of the early trade, however, was probably limited to flows of tribute among leaders of the various Shona-speaking confederacies of the times. The foreign imports, mainly cloth, beads, and ceramics, brought into the population centers at the largest

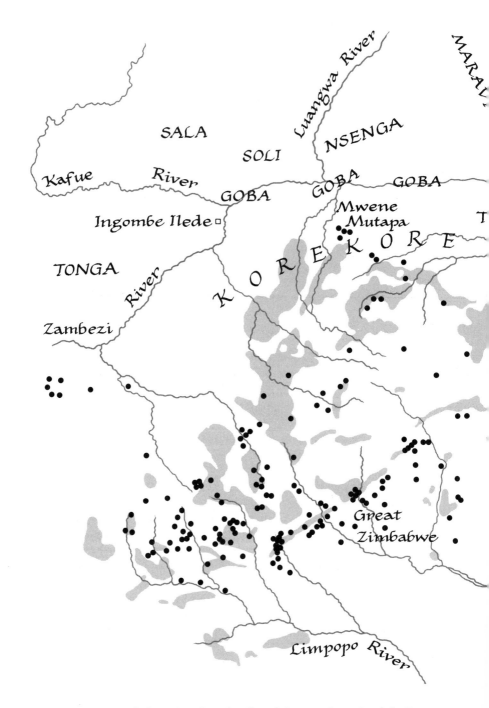

Fig. 8. Zimbabwe (Mashonaland) and the Southern Swahili Coast

Lake Nyasa

YAO

MOSSURIL

MOZAMBIQUE

ANGANJA

MAKUA

ANGOCHE

ezi

Sena o

QUELIMANE

River

INDIAN   OCEAN

Sofala

0   100   200

Miles

- Great Zimbabwe and Khami-style Ruins
- Areas with Gold ore and Pre-colonial mines

and most-senior land-shrine villages by Swahili and Shona middlemen were probably largely redistributed to offset tribute payments. As Garlake noted, the palace economy of Great Zimbabwe and its foreign trade probably served as important props for the leadership but had little impact at the subsistence level and no long-term effect on population densities (Garlake 1973).

7
Modern Political Organization and Contexts of Change

The political system in which the Goba find themselves today is very different from that of the precolonial past. In part it is based on arbitrary administrative boundaries established during the colonial era. The first of these boundaries were established by the British South Africa Company, a private venture chartered in 1889 to achieve imperial annexation without burdening the British taxpayer. It was a common device of the times, following the examples of the British North Borneo Company, chartered in 1881; the Royal Niger Company, chartered in 1886; and the Imperial British East Africa Company, chartered in 1888. Even before important gold discoveries were made on the Rand south of the Limpopo in 1886, Carl Mauch, Thomas Baines, and other explorers had belatedly discovered for England that there was gold in the Zimbabwe highlands on the far north (the Indian Ocean merchants and Portuguese had known it for centuries). Because African groups were in no position to gain final victory over European weaponry, northward British expansion became inevitable to secure this wealth from the encroachment of other European powers. There was also a need to tap the cheap unskilled labor resources of southern Africa for the expanding Rand mines and the South African diamond fields controlled by Cecil Rhodes.

As first steps in that direction, British Bechuanaland (now independent Botswana) was annexed in 1885, and a series of agreements was concluded with Lobengula, paramount chief of the Matabele, who had military control over much of the Zimbabwe highlands. The British South Africa Company grew out of this northward movement. It became the most successful and long lived of the late-nineteenth-century British chartered companies and laid the basis for British control of what later became Northern and Southern Rhodesia (Gann 1958). The Zambezi River became the boundary between the two colonies, dividing the Goba into two administrative districts. With its great mineral wealth and proximity to South Africa, Prime Minister Rhodes's main gateway to the interior, Southern Rhodesia always had a much larger white-settler population than its sister colony north of the river. Except for the rich Copperbelt on its northern border with Katanga province of Zaire (formerly the Republic of the Congo), vast areas of Northern Rhodesia were known to the Western world only as an undeveloped preserve for the anthropological field research conducted, mostly in the late 1930s to 1950s, under the auspices of the Rhodes-Livingstone Institute in cooperation with Manchester University (Gluckman 1956).

Colonial Administrative Organization

The first administrative boundaries established in Northern Rhodesia by the British South Africa Company were drawn to demarcate the jurisdictions of magistrates' courts. They were established in 1911, largely on the basis of astronomical lines, rivers, watersheds, and other physical features. Little was known about indigenous political boundaries (Davies 1972, pp. 50–51). By 1937 these areas had been reorganized into provinces, most of which were larger than many west African colonies. Each province was subdivided into a more or less arbitrary number of rural districts whose mean size was still more than 8,000 square miles. District Officers were given responsibility for these vast areas; they were assisted by local African courts operating by a system of "customary law" under the chiefs and local officials appointed in the chief's areas. In Northern Rhodesia the lower Kafue River was used as the boundary between Southern Province on the west and Central Province on the east. Within Southern Province the Zambezi Valley and the escarpment country separating it from the high plains became Gwembe Rural District, after the Matabele word for Zambezi. The Gwembe District was about 200 miles long and, like most other rural districts, encompassed an area of roughly 8,000 square miles (see fig. 2).

Little is known about the precolonial history of most of this district. Except for the Kafue confluence zone, most of the district was inhabited by the Valley, or Gwembe, Tonga, and in the nineteenth century they apparently managed to live in independent land-shrine realms unconnected to formal political confederacies of the kind discussed in the previous chapter (Lancaster 1974b). Only in the extreme western portion of the Gwembe do we find clear evidence of a chiefdom organized with subrealms in a pattern similar to that of the Goba (Colson 1960, p. 28). Elsewhere in the Gwembe the independent land-shrine areas were too small and numerous to serve as convenient units of indirect rule for the British District Officer, and the district was therefore reorganized into seven largely artificial "chiefly areas." But among the Goba at the Kafue confluence, in the territory known as Namainga, one of the new chiefly areas recognized by the colonial regime did in fact correspond to an established precolonial chiefdom. The same was true of Chiava in Central Province, east of the Kafue.

Oral traditions make it clear that something close to the present boundaries of Namainga chiefdom existed in the late nineteenth century, before the start of the British era. Namainga Territory waxed and waned in still earlier times, however. Smith and Dale's map of the Ila-Tonga peoples of Northern Rhodesia indicates that Namainga once occupied substantially more of the highlands northwest of the present chiefdom, and many European explorers recorded compatible observations (Smith and Dale 1920; Lancaster 1971). But the present borders of Namainga roughly coincide with part of a Portuguese concession granted to a Captain J. C. Paiva da Andrada in 1878. The western border of this concession, lying between the Kafue and Zambezi rivers, is shown in a map attributed to the Portuguese explorer Serpa Pinto (Ribeiro 1879; Axelson 1967; p. 120). The Portuguese normally found it convenient to use local chiefly realms as the basis for their crown estates (*prazao da coroa*) when attempting to advance their territorial ambitions in the interior. In the process they came to an understanding with the chief, set up stockades near his village, raised the flag, sometimes raided the chief's enemies, and encouraged the lucrative ivory trade. A more detailed map prepared by M. A. de Lacerda and L. Ignacio in 1890 shows the location of late-nineteenth-century Portuguese crown estates in this region and confirms that the Goba chiefdoms later recognized by the British on both the north and the south banks were not simply administrative creations of their own (Axelson 1967, map facing p. 260; J. D. White 1971, map facing p. 35; Lancaster and Pohorilenko 1977).

Although lone individuals and small groups of Portuguese, Goanese, and coastal Swahili were occasionally in the area from the sixteenth century on—and the Swahili probably earlier—most of them came from peasant backgrounds fairly close to that of the local Africans. Unlike the Englishmen who came later, they had little alternative to using local African institutions as guides for their own actions in the interior. There is little doubt that these traditionally organized chiefly realms were both old and indigenous. The territorial framework, based on a hierarchy of vast colonial provinces divided into large rural districts composed of a combination of newly created and traditional chiefly areas, was inherited by the independent government of Zambia when it came to power in 1964.

Fieldwork and Guerrilla Warfare

By the time my field study began in 1967, all the inhabitants of the south-bank Goba chiefdoms from the Kariba Dam in the west to the Mozambique border in the east had been resettled elsewhere by Southern Rhodesian authorities. That had occurred in the late 1950s in connection with plans to develop the valley agriculturally as an aftermath of the construction of Lake Kariba, then the largest man-made lake in the world. The plans were later tabled by events leading to the emergence of Northern Rhodesia as independent Zambia in October, 1964. In a move to forestall further African political gains, Southern Rhodesia succeeded in declaring independence from Great Britain in November, 1965. Since I was working as a research affiliate of the Institute for Social Research in the University of Zambia, the rift made it impossible for me to cross the Zambezi to work among resettled south-bank Goba populations. Freedom fighters waging guerrilla warfare had begun moving south from the independent African nations in the north, and many were crossing the river precisely where I had to work (Shamuyarira 1967; Maxey 1975, p. 107). I could see that the south bank of the Zambezi was guarded by Southern Rhodesian troops. Travelers in dugout canoes had been fired upon before my arrival, and during my fieldwork Goba villages in Zambia were littered from the air with leaflets warning of the futility of movement southward.

For these reasons my field study was limited to north-bank populations. Among those groups only two Goba chiefdoms, both straddling the Kafue-Zambezi junction, remained to be studied. Upstream on the west lay Lake Kariba and the Valley Tonga peoples studied by Colson, Scudder, and Reynolds (Colson 1971, pp. 7–10). Downstream on the east between the Chongwe River tributary to the Zambezi and the Mozambique border at the Luangwa River, the sparse north-bank population of Goba and Nsenga peoples under Chief Mburuma had also been completely resettled in the early 1950s because of a severe outbreak of human sleeping sickness. Although I worked in both north-bank chiefdoms, the largest remaining north-bank population was west of Kafue, where I concentrated my attention. In describing modern political organization as it has developed since Zambia's independence, it is convenient to restrict myself to this chiefdom, though similar conditions existed on the east.

Modern Ward Organization

In the late 1960s the Gwembe Rural District of colonial times still existed as a unit of local government; it is now called the Gwembe Regional Council. Its seven chiefly subareas, with courts operating under customary law, had also been retained, but it is important to note that the courts are no longer run by the chief and village elders. British ideas of justice have also been removed, though the new government-trained court officers represent ideas sometimes opposed to those of their elders.

Each of the chiefly subareas had been newly subdivided into three wards. The wards had no clear or consistent relationship to population densities or to former indigenous territories. In Namainga under Chief Sikaongo the ward known as Sikaongo South coincided with the old spirit realm of Nanyanga that had once been ruled by a subchief, Muzambi Bagasa (see figs. 7 and 9). At times in its remembered history it had been part of neighboring chiefdoms and had once been independent. In the late 1960s most of its cultivable lands lay fallow, and there were only six villages in the ward. Sikaongo Central represented the refugee Valley Tonga of the Lusitu Resettlement Area. The ward known as Sikaongo North comprised the rest of the chiefdom, including six former spirit realms, about 80 percent of the chiefdom's land area and forty-four of its fifty villages (88 percent).

The wards are now the basic units of local government. Each is run by a ward committee elected by the villagers. In addition to the chairman there should be two members from each village. One is usually an elder male representing the village's main descent group; the other is a younger man. If the local government court is within the ward, the well-trained young court officers, drawn from the local population, are automatically members of the committee. They are a valuable addition because their knowledge and modern sophistication are still sympathetically oriented to the local concerns of their kin and neighbors. They usually do not attend committee meetings in wards other than their own unless there is a special need. Since, in Namainga at least, the court serves within the old chiefly boundaries, and since male village elders tend to

August 10th, 1967

PRINTED BY THE GOVERNMENT PRINTER, SALISBURY

During my study Goba villages in Zambia were littered from the air with warnings against the futility of travel across the Zambezi.

become important ward committee members, there obviously is a significant admixture of familiar organization at the ward level.

Schools and the Outside World

Today most of the larger population clusters, though not all the old land-shrine realms, have access to a local government grade school. Families wishing to educate their children send them to live with relatives near a school or move there themselves. Everyone is aware that good jobs, security, and advancement in both the

NOTICE

are far from your home Do you want to die? You have
sent by your leaders in Lusaka to fight against us in Rho-
These men refuse to come themselves because they know
rength and do not want to die. They have sent you to die
em. You will die if you do not obey the orders which we
ow giving you. You will save your life if you do as we tell
To refuse is death. You will never be seen or heard of again.

ARE ORDERED TO SURRENDER AT ONCE. If you
der you will not be killed. Your comrades whose photo-
s are shown were not killed because they wisely did as they
old and they surrendered.

ARE ORDERED TO BURY YOUR ARMS AND
UNITION. If you are seen with these things your life will
Bury them at once and remember where you have hidden

WILL COME OUT ON TO THE PATHS AND THE
PLACES AND WILL KEEP SHOUTING THE WORDS
DO NOT WANT TO DIE — SAVE US — WE ARE
". You will shout so that our soldiers will know who you
d where you are. Remain silent and you will be shot as
ho creeps about with evil in his heart.

N YOU SEE THE SOLDIERS COMING YOU WILL
W YOURSELVES WITH YOUR ARMS HELD HIGH
VE YOUR HEADS TO SHOW THE SOLDIERS THAT
DO NOT WANT TO FIGHT. If they see your hands are
they will think you are carrying arms and they will kill you

T THE SOLDIERS AT ONCE WHEN THEY COME. They
orders to kill anyone who opposes them.

we have told you and your life will be spared. Remember
ur soldiers are better than you are and that they are every-
, You are all very far from your home and they have orders
you if you resist or are seen with arms.

Do not die for those in Lusaka — live for your families.

Muri kure nomusha wenyu. Munoda kufa here? Makatumwa
navatungamiri venyu vari muLusaka kuti muzorwisana nesu vomu-
Rhodesia. Vanhu ava vanoramba kuuya ivo pachavo nokuti
vanoziva simba redu nokudaro havadi kufa. Vakakutumai imi
kuti muzovafira. Munofa zvechokwadi kana musingaterere zvatiri
kukurayai kuti muite iye zvino. Munozviponesa kana mukaita
sezvatinokutaurirai. Kusazviita rufu. Hamuzomboonekwa kana
kunzwika pakare.

MUNORAIRWA KUTI MUZVIPIRE PACHENYU IYE
ZVINO. Kana mukazvipira hamuzopfurwi. Vamwe venyu vane
mifananidzo yakarakidzwa iyi havana kuuraiwa nokuti vakaita
zvine njere nokuita zvavakaudzwa. Vaka zvipira.

MUNORAIRWA KUCHERERA PASI ZVOMBO NAMABARA
ZVAMUNAZVO. Kana mukangoonekwa mune zvinhu izvi
rupenyu rwenyu rwapera. Zvichererei pasi iye zvino asi muyeuke
pamunozviviga.

ENDAI PANOONEKWA MUTUNZIRA NENZVIMBO DZIRI
PACHENA MURAMBE MUCHIGUWA KANA KUDAIDZIRA
ZVINOENDA KURE MUCHITI "HATIDI KUFA—TIPO-
NESEI—TIRI PANO". Munozodaidzirisa kuti masoja edu
agoziva kuti ndimi vana ani, zvekare kuti muri papi. Mukaramba
makanyarara munopfurwa souyo anovererera ane mwoyo wokuda
kuita zvakaipa.

KANA MAONA MASODYA ACHIUYA BUDAI PACHENA
MUZVIRAKIDZE MAKASUMUDZA MAOKO ENYU OSE
PAMUSOROSORO KURAKIDZA MASODYA KUTI HAMUDI
KURWA. Vakararirwa kuuraya munhu ari ose anorwisana navo.
Itai sezvatakuudzai ndokuti mupone.

Yeukai kuti masodya edu ari nani panemi, pakare vari kwose
kwose. Mose muri kure nemisha yenyu, ivo vakararirwa kuti
vauraye wose munhu anorwisana navo kana kuti uyo anoonekwa
ane zvombo.

Musafire avo vari kuLusaka. Rambai muri vapenyu kuti zvibatsire
mhuri dzenyu.

cash economy and the government sector are correlated with
schooling. The first schools were opened in 1961 by the Salvation
Army, and since 1965 they have been operated by the Ministry of
Education. Local schools now go to the equivalent of grade seven.
Secondary schools are outside the valley, and places are extremely
hard to get in the accelerating scramble for advancement. Local
students are clearly handicapped in this struggle. When local
teachers write letters of recommendation for promising students,
to the Ministry of Education regional headquarters in Mazabuka
District, answers are unlikely.

It has become an accepted part of the male life cycle for lads
aged fourteen or fifteen, who have gone as far as local educational

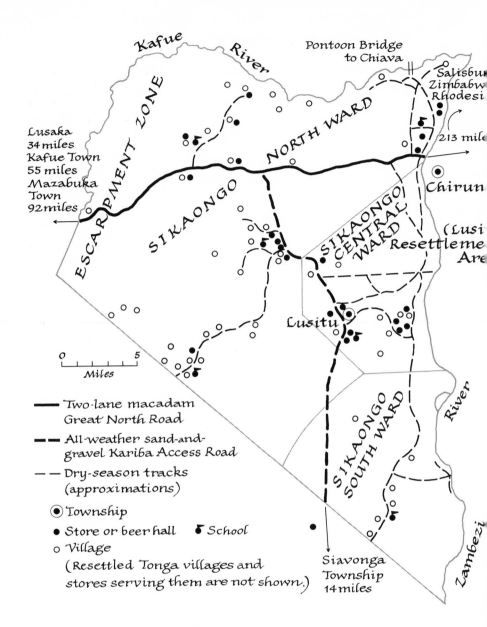

Fig. 9. Namainga Today

facilities can take them to migrate to the Tonga highlands. There they seek relatives from earlier migrations who may be able to find them a place in school. Sometimes they simply appear at the school opening day, among the horde of local applicants, and in the confusion such tactics occasionally work. Most of them must seek minor jobs in return for room and board or petty wages, and they drift among the small towns along the highway and railway running from Victoria Falls to Lusaka. Some reach Kabwe (Broken Hill) and the larger cities on the Copperbelt, though permanent jobs there as elsewhere are available only to those with experience and education that seem fantastic to village boys. Now that the border with Zimbabwe-Rhodesia, has been closed, a large number of Goba gather in Lusaka and surrounding periurban areas in Central Province rather than going south as they used to. There they can communicate relatively easily with linguistically related groups of long settled Shona-, Nsenga-, Sena-, and Nyanja-speaking peoples from the Soli, Nsenga, Chikunda, and Maravi ethnic areas of Zambia's Central and Eastern provinces, Mozambique, and Malawi. By 1967 the greater Lusaka area had attracted particularly large numbers of Shona-speaking political refugees from the south. The search for advancement has been linked in this way to schooling, townward migration, and a draining of young manpower from remote rural areas in many parts of modern Zambia.

An unknown number of these migrating men never return to their childhood homes in the valley except for short visits. Girls often accompany their relatives on short visits to town. But girls are fully employed helping their mothers in the fields, cooking, and taking care of children, and they do not really join this exodus to modern life until their later teens, one or two years after most boys have started traveling. Then they generally elope to town with older men and stay as long as their family responsibilities as mothers, and their purses, permit. Schools are an important aspect of the young villagers' relationship to a changing and attractive outside world, but there have been few openings for village women in the businesses and bureaucracies of the towns. Town life after schooling has become part of the new prestige sphere ideal for most successful modern males, replacing hunting, trade, crafts, and a viable political system able to validate male status yearnings in a satisfactory way. After a few years local girls begin dropping out of school, just as they must return from the towns, to rejoin their mothers and sisters in their domestic chores to support their children. While schools are more important for outward-looking young males, they also play a role for older men who have finally given up on town life, returned to the valley, and become active in the local political arena. Since villagers are no longer taxed as they were under colonial rule, each school now has a local governing board and a parents' committee to help raise money and work for special projects. In the late 1960s these projects usually involved making bricks for additional classrooms as grades were added. One or more members of the school board also sit on the local ward committee.

The Gwembe Regional Council

The ward committee's membership consists of school board members; court officers, if the court is situated in the ward; village representatives; and a chairman. They are usually among the most progressive people in the area. The chairman is often a storekeeper and an "improved" cash-cropping farmer. In their meetings the ward committees discuss such things as how to bring to the area new stores with large inventories and low prices. They also discuss the problem of keeping well-stocked stores running in the face of competition when bookkeeping is an unknown skill, inventory credit is difficult to obtain, transportation is costly, and the semisedentary village market sometimes drifts away from the fixed location of costly brick stores. Lobbying for famine relief and bore holes for dry-season water are also recurrent activities, as are preparations for the occasional visits of political dignitaries from the nation's capital, Lusaka. The chairman acts as the ward's delegate to the Gwembe Regional Council, which encompasses the former Gwembe District of colonial times.

In addition to the ward chairmen, or "councilors," as they are known, Gwembe Regional Council meetings are attended by the seven regional chiefs originally designated by the colonial administration in 1937. Because Regional Council meetings are largely devoted to development goals and the activities of government agencies that tend to bypass and undermine the chiefs as focal points of activity and authority, and because the meetings are conducted in English, the chiefs play a fairly passive role and must rely on interpreters. Upon their return from these meetings information ward meetings are convened by the ward chairmen. These meetings consist largely of the chairman's reports on the Regional Council meeting. His message usually includes exhortations to take greater individual initiative in applying for loans and joining local development efforts.

Based as it is on the old chiefly territories, the ward system is considered fairly marginal by knowledgeable younger progressives. The system is not directly connected to national party politics and machinery. The ward members are elected democratically by the local villagers with only local representation in mind. But one step up the ladder, at the level of the Gwembe Regional Council, the local ward system intersects with the national system of civil service and administration. This system is vertically integrated all the way up to the President's Office in Lusaka and has its own parallel organization leading back down to the villages. At every level this national system is coterminous with the structure of the United National Independence Party (UNIP), the group in power when independence came to Zambia. As UNIP likes to point out, advancement for public servants and rewards for the community of local adherents depends on participation in UNIP. Since UNIP has also organized itself at the grass-roots level in a system of constituencies and branches, the ward system understandingly attracts considerably less attention.

The United National Independence Party

Let us consider the UNIP system from the perspective of the villager (Government Reports 1967). The component units of each regional council are known as the "constituency" and the "branch." At the time of my stay in the valley, Gwembe Region had a total of six constituencies. Constituency leaders must be loyal, long-term UNIP members. Since the Constituency is part of UNIP, constituencies are formed only in areas with large populations supporting the party in the general elections. Within each constituency, party branches are based on a variable number of villages, depending on the availability of leaders and the size of the population. Each party branch has a chairman, one or more vice-chairmen, a secretary, a treasurer, and two or more influential members-at-large. As in the ward system, they are elective positions. Together the officers comprise what is known as the branch executive. Since in the early days of the struggle for independence the Goba supported the African National Congress (ANC) rather than UNIP, which was formed later, and since they continue to vote ANC, the UNIP party branch and constituency organization bypasses them and is oriented instead to the Valley Tonga in the Lusitu Resettlement Area.

The constituency is run by a constituency executive composed of the chairmen of each party branch. An assistant regional secretary attends meetings of the constituency executive. The Gwembe

Regional Council, in turn, is headed by a regional secretary appointed by national party headquarters. He chairs an advisory council composed of three trustees and the chairmen of each of the six component constituency executive committees, who also sit in the National Assembly in Lusaka. Gwembe Region is also represented by two members of Parliament. The Gwembe regional secretary is a member of the Zambian National Council, along with the president of Zambia, the members of the Central Committee, the national party chairman, the Youth Brigade directors, and the other regional secretaries. Above the Regional Council is the Central Committee, composed of an eleven-man cabinet of senior party members holding ministerial positions. The cabinet is headed by the president, who is president of both the party and the nation.

The UNIP organization is geared for economic development as well as political action. Even in the once-remote valley UNIP's constituencies are well provided with essential modernizing services and facilities. Conditions today are in sharp contrast to those of the long colonial era, when nothing comparable existed despite taxation. Modernization is beginning to provide a new network of occupations and titled positions for the people. The old realm of Namainga, for example, is served by a network of all-weather roads and graded dry-season tracks maintained by the national Ministry of Works and Housing through its local headquarters in the emerging township at Lusitu. The Roads Department at Lusitu provides year-round jobs for fiteen local men. In addition the Gwembe Rural Council maintains its own local office to service a network of simpler dirt tracks connecting all the major population centers. The Ministry of Education maintains twelve local grade schools, six of which serve the Goba. There is an agricultural extension service to help farmers develop and market new cash crops and subsistence foods. Local employees of the Game and Tsetse Department work at reducing the danger of human and cattle sleeping sickness and also cull the elephant population when it takes too great a toll on local crops. The Gwembe Regional Council has established an irrigation school and facilities for cotton marketing and commercial fishing. The Lusitu Credit Organization, a branch of the Credit Organization of Zambia, operates through the Lusaka Land Bank in offering small loans to local men wishing to purchase plows and oxen, grow cotton, open retail dry-goods stores, establish small-scale irrigation schemes for fruits and vegetables, raise poultry, or operate commercial corn grinders. The area is now served by a regular mail and bus service.

Conclusion

At the time of my field work in 1967–69 cash was still derived mainly from migrant wage work and the seasonal sale of local tobacco to itinerant long-distance traders. Despite great advances since independence, participation in the cash economy of the outside world was still more or less insulated from daily village life. Tobacco gardening in riverside gardens represented no break from the past; since precolonial times it had been integrated into accepted sex roles, work schedules, man-land relationships, and settlement patterns. Migrant wage labor had certainly drawn men away from the local scene, though perhaps no more than had precolonial trade and political activities. While migrant labor has been used to maintain the traditional bride-service marriage system in the twentieth century, as we shall see in chapter 8, it is difficult to assess the possibly great impact of this essentially colonial experience on local values and institutions. But until Kariba Dam and its aftermath, when the refugee Tonga in the Lusitu resettlement area clearly needed immediate help in intensifying food production from an inadequate land base and in learning how to derive local, *in situ* benefits from the cash economy, there had been no direct confrontation with the new order. Yet that is exactly what happened after the Kariba refugee resettlement of 1957–58, when government agencies, new roads, a greater number of stores, local wage-work opportunities, and cash-cropping facilities suddenly came to the country to help the resettled Valley Tonga in their new home in Namainga and also inevitably influenced their Goba neighbors. Such a confrontation with a new order eventually brings great changes in land-use and settlement patterns, sex-role relationships, and, perhaps most important, the locus of power in the local political economy. The advent of modern representative government, which began in Zambia only after independence in late 1964, is also affecting sex roles and the balance of power in the local political economy by limiting access to new institutions. But the spread of the cash economy, and the development of new government institutions at the local level were just beginning at the time of my field study in 1967–69. Only a few individuals were engaging in cash cropping and participating directly in the new political system, though the schools, migrant-labor experiences, and reorganization of the court had begun changing attitudes and social organization, as will be shown in chapters 9 to 11.

8

Social Dynamics and Female Authority in a Matrilocal Village System

Because the Goba recognize dual lines of descent and because this is an unusual ethnographic feature, there are several reasons why it is desirable to approach their social system from a broader perspective than would ordinarily be called for.

The cross-cultural approach taken in the first sections of this chapter are designed to explain a system that might otherwise seem to be an oddity whose interpretation has perhaps been overinfluenced by recent trends in women's studies. But the matrifocality that gives rise to dual descent among the Goba is an element that is known to exist in most human societies, whether or not recognized formally by the people or ethnographically by anthropologists. This is a significant ethnographic fact that has long been neglected and it is necessary to develop the point in order to place Goba social organization in proper perspective.

The Zambezi Goba are also notable for the formal, institutionalized authority, rather than mere influence, traditionally enjoyed by their senior women. It is important to recognize the basis for this unusual authority and to review the forces that may give rise to it in various ethnographic situations.

Finally, this project was initiated to study the role of economics in social organization. My working hypothesis has been that practical, material economic forces will have an impact on the social patterns observed by the field anthropologist, wherever he may go and whatever slice of time becomes his ethnographic present. Much of the research therefore focuses on the Goba system of subsistence cultivation. Environment, settlement patterns, man-land relationships, and work patterns have been treated in the previous chapters, and agricultural production, consumption, and exchange are analyzed in those that follow. The emergence of the local cash economy will be documented equally carefully. The subsistence

cultivation practiced in low-density societies is known to be noto-
riously woman-centered. It is important to determine whether this
is linked to the high status of Goba women and their unusual system of dual descent. On the other hand it is equally clear that the
development of a cash economy is likely to alter sex-role relationships and, inevitably, social organization, as we shall see in later
chapters. To understand the role of woman-centered agriculture
and these modern changes—which of course parallel those in many
parts of the world—it is necessary to preface this chapter with a
brief review of the roles played by property and economics in the
social organization of low-density precapitalistic societies.

Marriage, Residence, and Descent in Comparative Perspective

In a broad sense the categories of kinsmen likely to be involved in
daily patterns of face-to-face interaction are determined by rules of
marriage and post-marital residence. These factors are critical in
the recruitment of local groups in low-density kin-oriented societies, because settlements are comparatively small, scattered, and
composed of a core of related families. The Goba have practiced a
form of protracted uxorilocal bride-service marriage, known as *kugarira*, which filiates children to their mother's localized kin group
and which formerly incorporated their father as well. Uxorilocal
bride service marriage creates matrilocal extended families and
gives their society a decidedly matrilineal bias very much like that
once found throughout the Central African matrilineal belt (see
fig. 10).

On the other hand, most of the Shona-speaking peoples most
closely related to the Goba in the linguistic and cultural sense,
have preferred bridewealth marriage. Most of the Shona-speaking
peoples live in present-day Zimbabwe-Rhodesia. Upon delivery of
bridewealth the husband's residence is patrilocal, and the children
are formally filiated to his descent group rather than to their
mother's. This practice gives Shona society a patrilineal bias (Radcliffe-Brown 1950, pp. 34–36; Holleman 1951, 1952). In an ethnol-
ogical sense the Shona-speaking Zimbabwe peoples have usually
been classified with the patrilineal southern Bantu-speaking
peoples of Botswana, southern Mozambique, the Republic of
South Africa, Swaziland, and Lesotho (Schapera 1937; Wilson and
Thompson 1969). It is true that other prestige items may be substituted for cattle in bridewealth exchanges, among both Shona
and other groups exhibiting the patrilineal bridewealth complex in
West, Central, East, and Southern Africa. In recent times, how-

ever, the distribution of bridewealth marriage in many areas has in fact been closely related to the availability of cattle (Goody 1973; A. Kuper 1975, p. 142n.1; Lancaster 1976). This distribution has been applicable to the Zambezi Valley.

Most of the middle and lower Zambezi Valley, from below Victoria Falls to the Indian Ocean, has been a tsetse zone since precolonial times, and its inhabitants have not possessed sufficient cattle for exchange in a bride-wealth marriage system. Consequently various forms of uxorilocal bride-service marriage have predominated. From west to east the region is the home of the Valley Tonga of the Gwembe District below Victoria Falls, the Shangwe and Valley Korekore (or Goba), the Nsenga, the Chikunda (or Nyungwe), the Tavara, the Lower Zambezi Tonga between Tete and Sena, the Sena (or Chuabo), and the Podzo (Posselt 1926, 1927, 1929; Chigumi 1923; Bullock 1928; Schapera 1929; H. Kuper 1954; Lancaster 1971, 1974a; Stefaniszyn 1964; Bocarro 1876, p. 357; Bourdillon 1972; Lacerda 1944; Lopes 1907). Some lower Zambezi groups have been exposed to centuries of Arab-Swahili, Indian, and Portuguese ideas of father-right, though uxorilocal marriage has generally persisted. In recent times it has been common for youths to practice infant betrothal in order to commence their bride-service early with the aim of earning the right to remove the bride by the time she comes of age. In some groups a bride-service husband could eventually erase his debt for a woman (his wife) by assigning a mature marriageable daughter to his in-laws, while in other groups his service obligations have been perpetual.[1]

Even in regions less seriously affected by tsetse, such as the middle and high plains of Zimbabwe-Rhodesia, uxorilocal brideservice marriage has nonetheless been practiced as a result of cattle raiding, slave raiding, and poverty. Like slaves, poor people without cattle were commonly married in an uxorilocal manner. Some

[1]Among many of these peoples the use of cash for marriage prestations had gradually begun to give a man more latitude and to change post-marital residence to more virilocal forms as early as the 1920s. For example, among the Valley or Gwembe Tonga around the turn of the twentieth century it was still customary for husbands to take up residence with their wives' families. "The custom is for the men in this District to go live at their mother-in-law's as part payment of 'luselo'" (Guimbi Sub-District Inquiry, Secretary for Native Affairs, memorandum 28 October 1909 on the "Sigongo Uprising"). The unpublished Gwembe District Notebook maintained by the early colonial administrators and preserved in the Zambian National Archives, Lusaka, like the memorandum quoted above, similarly records that uxorilocal bride-service marriage was common throughout the

form of service marriage has thus been known among most of the Shona-speaking peoples, and Bullock noted that a large proportion of the Shona married that way (Bullock 1928, pp. 214–44, 355). Among most Shona groups, however, men have preferred either marriage by capture (*wutapa*) or bridewealth marriage (*ukulobola*), for both gave men higher status and more independence in making residential and political commitments. How Shona women viewed this situation has not been recorded. But it should be kept in mind that while the Shona-speaking peoples have always been placed in the patrilineal category for classification purposes, large numbers practiced uxorilocal bride-service marriage in precolonial times. Their children must therefore have been influenced by matrilocal residence and the importance of matrilineal kinship links, like their uxorilocal relatives in the Zambezi Valley, where the status of women has been high (Andrade 1955, p. 312; Barros 1552, p. 272; Conceicao 1696, p. 66).

In this connection it might be ventured that the way in which localized descent-group segments are organized is relatively open, depending on the sex of the married children who remain at home with their parents in the extended family. The critical question seems to be whether parents are regularly willing to accept some exchange equivalent to compensate for losing the company of their married daughters. If they are not, married daughters stay at home. The system of social relations is then largely based on uxorilocal marriage and on settlements composed of matrilocal family segments where matrilineal orientations are important. Identification with maternal kin is then strengthened, and the status of women is comparatively high. That has been the general situation throughout the Central African matrilineal belt, including the middle and lower Zambezi Valley. But among the Southern Bantu as among most other peoples of Africa, most parents have preferred to accept exchange equivalents for their departing married daughters and to keep married sons at home in patrilocal, patrilin-

---

early twentieth century Gwembe, though the practice was avoided by wealthy men and chiefs. Anthropologists have found it useful to use local district notebooks for information on earlier time levels, as seen in Colson's use of the Mazabuka District Notebook (1958) and Scudder's use of the Gwembe District Notebook (1962). But Scudder, who has collected family histories among the Gwembe Tonga since the mid-1950s, notes that "strong patrilateral tendencies, including virilocal residence, go back a good fifty years" among the Gwembe Tonga (Scudder; personal communication, October 1978).

■ Bride-service ,uxorilocal residence,
and matrilineal descent.

☐ Bridewealth, patrilocal residence,
and patrilineal descent.

▨ Double descent.

▩ Bilateral descent.

Fig. 10. Bridewealth and Brideservice in Sub-Saharan Africa. Modified
from Mair (1969) Murdock (1959a), and Vansina (1966).

eal extended families, .although, as noted, the Shona have not always succeeded in doing so.

Low-Density Flexibility Versus High-Density Restrictions

The notion that lineality in descent organization may thus, swing fairly easily from one apparent extreme to the other raises the important questions of descent-group corporacy and structural permanence. It has long been noted that kin-based groups in the middle range of relatively homogeneous precapitalistic societies tend to become stronger, unilineal, and longer lived where there is some degree of technological sophistication and when their organization is based on rights to durable property. But it is well known that most low-density cultivators have depended successfully on a comparatively rudimentary technology, that they have had little durable property, and that descent groupings larger than the coresident family are only weakly organized. Corporate social groupings based on rights to durable, relatively scarce, highly valued property are not found. Instead, social forms are comparatively labile, and bilateral flexibility in social action predominates over unilineal rigidities. This is known to be typical of low-density cultivators in general and of Central African societies in particular (Fortes 1953; Gluckman, Barnes, and Mitchell 1949; Lancaster 1976, 1979).

Under these circumstances social position in the family structure has had priority over material possessions. Both family position and material possessions are transmitted between individuals in a sex-linked manner. The proper functioning of the family system is commonly believed to depend on ancestral cult sanctions. Both males and females attain key positions in the cult through processes of positional succession, which are considered extremely important. In addition, each sex may inherit appropriate material possessions from same-sex relatives, but that is not accorded equal importance, because when they are needed most such items can simply be found, borrowed, bartered, fabricated, or obtained through wage work in the money economy. A few especially valued status symbols, like cattle and exotic trade goods, have been transmitted along with senior social position. Among most low-density cultivators cattle have been limited because of raiding and disease. Rather than accumulating more cattle, those that a family has possessed have typically been paid out to settle debts and legal claims or loaned out to help seal personal alliances formed through cattle pacts and bridewealth transactions. When the original parties to these transactions die, alliances important to the survivors are maintained through positional succession. In this event the heir to the social position in question will come to possess the appropriate status symbols and rights associated with it. Precolonial raiding and disease made cattle a fairly rare commodity in most Central and Southern African societies subsisting principally by low-density cultivation, though cattle have always been highly valued. Rather than being expended as a regular subsistence staple or retained as a visible basis for extended family corporacy and prestige, the few that have been owned have generally been distributed to reinforce important personal relationships in societies lacking tightly structured corporate groups (Colson 1969). Other status objects have been used in similar fashion.

As opposed to adaptive systems where sex-linked estates of scarce land or livestock form the material basis for both subsistence and the organization of corporate groups, access to food and relevant material goods has generally been less problematic and less important in the family structure of low-density cultivators (Goody 1976). Neither sex then gains the materialist and political advantages that males alone almost universally have acquired under conditions of heightened scarcity, when subsistence comes to be based on plow agriculture and other forms of work- and capital-intensive farming, nomadic pastoralism, or even hunting and gathering under conditions where male sex-role contributions may be considered especially important (see Lancaster 1976). Kinship seniority then remains the principal basis of descent-group organization, and since neither sex can have a monopoly on ancestral-cult seniority, the organization of the social system is seldom rigidly tied to sex-linked characteristics. Same sex, or unilineal, descent-group structuring is therefore less overpowering among low-density cultivators than it is among fixed-farming peasants and nomadic pastoralists. Males and females are free to identify their most important ancestors and living associates on a more situational, less materialistic basis. Women may choose to associate more with their women friends and relatives and to think of descent groupings and religious sanctions as stemming primarily from female ancestors. This is especially likely in an uxori-matrilocal residence system. Males may take an opposite view and stress male-male associations and descent through men, especially in a viri-patrilocal system. But while descent principles may still be recognized, closed corporate unilineal descent groupings are unlikely to dominate the patterns of social action.

Dual Descent and Matrifocality

While lineality in family orientations may thus swing from one extreme to the other, lineal thinking may frequently be dual in any event, particularly if female perspectives are taken into account. As we shall see, Goba social organization is based on uxorilocal residence, the idea of "brother-sister" marriage, and the symbolism of dual descent lines passing through both the father and the mother. That is the ideal for the organization of important descent groups. Goba women have tended to identify with members of their own sex, especially their sisters, mothers, aunts, and maternal grandmothers. For them the major structuring element in their descent groups and villages is conceived as a mother line. The men, for their part, recognize the importance of the mother line but in addition stress the dominance of the father line stemming from father and father's father in ordering major descent-group affairs.

Although better cross-cultural data are needed, there is some suggestion that similar dual orientations have existed elsewhere in low-density Africa. The matrilineal Bemba recognized a latent father line, which has assumed greater importance under conditions of modern cash wealth. The Bemba are an important group in northern Zambia, and similar tendencies seem likely to exist among the Bisa, southern Lunda, Lala, and Lamba peoples of northern Zambia and Zaire (Richards 1934; 1939, pp. 16–17; Turner 1957, pp. 61–62, 265; Chock 1967). Similarly, the matrilineal Plateau Tonga of southern Zambia have also developed patrilineal tendencies through the advent of cash wealth used in bride-wealth transactions (Colson 1958, pp. 25, 328, 333–34). There is clear evidence for dual descent among the Ila and Lumbu peoples, who intergrade with the Plateau Tonga (Smith 1949, pp. 58–59). And the Goba intergrade with groups of Valley Tonga in Zambia and Zimbabwe-Rhodesia, making dual descent lines a possibility there too (Lancaster 1971, 1974b). The matrilineal Valley Tonga north of the Zambezi in Zambia have recently developed patrilineal tendencies through the use of bride-wealth payments in cash, like the Bemba-speaking peoples of northern Zambia and their Plateau Tonga relatives. The matrilineal Shona-speaking Tonga south of the Zambezi have been influenced by neighboring patrilineal Shona groups.

Among the Shona-speaking peoples, dual descent can be inferred from the fact that royals in the Mwene Mutapa's Korekore

confederacy married real or classificatory queen sisters in an uxorilocal bride-service system that probably resembled that of the related Goba. Royal sister marriage has also been reported for the
coastal lowlands of southern Mozambique, between the Sabi and
Zambezi rivers, and in the adjacent highlands of Quiteve (Faria y
Sousa 1674, p. 24; Bocarro 1876, pp. 357–58; Santos 1609, p. 191;
Theal 1901, 7:305, Andrade 1955, p. 312). Cattle probably were
scarce in both regions, and uxorilocal bride-service marriage seems
to have been practiced. Dual descent also seems to have been recognized among the Lozi in the upper Zambezi Valley (Gluckman
1950, pp. 167, 177; 1951, pp. 81–82) and among the Yao of Malawi
and northern Mozambique (Mitchel 1956, pp. 69–70, 162). Many
other examples could be cited from farther afield.

Dual descent lines based on same-sex identification seem reasonably common in the literature, though many anthropologists
have assumed that men dominate social and political systems, and
many ethnographies have stressed male viewpoints only. Though
not necessarily forming corporate lineages, most human societies
probably implicitly recognize dual descent (Radcliffe-Brown 1935;
Fortes 1969, p. 274). As Stanner (1961) suggested, following Radcliffe-Brown's observations on the Murngin (1951), there is always
some recognition of matrilineal descent. Based as it is on the obvious mammalian mother-young tie, Stanner noted that matrilineal
descent is more concrete than patrilineal descent; matrilineal descent, at least in the minimal sense of connection to one's mother
or mother surrogates, is commonly a palpable and observable daily
relationship, while patrilineal descent and patrifiliation is more
often an artificial construct related to questions of formal status.
The facts of the latter must usually be determined by cultural processes of a legal and political nature, while the former (matrifiliation or matrilineal descent) need not be.

It is the frequency of this kind of matrilineal descent that led J.
R. Goody to adopt stiff criteria for "descent" when attempting to
classify the world's double-descent systems. While an awareness of
matrilineal descent stemming from the mother-young tie commonly creates sentimental mother lines of the kind I have been
referring to, it does not necessarily create *descent groups* in the
formal sense generally used in social anthropology (Goody 1961).
In identifying double descent as a meaningfully distinctive taxonomic category, Goody found it necessary to narrow his definitional
criteria, requiring the presence of separate institutionalized named
groups based on both matrilineal and patrilineal descent, where
the processes of unilineal descent in each instance are linked to

property inheritance. Even with these definitional limitations, Goody observes that the number of double descent systems is much larger than supposed. Goody found that double descent systems (and therefore dual descent line systems, which are less stringently defined) are common throughout all of West Africa and aboriginal east Australia. It can of course be questioned how appropriate it is to require the presence of named as opposed to unnamed groups if both are institutionalized. Similarly, nonmaterial inheritance involving status position is especially important in most of the low-density societies known to the ethnographic record. If we decide to allow nonmaterial criteria to have importance, the distribution of double descent systems is even wider, as Goody noted (1961, pp. 21–24). In that event, he wrote, "it seems that all, or nearly all, societies with UDGs [unilineal descent systems] would be classified as double descent."

R. T. Smith, writing in general about "matrifocality," noted the strength of the mother-child relationship and the tendency for the unit of a woman, her children, and her daughters' children to emerge as a particularly solidary unit, often constituting the core of a domestic group (Smith 1973). Here the woman in her role as mother becomes the focus of affective ties and the center of decision-making coalition with her children. This matrifocal quality develops in the domestic sphere whether or not a husband-father is present, even in male-headed households. Domestic matrifocality thus appears, in varying degrees and forms, in a wide range of cultural situations, ranging from those where males virtually monopolize political, economic, and ritual life, as in China and India, to those where women are active in some or all of these activities, as in the Caribbean, Java, or West and Central Africa. The reason is that "mothering" is the central activity of the domestic domain, where it is "productive of intense affective relations which pervade it" (Smith 1973, p. 140).

Smith noted that a relative absence of (or culturally fashionable disregard for) male property and male status considerations in the domestic realm is particularly conducive to the development of a matrifocal domestic system, for then older males concerning themselves with supradomestic legal-political roles tend to be less interested and competitive in domestic matters. They may even be tolerant of unstable marriages, such as Smith described for the West Indian lower class. In such cases women may hold and manage property equally with men and be capable of holding together a diverse household group or kin network. On the other hand, where males perceive a close link between their status in the domestic domain and their standing in the wider community, the focus of legal-political decisions in the kinship system as a whole and *formal* authority within the domestic sphere tend to shift away from mothers and their matrifocal coalitions to men, despite the continuing and often competitive intensity and influence of affective relationships centering on mothers (Smith 1973, p. 142). This inherent, sometimes informal matrifocality is undoubtedly the fundamental force underlying the ubiquity of *double* descent in unilineal-descent systems and of mother lines in more bilateral situations (for example, see Bott 1957; Yanagisako 1977).

Among the Goba dual descent lines help each individual organize an essentially bilateral kin grid, and they serve as latent axes of social organization to be brought into play in varying circumstances. As we shall see, the uxorilocal Goba have generally found matrilateral connections more useful than patrilateral ones in daily life, though closely related Shona-speaking peoples marrying with bride wealth have found the opposite to be true. Over the long term the predominance of one line of descent over another in a low-density society seems to be a matter of local cultural adjustment and style, as expressed in marriage-exchange preferences affecting post-marital residence, the relative positions of husband and wife, and the filiation of children. The matter will be discussed again in chapters 10 and 11, because Goba preferences in this regard have been changing through time. The purpose of this discussion has been to suggest that such basic and sometimes painful changes can come about fairly easily.

Matrilocal Extended Families and Female Village Cores

Under the Goba system of uxorilocal bride-service marriage, men generally marry for the first time in their mid- to late twenties. On the average, a man today can expect to complete his brideservice and, if he wishes, remove his wife and children from the compound of his senior in-laws by the age of thirty-eight. The age varies widely in individual cases, but 74 percent of men under age forty still find their choice of residence determined primarily by the uxorilocal rule (see table 9). The life expectancy for male live births is probably thirty-two to thirty-three years, rising to about fifty-two years for those who survive to age ten (Coale and Demeny 1966). The rule of uxorilocal bride-service marriage therefore has a decisive effect on the male life cycle, dominating 75 to 100 percent of it on the average. Men over forty still exhibit a significant tendency toward uxorilocality (26 percent in table 9), though by

Table 9
The Goba Residence Pattern

Men under Age 40			Men over Age 40		
Principal Residence Tie	Number of Cases	Percentage Marrying Kin	Principal Residence Tie	Number of Cases	Percentage Marrying Kin
			self	5	
			S	2	
			D	2	
	7	57	B	15 }14%	
			Z	8	38
	4	100	MB	6	
	1		MF		
	11 }	91	M	18 }	11
F	19 }20%	95	M & F	42 }51%	48
	10 }	40	F	21 }	43
	146—74%	29	uxor.	41—26%	24
Total	198	42	Total	160	28

Women under Age 35		Women over Age 35		
Principal Residence Tie	Number of Cases	Principal Residence Tie	Number of Cases	Percentage Marrying Kin
	5	D	4 }	27
	1	B	15 }19%	
	4	Z	7 }	
	1	MB	4 }	
	32 }	MM		
F	104 }86%	M	27 }	41
	18 }	M & F	30 }46%	57
	15—15%	F	14 }	21
		H	54—35%	9
Total	180	Total	155	26

Unmarried Children	
Principal Residence Tie	Number of Cases
MM & MF	17 }
B	5 }
Z	1 } 16%
MB	21 }
MZ	2 }
M	61 }
M & F	557—81%
F	16
FZ	2
FM	5
Total	687

Source: Lancaster (1974a–56).

that age most husbands have been able to finish their service cycle and make other residential arrangements.

Most women under age thirty-five (86 percent) are residentially tied to their parents or other close uterine kin. Women are taken away from home beginning at an average age of thirty-three, but even in older age most women over thirty-five live either with their parents (46 percent) or close uterine kin (an additional 19 percent). Among the Goba this is much the preferred life for a woman. Marriage to a kinsman or neighbor increases the likelihood that her spouse will not want to take her away to live with strangers in her old age. Men also prefer to practice local endogamy among kinsmen and friends, because it appreciably ameliorates their bride-service experience, improves their status, and enhances their chances for a happy and lasting marriage. In a study of 217 marriages, 53 percent were among neighbors and local kinsmen (Lancaster 1974a).

This pattern of marriage and residence, repeated in each generation, promotes long-lasting matrilocal extended families and makes matrilateral ties more important than patrilateral ones. In a sample of 261 married men of all ages, 150 men (57 percent; see table 10) lived as sons-in-law and junior dependents in the matrilocal extended-family homes of their wives, where they and their children were under the authority of one or both wives' parents and in the company of other affines. An additional 18 married men (7 percent) lived with their wives' mothers' brothers, brothers, or sisters, usually after their wives' parents died or separated. About 64 percent of the men were thus living uxorilocally. The remainder of the married men (36 percent), had either terminated their bride-service sequence and been allowed to remove their wives and children to new locations or had entered into endogamous service marriages allowing them to live among their own kin in the first place (see table 9). Some of these men (11 percent) were found living in the homesteads of their own parents, and 14 percent of the older men had had time to establish their own independent village sections and villages or, more likely had succeeded to senior positions in existing units.

Similarly in a study of 292 married women of all ages, 52 percent were living with their parents and uterine kin. The percentage rises to 64 when we include married women living with their mothers' brothers, brothers, and sisters, usually after the deaths of their parents. Most of the remaining 36 percent were living with their husbands' immediate kin or were older women living with their

Table 10

The Composition of Extended Families

	Totals
Married Men living with their wives'	
M &/or F etc	150 = 57%
MB etc	9
B etc	7 } = 7%
Z etc	2 } 64%
Married Men living with their own	
M &/or F etc	29 = 11%
MB etc	3
B etc	14
Z etc	6 } 36%
Child/children etc	5
Older Men heading independent compounds	36 = 14%
	261
Married Women living with their own	
M &/or F etc	151 = 52%
MB etc	8
B etc	22 } = 12%
Z etc	4 } 64%
Married Women living with their husband's	
M &/or F etc	22 = 7%
MB etc	6
B etc	0
Z etc	2 } 36%
Child/children	15
Women in their own or husband's independent compound	62 = 21%
	292

married children. Because the unusually high rate of in-marriage makes Goba kin groups essentially bilateral, a woman's matrilateral kin ties are usually important in daily affairs even when she is living with her husband's people. Matrilateral ties are typically found to provide the distant linkages recognized between comparatively remote groups of people where one has to reckon through considerable genealogical distance to make a connection. Matrilateral ties generally provide the framework for daily action and the common idiom for expressing ties within the village.

The prevalence of uxorilocal marriage means that in every generation localized descent groupings are principally composed of solidary blocks of coresident sisters and their female kin. Especially in the case of larger and older settlements where this pattern has had time to develop, age-graded sorority groups, together with their guardian brothers who represent them in affairs outside the family compounds, are thought of as the heart of the village and as the living representatives of the original founding core of village women. These women—grandmothers, mothers, sisters, daughters, and granddaughters to one another—prefer to remain together, as they believe their ancestors did. Praise names, family names, inheritance, succession, descent, and less formal acts of patronage all tend to flow along matrilineal lines in a residential system of matrilocal extended families intimately influenced by connecting ties through women.

Kinship and the Family Cycle

In thinking about potential marriage partners and village neighbors, the Goba like to cast as wide a net as possible. The sometimes harsh demands of uxorilocal brideservice has commonly led men to marry half-sisters and other close kin. Elders claim that in the days of long-distance trade and the Zimbabwe confederacies great leaders married their full sisters and imply that this is still common, though I was unable to document any instances of it in 1967–69 (Lancaster 1974a, pp. 55–58). But aside from full sisters, Goba men can and do marry all women of their own generation descended from their fathers and their siblings, from their mothers and their siblings, and from both sets of grandparents and their siblings and children of both sexes. Any of these marriageable women may be called "sister." When necessary, a classificatory "father," "mother," or "grandparent" may be used in defining the relationship of the "sister" one wishes to marry, so that in effect most local women of appropriate age are marriageable.

The mechanics of a high rate of marriage to real or classificatory siblings and cousins favors bilateral kinship reckoning through both one's mother and father. Goba do, in fact, think in terms of a kindred (hama) in which all genealogically expressed connections of descent are potentially important. In functional terms one might speculate that bilaterality makes sense for low-density cultivators. But in practice the favored uxorilocal-residence pattern generally causes the *nhundu* to crystallize out of the broader potentialities represented by the kindred. The *nhundu* is normally composed of a married brother living with one or more sisters and their married daughters in a matrilocal extended family.

This brother-sister-sister's children combination is the minimal descent group among the Goba, in both a statistical and a cognitive sense. As we have seen, it is the commonest statistical outcome of marriage and residence practices. It is also the preferred pattern. If necessary, a minimal coresident lineage segment composed of a married brother-sister pair can be self-sufficient in economic, legal, and religious terms. But the ideal is to see this unit grow as daughters marry and raise children of their own. Fathers and mothers benefit in emotional, social, and political terms from the presence of their daughters and grandchildren and obtain years of valuable service from their sons-in-law, which may include help with the clearing of fresh fields and garden plots, critical heavy weeding during the early rains, construction of buildings, and, most important nowadays, cash-wage remittances. Mothers retain the good company of their daughters as they work through the agricultural year in neighboring fields and gardens. Sisters, daughters, and grandchildren live in a supportive family setting offering many play-group opportunities and enjoy aristocratic status when they are members of the stable core of a large and well-known village.

Even the service husbands have had a rewarding life, especially in precolonial times, when they provided meat, skins, ivory, and other goods from long hunting forays; protected the village; and participated in trading, raiding, and diplomatic activities centered at the courts of political leaders. These were prestigious activities that men still like to remember. Service obligations and the matrilineal organization of women, children, and old people toiling in the fields back home would hardly seem to have concerned the younger men. And today migrant wage labor, petty trade, hunting, fishing, and local-level politics occupy their time, call them away, and reduce the daily service demands their in-laws can make. And because slash-and-burn cultivation is land-extensive rather than capital- or labor-intensive, the actual physical labor demanded of service husbands in the family fields and compounds has actually been low by cross-cultural standards.

When listing the members of their scattered personal kindred (*hama*) for the anthropologist, Goba of both sexes commonly mention their sisters and their sisters' children first. In listing the members of their coresident family groupings (*mhuri*), Goba of both sexes similarly think primarily of their sisters and their sisters' children (*vazukuru*) and typically voice the truism: "Sisters' children are the family, and they can make a village for me someday." Under the service-marriage system, a man's children belong to their mother's consanguineal kin group. Their male representative and guardian (*dundumuntuli*) in legal, political, and spiritual matters is the same maternal kinsman living with their mother who represents her. He is usually either her father, her mother's brother, or her brother (Lancaster 1974a, 1977). If a man is able to satisfy his bride-service requirements and is able to deliver a final bridewealth payment in his marriage, the children then become filiated to his own descent group as well as to their mother's. If he wishes, the father can then act as guardian of his children and represent them in public and spiritual affairs. At this point he can remove his wife and children to a residence of his own choice. Later, if his sons do not practice village endogamy, they move out of the settlement to join their wives' extended-family compounds (*chimana*). There they become incorporated as dependents in their wives' groups until and unless they can extricate themselves and their children many years later with a final bridewealth payment in their own marriages. When his daughters marry, they, of course, remain with their father and mother, and their father, having paid bridewealth and become his daughters' principal male guardian, also acts as guardian for his daughters' children in the matrilocal extended-family compound until satisfactory brideservice and bridewealth have been accepted for their mothers. If a son-in-law never manages this, a man receives brideservice from the spouses of each of his coresident granddaughters until satisfactory brideservice and bridewealth have been delivered in *their* own marriages.

Because the brideservice period for their daughters and granddaughters is generally rather long, and because practices of positional succession entitle surviving older men to look after the daughters of deceased male relatives, a man's residential compound and role in public and spiritual affairs is likely to be enlarged by the presence of these women and their dependent families on a fairly permanent basis. His public role as representative of family dependents centers on ancestral-cult responsibilities connected with a wide range of important life-crisis activities for each family dependent, which must be conducted in consultation with diviners, herbalists, shamans, spirit masters, descent-group elders, and affines who are sometimes scattered fairly widely over the social landscape. These time-consuming activities, plus the need to recruit new residents and allies as others die or move away, keeps adult male elders in large extended-family settlements constantly on the move. In the meantime, their female compound associates—their grandmothers, mothers, aunts, wives, sisters, and daughters—usually stay closer to home to manage the domestic sphere and subsistence cultivation pretty much on their own. Such local prominence usually causes a man to be included in local council meetings concerning other compounds in his village, while even busier men with still more dependents and family responsibilities are included in the more distant councils of the subchief and chief and may themselves become village leaders, subchiefs, and chiefs.

As a male elder ages, the prestige of his responsible position as senior male compound representative is a legacy his brothers, sons, and sisters' sons usually fight for, especially if the settlement is an important one and the elder has occupied an important position in a large descent group. It is precisely this legacy that motivates ambitious men not seeking a permanent life as a wage worker to finish their bride-service years and return to their natal compound. And it is well known that the man who marries a half-sister or cousin in his natal village and lives there most of his life is usually in a better position to succeed the male elders later, because it is the people of the village, and the women in particular, who must be willing to accept him in that role. Having succeeded his male compound elder (usually the father or mother's brother), he can move up a generation in the kinship grid of his descent group and act as guardian brother for any of his mother's sisters who are co-resident, as mother's brother for their coresident female descendants, and of course he can do the same for his own core of sisters and their children, while keeping his own daughters and granddaughters at home as well. Because groups of coresident women are basic to Goba village organization, succession to the position of father, brother, and mother's brother is the surest way for a man to achieve social and political prominence. Groups of women living with their growing offspring, and possibly with affines and friends, are invariably accompanied by competitive coresident male kinsmen seeking to affiliate themselves in order to act as their father, brother, or mother's brother.

Descent-Group Organization

Though some people find their ambitions thwarted by the maneuvers of competitors, most men and women have ample opportunity to share the advantages of forming these basic units of related co-

resident women. We have seen that all the women of a man's generation descended from both sets of grandparents can be called
"sister" (hanzadzi). In addition terms of close relationship may also
be applied to distant members of the kindred and even to "fictive"
kin beyond it. The result is that men can marry most women ("sisters") of appropriate age and inclination in the home village or its
immediate vicinity and may never have to lose touch with their
female relatives, provided they are able to withstand the jealousy
(witchcraft and sorcery) this stimulates in competitors. It also
means that persuasive men without many full sisters and daughters
can still piece together impressive blocks of solidary females willing to act as "sisters" and "daughters" in an aristocratic settlement
core. For both men and women the alternatives are generally un-
attractive.

Men living isolated from their own kin as service husbands in
distant villages are still justly regarded as equivalent to debtors or
domestic slaves (varanda). In precolonial times domestic slavery
was common, and that experience still provides a model for current
patterns. Nubile female slaves were a valued prize sought in raids,
long-distance trade, and local court decisions. Generally they were
assimilated as junior kinsmen in localized descent groups and taken
as junior wives by the men. Their descendants formed matrilineal-
descent groups perpetually attached to their husbands' families.
Though considerably less common, male slaves taken as youngsters
generally grew to serve as permanent service husbands married to
female slaves. Their offspring were also considered to be perpetual
fictive descendants of their mother's "owners" or guardians, from
whose kin group they took their praise names (or "clan") and family
or descent names. Like their mother and father, they were given
individual ancestral guardian spirits selected from those belonging
to the adopting kin group. This made their owners their interces-
sors, guardians, and fictive elder kinsmen in important spiritual
matters throughout the life cycle. It also made them their legal
representatives in social and political affairs, just as they were for
all their junior kinsmen. In fact, it appears that a slave's descendants became fully assimilated as kinsmen within three or four generations, inasmuch as their patron's goal was to amass as large a
family as possible. While not treated as economic chattel, as may
happen in stratified societies with denser populations, slave husbands, like ordinary service husbands, were consigned to a status
of permanent dependency. Until relatively recently, when a bridewealth prestation was added onto the end of the long bride-service
cycle, service husbands, like their offspring, continued to be incor-

porated into their wife's matrilocal, matrilineal descent group. Men in particular have thus associated uxorilocal "slave" or service marriage and matrilineal descent with slavery and dependency. Endogamy has been popular for ambitious men, whether free or of slave origin, precisely because it may act to convert uxorilocal "slave" marriage into something approaching viri-patrilocal marriage. Even though service is still due, the husband's status is likely to be higher in an endogamous marriage, since he has the support of his coresident kinsmen, if they are numerous and influential, and especially the support of his kinswomen. When repreated through generations, the combined practice of daughters marrying their half-brothers or other reasonably close male relatives and ambitious sons marrying their village dwelling "sisters" simultaneously creates matrilines and patrilines within the village.

The practice of endogamy to create the presence of a patriline is still a matter of significance among conservative Goba not intent on becoming Zambian Tonga. Viri-patrilocal marriage and patrilineal descent have been hallmarks of prestige and good social standing in the Shona-speaking world. The predominance of uxorilocal "slave" marriage in the tsetse-infested Zambezi Valley has given the Goba a "slave" image in the eyes of their Shona neighbors. In Goba thought it has been the presence of the endogamous patriline that has distinguished aristocrats (the Vachinda or Korekore) from peripheral followers of matrilineal slave backgrounds (referred to as ordinary Goba, Chikunda, or Tonga [Lancaster 1974b]). Under the circumstances the notion of a father-son line of descent has been especially meaningful, and ambitious families have attempted to marry within their own localized descent groups.

For her part, the woman with no strong localized kin group to keep her at home while enforcing her husband's cycle of brideservice obligations must usually accede to her husband in choice of residence. Often she must live among *his* solidary female kin as a comparative stranger and outsider, even as she ages and yearns for more status. She will frequently be accused of witchcraft and driven from the village, her grown children, and household when her husband dies, permitted to take only her infants. Unless accompanied by a sister or sister-in-law in the same situation, she will usually feel lonely and neglected. This of course was the common lot of the poorly assimilated precolonial slave woman. Jealous old women in this "slave" position today are still the butts of gossip and folklore. Just as it may benefit a man, the endogamous marriage of real or classificatory brothers to their localized sisters acts to strengthen the matriline of coresident women by adding the concurrent interests of the localized patriline composed of their male relatives. The symbolism and ideology associated with this dual structure considerably improves the status of each woman involved. It also resolves one of the classic weaknesses of matrilineal organization by giving the men and their children a real and continuing interest in the welfare of their sisters' matrilineal group (Schneider 1962). The matrilineal puzzle is solved by creating a dual system derived from sexual differences, though the women and their younger children tend to consider the matriline more important than the patriline.

Senior women in localized aristocratic descent-group cores are normally too busy with domestic affairs and subsistence cultivation to accompany their senior male colleague and representative (*dundumuntuli*) as he travels about on all of his family business, though a delegation of one or two married women may accompany him on particularly important matters. A delegation of senior women always goes along when death divinations are involved. A death in the village is a particularly serious matter. Propinquity and the interweaving of interests always implicates kinsmen in the death of a kinsman, and it is a reflection of this fact that leads Goba to observe that witchcraft and sorcery (which run together in Goba philosophy) follow family lines. If deaths occur too frequently, Goba are likely to sever even their closest kin ties and move away. Because the *dundumuntuli* is often suspected of using his sensitive position in the ancestral cult to advance his own ends, and because he may simply be an unsuspecting witch, the accompanying women act as a check on his behavior, and at the same time their presence lends weight to his representations, inasmuch as his influence is so largely derived from the cooperation of the women. When the ranking *dundumuntuli* is absent, ill, or unsuited to the women, another male kinsman can always be found to take his place.

This then is how a localized descent group is structured. Many related males compete to become descent-group (*nhundu*) representatives for sibling blocks of sisters and their daughters. The winners are selected by their coresident female kin, and no male has absolute power. Decisions are made in consultation with all the group members, and even the senior *dundumuntuli* for the descent group must exercise his office on a situational basis. He usually has to share his responsibilities with the male representatives of constituent sorority groups, and he always needs the cooperation of the women in carrying out his duties in the ancestral cult. Both a male and a female elder must be present during communication with the ancestral spirits, and there can be no ceremony at all unless the women have agreed to brew beer. While males take the leading role in addressing the guardian spirits of male group members, females do so for female members. Males who abuse their followers and are unpopular are quickly suspected of witchcraft and sorcery and are replaced or passed over. Only a few males in each generation have the opportunity to act as *dundumuntuli*. Most males not chosen by their sisters remain scattered by the rule of uxorilocal residence and live as service husbands in other villages, though some may eventually succeed in attracting a few followers dissatisfied with conditions in the main group. In contrast, their female kin fare considerably better, provided they remain together. They usually accomplish that by marrying pliable service husbands or ambitious brothers who are willing to marry kinswomen and compete for leadership against the jealousy and opposition of rivals.

In the example shown in figure 11, Gasulamate has descent-group responsibilities for all the sisters and their descendants of both sexes who choose to live with him and continue to accept him in his role as male representative of the "effective" descent group. For those of his sisters and their descendents in the wider nonresident descent group who do not live with him for various reasons, he may still be called upon from time to time to act as *dundumuntuli* when their more immediate descent-group leaders are unavailable or being held in check. Otherwise he may be summoned to attend important life-crisis rites and other events as a senior consultant. Descent-group members living at some distance are less likely to benefit from positional succession awards entailing descent group responsibilities. These are generally offered first to confirmed coresident members of the "effective" or localized descent group. This preference tends to keep the group from splitting up under the leadership of rival males and females seeking to establish residential followings elsewhere. Unlike a service husband-father, such as White, Gasulamate also has descent-group responsibilities for all his daughters (the children of his classificatory sister-wife) and their offspring. Rice will one day succeed Mututa and Gasulamate, and he will try to keep their well-known descent group together. He also has his own daughters to look after. With Mututa ill and out of favor, Rice will assume Gasulamate's dynastic descent names and kinship responsibilities when the current title-holder, Ngoro, dies. Rice will then personify the main patriline in the village.

As a son in the patriline of senior male descent-group heads

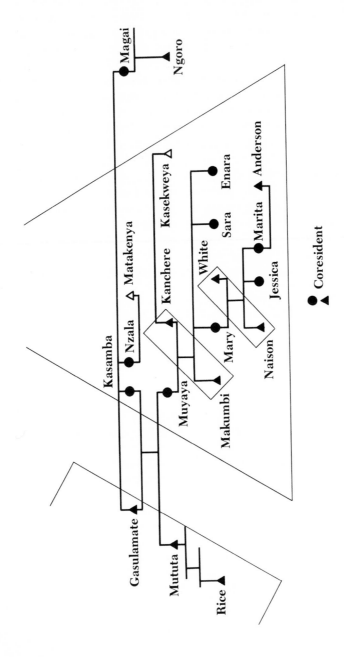

Figure 11. The Descent Group of Gasulamate (Shown in part)

(*dundumuntuli*), Rice will outrank Makumbi in important group matters. But Rice will have to be patient and skillful. In time he will be expected to arrange marriages between the children of his own sibling block and those of Makumbi's to prevent the growth of genealogical distance and avoid a schism. With the backing of Muyaya, Mary, and the other women of Kasamba's matriline, Makumbi could try to interrupt Gasulamate's patriline and forestall Rice, just as Ngoro and the women forestalled Mututa from succeeding his father as senior *dundumuntuli*. Makumbi could try to replace his mother's father, Gasulamate, or his mother's brother, Mututa, when their positions become vacant. Such a move would probably cause a major upheaval and split the village, since Mututa's descendants are numerous, and the descendants of Gasulamate's other coresident sisters (not shown) would probably resent such an exclusive move. If that stratagem fails, Makumbi could move his impressive following to the aging Matakenya's rival village in hopes of establishing himself there as a link in the main patriline of that village. Matakenya occupies a position as his father's father. Whatever eventually happens will largely depend on the wishes of the coresident women who comprise most of the settlement. Unless serious interpersonal conflicts develop, they will probably prefer to keep things as they are and assure the survival of the village rather than split up.

The Village Developmental Cycle

In explaining why they choose to live in villages rather than isolated homesteads, Goba are likely to mention soils, water, protection from game, and access to roads, stores, and wells. Whatever may have influenced the location of a particular village, however, the truth is that the Goba are gregarious people who prefer to live among as many congenial village neighbors as they can manage. Yet because of inevitable personal frictions, their villages are composed of slowly changing, recombining collections of individual living places, since there have been ample lands for dissidents to farm and many villages to choose from. As villages move about in search of fresher fields or cleaner building sites—or perhaps remain in a favored spot—the internal composition of each settlement varies considerably according to a distinct developmental cycle that is influenced by the personalities and relationships of its inhabitants. The cycle is basically unconnected with farming problems.

That is true even though villagers typically blame tired soil for a change of residence that leaves their quarrels behind them. Of course, most people planning to move wait until the slack months after the main harvests of May and June before undertaking the considerable task of building anew and clearing fresh fields in a new village. That work must be done periodically in any event, since buildings are short lived, and fields must eventually be fallowed, and the work does not deter most families from moving if they really want to. Since villages tend to be within fairly compact population clusters exploiting good soils, quarreling villagers can simply move to a neighboring settlement nearby. When a whole village section leaves as a unit for the village next door, old field neighbors who farmed and lived together before the residence shift often can make their initial adjustment simply by relocating their village buildings without altering their farmsteads. The individual who makes such a short move with only his nuclear family for company is often able to borrow a temporarily unused hut and field for a year or two, which eases his transition. In this way localized kin and friendship networks can be maintained by repeated short-distance moves, and that makes it easier for the service husband to find congenial in-laws among supportive allies.

Of course, many people shift between villages voluntarily and happily. Children and old people seem to have the highest circuit velocity in this respect. Children commonly move about neighboring villages and subchiefdoms to stay for a few months or a year with various relatives, helping out as cowherds, babysitters, and companions for the elderly or moving to locations where large play groups are available or government grade schools are in operation. Children of broken marriages also shift about when their parents remarry, and others are redistributed throughout the villages when their parents go off to the towns to seek wage-work opportunities. Older people and widows in particular like to take turns staying with adult children living in different villages. In such cases fields are even less important in limiting movement. They eat comparatively little, and much of the food required by children and oldsters is obtained by foraging in any case. Newcomers to an area and unfortunate people whose relatives have not multiplied also tend to move a good deal, perhaps every five years or so.

The most stable residential arrangements are those of satisfied members of well-entrenched matrilineal descent groups who dominate their own villages and can bring pressure to bear against those they dislike. Fortunate people in this position, especially the women, may stay with the same village all their lives and follow it, if necessary, through a succession of sites. Then as age takes its toll and new factions spring up within the group, the remnants of proud old village cores may become quite small, often preferring to die out by themselves before passing on their authority and merging their identity with a larger collection of younger kin with interests of their own. By the time the old village core has died out, one ambitious splinter group of younger dissidents is likely to have absorbed the name, dynastic titles, and many of the descendants of the parent village and may even have occupied one of its former sites (*matongo*). Most new villages, and many smaller ones in particular, are more or less temporary groups splintered off from older settlements in this manner.

The typical pattern is as follows: one or more spatially segregated descent-group subcores (*chimana*) based on the matrilocal extended-family pattern develops within the parent village as it becomes large. Some remain, and some eventually leave to join other villages, but one of the leading subcores gradually develops its own identity, farming in an area traditionally associated with the parent village, where it is recognized as a satellite, rival, and home for refugees from the older village if it declines. Finally, as the parent core dies out, leading elements of the successor core begin to filter back in to take over, or the fragments of the old core move to the outskirts of another large, prestigious settlement, commonly that of the chief, where they may maintain a semiindependent identity and act as respected elder councilors, while the former satellite gradually assumes the place of the original settlement.

A time-lapse camera focused on any village would thus reveal an active pattern of accretion and diminution comparable in many ways to the much more rapid and marked flux in a hunter-gatherer camp (Turnbull 1968). The villages to be found at any one time range from tiny hamlets containing only a few individuals to the prestigious settlement of a chief, which today may still exceed five hundred inhabitants. The core of the village will be composed of an aggregation of one or more related matrilocal extended-family segments, and even a large village including a fringe of many affines and unrelated friends will be referred to as if it were a large, unified matrilocal extended family (*nhundu*), in reflection of its dominant central core and most stable element.

Statistical trends in the village developmental cycle can be summarized briefly (see table 11). Once a man has ended his uxorilocal bride-service and established an independent family compound, he is most likely to be living with his own wives and daughters. The wives and daughters of the male village leader (*dundumuntuli*) account for 56 percent of the nuclear-family cooking hearths in the small settlement of Muinga, 75 percent in Nyampereka, and 100

Table 11

The Village Developmental Cycle

Village Name*	Total Population	Descent-Group Hearths	Percent of Descent-Group Hearths Formed by Female Kin	Allied Hearths	Allied Hearths as Percent of Total
Muinga	33	7	100	0	0
Nyampereka	34	12	42	0	0
Kayakila	62	14	43	0	0
Kalipanyo	100	23	74	2	7
Matope	164	26	62	21	45
Jakafumba	230	37	70	24	39
Bwenangoma	261	43	77	41	49
Shamutapa	112	18	78	19	51
Sichiverere	42	14	57	0	0
Sianjami	5	3	33	0	0

*Village names have been changed.

percent in Kayakila. These figures rise to 100 percent in all three settlements if we include the *dundumuntuli's* sisters. In terms of the developmental cycle these are all "young" settlements. Because female cousins are more difficult to control residentially and win away from competing elders than are wives, daughters, sisters, and nieces, small settlements in early stages of the developmental cycle are also likely to include an unusually high proportion of male kinsmen—brothers, sons, grandsons, and nephews. That is not true in Muinga, but in Nyampereka male descendants form 58 percent of the hearths, while in Kayakila they form 57 percent of the hearths.

Villages in a more advanced stage of the cycle have been successful in amassing a fairly large female core of grandmothers, mothers, aunts, and cousins to go along with a growing number of wives, daughters, granddaughters, sisters, and nieces. Male descendants are always outnumbered in these larger settlements. In Kalipanyo, for example, all the descent-group hearths are formed by the descendants of female kin (though some are males), and female kin account for 74 percent of the descent-group hearths. Another feature of the developmental cycle at this stage is that a float of unattached affines (*vatezwara*) and unrelated friends (*vato-wah*) begins to be attracted to the large village. These trends are characteristic of the larger, more mature villages, which constitute the Goba ideal in settlement size and composition. For example, all the descent-group hearths trace matrilineal links in Matope, Jakafumba, and Bwenangoma. The percentage of descent-group hearths formed by female kin range from 62 to 77 percent in these mature villages, and hearths of affines and friends account for a substantial 21, 24, and 41 percent of all hearths, respectively. In smaller, declining villages like Shamutapa and Sichiverere, the headman's own wives and daughters again comprise a larger proportion of total hearths (17 percent in Shamutapa and 36 percent in Sichiverere). At the very end of the cycle, as seen in Sianjami, all that is likely to remain is the original brother-sister nucleus.

While relatively stable coresident matrilineal segments comprise the core of the community and are especially prominent in larger settlements, the father line of senior male descent-group leaders (*dundumuntuli*) is often represented by only one or two coresident men, even in the largest settlements. Wage-work requirements in the marriage cycle, personality conflicts, and the need to please the women in a woman-centered residence pattern often result in the breaking or interruption of the father-son succession. As in the case of Gasulamate (fig. 11), the man occupying the office of senior *dundumuntuli* for a time may actually be a sister's son. When a son is too young or otherwise unacceptable to the women, the stop-gap elevation of a sister's son is usually corrected later, if possible, and the temporary succession of a sister's son may be forgotten altogether many years later when *men* recount the names of the principal officeholders in their descent group's father line.

In the eyes of the women, however, maintaining an unbroken father-son succession in the line of *dundumuntuli* is less important than maintaining large, stable blocks of coresident sisters and other female kin in each generation. Some examples of father lines in large localized descent groups are shown in figure 12. Each sorority block is headed by a senior sister (*samukadzi*), who requires the ritual assistance of a male counterpart (*dundumuntuli*) in her ancestral-cult duties. He should be a real or classificatory brother descended at some point from the same womb as his senior sister. In the next-descending generation his successor should always be a sister's son (born of a related woman) in the matriline associated with the numerically preponderant women. If he is away in town or otherwise unavailable or unsuitable, a matrilineally related *dun-*

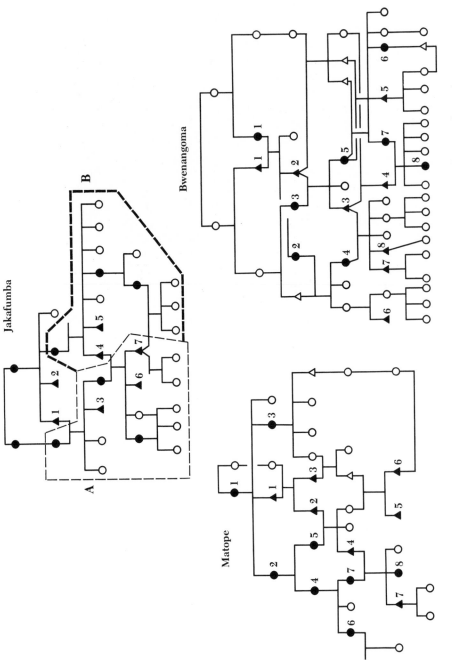

Figure 12. Mother Lines and Father Lines in Three Large Villages (Simplified Genealogies)

dumuntili from a senior generation who has grown too old for migrant wage labor is commonly asked to serve in his place. In the eyes of the women, then, the *dundumuntuli* should always be a matrilineal kinsman, a brother or sister's son of the matriline, and his patrilineal credentials may be less significant under the circumstances.

The senior descent-group males in Matope village conceive of their descent group in terms of a structuring line of *dundumuntuli*, including males numbered 1, 2, 4, and 7. In the long run number 3 will be forgotten because he simply represents an extension and temporary replacement for his brother, number 2. When number 4 needed a replacement and had no suitable full brothers or elder sons, number 5 was chosen because he was a son of the father line. His brother, number 6, had the same credentials. Succession by number 7 might have split the village if 5 and 6 had had a suitable brother, son, or sister's son and a large coresident sorority group of sisters wishing to retain immediate control. Since they did not, there was no reason to pass over number 7 when the time came for the next succession.

In Jakafumba village the father line of males numbered 1 and 3 was broken when 3 left an unpopular son as a candidate in the succession. Number 4 was still young enough to succeed, and he had many coresident sisters to support him. He managed to succeed to the positions of his mother's brothers, numbers 1 and 2, and take their places in the genealogy. Number 4's succession was a major event in the history of the descent group, but number 5's succession occasioned little controversy. Full brothers are rarely passed over in a succession of this kind. But number 6's succession caused quite a few people to leave the village because some of number 3's sisters' children wanted to reestablish the father line of numbers 1 and 3 and have the line of *dundumuntuli* revert to their side (*chipani*) of the descent group. By this time the core group was fairly large, and the descendants of *samukadzi A* (see fig. 12) saw themselves opposed to those of *samukadzi B*. Number 4's marriage to a sister in *chipani A* had resolved the problem only in part. Those who left upon 6's succession have formed their own temporary splinter village and are waiting for the parent settlement to die out when old number 7 passes away. Number 7 considers himself the son of *dundumuntuli* number 1, through 4's positional succession. But his succession from 4 and 5 reasserts that number 1's direct line has in fact been broken, and number 7's marriage underscores his orientation toward *chipani B*. He is unpopular as well.

In Bwenangoma village, male number 5 succeeded his father and his father's brother, making good a patrilineal claim the father had never managed to assert in his lifetime. That he was also number 3's sister's son made this possible. Number 6 stepped in after 4, and 5 had occupied the position only a short time; he did so as a "sister's son" to the line of *dundumuntili* 1, 2, and 3. By the time 6 died, 7 was old enough to resume the father-son succession from 3. Number 8 now recites the line of succession as 1, 2, 3, and 8. Number 1's name has become the dynastic title designating the entire descent group and village, though the women have preserved the descent name of his sister-wife in their own successions in her mother-daughter line. It was number 1 and his sisters who first won prominence for the family, and number 1's less-renowned male antecedents have been forgotten as individuals. The same is true of relatively obscure successors in his own generation. The aura of number 1's office has absorbed these obscure incumbents. Their guardian spirits and those of their male predecessors, cognates, and descendants are communicated with through number 1's spirit, which has been vested in each successive senior *dundumuntuli*. Similarly, number 8 fails to mention numbers 4, 5, 6, and 7. He has absorbed the relevant aspects of their positions as senior *dundumuntuli* for the entire group, and there is no need to remember them in that capacity, though of course their own immediate descendants will remember them as ancestral guardian spirits. The relative fertility of individual women, and especially of united sisters, and the rival fortunes of their descendants will probably determine which male in number 8's own generation will be remembered after the next generation has taken over. In the longer run they may all turn out to have been relatively obscure, and their uneventful generation may be telescoped and forgotten.

9

The Organization
of Work and the
Circulation of Grain

The ideal culmination of the Goba life cycle is the creation of the large grandparental households previously discussed in connection with per capita acreages kept under active cultivation (chapter 5, table 7). These households have normally developed a lasting attachment to a particular village. The shifting about associated with the transition from dependent status, while the brideservice cycle is still unfinished, to prime adult independence as a household still engaged in making its longer-term social and political commitments is usually over. Now the household heads may be leading their own villages (*musha*), leading their own sections (*chimana*) within a village headed by others, or acting as senior friends and allies of their village and section leaders. The husband, or a successor, will still be alive. With his days of regular migrant wage work behind him, he will be relying on marriage prestations from his sons-in-law and, to a lesser extent, gifts from sons working in the towns and other job centers. He will also be relying on cash sales from his tobacco garden and livestock pens to get the household by when crops run short and food must be purchased or bartered. His wife's beer-brewing activities may also be helpful in that respect. With both spouses still alive and healthy, acreages will be large and productive enough to feed the old couple well when rainfall is adequate. They will of course also be supporting any unmarried younger children, plus daughters divorced or separated from their husbands. Even if their daughter's marriage is running smoothly while the son-in-law is away seeking cash to end his brideservice and enlarge his own nuclear family's cash reserves and livestock holdings, the grandparental mainstay household will still be prepared to help if the daughter's fields fail her or if she is away in town at planting time. If good relations prevail, the same may be true of siblings and other relatives.

The ideal subsistence work group is derived from the structure of this ideal, successful old family. Work in field and garden is the task of both husband and wife. They work together in the same plot much of the time, along with their unmarried children, if they still have many mouths to feed. Or they work separately if most of the children are independent and the husband maintains his own plots to provide for production of beer or an exchangeable surplus. There may be a crowd of married children, grandchildren, and other relatives nearby to help the mainstay couple bring their annual sorghum harvest home to the village granary, to keep them company from time to time in their field shelter, or to help with the daily work if trouble has struck in their own nuclear family fields. But most of the time the couple works alone, aided only by the remaining unmarried children. In a younger family from which the husband is absent, working in the towns, the woman works by herself, as does the widow, though both will also be aided by unmarried children if they are old enough.

Adult Work Inputs

Work inputs in the fields and gardens can only be estimated, since household schedules vary. Beginning in late September, older women no longer expecting to travel with their migrant men begin returning to their plots to prepare for the coming season. They leave the village at 6:30 or 7:00 A.M. at the latest and work fairly steadily until 10:30 or 11:00 A.M., when it begins to get hot and uncomfortable. This four-hour schedule is typical of late September, October, and most of November. A few women prefer to start as much as an hour earlier and quit by 9:30, just as the sun begins to feel hot on their backs. The fields are seldom more than three miles from the village. If a choice winter-garden site is farther away, a village section is likely to move closer to it. The women lose little time traveling to their workplaces. For late November and December planting and weeding the women are generally to their workplaces by 5:00 A.M., just at dawn, and most stay on until eleven or so. After a short rest, some may work until three in the afternoon. But from January through May most women work a fairly steady 5:00 to 10:00 A.M. schedule.

Altogether this work pattern adds up to about 1,185 hours a year for an able-bodied adult female subsistence cultivator. This averages almost 3½ hours a day, giving an average work week in the fields and gardens on the order of 23 hours. If anything, these estimates may err slightly on the high side, since daily work patterns are readily interrupted for important disputes, deaths, buri-als, possession dances, major festivities, heavy rain, and family ill-ness. Balancing this, perhaps, is the amount of afternoon and evening time the women spend in their plots when they are living in their convenient field shelters and guarding the crops. Because of the many other demands on their time, there is no rigidly fol-lowed "normal working day" for an adult female cultivator. In ad-dition the women, aided significantly by their children, do most of the periagricultural work of crop protection as well as the nonagri-cultural work of the household, which is also time-consuming: gathering of firewood, water, and wild vegetables; preparing food; penning the small stock in the evening; and doing other chores such as sweeping, bathing the children, and doing the laundry and dishes. Fetching the daily water may take two hours in an upland village.

These estimates of agricultural subsistence work inputs by adult Goba women are similar to those reported by Richards (1939) in her study of the Bemba of northern Zambia. Since slash-and-burn subsistence systems have much in common throughout the lightly populated savannas of western, central, eastern, and southern Af-rica, much the same work pattern has been projected for these areas (Dumont 1968). It had already been clearly suggested by Richards for the Bantu-speaking region south of the Zambezi (Rich-ards 1932). Farther afield, an average slash-and-burn subsistence cultivation work year of about 1,200 hours was reported for the Hanunoo of the Philippine Islands (Conklin 1957, p. 151). In con-trast, adult workers among the hunting-gathering !Kung in Bots-wana put in an average of only 2 ½ days' labor a week. Since their day's work is only about 6 hours, their work week amounts to no more than 15 hours (Lee 1969).

So far we have been considering only woman's work in subsis-tence cultivation. In the older, established prime-adult and main-stay households men also make a significant contribution. That is clearly reflected in the larger *temwa* and *matoro* acreages culti-vated by older husband and wife teams (See Chapter 4, tables 2 and 4). It is more difficult to arrive at a representative estimate of adult subsistence-cultivation inputs for men than for women, since older men are much more likely to be away from the fields and gardens during the crop year to attend to social and political mat-ters. Younger established men spend considerable time hunting and foraging for game and herbal remedies as well as suitable con-struction materials for village buildings. Men also devote a dispro-portionate share of their agricultural time to tobacco cultivation.

My notes show that able-bodied older men who have given up migrant wage labor put in a yearly average of 800 to 950 work hours in subsistence farming, an average of 2 to 3 hours a day. This represents 67 to 80 percent of the average for an able-bodied older woman. In 1967–69 most of this male contribution took place during the early stages of field clearing, plowing, planting, and critical early weeding; much of the remainder came at the end of the sorghum cycle, when male presence was again particularly valuable for crop protection and help in bringing grain home to the village. On the other hand, the few men who maintained their own *temwa* fields and *matoro* gardens put in longer farm hours and probably worked just as hard and long as the average woman, perhaps 1,000 to 1,200 hours a year.

Boyhood Activities

In upland villages most of the boys' work consists of herding cattle and looking after the families' animals. They usually do this between noon and the evening meal, so there is no conflict when school is in session. In the mornings their fathers take care of the village herd in turns. Not all boys go off herding every day. If they live in a large village or a crowded neighborhood, they can trade off their duties, so long as there is a large enough group to see to the cattle. The herding group is also a large play group, and it is like a magnet, causing boys to join even if their parents have no cattle or have other chores for them. Boys from nearby settlements often bring their herds together to feed quietly in natural parkland. Then they join forces to play endless games of soccer. A lot of time is spent in fruiting trees, the bigger lads shaking fruit and nuts down to the smaller ones. They often look for honey or swim at waterholes. Many waterholes have fingerling fish, which the boys catch with bent-wire hooks, short lines, and pieces of porridge for bait. Everything they catch is cooked and eaten on the spot.

There is seldom any serious herding of goats or sheep, which rarely wander far from the village, though nearer fields and gardens are highly vulnerable. Garden owners are considered responsible for keeping small stock away from crops, and the owners are allowed to kill and eat them like wild game, which they do if they become angry enough and can kill the animals in the garden. Because cattle are more valuable and cause more damage, they are herded. Responsible older boys chase small stock away from crops when they get the chance, however, and in areas lacking cattle boys are likely to spend some time herding the sheep and goats instead.

Hunting boys are allowed to place snares for guinea fowl and other game in fields and gardens. The traps are usually set at the edge of the plot along some barely visible pathway. Small birds, young chicks, and young ungulates are sometimes kept as pets. Nets are placed high in tall trees to catch larger birds and pigeons. Boys also become adept at digging tasty field mice out of their burrows. All of them are skillful with powerful rubber slingshots, which they use on birds and green monkeys (vervets). Even in hunger months dusty little boys with slingshots hanging round their necks are likely to have full stomachs and small game bulging in their trouser pockets when they rejoin the family fire at dusk after a full day on their own.

The young boys of the village are responsible for penning the stock each evening, while their mothers and sisters bathe the tots and toddlers by the cooking fires. The penning usually results in a wild chase of cows, pigs, chickens, goats, and sheep, which younger children dearly enjoy, especially if there are bulls to bait into battle. When they are not busy herding, playing soccer, or hunting, the boys love to build complex wire models of automobiles (*motokari*). They also enjoy modeling clay cattle figurines and practicing spear throwing. When crops are ripening, bands of little boys raid the fields for tasty fresh maize and sorghum.

Boys eight to ten years old help their fathers in special male projects, such as building sleeping shelters and animal pens. By this time they can swing the light Goba ax with skill and surprising strength and have mastered many building techniques. They also flock to help their fathers and uncles plow and bring home the sorghum in ox-drawn sledges. Boys also spend a lot of time running errands for their elders. Socially invisible young boys are often sent to see and hear what so-and-so are quarreling about or gossiping about—or eating, if it is suspected that game meat is not being shared. In a large family it is far more likely that a boy will be "idle" in the ways just described than that a girl will be unoccupied. He may be playing, or helping fix a bicycle (a man's possession), but if he is nearby, he is at his parents' beck and call to run to the store or carry a message, especially since few girls can ride a bicycle. Mothers are far more likely to turn to a daughter for help, just as fathers turn to sons, but all agree that sons have the least serious work to do. Yet the sons do help plant and cultivate when the family has much to accomplish in a short time. And in unfortunate households where there are no daughters, I have seen young boys happily carrying babies on their backs to help their busy mothers.

There is very little age grading. Boys and young men work together to repair a bicycle, and boys from four to nineteen play together with their wire *motokari*. The boys recognize their age differences but often pass the time together in the same way, gathering nuts and fruit, hunting with slingshots, running errands, and hanging about at dances. If there are only a few unmarried males in the village section or settlement, all may sleep together in the boys' hut (*dare*) and spend a lot of time lazing about in the shade of its eaves, just as older men of all ages gather to smoke, gossip, and drink at the men's hut (*ingazi*). If the settlement is larger and there are unused huts, older boys from age ten up are likely to live together, leaving lads from about age three to ten to sleep and band together separately.

Today the big break from boyhood comes when the boys finish the equivalent of grade 6 in the local government elementary school. Those who finish suddenly feel that they have no place to go and sadly watch younger children flock to school. A few repeat grade 6, hoping for better grades, and almost all apply for coveted places in secondary schools on the Zambian plateau. Some are honored before they leave with an offering to their ancestral guardian spirit in recognition that they are now ready to travel. If they are lucky, they go off in small groups to secondary schools at Chikenkata, Chivuna, Chisekesi, Mazabuka, Monze, Choma, Mapanza, Namwala, and Kalomo on the Zambian plateau and to old Chipepo in the western Gwembe Valley. The children who see them off at the bus stop shout, "Good-by, Form 2! Who will beat the drums now?" That night a new crowd of boys will take over the flutes and drums on the village dance floor. Some of the young men will eventually find wives, jobs, and new homes on the Tonga plateau and never return.

The Chores of Girlhood

The nature of chores assigned to young girls generally keeps them too busy to form play groups as large as the boys', though in later life female groupings rival those of males. While boys' chores are largely play, light, and only sporadically demanding, even when herding, girls are soon taught to incorporate hard work routines into their more disciplined lives. From the age of four or five girls are entrusted with the care of siblings or cousins so heavy they can scarcely lift them. They prepare and cook their own lunch, wash

Two little girls guard the sorghum harvest while mother brings home another load.

the dishes, feed and bathe the babies and dress them afterward. A seven-year-old is expert at swinging a baby onto her back, fastening it in a sling, and carrying it all day. An eight-year-old is already adept at child care, the full range of domestic chores, and gardening. She is a full work partner and companion for her mother, chopping and carrying the daily firewood and bringing home the four to six gallons of water the average family uses each day, even though the distances she travels may be considerable. The skills required are the relatively simple ones she has seen her mother perform repeatedly; her limitations are mostly those of size and strength. If no girls have been born into the nuclear family, a boy may do some of these chores, though never the cooking or fetching water. It is more common for another girl in the extended family to act as mother's helper, and since many nuclear families are broken by death or divorce, girls and boys are redistributed among related families needing herdsboys or mother's or grandmother's companions and helpers.

A little girl with no younger siblings is often a great favorite, especially if she is the last child, who may remain with her mother in her old age. She is freer to play in mother's shadow, learning the skills she will someday need. She imitates her mother on the way to the well or spring, learning to balance a small cup on her head, mind the pot, and tend the fire when her mother is busy, and help pound sorghum with a tiny mortar and pestle or stand on a stool and use her mother's large stamping block. Like all the other girls, she always has a small hoe with a blade too worn for adult use, which she wields next to her mother, sister, or grandmother. More rarely, small groups of girls age six to eight will go off to gather wild greens or pick garden vegetables for the next meal.

Girls do not invent games or make toys out of wire, clay, or sorghum stalks as boys do, nor do they have the time for as much formal schooling. Their play involves making a daily contribution to mother's domestic routines, using the same utilitarian objects she uses. Especially if she is the only daughter in a large family, a ten-year-old is never seen playing away from her mother's compound or engaged in an activity that is not work, except perhaps in the evening when there is a dance after dinner or on some other special occasion. While boys range widely, fairly freely, and sometimes wildly over the entire village and throughout the surrounding countryside for miles around, girls are largely tied to their mothers, the mothers' compounds, their mothers' fields and gardens, the village well, and the public pathways lying in between. The same pattern is strikingly true of the older women the girls use as their models. This pattern reflects certain facts of village etiquette and social organization that are expressed by the careful, if irregular, arrangement of buildings, clearings, and pathways. It is also related to the organization of work.

The Ecology of Village Space

The main village paths that connect family compounds and link a village to external points are thoroughfares free to all persons. The living places, or family compounds (*chimana*), along the paths are private places to be entered only with a purpose. This rule confounds the intruder unaccustomed to living spaces without manmade walls or ceilings. As a rule, only sleeping places, granaries, and animal pens are enclosed, though some families may fence off small latrine areas, and youngsters sometimes like to fence off their

A trim circular sleeping hut (*imba*) with thick thatching and a fenced veranda to protect family belongings from goats. The wife's cooking hearth and grinding stones are in the clearing (*dare*) before the entrance. On other occasions the *dare* will be the scene of legal discussions, religious ceremonies, dances, beer drinking, and other meetings.

dance floors. The rest of the domestic boundary, which may merge with the almost equally frequented countryside, must be gleaned by signs of constant human use, such as the widening of a path into a clearing and the curving away of major, more deeply incised pathways as they run from compound to compound (see fig. 13, where compounds are outlined for illustrative purposes). Most important, purposeful intravillage visits to an individual family compound are made by older married men or even by the busy older women with status in the core descent group. The mundane message or errand can be entrusted to a socially inconsequential messenger child. While major pathways are open to all, adult passersby keep their eyes ahead when the route goes close to living space,

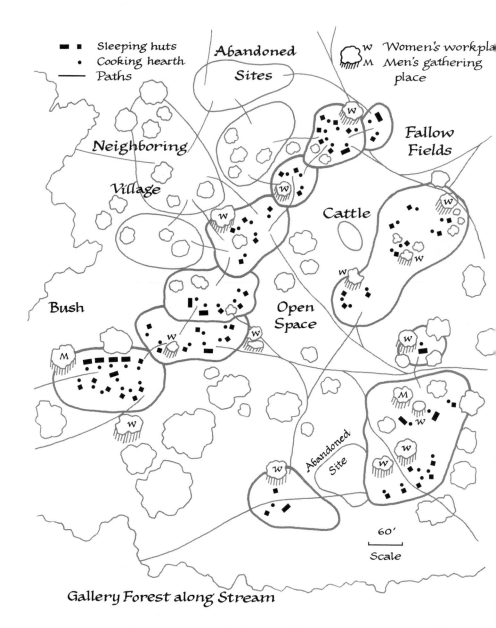

Legend:
- ▬ ▪ Sleeping huts
- • Cooking hearth
- —— Paths

Abandoned Sites

w Women's workpla[ce]
M Men's gathering place

Neighboring Village

Fallow Fields

Cattle

Bush

Open Space

Abandoned Site

60'
Scale

Gallery Forest along Stream

Fig. 13. Sleeping Huts and *Chimana* Clusters in Bwenangoma Village

A pen (*bondo*) for goats, sheep, or pigs shaped like a miniature sleeping hut. The entrance is barred at night. Thorny brush protects the roof from hungry livestock. Another hearth lies in the clearing.

whether or not it is occupied at the moment. There is a fine network of smaller paths that only members of the immediate family, children, and household animals are to use. These branch off from the main thoroughfares and enter individual compounds from various directions, leading to buildings, activity sites, and backstage areas not open for casual visitors.

Because most larger settlements are decentralized, there is normally a good deal of privacy. Most family compounds are deliberately planned so that people sitting at their accustomed places by the hearth or sleeping hut cannot see or hear much about the personal lives of those in other compounds. It is within this semiisolated setting that adult village women and their helpers are typically encountered. Women and their coresident female associates stay fairly close together as they work through the average dry-season day in their village compound, and it is much the same in their equally segregated living quarters in the fields and gardens during the crop year. Village women from other compounds may greet one another as they pass by during the daily round of work, but they rarely find time to enter each other's compounds to sit and visit any length of time, unless there is a special occasion and they are on intimate terms. Women sharing an extended-family compound may choose to visit all day and often work side by side in the same shade in a place reserved for women, unless friction has developed. But except on special occasions when normal work-day patterns are suspended, it is rare for women of different compounds to spend any part of the day together in one another's domestic living space.

During the normal course of events women from different compounds visit on neutral public grounds, principally on major pathways or at the village water source. Since the busy women on the pathways often have loads on their heads and some destination in mind, and because adult men may soon be approaching, meetings on pathways are brief and restrained. Long queues at the water source because of the time required to fill up when the water table is low, and the women's habit of waiting for everyone in the compound to load up before moving off in unison, make the village water source the primary setting for feminine social life. In slack times women may spend well over an hour congregated there each day, the more important elders taking turns dominating the bucket and pouring for the others until their compound group is satisfied and moves off. Since men never approach the water source unless it has been fouled and needs cleaning, the scene at the well is animated and noisy. Women also bathe there modestly, while mar-

An assembly of women and children filling a shady spot during a village beer drink.

ried men go off to water holes in the bush when it is convenient or wash down in their sleeping huts with water from pots supplied by their wives.

Otherwise, feminine socializing across compound lines is restricted to special events, notably when people gather in the hearth clearing for dances of various kinds during free time after dark. In the daytime they also gather to discuss an impending death; to mourn during burial ceremonies; to settle disputes of various kinds and discuss important divinations; to celebrate births, successions and girls' coming-of-age ceremonies; or to attend village-wide beer parties. Most of these events last all day. In the slack months of the dry season such a gathering is likely to be the occasion of a mob scene lasting several days and sometimes as long as two weeks, filling the clearing of the host compound with visitors from all sections of the village, as well as relatives and

Part of a large throng of women waiting in the shade during a coming-of-age ceremony.

friends from neighboring villages and more distant subchiefdoms, dignitaries called in to play special roles, casual passers-by, and even itinerant traders who happen to be in the vicinity.

In all of these large intercompound gatherings, which constitute the high points of social and political life, the women segregate themselves from the clusterings of men, during both serious business and more lighthearted moments. Moreover, the older women play important and conspicuous roles. When initial approaches are made to the land-shrine spirits for rain, it is the women of the village who assemble with beer and songs at the Shaman's sleeping hut to beseech the spirit to appear. The senior women of the assemblage sit in the clearing beside the entranceway, surrounded by a flock of older girls and young wives who serve as singers, backed by an impressive array of older married women. The men sit farther back and usually let the senior women address the spirit. In possession dances (*ngozi*), when the village is being cleansed of harmful spirits and witches may be identified, it is the senior women who are most prominent and hold court with the spirits, while young men beat the drums and older men generally sit off to one side by the fire ready to bear witness to any significant revelations. At succession ceremonies it is the widow of a deceased male, or a high-ranking female relative of a female who has died, who points the spear to identify the chosen successor, while separate clusterings of male and female descent-group elders sit and watch. And it is the throng of seated women less closely involved in the politics of the situation who end the scene and dissolve the tension by breaking into a beautiful wailing cry. Meanwhile, other women signal the remaining days of festivities by waving spearlike sorghum stalks to start the beer-capturing dance and mock assault on the stockade, where large drums of beer are waiting. Again, it is the assembled women, squared off against the grouped men, who mourn at a stricken mother's hut to judge the report of the deputation sent to bury a child and seek out the mystical causes of death. In the same way, the elder women, like the men, assemble separately to hear and judge all important decisions and disputes affecting their own and allied descent groups.

The privacy of household compounds is also invaded on more humorous, though rare, occasions when there is an open argument in the village, usually between a man and wife. Women (but never married men) may then drop their normal activities and approach the wife's hearth in the clearing, the place where fights usually occur. But they do so only in the later stages of the quarrel, after both husband and wife have begun broadcasting appeals for support. Now that interference has been sanctioned, the elders begin edging closer. The senior *samukadzi* may then enter the clearing and speak to the issues with some authority. Girls and young wives pretend to go on grinding their flour like unseeing machines while the battle rages, though they too listen with great attention. If one of the battlers is thought of affectionately as a bit of a fool, though a nice one, for losing emotional control, even the younger women may put their babies aside, drop their pretensions, and stand to watch and laugh into their hands, thus helping ease the tension. When the quarrel is too far away, or is not amusing, or when the parties are not on particularly good terms with the onlookers, the village studiously ignores the din. Then some lad may be sent to play nearby, innocently rolling his *motokari* or chasing a stray hen, to report back later. Otherwise, household boundaries are meaningful and respected. Adult visitors who stay long hours, eat, and spend the night, are invariably nonresidents from some distance away who cannot return home the same day.

Men get around a good deal more than women do. Freer of domestic and gardening chores, they have time to attend disputes and beer parties. That is considered part of their proper role behavior. They also congregate at the country stores, especially those selling beer. Children, of course, can come and go the most freely. In addition to the press of work, sex avoidances effectively keep women from straying far from their usual places. If at all possible, they carefully avoid coming close enough to adult men to require a greeting, choosing different paths, ducking into the bushes, or moving off the path and averting their faces if no other choice is available. This custom places a premium on youthful messengers and errand runners. A large group of women may go to the store and make other trips together. On those relatively rare occasions, men avoid the women or squat and clap deferentially as the women parade by following their *vasamukadzi*. Sex avoidances are another reason why women do not visit freely in other compounds, even in joint family households. It is considered very poor form for a woman to be seen alone with men or to frequent a man's place when he is there, especially if he is a kinsman or a potential future husband.

For these reasons messages and errands require special handling. Important errands that cannot be entrusted to children or unmarried subadults are carried out by an adult *sadombo*, a neutral intermediary of good standing from outside the village who is commissioned to wait outside the compound until the husband or the elders of the compound come home. Important transactions of a more routine nature are handled by a husband who normally represents his nuclear family or extended-family compound in this way. The use of mere children as bearers of minor messages and gifts is considered a sign of the sender's prosperity and good will. It also shows that the two households communicating in this way are on such close terms that they can afford to be spontaneous and informal.

The Family Compound

A typical family compound of the late 1960s is illustrated in Figure 14. The senior nuclear family heading the compound occupies a fairly roomy rectangular sleeping hut made of sun-dried adobe bricks. While many families still use circular structures made of

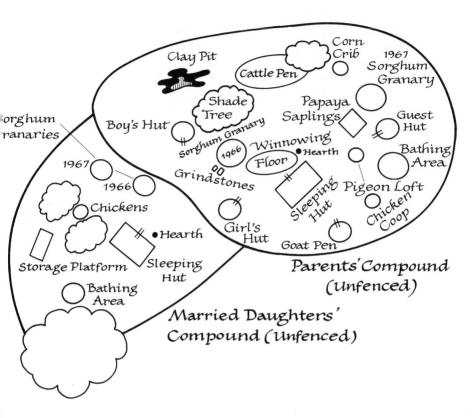

Fig. 14. A Matrilocal Extended Family Compound

upright logs, a growing number think that adobe is more modern and longer lasting. The other large compound buildings are still made of upright logs, however (Reynolds 1968). Three river cobbles, forming the hearth, are near the doorway. A spirit tree dedicated to the ancestors often stands nearby, but this family prefers to make its offerings in the hut beside the bed, as is common. There is also a sleeping hut for the unmarried youngsters of each sex, a cattle pen (found only in a few upland locations in Namainga), a goat pen, lofts for chickens and pigeons, and an enclosed bathing area. Some compounds also have pens for sheep and pigs. Some fledgling papaya trees have been protected by a fence, and a fairly dilapidated girls' hut is occasionally used for cooking on windy days or for housing children returning from town and overnight guests. The maize and tobacco storage area is built on stilts, providing a shady area for the father and his older sons to rest, smoke, entertain male guests, carve wooden household utensils, and make repairs. The father keeps his drums and herbal medicines there. The mother stores her herbal medicine chest, her household wares, and the couple's clothes in the main sleeping hut, where the father keeps his muzzle-loader and an assortment of spears.

The large sorghum granary where the 1966 harvest was stored stands near the center of the compound clearing. That was a bumper year, and because the granary was still fairly full when the 1967 crop was harvested, a second granary was built to accommodate that harvest. It was placed along the back row of utilitarian outbuildings. No strict floor plan is adhered to when structures are added in this way, since termites and other insects make it necessary to relocate buildings. This irregularity gives most compounds an "ad hoc" appearance. Granaries quickly become infested and are generally used no more than three or four years. Most sleeping huts built of wood last no more than seven years. Nevertheless, the Goba like to think that the entire compound may someday be ringed with buildings as the family prospers; adds children, granaries, livestock; and attracts more residents. The ideal for the prosperous family is to be ringed by followers, much as a significant chiefdom is surrounded by friendly subchiefdoms. Once it is empty, the 1966 granary will be reused for subsequent harvests until it is no longer serviceable. Then it will be rebuilt in a different spot if necessary. The average family compound also contains shade trees, a small ash pile for refuse, and a pit where clay is dug when new buildings need to be sealed and old ones resealed against mosquitoes and other pests.

Each married woman keeps a large, hard-packed area (*lubuwa*) swept clean in front of her doorway. That is where she prepares her family's daily sorghum requirements. The first step is to remove dried sorghum seed heads from the granary and pound (*kudzura*) them in her wooden mortar to loosen the small grains from the stem and remove the hard outer covering. The work is done in two stages. Once the contents of the mortar are cleanly threshed, they are winnowed (*kupepeta*) to remove the chaff. Then grinding (*kukwiya*) the grain into fine flour. The shade of the 1966 granary and the threshing floor constitute the woman's workplace in this particular compound.

A married daughter grinds flour alongside the men's hut (*ingazi*) in her extended family's compound. The older men generally lounge and pursue crafts here. Maize, tobacco, and herbal remedies are stored under the eaves. A drum can be seen suspended under the drying rack used for household pottery and other items that livestock might like to nibble.

As figure 13 illustrates, each compound in a village contains its own woman's workplace, where the women of the compound thresh and winnow together. Though the women work together, the wife of each nuclear family normally prepares the family's own food from its own fields and granaries. In the work area described here, the mother works along with her daughters. As figure 14 shows, one of the daughters is married and living next to her parents. Her "junior" compound contains its own sleeping quarters, hearth, granaries, chicken loft, bathing area, shady rest areas, and clearings used when the couple play host to a beer party or some other gathering. The husband has ended his bride-service cycle, he will continue to work for cash until he has acquired, or perhaps inherited some cattle, goats, and sheep. Then his compound may begin to grow and to resemble the mature compound of his in-laws. The junior compound shown in figure 14 also has a high scaffold for the temporary storage of grain while new granaries are being prepared or old ones rebuilt to receive the staple harvest. In the illustration used here, the married daughter's compound is simply a junior appendage to that of her parents. In contrast to the separate compounds, the women usually share a single workplace, and there is a great deal of casual visiting back and forth within the extended family created by the daughter's coresidence, though it will be many years before an unrelated son-in-law can feel completely relaxed among his in-laws. If the daughter's smaller fields and granaries fail her, this togetherness makes it a simple matter for the junior household to eat from the granaries of the senior couple, just as the daughter did before she married and established her own fields, granaries, and hearth.

The women who choose to live and work together in their village compounds prefer to do so, if possible, during the long months from early January to May, when they are living alongside their crops. The preferred pattern is for the members of a compound to cultivate *temwa* fields close together (see fig. 15). Each *temwa*-field shelter (*tsaka*) is a duplicate in miniature of the nuclear-family household in the village compound. During the crop year everything needed for daily life, including pots, baskets, grindstones, mortars, and pestles, is transported to the *tsaka*. A few families even take their goats, sheep, and chickens with them and build huts and granaries identical to village structures though others just build temporary structures for use during the warm months. If the *matoro* garden is some distance from both the *temwa* and the village, there are also facilities there. Most of the crop season is spent at the *temwa*, however, since it is larger and provides the staple

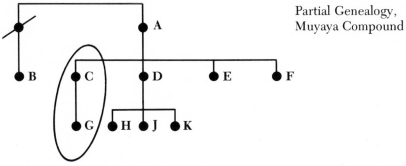

Partial Genealogy,
Muyaya Compound

C and G live in an adjacent compound.

Temwa-field Relationships

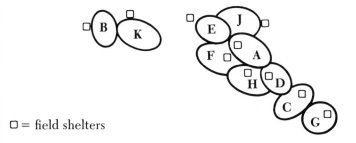

□ = field shelters

Figure 15. *Temwa*-field Relationships

Each family compound in a village has a shady woman's workplace where daily chores can be accomplished in good company. Here the married women in a large compound pound sorghum in their wooden mortars to make beer to please the ancestral guardian spirit of a sister who has been feeling badly.

crop. If possible, the *matoro* is nearby and is served from the same shelter. Most family compound groups try to cluster their *matoro* holdings close together along the watercourse the village is exploiting at the time. Since because of the topography good garden sites can be difficult to find, *matoro* clusterings do not correspond as closely to compound relationships as *temwa* sites do. The *temwa* are on level ground behind the *matoro* and are more easily grouped together because of the ample acreage normally available. As a result, the spatial relationships between *temwa*-field shelters tend to be close copies of the spatial orientations of sleeping huts in the village compound. For that reason the coresident descent-group segment occupying a village compound is commonly known

A mother and her children in her field shelter (*tsaka*) during the long crop year. Note the winnowing baskets and other household utensils. The man on the right is my assistant.

as a *tsaka*, a group of close relatives who like to farm near one another.

The Sociology of Field and Garden Sites

The uxorilocal brideservice system, which has a dominant effect on the family and village developmental cycles, also affects the siting of fields and gardens. The overwhelming influence of the uxorilocal brideservice complex is evident in table 12. People who live together prefer to farm together, though in larger, extended-family compounds, where there is an inevitable fluidity of membership through time as people come and go and children return from the

Table 12
The Relation of Field and Garden Siting to Compound Residence

Key Compound Neighbor	Number of Cases	Key Farm Neighbor Temwa Field	Key Farm Neighbor Matoro garden
Mother's mother	2 ⎫ 22%	2 ⎫ 27%	− ⎫ 10%
Mother	31 ⎭	20 ⎭	11 ⎭
Mother's brother	5	2	3
Father	6	3	3
Father's sister	1	−	1
Father's sister's son	1	−	1
Sister	14 ⎫	9 ⎫	5 ⎫
Sister (in village, not compound)	4 ⎭ 12%	2 ⎭ 13%	2 ⎭ 10%
Brother	12	6	6
Brother's daughter	2 ⎫ 15%	1 ⎫ 18%	1 ⎫ 12%
Daughter	21 ⎭	14 ⎭	7 ⎭
Son	1	1	−
Wife	3	2	1
Husband	6	4	2
Unrelated	3	−	3
Special Cases	7	5	2
Temporary plots	31 (21%)	12 (15%)	19 (28%)
Total sample	150	83	67

towns, the entire compound is unlikely to be able to maintain itself intact among the fields and gardens.

A field or garden that is not adjacent to those of compound mates in the preferred manner is likely to be an old plot hastily pressed into service by someone who has recently returned from town or has shifted from another settlement and has not had time to establish a site near compound mates. In such a case a conveniently cleared old plot still in a grass-fallow stage of regeneration is commonly taken up on a temporary basis until a more suitable choice can be made. This normally involves switching later to fresher soil nearer one's compound mates. In the meantime there may be few other workers in the immediate vicinity, since the practice of clustering fields for defensive purposes against game means that whole sections of land tend to be abandoned at the same time.

This fluidity in village population accounts for a sizable proportion (21 percent) of temporary plots listed in table 12. Most of the users are younger women just returned from visits to their husbands in town or aged widows not anchored to large coresident descent-group cores who have recently arrived to be near their daughters. Because of their age, the likelihood that they will soon be off to visit children elsewhere, and their disinclination to labor overhard after a lifetime of toil, the peripatetic widows obtain poor yields from the old plots. The same is true of the younger women, most of whom hope to return to town. There is usually a large number of such marginal workers temporarily using old plots, and while their locations are not closely tied to those of their compound mates, the old plots always lie within shouting distance of those of other village residents. While this float of marginal workers crosscuts the tendency for farm residence to correlate closely with village residence, there is an additional crosscutting factor in the tendency for farm sites to be chosen on an age basis within the village population. People of like age tend to have more in common and to prefer each other's company. Finally, when a family compound loses popularity or begins to disintegrate with age, mature married children and other coresidents depart, leaving the fields and gardens of the remnants isolated like those of relative newcomers and at a disadvantage in the perennial battle against animal predators. In addition, many of the temporary plots (28 percent) listed in table 12 are *matoro* gardens that could not be sited near those of compound mates for natural reasons.

Table 12 also lists a few instances of special farm-site locations. Most of these are used by storekeepers, who tend to locate their subsistence plots near their places of business rather than relatives. Two of these are large cotton fields. One or two plots tilled by men independently of their wives are included in this category, since the fields are sometimes taken up as an afterthought in odd, available locations once the large staple fields of their wives have been advantageously situated.

A large village usually has *matoro* and *temwa* strung out for a mile or more along a watercourse. There may be an outlying cluster of fields where new directions are being explored by a subgroup with fission in mind, and fields may be pioneered in new directions if the main farm area is aging and crowded. Other outlying farm clusters may be those of newcomers who are still using plots cleared when they were living in a neighboring settlement. Thus not all of a village's fields and gardens will be tightly grouped, though most will be. That is especially apparent in the leading edge of prime-adult and mainstay farming households. Such households, with able-bodied husbands and fathers permanently at home to help maintain large acreages for their women, lead the slowly moving group in pioneering fresh tracts in the long-term effort to maintain high yields. It is among this compact cutting edge of superior farmers that yields are highest, while plots farther back along the course of gradual movement are generally tended by older, infirm, or less attentive workers or young householders still orienting to the towns or headed for divorce court.

Though it is still commonly said that the chief or subchief is "owner of the land" in a mystical and political sense through his connection to royal land spirits, farmers take up sites today without necessarily having to ask permission of someone in authority. Man-land ratios have assured both hosts and newcomers to a village that there will always be good land for the taking, though most newcomers find it both courteous and wise to ask their new neighbors for guidance in making a choice. In doing so they capitalize on the experiences of those used to farming in a particular area and avoid conflict if it is known that a neighbor plans to extend his field in that direction or if the temporarily absent user of a plot expects to continue using upon returning that year, or perhaps the next. Otherwise the only authorization needed for land use and tenure is acceptance into village membership as a relative or friend. That voluntary association carries with it the right to use all of the neighboring land and forest for an extended distance, as long as there are no other settlements in the region. Each village farms, gathers, herds, and hunts in particular sectors of the countryside, which vary by activity type and with the seasons. To my knowledge these zones are not delimited sharply unless those of adjacent settlements begin to encroach too closely.

In ending this section, I believe it is worth emphasizing again that, like village residence, the most important workplaces chosen by adults in the subsistence economy are sited on the basis of personal preference, including social and political factors, rather than with an eye to economic specialization, the requirements of complicated cooperative work patterns, or the demands of a high-impact technology.

The Movement of Grain from Field to Granary

According to reports left in the district notebook by colonial administrative officers in Feira district, centered at the Luangwa-Zambezi confluence about one hundred miles below the Kafue confluence, chiefs had certain traditional rights over the labor of others.
A chief had rights to a part of any larger game animal killed in his
district. When visiting far from home, the chief had the right to
overnight hospitality in any village in his realm. The chief could
also call for labor by neighboring men and women who lived close
enough to be able to return to their own homes at night. This right
to labor was known as *budzi* right. Presumably it included men
and women from all the villages in the chiefdom. Adult male
householders could be called upon to clear fresh fields and help in
construction projects, while adult women could be summoned to
plaster huts with clay and cut bundles of thatching grass. Presumably they also helped cultivate the chief's fields, though that labor
is not specifically mentioned. Cultivation of the chief's fields may
also have been a responsibility of the chief's domestic slaves, as
seems to have been the case in the Kafue confluence area. The
chief rewarded all his laborers with food.

The right to labor was limited. When the district officer mentioned this "immemorial" right in his records, he noted that the
chief and his people agreed that it amounted to only two days' labor
a month by two men and two women from each village. Assuming
that three hours would constitute a full day's work for people having to travel as well, each village would owe about twenty-four
hours of combined male and female labor a year. Forty to fifty villages would therefore provide enough labor, 960 to 1,200 hours, to
support the annual subsistence needs of the household of the
chief's great wife. The labor of his domestic slaves presumably augmented this labor to permit occasional feasting and support of a
large group of henchmen.

Customs in Feira district often resembled those in the neighboring Zambezi-Kafue confluence area, though the local district notebook is less informative on this particular point. *Mbudzi* work parties are still known, though today they are recruited through
coveted social invitations, however things may have been phrased
in earlier times. The event is now limited to women and is properly
called *mbudzi ye kurima*, implying that it mainly involves weeding
and cultivating. The Banamainga had an *mbudzi* work party in
January, 1968. The hostess was the chief's principal wife, who summoned the women to her *temwa* shelter for the purpose of replant-

ing bare spots, weeding, and cultivating. Only five or six leading women from the chief's village were invited to help with the work, and afterward they ate a goat (*mbudzi*) from the chief's herd. Such an event is today an isolated annual ritual that clearly has little economic impact. In the past, *mbudzi* labor may have supported the chief's main household at most, though the labor of domestic slaves is likely to have been considerably more important. Some compounds are still hosts to work parties (*hwahwa we kurima*) at which beer (*hwahwa*) is substituted for goat flesh. Because of the beer, these parties are rather more crowded with older men and women, though little work is accomplished, and everyone agrees that the goals are social rather than economic. Today most often labor is hired for money (*mari*). In 1967–69 such parties were generally limited to work in the new cotton industry. Even beer for work parties is now rare, since everyone has as much fun, and the hosts probably derive as much prestige, from beer parties (*hwahwe ye mari*) at which a small fee is charged to cover costs and allow a modest profit. To please everyone even more, the hosts always seem to brew more beer when cash income is at stake.

As sorghum from the granary is sown back into the land to ripen in tall stands in the *temwa*, it is usually the mother, her unmarried daughters, and, ideally, her husband who share in the work. Though the political economy centering on the precolonial chief's establishment, including his warriors, was more elaborate, subsistence production for most of the population has normally been the business of the nuclear family. From planting time until the last of the sorghum is consumed and the storehouse stands empty once again, the circulation of grain is essentially in the hands of the nuclear family. The only exceptions occur when junior nuclear families and other relatives fail to produce enough food and turn to their more fortunate kinsmen, when cooperating compound mates help each other bring home the harvests, or small amounts of nuclear-family grain are sold or exchanged.

Sorghum is usually cut in May. If it is not properly dried, it is susceptible to deterioration in storage. Once the stalks are hoed down, therefore, they are carefully laid in neat squares, and the detached seed heads are placed over them in shallow piles protected from the ground. After drying in the sun for up to two weeks, the seed heads are dried further on a large platform (*bamha*) at the edge of the field. There they are piled in a truncated pyramid, which most families take great care and personal satisfaction in arranging neatly. The careful handling allows each family to estimate fairly accurately how many months' food can be expected

Sorghum seed heads drying on platforms at the edge of a cluster of harvested *temwa* fields in May, 1967. Note that the mature stalks have been
removed and preserved for later uses.

from the crop. Next to each display is always a messy pile of
mapese, sorghum that was picked over and damaged by birds,
monkeys, or goats and harvested after the prime tassels have been
cut down and protected from further inroads. These seconds are
dumped unceremoniously onto a mat next to the display pyramid.
Then, usually in June, when the grain is thoroughly dry and cannot
be dented with the thumbnail, the pyramid is dismantled, and the
sorghum is taken to the village granaries. The *mapese* is carried
home last, since further loss will be minimal.

Some families use old-style ox-drawn sledges (*chilayi*) or modern
two-wheeled carts to haul the sorghum home. Some men charge a
small fee for this service, but most families still head-carry their
crops. Even in the uplands oxen are often difficult to harness.
Head loads are carried in the broad, flat baskets used daily for

A married woman at her field shelter starting back to the village with a sixty-pound head load of sorghum seed heads in June, 1968. Most of the drought-stricken stalks have been left standing. Mature acacia trees in the background mark the edge of the village's clustered group of fields.

winnowing, and while the loads vary somewhat in size, there is a fairly standardized load for an adult woman. When the basket is filled for transportation purposes, a head load (*muso*) of seed heads may exceed 60 pounds, and test samples were found to average about 50 pounds each. It is much more comfortable to balance weights of this kind on the spinal cord and pelvis than to carry them in the arms or on the back which places unusual strains on the body. In watching the wife and daughters of an extended-family compound bring home their sorghum in 1967, I counted 145 head loads averaging 50 pounds apiece, not counting *mapese*, loads taken in for earlier use, and grain eaten green in the field shelter in late March and early April. The family's field platform lay about

The large granary of a grandparental mainstay family with its conical roof tipped back to receive the annual crop. Note the adobe stepping block and small window at the top of the cylinder. The author's wife is in the foreground.

three-quarters of a mile from their granary, requiring 217 miles of round-trip walks to finish the job. The total weight was about 7,250 pounds of seed heads. That of course explains why so many women band together for this work or much more rarely, seek help from the men.

Most granaries are large enough to hold the entire crop. The storage container is a sturdy cylinder braced with strong, slender poles wedged firmly into the ground. The walls of the cylinder are usually composed of sorghum stalks, which are strengthened with several horizontal bands of interlaced saplings, though some granary cylinders are woven entirely out of saplings like a huge basket or built up from thick spirals of woven grass that are tied into place. The inside is thoroughly sealed with a thick layer of clay. In large households the cylinder may be nine feet in diameter and six feet high. The cylinder is placed on a raised platform two or three feet high usually supported by wooden stilts, though many families prefer to trim slabs of rock to serve as a foundation impervious to termites. The head loads of incoming grain are emptied onto the clean-swept, hard-packed ground facing the tiny window-like entrance at the top of the cylinder. In larger structures the entrance is usually reached by a series of footholds built into the cylinder wall. There may be a mound of adobe on the ground below to serve as a first step. When the cylinder is to be filled with the new crop, the large, grass-thatched conical roof is lifted by its eave supports and tilted back to expose the open cylinder, and the interior is carefully picked clean and resealed if necessary.

Sorghum Yields

I calculated and checked sorghum yields in several ways. The large *temwa* platform displays could be measured in 1967 (no platform displays were prepared for the drought-stricken 1968 harvest, even by fortunate families with substantial grain to reap). Homeward-bound head loads were also measured and counted. When individual granaries could be linked to specific fields, growers, and crop years, these too were measured and compared with the contents immediately after filling. Finally, in a measure designed to make myself useful and gain access to the granaries, I brought home a large number of harvests in my pickup truck, using a specially prepared enclosure to facilitate measurement. The results are summarized in table 13. As before, the material has been arranged to reflect the five basic stages in the developmental cycle of domestic groups, as well as to show over-all averages. All figures are expressed in terms of net pounds of threshed sorghum grain detached from the stalklike seed head. Some interesting facts emerged. In all stages of the family developmental cycle, subsistence production of staple grains is unreliable and irregular, on both a per capita and a per acre basis. The Goba assured me that this is the normal condition, unavoidable for two reasons. The first is that household production varies with the random incidence of animal predation and illness in the workforce during the crop year. The second is insufficient rainfall. Yet despite these problems the Goba consider themselves successful farmers. The evidence suggests that they are right. Scudder convincingly described the valley as far more suitable for hunters and gatherers than for farming

Dried sorghum from a drying platform being loaded into the author's 4-wheel-drive truck for measurement and the trip back to the village.

communities, regardless of size. Every year there are insufficient harvests somewhere in the valley, mainly because of lack of rainfall (Scudder 1960, 1962). Yet when they can harvest, yield figures suggest that the Goba enjoy at least average success in sorghum farming.

African studies have been as remiss as any other branch of anthropology in collecting information on subsistence matters, but some guidelines are available for comparative use. Figures are most easily obtained for African market farmers, or "improved farmers," as they have been called in Zambia and Zimbabwe-Rhodesia. Among Plateau Tonga market farmers in 1943–44, mean maize yields ranged from 322 pounds to as much as 1,202 pounds per acre on fresh soils, while older fields no longer fresh enough for large maize cash crops gave a mean of just under 400 pounds of

Table 13
Staple Sorghum (*Temwa* Field) Yields

Household Type	1967 Harvest (Reasonably Good) Lbs. of Grain per Acre	Lbs. of Grain per Mouth 1 Lb. per Capita	Adjusted	1968 Harvest (Drough) Lbs. of Grain per Acre	Lbs. of Grain per Mou
Type 1					
Veteran					
Mainstay					
Chiboya	NA	NA	NA	493	179
Siandaro	823	230	369	139	21
Kapitao	544	370	528	93	63
va Sara	424	161	268	304	116
Isaac	288	110	173	Negligible	Negligib
Makazana	562	93	126	"	"
Mukombe	423	161	222	151	58
Ngoro (Zunde)	522	. . .	. . .	Negligible	Negligib
Laika	678	347	520	"	"
Kodzere	181	68	114	"	"
Chipangula	750	375	900	500	174
Laina	560	266	426	Negligible	Negligib
Averages	523	218	365	140	51
Type 2					
Partial					
Households					
Elena Miria	508	216	345	141	0.2
Kakono	245	133	240	Negligible	Negligib
Alec	279	173	247	"	"
Velina	67	40	60	"	"
Langson	554	190	266	"	"
Andriek	367	110	132	"	"
Samaria	661	418	837	"	"
David	443	222	332	"	"
Makaya	572	432	648	"	"
Violet	569	424	667	"	"
July	660	297	396	"	"
Marita	498	237	315	"	"
Esnati	468	170	267	"	"
Jesnara	358	172	215	"	"
Averages	446	231	335	"	"

Table 13 (continued)
Staple Sorghum (*Temwa* Field) Yields

usehold e	1967 Harvest (Reasonably Good)			1968 Harvest (Drought)	
	Lbs. of Grain per Acre	Lbs. of Grain per Mouth		Lbs. of Grain per Acre	Lbs. of Grain per Mouth
		1 Lb. per Capita	Adjusted		
e 3 *ne-Adult* *Households*					
son David	454	579	771	88	112.5
ion	483	370	370	Did not plant	Did not plant
pulanga	491	168	262	404	138
leon	325	347	416	Negligible	Negligible
siya	1,010	437	525	161	70
os	477	123	191	86	22
ert	426	250	388	Negligible	Negligible
ki	378	290	435	"	"
rages	506	321	420	92	43
e 4 *nen* *Working* *lone*					
mudza	275	440	587	Negligible	Negligible
ombo	357	1,142	1,142	"	"
tegwa	694	694	694	"	"
su	125	407	407	"	"
yaya	246	982	982	138	550
y	129	84	335	14	9
rages	304	625	691	25	93
e 5 *Women or* *ouples with* *ew* *ependents*					
i	460	345	394	Negligible	Negligible
sooli	440	153	217	"	"
bo	399	295	452	18	13
ka	302	288	383	Negligible	Negligible
ngo	808	323	388	"	"
wate	328	317	381	28	27
sera	293	169	270	Negligible	Negligible
rages	433	270	355	7	6
ERALL VERAGES	442.4	333	437.2	52.8	38.6

sorghum per acre (Allan et al. 1948; p. 139). In comparison to this, the Goba average (from table 13) 442 pounds per acre.

About 400 pounds per acre can tentatively be taken as a modal-yield figure for African subsistence grain production in Zambia. In support of this figure Scudder reported modal staple-grain yields of about 400 pounds per acre among the Valley Tonga (Scudder 1971, p. 47 n. 14), though they experience as wide a range of yields as the Goba do. On fresh *temwa* soils Valley Tonga millet yields have been as high as 800 pounds per acre. Older rains fields seem capable of yielding between 200 and 400 pounds per acre almost indefinitely (Montgomery, Bennett, and Scudder 1973, p. 39).

Since Plateau Tonga try to retain an average of at least 400 pounds of grain per capita for subsistence (Allan et al. 1948, p. 138), and since an average per capita cultivation factor approximating one acre has been found in a wide variety of African woodland savanna land-use systems, as discussed earlier, it seems reasonable to think in terms of 400 modal pounds of grain from an average-acre plot. For the Valley Tonga, Scudder observed that in most years, though by no means all, one acre produces sufficient grain— about 400 pounds—to last one person until the next staple-grain harvest (Scudder 1962, pp. 218–19). It is tempting to imagine that some 400 pounds of grain per adult per acre may be fairly standard among African savanna cultivators under similar general conditions of reasonably low population pressure, where fields can be fallowed or otherwise kept sufficiently fresh, and work inputs can be minimized. Unfortunately, there is not a great deal of evidence for this proposition beyond Zambia itself, though some figures can be cited. In Zimbabwe-Rhodesia annual yields of "ordinary native farmers" (versus "improved farmers") from 1948 to 1958 centered on a figure of 400 pounds per acre (or two 200-pound bags). This figure has been influenced to an unknown extent by land pressure in the unsatisfactorily crowded "native" reserves and the more intensive labor and capital inputs it has required (Yudelman 1964, p. 243, table 18). Farther afield, the Hill Kofyar of Nigeria obtain yields of 200 to 450 pounds on their lower-density long-fallow bush farms, in contrast to an average of at least 1,000 pounds of food per acre from their more intensively worked, manured farms, though such yields require close to twice as much labor (Netting 1968, pp. 97–98, 100, 133). Similarly, with greater work and capital inputs, modern African market farmers in Zimbabwe-Rhodesia reportedly produce up to 6,600 pounds of maize per acre (Weinrich 1975, p. 270), though the world record for sorghum is said to be only 2,240 pounds per acre (Wittwer 1975, p. 580).

If we use 400 pounds per acre as a modal subsistence-yield figure for Africa, the Goba average of 442 pounds is slightly above average. Goba performance compares even more favorably with the 1974 world average production of only 317 pounds of sorghum per acre (Wittwer 1975, p. 580). This productivity may account for the lower figure for average per capital acreage, which I found to be 0.83 acres versus Allan's more generous figure of 1.07 acres for Zambia as a whole (tables 7 and 8). This may suggest that with a fairly low man-land ratio the Goba selectively farm relatively small plots on only the better soils and either abandon or plow them when yields decline.

It may also be supposed that Goba farming is relatively intensive. Land-extensive, or slash-and-burn shifting cultivation, as it is commonly called, is still characteristic of much of rural Zambia. Except for more permanent riverside gardening among such groups as the Lozi on the Upper Zambezi and the Valley Tonga on the middle Zambezi before Kariba, extensive shifting cultivation is still the wisest policy in many rural areas (Lancaster 1979b). It is associated with large rain-fed acreages, long fallow periods, natural regeneration, low population density, largely female labor, minimal capital inputs and improvements, and short work days. In contrast, intensive cultivation is associated with smaller acreages, shorter fallows or permanent cultivation, higher population figures, higher capital inputs and improvements in the form of plowing, terracing or irrigation, and longer work hours, accounted for by substantially increased male work inputs to supplement the work of the women (Lancaster 1976). The Hill Kofyar of Nigeria fit this description, and their high-yielding, intensively farmed plots average just over half an acre per person (Netting 1968, p. 100). With their smaller-than-average plots, shorter-than-average fallow periods, use of the plow, and work input of older males almost equaling that of their wives, the Goba may also seem to fit this description. But since both older men and women work short hours in the fields, and since adequate comparative data for inputs from older males in extensive systems are lacking in any case, the Goba should probably be classed as selective extensive cultivators on above-average soils whose shifts, like those of other groups, are often only voluntary or political rather than strictly necessary from an ecological standpoint. It is also possible, and probably likely, that the somewhat higher per capita acreage figures cited for the better-developed Zambian plateau of earlier years reflect, at least in part, earlier African responses to cash markets for their crops, improved transportation, and larger fields made practicable by use of the plow. Eventually Goba acreages may be forced to catch up if agricultural subsistence production ever becomes more directly involved in the cash economy.

Additional points emerge if we examine Goba yield figures more closely. As noted earlier, per acre yields vary widely on a household and yearly basis, ranging from over 1,000 pounds to virtually nothing (table 13). Even the most important households can experience hunger in a good year for reasons beyond their control. The mainstay household of Kodzere and Honzoli produced only 181 pounds per acre, or 68 pounds of sorghum per mouth in 1967. But by 1968, Honzoli had become the leader of his village and an important elder in his prominent descent group. Furthermore, if we take some 400 pounds of grain as an adult's average annual requirement, or even only 365 pounds (allowing a pound of grain a day for an adult), only two of ten mainstay households achieved this goal in the reasonably good year 1967; only thirteen of forty-five (29 percent) did so if we include all the household categories enumerated in table 13.

Unreliable as typical unimproved slash-and-burn cultivation may be, these stark results suggest some revision in our tentative modal figure of 400 pounds of subsistence grain per person per year. Adjusted 1967 figures for per capita grain yields are shown in column 3 of table 13. A figure of 1 pound of grain a day per adult has been retained, since it closely approximates local norms and practices, as verified by measurements made in the field. But by the same token per capita food requirements have been adjusted downward for older people (to an average of 0.75 pounds a day) and children (an average of 0.5 pounds a day).

It is also unrealistic to require the family sorghum granary to feed each person 365 days a year. Sorghum is harvested in May and brought home in June, but before they bring home the harvest the people eat fresh green sorghum from mid-March through April, and they consume riper sorghum throughout May at least, all in amounts unmeasured in table 13. Seventy-five days may therefore be deducted from the time that harvested sorghum in the village granary should be expected to feed the people. An adjusted per capita figure approximating 290 pounds is therefore a more realistic measure of the sorghum subsistence harvest than 400 pounds. This lower target figure also takes *matoro* gardens into account. While the average *matoro* holding is 0.7 acre per family, there was no practicable way for a lone fieldworker to measure the average output and incorporate yields from this significant acreage (table 13). Even without flooding, we can assume that *matoro* contributes significantly while the people are eating green sorghum in their field shelters. The same is true of general foraging. The busy months March through May are just the time that older men complain bitterly about the lack of cooked meals. They are also the "folklore" months, when grandparents relate traditional scare stories about mythical lions and snakes to keep the children from overindulging themselves in the fields and gardens.

If we consult these adjusted figures in table 13, only five of ten mainstay families failed to reach the per capita sorghum target of 290 pounds in the good year 1967, while the adjusted average for mainstay households that year reached a more-than-adequate 365 pounds per capita. On this new basis the average for each household category exceeded the 290-pound target, and the over-all average for forty-five households was a solid 437 pounds of sorghum per capita. Even so, sixteen households (36 percent) failed to meet the target.

The recurrent failure to produce enough food inevitably stems from insufficient local rainfall, unexpected illness, and the equally uncontrollable inroads of game, roughly in that order. All three factors may combine to cripple a household's output in any one crop year, though the year can accurately be described as good for the chiefdom as a whole. Scudder's work leads us to expect this as normal for the valley as a whole. The Goba have certainly learned to expect it. That is clearly demonstrated by the size of new granaries built to accommodate the sorghum harvest expected from the nuclear family' plots. They are often too small to house a pound of grain a day for each adult in the family. Of course, children and oldsters eat less than prime-age adults do, much food is eaten from the vine during the growing season, boys generally forage for themselves much of the time, and cash purchases, barter, hunting, fishing, and the gathering of wild and semiwild volunteer crops are always relied upon.

In this connection it is important to remember that farming is not the sole base of the local economy any more than it is the sole subsistence base. Political maneuverings and rewards are geared to the acquisition of influence over others in the kinship system. The focus is on the acquisition of dynastic family titles and key spirit names reflecting formally sanctioned positional succession to seniority in the ancestral cult. Chronically infirm, lazy, and inept individuals perpetually unable to feed themselves and their dependents eventually lose influence despite bona fide title claims. Those who continue to enjoy relatively high social standing conform to local cultural norms and behavior, including at least mod-

erately successful and always diligent farming efforts. But prominent leaders do not accumulate unusually large acreages incommensurate with their stage in the life cycle, nor do they personally
control unusually large labor pools or crop yields for their own
benefit.

Despite these strictures, mainstay households generally produce above-average yields per acre in both good years and bad, as
the word "mainstay" is meant to imply (523 pounds versus a sample
average of 442 in 1967; 140 pounds versus 53 in 1968). Even in
1968, the worst drought year remembered, two of the mainstay
households I followed closely had acreage yields above the 1967
average. Mainstay households tend to have lower-than-average
yields on a per capita basis, but that is because of the greater number of unmarried dependent children and grandchildren they typically support. Mainstay households are less likely to lend out their
children to others who need company or may be better able to feed
them. Since mainstay households are large and ringed by the
households of others, children prefer them because of their large
play groups and willingly join them for extended stays when their
parents are away or when the elders succeed to new kinship responsibilities upon death or divorce in related families. Though
per capita sorghum yields decline as the number of subadult dependents increases, mainstay households more than offset this
strain by drawing on the cash earnings provided by their sons-in-
law and older sons. In addition, older men forming veteran mainstay and prime-adult households occasionally tend large fields and
gardens of their own (zunde) and substantially augment the acreage
worked separately by their wives. Only one of these is enumerated
in table 13, but it can be seen that such acreage can provide a
valuable margin of family safety in case of need.

Partial households, which still rely largely on town money as the
husband works his way through the uxorilocal brideservice cycle,
experience much the worst results in poorer years, for then the
wife is quicker to abandon her inferior acreage and rejoin her
mother or go to town to live with relatives in periurban areas. As
groups prime-adult households enjoy above-average results, though
the more experienced mainstay households tend to enjoy even
higher acreage yields. Older women working alone in older, un-
plowed plots (household type 4) often experience low acreage
yields, and that is especially noticeable in poor years. Yet their high
per capita yields are indicative of the large surpluses they can share
with close allies when necessary. This advantage undoubtedly
helps underwrite their social and political importance. Older in-

A daughter stirs the evening's porridge in the shade of her mother's granary while the others bring home the harvest. A pot of vegetable relish dip lies in the foreground. Drying sorghum covers the clearing.

firm single women and older couples in smaller, less prominent households show roughly average results (household type 5), though in poor years the yields from their older plots decline more sharply, and the loss is less likely to be offset by cash from dependents in town.

Food Consumption and Eating Arrangements

The ideal eating arrangement is three meals a day: at dawn during the crop year or a little later during the less active dry season; at noon; and in the evening around seven. The morning meal is likely to be a bit of cold leftover porridge when the wife is working her crops or living at her field shelter, and this snack may be skipped altogether. Young men may also gather and eat their lunches casually, in small portions, while they go about their business, though adults generally expect a sit-down lunch and dinner. The noon and evening meal is usually a very thick, slabby porridge (*sadza*), of which the average adult consumes about one pound a day, while youngsters and older people take proportionately less. Whenever possible the main meals are eaten with some savory or relish (*muriwo*), the main source of vitamins, minerals, animal and plant proteins, and fats. The stiff porridge is rather tasteless, since no condiment or flavoring is added. It is served in a central bowl, which is placed before each eating group. The diner takes up a small portion with the fingertips, quickly rolls it into a dry ball, and dips it into a small dish of relish. The relish is usually salted and quite tasty. Scudder showed for the Valley Tonga that food gathering, fishing, and hunting provide a much higher proportion of the relishes consumed during the year than do farming and animal husbandry combined, and the same is probably true of the Goba and many other African peoples (Allan 1965, p. 256). Nowadays young progressives with a little cash like to thin their sorghum meal with a little water, add sugar from the store, and eat it with a cup of tea. It is even more prestigious to make porridge from ground maize ("mealie meal") in imitation of prosperous market farmers on the Tonga Plateau in Mazabuka District.

In chapter 10, I will consider grain that is exchanged beyond the confines of the nuclear family. But most grain by far begins and ends its circulation within the control of the nuclear family that produces it. The mother who spends so much of her time working in her plots, living in them, and guarding them, is also the one responsible for food preparation and cooking, aided always by her helpers. In a sample of ninety-three unmarried village children, seventy-three (78 percent) ate from their mother's granary and hearth. This figure included girls up to sixteen and one boy as old as seventeen. The older girls had gone to stay with their wage-working men, and the older boys had gone to seek places in secondary school or wage-paying jobs. Eight of the children (9 percent) had been fathered by their mothers' earlier spouses, and five of the youngsters (5 percent) had been born of their fathers' previous marriages. One older boy was living with his divorced mother's sister, and six children (6 percent) were grandchildren being fed either by their maternal grandmothers or mothers' sisters while their mothers were permanently absent, living with fathers in town.

While dependent children and the husband always eat from the mother's nuclear family hearth and granary, seating arrangements within the compound are broken up along age and sex lines. In an independent nuclear-family compound, the mother sits with her daughters and the very young male toddlers, where they are joined by the mother's mother when she is present. This group chooses any convenient shady spot in the main clearing by the hearth. If an adult female visitor is present, unless she is a close consanguineal relative of the mother, she sits by herself and eats from her own portion. The father joins his wife and children if the compound is secluded and his wife's mother or other visitors are not present. Otherwise he sits nearby, in another convenient shady spot, where his wife brings him his own bowl of porridge and a separate small dish of relish. He is joined there by his older sons, though all but the oldest sons will return to the mother or form yet another group if the father has adult male company from outside the compound. In larger extended-family compounds formed by married male siblings, the brothers and their older sons form a single eating group, joined perhaps by their older brothers-in-law and their older boys, while all the women join together. In all joint seating arrangements of this kind each married woman or her cooking daughter is careful to supply sufficient food for her own dependents. Strained relations may quickly develop in separate dining arrangements, however, in which case each family is likely to revert to the basic nuclear-family pattern.

In matrilocal extended-family compounds coresident married daughters and their own daughters join their sisters and mother, and perhaps their mother's mother, in a single large group. The father sits with compound boys too old to remain with the women, though a third group of teenage boys may form if there are enough of them. Any of the younger sons-in-law who are home for a visit may sit together in a fourth cluster, though a single son-in-law is likely to join the teenage boys. Only an older, very well established son-in-law would ever sit with his wife's father, they say, and I never saw one do so. If there are no older boys for company, a well-liked son-in-law may be permitted to sit separately with his wife and children at mealtimes. In polygynous compounds each wife sits apart, at the head of her own group, though the boys band together or join the father, who is fed equally by each wife, either in turns or in equal portions.

10

Trade, the Cash Economy, and Social Change

As shown in chapter 9, while members of extended-family households often eat together in an age-sex arrangement, and while occasional outside visitors are fed and entertained, the movement of seed grain from mother's granary to the field, then back in larger amounts to the granary, out to the mother's workplace in small daily increments, and on to various eating groups, is largely a closed nuclear-family subsistence circuit. Nevertheless, some grain does move beyond this tight domestic sphere. The question is how much and with what impact.

In 1967, working with a sample of forty-six sorghum fields (table 13), I found an aggregate movement of 49,769 pounds of threshed sorghum grain from the fields of the growers to their respective village granaries. The growers in the sample had an average sorghum yield of 442 pounds per acre and an adjusted average per capita production of 437 pounds. Since it was calculated that a per capita figure of only 290 pounds would on average be sufficient to feed an adult until the next annual sorghum harvest, the average yield would seem to include a theoretically exchangeable "surplus" of 147 pounds per mouth, representing a substantial 34 percent of the average per capita production safely harvested and stored in nuclear-family granaries.

This figure is actually too high. It has already been stated that most of the grain circulation and distribution is restricted to the confines of the grain-producing and consuming nuclear family, or matricentric cell in the case of widowed women and cowives in polygynous marriages. This easily measured family circulation normally includes much of any apparent "surplus" an individual household may reap, since nuclear-family grain is commonly shared within the extended-family compound or with other closely allied families living in separate compounds of their own. This casual "family" sharing is difficult to quantify, but when closely allied households fail to produce enough grain in any one year, the nuclear household with sufficient grain (or other resources convertible into grain) may temporarily expand to share its supply and, in effect, form a temporary joint eating unit. To a greater or lesser extent most nuclear families probably either give or receive grain in this way every year, whether or not it is desperately needed. Often it *is* needed. We have seen that in 1967, a reasonably good year, 36 percent of the growers in the sample failed to produce enough sorghum to meet the adjusted annual per capita demand target of 290 pounds. Much of this shortage had to be made up by extended-family sharing, and only a portion of the indicated "surplus" was really available for external circulation beyond the confines of the producing-consuming nuclear family, or slightly larger extended-family food-sharing unit.

In this chapter I will discuss the uses to which this "excess" grain is put and trace grain exchanges extending beyond the confines of the food-producing and food-sharing household. Particular attention will be paid to social and political factors, so that the connection of subsistence production to the political economy of the chiefdom and village can be assessed empirically rather than assumed on a priori grounds. Attention will also be paid to grain flows associated with the cash economy. The volume of the cash sector will be estimated, as will the extent to which subsistence production is involved with this sphere. While the cash economy is a twentieth-century phenomenon, it largely replaces the former element of inligenous trade in the male-dominated political economy (Watson 1958). This makes it necessary to investigate the extent to which ubsistence production can influence social and political organization through its connection to the modern cash sector of the political economy.

Before I discuss avenues of exchange and rates of flow, it is necessary to describe the basic units of measurement and exchange used by the Goba.

Units of Measurement and Exchange

The unit of measurement most commonly referred to and used in daily life is a "head load" (*muso*) of sorghum seed heads piled in a broad, shallow winnowing basket (table 14). The *muso* is a fairly standardized unit of measurement, though winnowing baskets vary in size. They are made not by specialists working to a set pattern but by older women in their spare time. Nevertheless, the use of

Table 14
Goba Standard Units and Rates of Exchange

Unit	Rate of Exchange
Muso	Informal head load of seedheads; should average about 50 pounds in a good year, or about 2.93 cubic feet, converts into about 17 pounds of threshed grain, though contents actually variable
Chiwoomba	Formal head load of seedheads used for trade; usually averages about 30 pounds, or 1.76 cubic feet, converts into about 10 pounds of threshed grain
Buketi	5-gallon tin holding 30 pounds of threshed sorghum grain in 0.61 cubic feet

head loads in more or less formal exchange has resulted in a rough degree of standardization that everyone finds acceptable. Since head loads seldom become involved in trade at the local country store, where balanced exchange and careful measurement are necessary, women like to appear casual about the size and generosity of their head loads. This attitude gives the head load some of the qualities of a gift. Though an equivalent and possibly adequate return may be accepted, the implication of unbusinesslike generosity paves the way for a return head load, or a gift, at some later time when household fortunes are reversed.

Despite this element of diplomatic variability in head-load sizes, a series of tests revealed that it is permissible to speak of an average winnowing basket (*dengu*). It measures twenty-two inches across the mouth, the widest point, and tapers evenly to a flat bottom about nine inches across and six inches deep. When a head load is being given to a close ally, relatively little attention is paid to its contents, since a return is available for the asking should there be need. But in bartering more formally with more distant associates, everyone is aware that the height of the pile of sorghum heads in the basket is crucial, and in poor years it tends to decline. For example, in late 1967, after two successive good harvests, the average head load weighed about 50 pounds, though work loads in the same basket often exceeded 60 pounds. Soon after the extremely poor harvest of 1968 the average weight of head loads was only 44½ pounds. Later that year, when hunger was common, I measured head loads of only 30 pounds.

When giving head loads of grain to closely linked allies, no price or immediate return is exacted. In dealing with more distant associates, the standard charge is five shillings. This fixed exchange rate does not vary from year to year, they tell me, despite well-known adjustments in head-load contents, which vary with social distance and quantity available. The five-shilling exchange rate is considered only a token. Grain exchange deliberately aimed at providing a little cash income or some other need, is handled differently as we shall see.

In keeping track of the uses to which households put their sorghum, and in measuring the exchanges shown in table 15, column 6, I found it impossible to keep an accurate record of head loads (muso) given or received. For example, nuclear household numbers 9, 14, 21, and 28, among others, showed sizable grain deficits in 1967 (table 15, column 4), compared with their estimated per capita requirements (column 2). The deficits ranged from 277 to 587 pounds, or 24 to 45 percent of the household's estimated annual subsistence grain needs. To a large extent these deficits were made good by uncounted head loads from extended-family compound mates; in each case it was the wife's coresident mother or husband who gave from the produce of his or her plot. Cash reserves and herds of small stock were also drawn upon to purchase food from other villagers or from local country stores. Despite the original deficit, each of the households was then able to exchange a modest amount of grain for necessities, such as a small amount of cloth from the store, or to brew beer for important religious and social purposes. No matter how bad the harvest, each nuclear family tries to brew beer at least once during the dry season to combine ancestral prayers with a more relaxed social aftermath. While this custom may seem improvident at first glance, grain consumed as beer probably has food value equivalent to porridge, and beer given to others is later returned through reciprocal parties.

Family sharing of grain is done so spontaneously that amounts given and received are forgotten and difficult to estimate and consequently have been omitted from table 15. Rather than helping fill an unfortunate compound mate's granary with a remembered number of measured loads, households within the same compound may simply pool their grain informally when meals are being prepared at the threshing floor. But a smaller head load piled in the same basket, or perhaps wisely loaded into a smaller one used by

Table 15
Grain Exchanged Beyond the Household—1967 Crop

Household	(1) Number of Mouths	(2) Subsistence Needs (1) × 290 lbs. (Lbs.)	(3) Total 1967 Sorghum Harvest (Threshed Lbs.)	(4) Exchangeable Surplus (deficit) (3) − (2) (Lbs.)	(5) Exchange-Surplus as Percentage of Needs (2) (Percent)	(6) Amounts Used in Chiwoomba (Lbs.)	Drums (Lbs.)	Bucketi (Lbs.)	(7) Total Used Beyond Household (Lbs.)	(8) Total Exchanged Beyond Household (7) as Percent of (3)
Wilson David	3	870	2,315.4	1,445.4	166	34 = 340	3 = 180		520	60
Lukombo	1	290	1,142.4	852.4	294		2 = 120		120	41
Musooli	4.25	1,232.5	924	(308.5)	−25		2 = 120		120	10
Jesnara	2	580	429	(151)	−26		2 = 120		120	21
Langson	2.5	725	664.8	(60.2)	−8		1 = 60		60	8
Zakeyo	4.5	1,305	1,847	542	42	22 = 220	1 = 60	18 = 540	820	63
Robert	4.5	1,305	1,746.6	441.6	34		6 = 360		360	28
Mutegwa	1	290	902.2	612.2	211	7 = 70			70	24
Siandaro	6.25	1,812.5	1,234.5	(578)	−32	10 = 100	2 = 120		220	12
Simon	3.5	1,015	1,376	361	36		1 = 60		60	6
Kapitao (Zunde)	.....	.....	1,110.9	1,110.9	100	28 = 280			280	25
Rodia	3.5	1,015	1,849.9	834.9	82	27 = 270	2 = 120		390	38
Sigongo	2.5	725	969.6	244.6	34		1 = 60		60	8
Kasamba	4.5	1,305	718.4	(586.5)	−45		½ = 30		30	2
Marita	3	870	946.2	76.2	9		2 = 120		20	14

Table 15 (continued)

Grain Exchanged Beyond the Household—1967 Crop

Household	(1) Number of Mouths	(2) Subsistence Needs (1) × 290 lbs. (Lbs.)	(3) Total 1967 Sorghum Harvest (Threshed Lbs.)	(4) Exchangeable Surplus (deficit) (3) − (2) (Lbs.)	(5) Surplus (4) as Percentage of Needs (2) (Percent)	(6) Amounts Used in Chiwoomba (Lbs.)	Drums (Lbs.)	Bucketi (Lbs.)	(7) Total Used Beyond Household (Lbs.)	(8) Total Exchanged Beyond Household (7) as Percent of (3)
Mary	2	580	670.8	90.8	16		3 = 180		180	31
Esnati	3.5	1,015	936	(79)	− 8		1 = 60	3 = 90	150	15
Isaac	3.5	1,015	604.8	(410.2)	−40		2 = 120	4 = 120	240	24
Makazana	8.5	2,465	1,067.8	(1,397.2)	−57		1 = 60	6 = 180	240	10
Makwate	2.5	725	951.2	226.2	31	6 = 60	2½ = 150		210	29
Mukombe	4	1,160	883.3	(276.7)	−24		1 = 60		60	5
Ngoro (Zunde)	. . . . .	. . . . .	1,305	1,305	100	29 = 290			290	22
Laika	3	870	1,559	689	79		4 = 240	4 = 120	360	41
Samson	5	1,450	1,269.7	(180.3)	−12		1 = 60		60	4
Mesiya	2.5	725	1,313	588	81	4 = 40	1 = 60		100	14
Chipangula	2.75	797.5	2,475	1,677.5	210		3½ = 210		210	26
Mbasera	2.5	725	673.9	(51.1)	− 7		2 = 120		120	17
Jailos	4.5	1,305	858.6	(446.4)	−34			1 = 30	30	2
Totals	90.25	26,172.5	32,745.0	6,572.6	25	167 = 1,670	47½ = 2,850	1,080	5,600	21

a daughter, is employed in more calculated exchanges, usually with villagers outside the compound and especially in barter with local shopkeepers and both local and itinerant traders. Technically, this more closely measured unit of exchange is known as a *chiwoomba*, though in general conversation it too is commonly referred to as just another head load (*muso*). There is no confusion, since everyone knows that the volume of the head load always depends on the social situation as well as the season. To avoid error in collecting statistical material I have employed the technically correct term *chiwoomba* for the more carefully measured head load.

Because the *chiwoomba* is exchanged in more balanced barter, including dealings at country stores and trading stations, and because it contains little if any "gift" quality designed to encourage future reciprocity, its volume is less variable than that of the *muso*. A standard *chiwoomba* holds 1.76 cubic feet of seed heads, numbering perhaps 186 seed heads, weighing about thirty pounds. When cleanly threshed, the load yields at least ten pounds of grain. The *muso*, in contrast, holds something like fifty pounds of seed heads and converts into some seventeen pounds of grain. The smaller amount of grain in a *chiwoomba* exchanges among villagers for the same standard equivalence as a *muso*, with the result that closer associates receiving a *muso* enjoy better terms of trade, as they are meant to. It is commonly alleged that one *muso* should equal two *chiwoombas*, as a standard equivalent, though many women say that in preparing the *chiwoomba* they fill it so that two *chiwoombas* are actually more than one *muso*. Rather than being mean about this more carefully calculated measure, they like to give the impression that a careful scrutiny of their *chiwoomba* only reveals how generous they are. In practice a standard *chiwoomba* may equal something like 60 percent of the standard *muso* exchanged in a good year, rather than 50 percent, as suggested by the alleged two-for-one equivalence. In poorer years the size of the *chiwoomba*, which does not vary, may actually equal that of the *muso*.

As shown in table 15, nine households traded off *chiwoomba* for various purposes in 1967. All but one of the households had reaped a crop surplus, and while household 9 had a deficit, it was made good by drawing down cash reserves and sharing the coresident mother's sizable surplus. Altogether this minor trade in head loads (*chiwoomba*) represented only 5 percent of the total harvest reaped by the twenty-eight growers in table 15. Since each *chiwoomba* trades for five shillings, or some other standard equivalent, the 167 *chiwoomba* enumerated in column 6 represent a gross cash flow of $100.20 in the 1967 rate of currency exchange.

The beer party is another use of sorghum that dissipates the grain beyond the confines of the producing household. The twenty-eight sorghum growers listed in table 15 brewed a total of 47½ drums of beer from the 1967 harvest. The drums are discarded gasoline containers holding 55 gallons (44 British gallons). A few small brews for religious and social gatherings in households with little grain to spare have been excluded from my calculations. Smaller brews are prepared in irregular pot sizes, and the negligible amount of grain consumed is difficult to estimate reliably. Almost all the beer brewed is sorghum beer (*chimera*), with an estimated alcoholic content of 3.5 percent. An average drum requires 60 pounds of sorghum. A negligible amount of millet is grown to provide a little variety in the form of porridge and millet beer (*mbidzo*). Only 30 pounds of millet are used in a drum of pure millet beer, though millet is generally used only as a flavor additive. My calculations were made on the basis of sorghum inputs only. After boiling, a full 55-gallon drum yields no more than 45 to 50 gallons of brew. A small private party (*kabicira*), where a pot or two of beer has been prepared for an ancestral prayer and descent-group communion, generally involves no exchange of cash. But if at all possible, households with sufficient grain, or with *muso* exchange networks, brew one or two drums at a time so that the drinking party can be opened to the public at large after the small religious ceremony has been held. Such large public parties are known as *hwahwa ho engonwa*, "parties just for the drinking."

At the prevailing rate of 60 pounds of sorghum per beer drum, the 47½ drums represented 2,850 pounds of grain, or 9 percent of the 1967 harvest (table 15). All but four of the households in my sample brewed at least one drum each. The four exceptions were one older widow sleeping with small granddaughters and sharing the compound of a married daughter who let her daughter do the brewing; one coresident young daughter who let her mother do the brewing; and two polygynous males with fields of their own who permitted their wives to use their own produce for the family brews. If necessary, such husbands later reimbursed their wives.

In terms of cash flow a survey of 176 drum-sized brewings revealed that the average drum yields a gross cash return of about $7.80. As indicated earlier, almost all large brews were open to the public in 1967–69, and after each drinker was given one or two free cups, a nominal charge was made for subsequent draughts.

Once the hosts decide that they have taken in enough cash, the rest of the drum's contents, which may be turning slightly sour, is given away.

Today the party at which beer is given as a reward for work is almost entirely a thing of the past. Most beer party customers are older adult men who have finally come home to stay from their years of migrant wage labor and bride-service remittances. They finance their beer consumption from tobacco sales and marriage prestations from sons-in-law. Large groups of older women also attend the parties in slacker months of the dry season, when most farming activity necessarily shuts down in locations lacking *matoro* gardens on larger watercourses. Women finance their own drinking from the minor cash trade in sorghum, which is largely a woman's affair, and from the proceeds of their brewing. Younger wives with smaller fields rarely have enough money from such sources to attend parties, and since their men usually are absent in towns, it is considered prudent for them to stay home from these mixed crowds. Older married couples who work together in the fields and gardens usually split the proceeds from grain sales and beer parties, though women fetch the water and do all the work connected with brewing. If a polygynist wife receives no contribution in grain from her husband's granary, she retains all her beer proceeds, just as a man may keep all his tobacco money if he works alone. The 47½ drums of beer listed in table 15 represent a cash flow of about $370.

Grain, Traders, and the Cash Economy

The trade in *bucketi* is the last major avenue through which grain is drawn out of the domestic orbit. In everyday talk the *bucketi, muso,* and *chiwoomba* are said to be mutually interchangeable. All are traded for the fixed equivalent of five shillings, and everyone will say that they represent equal amounts of grain, though all know that this is false. The close ally may receive almost twice as much in his *muso* in a good year, as a more distant trading partner obtains from a *chiwoomba*. This discrepancy in volume lies at the heart of village-level politics, where the general goal is to amass as many close allies as possible. While both the *muso* and the *chiwoomba* exchange for a nominal five shillings among villagers, a commercial trader or shopkeeper is wisely leery of the highly variable *muso*. While the *chiwoomba* is considered an adequately measured unit of exchange among villagers, who do not use scales or standard basket sizes among themselves, it too is unacceptable to the trader linked to the cash economy of the outside world. By the very nature of things the trader and the shopkeeper are out to make a profit from the average transaction and must rely on close calculations if they are to stay in business. This need has given rise to the *bucketi* ("bucket") as a more precise unit of measurement and exchange.

The *bucketi* used in such trade is a rectangular cooking-oil or paraffin tin obtained from a local country store. It measures 9 by 9 by 13 inches and contains 0.61 cubic feet, or 5 U.S. gallons. When filled level to the brim, a *bucketi* holds 30 pounds of threshed sorghum grain. When trading among themselves with various social, political, and economic motives in mind, villagers blandly equate the *muso*, *chiwoomba*, and *bucketi*, but my measurements (table 14) show these to be incommensurate units in a quantitative sense, representing 17, 10, and 30 pounds of threshed grain, respectively. Needless to say, villagers rarely trade in *bucketi* among themselves, for all their talk. The reason, they say, is that the *bucketi* trade requires that the grain be threshed, and that is a lot of work. They simply assert that their generous unthreshed head load (*muso*) equals one or more *bucketi*, and they claim to prefer the head load since it may represent a larger amount, while a *bucketi* can never hold more than a bucket. Head loads (both *muso* and *chiwoomba*) are exchanged among villagers for five shillings each and can only rarely be obtained from or bartered to commercial traders and shopkeepers. *Bucketi* generally involve only shopkeepers and traders, who stand ready to buy for 5 shillings ($0.60) and sell for 10 shillings ($1.20). In fact, in the hungry months, November to February, shopkeepers and traders are often able to sell them back to villagers for 15 shillings ($1.80) each. In the extremely hungry month of October, 1968, after the worst harvest remembered by elders, some local shopkeepers sold buckets of sorghum back to villagers for as much as $2.10 each.

While commercial traders can occasionally net spectacular 250 percent profits from the sorghum trade, the over-all volume on this bucket-by-bucket business is very low. Moreover, it is very time-consuming. During the slow dry season women love to pass the time bargaining for the items to be exchanged for each bucket. But a 250 percent profit representing only $1.50 to the trader earns commensurate hostility that damages future business even while the $1.50 fails to compensate the trader adequately for his time. Since he carries his inventory on credit, his time should be spent retailing more profitable items on a volume basis. The trader who buys a bucket of village sorghum can either hold it for months and resell it to villagers, possibly for the same price he paid, eat it himself, or sell it in town. If he seeks a buyer in town, as he normally must, he is often forced to sell to the wholesaler who controls his transportation service and supplies his regular line of goods on credit. In 1967–69 the wholesaler was invariably an Indian, with no large market or personal desire for African sorghum. Indeed, many if not all wholesalers discouraged the trade, preferring the more profitable beds, sewn clothing, and bicycles. In 1967–69, a rural shopkeeper spending his time on sorghum trading was likely to lose his transportation and credit, lower his inventory, and have his store taken over by another African apprentice to the wholesaler in town. For that reason rural shopkeepers either avoid the bothersome petty trade altogether or follow the example of itinerant African traders and sell their sorghum secretly in small lots to dealers catering to urban African populations. Most of the men who engage in this business are former shopkeepers whose stores have failed and to whom the petty sorghum trade is one of the few economic niches still available.

The established unit on the wholesale end of this trade in the towns is a bag holding six $0.60 buckets of seed. Since transportation to town costs $0.60 a bag, the trader's minimal cost per bag is $4.20, compared with a selling price in town of $5.10 to $5.40 at best. While that is not an insignificant profit in the local scale of things, it seldom represents a full-time occupation, even in densely settled neighborhoods where more grain is available. Women are fairly slow to trade off their tiny lots of sorghum in this way, the trader may have to wait several months in one locality before accumulating a worthwhile number of bags, and a quick cash sale in the towns is by no means assured. Many urban and periurban Africans are able to grow and collect their own food, and stores selling sorghum to Africans in town have many irregular sources of supply, making it necessary for the trader coming in from the country to spend a great deal of time shopping for an outlet. In doing so, he may be forced to spend cash to maintain himself in town. Often he must leave his grain at the outlet on a conditional basis or accept goods rather than cash in return.

A few traders are able to make quite a success of the business, however, by exchanging village sorghum for bolts of cloth in town. Most of the colorful cloth costs the trader from $0.18 to $0.21 a yard in town. Back in the village he trades one yard of material for a bucket of sorghum, for which he would otherwise give $0.60 in cash. Six yards equal a bag of sorghum, which he can sell in town for as much as $5.40. Assuming that he exchanges the cloth costing only $0.18 a yard, his costs amount to $1.68, including $0.60 in transportation for himself and the bag. This nets a profit of $3.72. When a local woman gives six $0.60 *bucketi* for six yards of cloth, she is giving up $3.60 of potential cash income for six yards costing the trader as little as $1.68, counting transport. The cheapest price she would have to pay for cloth from a local store is $0.54 a yard, or $3.24 for six yards. Therefore both the trader and his customers gain an advantage in this trade, for few women can spend as much as $3.24 in cash on clothes for themselves at the store, and few storekeepers can accept *bucketi* for cloth.

Because the Goba recognize that this trade is beneficial to themselves, and because it undermines local shopkeepers, many of whom are Africans from other ethnic areas and almost all of whom are unpopular, it affords a decent living by local standards. Except for occasional outsiders who wander through the villages offering similar terms but with only a small inventory, this trade is the monopoly of one or two resident traders per chiefdom.

The man who starts out with a cash investment of about $4.20 can accumulate a six-bucket bag of sorghum, transport it to Lusaka, and set himself up in business as a trader. Accumulating the initial $4.20 is no mean feat, however. Tobacco sales, the main source of cash income in the valley, is the business of older men who have finished the bride-service cycle and have settled down to life in the villages. Most traders are necessarily young, active, and mobile, and for them tobacco sales are unlikely to be the source of the initial stake, unless an elder is willing to provide financial backing from his savings. Soon after the formation of Lake Kariba, many men reaped large sums of money from the commercial fishing boomlet that followed. It had been the original economic base for many of the more successful Goba storekeepers whom I encountered in 1967–69. For some reason fish catches soon declined. By 1967–69 fishing on Lake Kariba had dwindled to the original low level along the Zambezi, leaving migrant wage labor the main cash source for most would-be young entrepreneurs (Scudder 1960b; Scudder and Colson 1972). As we shall see later, working for migrant wages is generally a slow way to save money.

A bag of sorghum transported to Lusaka at a total cost of $4.20 can with luck be sold for $5.40. The successful trader converts that sum into the cheapest cloth available, which wholesales for $0.18 a yard. At that price his $5.40 becomes thirty yards of cloth, if he can avoid using his meager capital for transportation and living expenses. Back in his village district once more, he can convert the thirty yards of cloth into thirty *bucketi*, or five bags of grain, which can be sold in Lusaka for a maximum of $27.00. After deducting the initial investment of $4.20 and transport fees of about $3.00, the trader has a profit of about $19.20, which is considered sizable. A careful trader can earn this much in a good active month of work after the harvests. During the slack, dry months, especially July and August, it is common to see groups of married women carrying their head loads of grain to the home of the local trader (unless there is a mechanical milling device nearby), where the women or the trader's wives and daughters thresh the grain on the spot and measure it into buckets. This is one of the few times "respectable" women are seen near a store or trading center, and even then their busy work area is always some distance from the places the men frequent. In both Namainga and Chiava chiefdoms successful traders augment this trade activity by collecting grain from outlying neighborhoods and bringing it home in their trucks.

Since the trader gives 5 shillings ($0.60) or a yard of cloth or some other equivalent for each 30-pound bucket of sorghum he takes in, the thirty-six *bucketi* listed in table 15 represent a gross cash flow to the villagers of about $21.60 and a physical flow of about 1,080 pounds of grain, only 3 percent of the total harvest represented in the table. With its twenty-six households and ninety people, the sample is the equivalent of a fair-sized settlement.

Grain and the Political Economy

As shown in table 15, the combined external trade in head loads (*chiwoomba*), beer, and *bucketi* accounts for about 17 percent of the total grain harvest, which represents a good crop year. I believe that these figures are reasonably representative of the population as a whole. They show that most of the subsistence grain production—about 83 percent, from this sample—is a household matter from beginning to end. The same can be said of subsistence farming in general, since only sorghum, plus a little millet, can be made into beer or exchanged to traders. Together with life-cycle factors previously discussed in connection with per capita acreages and sorghum yields, these figures are further evidence that subsistence production, with all of its irregularity, is not a major or determining factor in the local political economy, though its requirements determine settlement patterns and influence population density. The dynamics of household, descent group, and village organization described earlier are determined by cultural preferences in the system of marriage and residence, together with compatible ideas concerning descent and succession, rather than by the possibility of dominating grain supplies or grain-producing labor. Once the period of uxorilocal brideservice is completed, the developmental cycle of the domestic group continues to be influenced by the same set of cultural factors that determined its earlier stages. Within these general limits the household sustains itself as best it can through cultivation, gathering, hunting, fishing, animal husbandry, petty trade, migrant wage labor, and cash earnings from tobacco sales. Some households were even cash-cropping cotton in 1967–68.

The circulation of grain is largely a domestic concern, especially the uncounted "gift" head loads (*muso*) that circulate within larger compounds and between closely allied households. It is also true of the minor trade in head loads (*chiwoomba*) and the buckets the women trade to clothe themselves and the children and to buy occasional luxuries at the store. Together these minor avenues of exchange account for only 8 percent of the staple harvest. That is hardly the stuff upon which social and political systems are based. Beer parties are more important quantitatively, accounting for 9 percent of the harvest in the sample. Like prime-adult and veteran mainstay households that can feed more people and claim cash remittances from a greater number of young men working for wages, households that brew beer and give parties are likely to serve as focal points in the social landscape. But since each household controls only its own labor and that of hungry dependents when their own granaries fail and since all are equally subject to lack of rain, animal predation, and incapacitating illness, beer-party capacity is too irregular and unreliable to ensure lasting political alignments. It simply reflects age-linked factors in the developmental cycle common to all households. In time all mature households experience increases in numbers of dependents, acreages, harvests, and beer parties. They are not the prerogatives and responsibilities of social and political leaders. Conversely, leaders do not always fare outstandingly well in family size, farming success, and the ability to feast their followers. The ties that weld family groups together emanate from the philosophy and religious sanctions of the ancestral cult, together with the preference for large settlements and good company to isolation. In addition, the factors that attract a numerically important periphery of unrelated friends and affines to the most popular settlements have to do with relative numbers in the protective battle against animal predators and, nowadays, access to roads, stores, beer halls, schools, agricultural demonstrators, and other government services, rather than the possibility of economic largesse from the hands of the local leader.

In the past the circulation of grain was only incidentally connected to the male-oriented political economy, which was principally concerned with military power, raiding, long-distance trade, political alliances, and control over dependents through marriage prestations and ancestral-cult sanctions (Lancaster 1979b). Since the Pax Britannica males have been concerned with migrant labor to satisfy brideservice requirements in their younger years and ancestral-cult controls ("kinship" maneuverings) after becoming household heads and junior elders. Grain cultivation and distribution have continued to be largely domestic matters left to the women.

Throughout the low-density areas of eastern and southern Africa, including the middle Zambezi, there have been only a minor neighborhood trade in field and garden produce and little of the female-oriented market trade found in more densely settled regions. That is probably linked to population density coupled with the limited capacity for travel of child-bearing women in the days before inexpensive mass transportation. With low population densities most supralocal trade necessarily becomes in effect long-distance or regional trade. Throughout eastern and southern Africa such trade has usually been conducted by men. The residual local trade in foodstuffs has not been highly routinized or regularly channeled, since there have been so many potential producers of minor exchangeable surpluses and so many potential takers in any one locality. Yesterday's trader in surpluses has been tomorrow's beggar. Because its low volume has not been predictable and because small surpluses have been absorbed locally and fairly informally, the grain and produce trade has not been susceptible to highly developed social and political control. That could change fairly quickly, however, if production from the land were to become more important to cash-dependent families through creation of local produce markets that provided a viable alternative to migrant wage labor and the high rates of unemployment faced by most migrant men.

Measuring the Local Cash Economy, 1967 to 1969

The sample of twenty-eight sorghum growers shown in table 15 can be taken to represent an average settlement. In the sample about 17 percent of the sorghum harvest in a good year was exchanged beyond the confines of its basic producing-consuming nuclear or matricentric households. All of this trade in grain was involved with the cash sphere, directly or indirectly. In the long run we can assume that most of the cash value of the trade eventually finds its way into the hands of middlemen in towns on the Zambian plateau. As estimated earlier, the measurable trade in head loads represents an annual village-level cash flow of about $100.20, 20 percent of the total annual cash flow represented by the data in table 15.

Large-scale beer brewing in fifty-five-gallon metal drums accounted for an additional cash flow of $370.50, or 75 percent of the total. The trade in buckets of grain accounted for about $21.60 in cash terms, giving a total cash flow of $492.30. On a per capita basis, the trade works out to a traffic of $5.47 a person a year. If we generalize this figure for the fifty villages in Namainga chiefdom, the total cash flow associated with sorghum would be roughly $24,600 in a reasonably good year. Of course, we have to remember that the speed with which the small stock of cash actually on hand travels is rather rapid and that the dollar value of the cash circulation obviously includes a good deal of double counting. Nevertheless, the figures give a general picture of the average annual dollar volume of trade connected with sorghum in Namainga chiefdom.

Not all of the local cash economy is restricted to exchange value centering on sorghum. A possibly more accurate measure of the cash economy can be obtained by analyzing the main avenues through which funds are injected into the chiefdom. There were two main sources of outside cash in 1967–69: proceeds from migrant wage labor and tobacco sales. Cotton cropping was just beginning to show substantial promise. Balanced against these sources of cash input, we can estimate the amount of cash subtracted through the operations of local storekeepers and beerhall proprietors to gain an additional measure of the local cash economy. In addition to these major sources of cash injection and leakage, we can estimate the dollar value of livestock holdings and cash hoards held as insurance. Taken together, these figures will give us the best available picture of the local cash economy.

Inputs from Migrant Wage Labor

Migrant wage laborers must spend a good deal of money to maintain themselves in town, and many are unemployed much of the time. Moreover, it would seem that wage labor was never meant to be a lucrative occupation for the African. In the early days of the sister colonies Northern and Southern Rhodesia, wage labor was forced on Africans at a time when there was an acute demand for

cheap unskilled labor among white farmers, ranchers, mine owners, and government bureaucrats. In those early day coercive measures were used in the form of a compulsory head tax, payable only
in cash to generate a "positive" response to wage labor among Africans. Overhead costs and wages were kept low by deliberately
discouraging permanent town settlement by experienced African
workers and encouraging only relatively short work tours by perpetually unskilled men (Richards 1963; Weeks 1975). Taxes were
first imposed in 1898 in Southern Rhodesia and in 1904 in Northern Rhodesia. Married men were forced to leave their homes to
earn their taxes, and even in such remote areas as Namainga the
district officer tried to keep track of defaulters.

As early as 1915, when most of the initial overt resistance among
the Banamainga had died down, armed labor recruiters with gangs
of followers came to the villages to catch defaulters and promise
others safe-conduct to good jobs in the south. Among the recruiters were such well-known post-Livingstone hunters and travelers
as James Chapman, V. L. Cameron, and P. J. Pretorius (Northern
Rhodesia Government Reports, n.d.). Most of the Africans who
joined the caravans of the Rhodesia Native Labor Bureau, as it was
called, were taken to mines and farms in the south. Oral traditions
make it clear that the well-documented Namainga uprising of 1907
to 1914 was a response to the taxation and labor recruiting, as well
as to district officers who burned small villages and forced others
to move to more accessible sites.

These early work experiences were unfavorable and have become a rich part of local tradition, as have tales of early resistance
to colonialism (see van Onselen [1974] for an African's view of the
wage-work situation in the western Zambezi Valley.). All the elders
agree that in those early days the men's hands were tied as soon as
they left the chiefdom to prevent flight. A starter's wages were the
equivalent of $0.60 a month at 1967 rates plus food and clothing.
Carriers were paid $0.04 a working day; in 1915 a per diem of two
pounds of grain and a half-pound of salt was added. A carrier traveling forty-two miles to the Kafue Bridge near Lusaka and returning unloaded received $0.18 in 1915. Each married man had to pay
an annual tax of $1.20 (Gann 1958, p. 83).

Wages rose only slowly. Government laborers working on roads
and other tasks received $1.20 a month in 1926. They could earn
$1.44 a month if they signed up for three-month stints at the Zam-
bezi Sawmills above Victoria Falls. Harder-to-find positions with
the district engineer paid $1.86 a month. By the late 1960s, after
Zambia's independence, officially posted government wages had

risen substantially, but most Goba men lacked the advanced schooling and technical training required. Most worked only occasionally as ordinary farm laborers, earning the minimum of $17.00 a month. A lucky few obtained longer-term jobs as cooks in private homes for wages ranging from $15.00 to $22.00 a month, plus small allowances for food and housing. Today men holding good long-term jobs like these are housed in one-room concrete huts, which have running water at an outside tap but may not have electric lighting. Annual visits home are usually restricted to two weeks or ten days. Most cooks are called houseboys. Their duties usually include doing all the food shopping, food preparation and cooking; waiting tables, and dishwashing; housecleaning and bedmaking; hand laundering and drying; and daily floor waxing. Another choice job is that of garden boy, which in 1967–69 paid $7.80 to $10.00 a month.

With maintenance costs high in town most men save only one or two dollars a month from jobs like these. Both the houseboy and the garden boy are expected to keep themselves clean and reasonably well dressed. By the time a man remits enough money to satisfy his bride-service requirements, and after supporting himself in town, there is only a little cash left. Much of that disappears pretty quickly upon his return to the village. His wife, children, and parents will place many demands for his savings, and sometimes he must purchase a good deal of food from the local stores, since his return is likely to signal the end of his wife's dependence on her mother's granary.

I have estimated elsewhere that each man delivers an average of $96.00 in his total marriage prestations (Lancaster 1974a), and it is probably safe to assume that at the end of his wage work the average man comes home with cash savings of about $42.50. About $20.00 can be added to cover gifts he will remit over the years, together with sums of money spent on marriage cycles interrupted by separation or death. No special adjustment is made for polygynous marriages because most of them involve wife inheritance, and those few that do not normally involve smaller cash prestations. The average man therefore injects about $158.50 into the local cash economy from wage work in other areas. The amount is spread over a number of years. While boys begin their travels at the age of fifteen or so, most probably begin making significant remittances only when they are older, and many continue wage work well into their forties (Lancaster 1974a, p. 50). Most significant remittances are probably made between the ages of twenty and forty-four, and the wage-working career of the average man who eventually returns to Namainga is twenty-four years. During this time there are, of course, long periods when he will be ill or unemployed in the cash sector. In any one year the average man will inject about $6.60 of outside money into the cash economy of his home chiefdom.

The next task is to determine how many men are following this pattern in Namainga. Assuming that all men between the ages of twenty and thirty-nine and a third of those in the forty-to-forty-four-year bracket are making significant remittances, the total of the two groups should represent about 14 percent of the total population. This percentage is based on the estimated age distributions by sex for Africans born in Zambia, as reported in the 1963 census of Africans (Government of the Republic of Zambia 1964, p. 15). While a large number of Goba males and a smaller number of women and children are temporarily away in town and periurban areas outside Namainga at any one moment, that is true of all Zambian ethnic groups, and there is no reason to suppose that Goba population characteristics differ appreciably from those of the Zambian-born population at large. On this basis 14 percent of the Banamainga population is about 1,092 men, and their combined average annual cash remittance can be estimated as $7,207. If we divide this figure by 50, the average village receives on the order of $144.14 a year from migrant male wage workers. That works out to only $1.60 per capita for the composite sample village of 90 co-resident people shown in table 15, or $3.13 per adult. Of course, most of this money flows into the hands of the older men of the village, who are receiving marriage prestations and tracking down errant sons-in-law who have been slow to remit.

Inputs from Tobacco Sales

The other major source of money flowing into the village from the cash economy of the outside world is tobacco. The twenty-eight sorghum growers listed in table 15 also produced and sold an estimated 768 cones of tobacco in 1967, an average of 27 cones per grower.

Small cones of tobacco (*mbande* or *chilundu*, literally "small hill of tobacco") sell in the villages for an average price of $0.48 to $0.60 (1967–69 prices). In Mazabuka, where some Valley Tonga and Goba take their tobacco for sale, the same cones may fetch $1.80 apiece. In Lusaka, where there is greater demand and less competition from other tobacco-growing chiefdoms, a small *mbande* may sell for as much as $3.00. Larger cones may sell in the village

Large tobacco cones drying in the sun.

for $0.90 to $1.20, rising to about $2.76 in Mazabuka and $3.60 in Lusaka. In years of scarcity the price is higher. For example, small cones sold for $0.96 among villagers in April, 1968, after inadequate *matoro* flooding; identical cones shaped by the same mortar sold among villagers for $4.20 in October, 1968, when even fewer cones were to be found. A few growers make a larger return by selling in the towns themselves. Most wait for traders to visit them and either haggle patiently or wait until September and October, when supplies are lower and prices higher. At an average price of $0.90 a cone the 768 cones produced in my sample yielded a cash equivalent of $691.20 in the good year 1967. For the average household that represents a net tobacco income for the year of about $24.30, though there was nothing from this source in 1968.

Inputs from Cotton

Cotton is now a third significant source of cash from the outside world. Unsuccessful cotton-growing schemes were introduced or planned at various times during the colonial era, and it is known that native cotton was grown and woven in precolonial times (Lancaster and Pohorilenko 1977). The current situation dates from recent government efforts to aid the Valley Tonga in the Lusitu Resettlement Area. Rough figures kept by agricultural field officers are available for only the 1965–66, 1966–67, and 1967–68 growing seasons, though there was some very minor activity in the immediately preceding years. These figures show that the Goba, almost entirely on their own initiative, have consistently accounted for 29 to 30 percent of the registered cotton growers in each of these years, with the number rising from twenty in 1965–66 to seventy-one in 1967–68.

All these men had abandoned tobacco to have time for cotton. Not all the cotton growers have been successful; few of the growers received any income from the disastrous 1968 harvest, and most were forced to default on their small loans. That was expected to have an adverse impact on enthusiasm for the scheme, since some local development agents were claiming that future loans for seed, chemicals (which seldom arrive), oxen, and plows would be withheld until the arrears had been paid. Nevertheless, local attitudes suggest that cotton will be more important in the future. In 1967–68, the seventy-one Goba would-be cotton growers accounted for about 280 acres, or 43 percent, of the total acreage dedicated to cotton in that year in Namainga. The resettled Tonga accounted for the remainder.

If this trend continues, it seems likely that cotton will oversha-dow tobacco and put additional pressure on man-land ratios. Sev-eral growers now devote twenty or more acres to cotton production alone, and the government hopes to make Namainga a nationally important cotton center to help supply the new textile mill in nearby Kafue, between Mazabuka and Lusaka. As I left the field, the near-term goal was to reach an annual figure of nine hundred acres devoted to cotton in Namainga. The average Zambian com-mercial farmer reaps about 1,000 pounds of seed cotton per acre (Government of the Republic of Zambia, 1966). In the period from 1965 to 1967, Goba output averaged far less than that, because crops were not rotated, or always plowed, and expensive chemical sprays and fertilizers were not used. Most men have been content with a single woolpack of seed cotton per "acre" or field. The packs, averaging about 400 pounds each, sold for $0.08 a pound, or $32.00 a pack, at the Lusaka cotton gin in the late 1960s.

Despite the large number of men who were planning to grow cotton in 1967–68 until drought discouraged them, only a few (twenty in 1966 and thirty-four in 1967) had any kind of return from this activity, and I was unable to compile or find a totally reliable record of woolpack sales in those years. Some estimates can be made, however: if the twenty Goba growers of 1965–66 harvested one average 400-pound woolpack from each of the 72 "acres" planted in cotton that year, the gross receipts, at $0.08 a pound for class A seed cotton would total $2,304, less fees for seed, packs, and transport, which were deducted at the gin. On the same basis the thirty-four growers of 1966–67 would have grossed $3,936 from 123 "acres" of cotton. These growers were scattered through-out Namainga. There were none in Chiava chiefdom east of the Kafue River. If we divide this gross estimated return by fifty, we get rough pro forma figures of $46.00 and $79.00 per village for each of these years.

For 1967, then, we can say that the average Namainga village took in roughly $144 from migrant wage workers, $691 from to-bacco sales, and another $79 from cotton, a total of $914, while there was a capital value of about $500 worth of exchanges associ-ated with sorghum.

Estimated Dollar Volume of Country Stores

While traditional tobacco farming, migrant wage labor, and cotton cropping bring money into the chiefdom, country stores and beer halls are the main points at which cash flowing within the chiefdom leaks back to the outside world from which it was originally drawn. Until late 1967, Indian entrepreneurs frequently combined their retail operations in the larger towns on the plateau with a string of satellite "bush shops" in rural areas. In less remote rural locations serving a good-sized, reasonably concentrated African population with only moderate competition, the more profitable country stores were usually managed by another Indian, possibly a kinsman. In more remote, off-the-road areas or less desirable and competitive locations serving only scattered villages, the man behind the counter would usually be an African. Matters of store location, construction, inventory control, and bookkeeping were handled by the wholesaler in town, and the Indian or African agent simply served behind the counter.

The biggest problem for country stores has always been inventory control. The African storekeeper would typically receive a well-selected starting inventory of $1,200 on credit. If the country store could maintain that level of inventory, even with a slow turnover rate, the operation would be profitable, because the Indian wholesaler in town could do what few Africans could do, buy in bulk. As long as the rural outlet could maintain its inventory, make payments on its inventory credit charges, and continue to replenish supplies sold, the central wholesaler backing the store could turn a profit on the difference between his own buying costs and his wholesale selling price to the rural outlet. Volume was the key to his low buying costs and thus his profits, and the Indian wholesaler could get credit at the banks and act as buyer for his own relatively high volume town shop together with a string of several country stores.

Unfortunately, rural African storekeepers have often been unable to maintain their original inventory level, let alone enlarge it. Under tremendous social pressure and with too little commercial experience, they tend to give gifts to friends, consume their own inventory, and pocket sales proceeds. In time the wholesaler fails to collect on his loan, the store is left with an unbalanced and picked-over inventory, and relations deteriorate. Low-profit items designed to lure customers into the shop, such as cigarettes, soap, cooking oil, paraffin, sweets, razor blades, and soft drinks, tend to move quickly, but unprofitably. Smaller rural stores often have to buy these items at or near the retail price in town, and the sales volume does nothing to maintain the store, especially when the inexperienced shopman gives them away for good will. Once the items have run out, traffic at the store tends to dry up and the leftover inventory of higher-priced profitable items collects dust.

If the shopman reduces his generosity, the trade quickly shifts to other small local shops, inasmuch as African shopkeepers have usually had to manage in highly competitive locations. In time the villages near the shop are likely to move away anyway, leaving the expensively built store in limbo. Many abandoned sites of large Banamainga villages show traces of old cement floors from stores that failed in this way.

Because of these difficulties, together with the limited purchasing power of the typical villager, the situation has not been favorable for small outlets in rural areas. Moreover, rural business was adversely affected, at least for a time, by the sweeping economic reforms announced by the government at the Mulungushi Conference in August, 1967 (see Government of the Republic of Zambia 1967). Among other goals the Mulungushi reforms had the much-needed aim of improving the African's position in retail and wholesale trade and opening up direct lines of bank credit for small-scale African entrepreneurs. Indian merchants were restricted to a few large centers along the highway and rail line on the northern highlands, such as Livingstone, Choma, Mazabuka, Lusaka, and Kabwe and larger towns in the Copperbelt mining areas. Because of their experience they were directed into more specialized lines of business deemed preferable for balanced national development. In the turmoil accompanying this major transition, retail business in Namainga temporarily slowed down. Some local stores dependent on urban Indian wholesalers for goods and credit had to close down for a while or operate under reduced circumstances. In the years of my field study two stores formerly run by local Indian traders had to close for protracted periods. These background factors have to be taken into account in assessing store volume.

At one time the typical rural outlet established by an urban wholesaler as a captive market for his goods was set up with a $1,200 starting inventory. A few stores did better than that, opening with inventories of $2,000 or more. Other independent operations open with as little as $120 in stock. Many of the owners of these last have gained some experience working in stores in town. Other small shops are opened by men who have failed as rural agents for a wholesaler or who started as itinerant traders and by schoolteachers who have saved some cash or lost their jobs. Still others are opened by ordinary villagers who invest their tobacco money and manage to keep afloat by annual subsidies from their *mbande* sales. Larger shopkeepers tend to give up "old-fashioned" tobacco growing in favor of cotton. Since the large storekeepers can afford to grow cotton without recourse to government loans, which pose a

A new store being built near the steep valley escarpment in the prosperous uplands of Jamba, where cattle could be kept in the years from 1967 to 1969.

major obstacle for most potential growers, larger shopkeepers are in the forefront of the movement into cotton—as well as local-level national party politics.

The smallest shops are rectangular huts built of vertical timbers laced together with saplings and coated with clay. Corrugated-metal roofs protect the goods—and transmit intense heat. Larger stores are built of adobe brick plastered with cement or locally fired bricks. Whatever the original cost of the store, inventories tend to run down and move slowly.

It has been estimated that the average shop operated by an African in Zambia has an inventory no greater than about $360.00,

The Lusitu General Grocery and Bottle Store run by Johnny Mwanja in the Lusitu township. Johnny is active in cash cropping and local politics.

and most have far less than that (Dotson and Dotson 1968, p. 81). My own figures show that the seventeen stores serving the Goba in Namainga in 1967–69 had a combined daily gross of $44.00, or about $2.60 per store a day. In the long run we can assume that most of this money drains off to middlemen in the towns on the plateau. Most stores are short-lived, and even older, established shops need subsidies during critical months of the growing season when villagers are busy with their crops. The stores in Namainga had an estimated combined annual volume of some $16,000.00. In 1967–69 none of the stores frequented by the Goba did any appreciable business with the resettled Valley Tonga, nor did the Goba

Table 16
Estimated Livestock Holdings, Namainga

Year	Cattle					Other				
	Bulls	Cows and Heifers	Oxen and Tollies	Calves	Total	Sheep	Goats	Pigs	Fowl	C
1963	11	267	216	106	600	831	2,817	218	NR	€
1964	9	134	159	51	353	811	2,876	131	NR	€
1965	11	180	185	51	427	796	2,471	123	5,036	4
1966	15	220	212	113	560	1,110	3,842	83	6,507	5
1967	8	112	209	107	436	1,225	4,120	NR	2,130	N

Figures Used in Calculating
Average Values for Table 16

Adjusted Estimated Price per Animal, 1967		Total Value of Estimated Holdings		
16	bulls	$65.00	$1,040⎫		
224	cows and heifers	70.00	15,680⎮ cattle	(68%)
418	oxen and tollies	40.00	16,720⎰ $40,716	
214	calves	34.00	7,276⎭	
1,225	sheep	6.30	7,718⎫ small stock	
4,120	goats	2.85	11,742⎭ $19,460	(32%)
			$60,176	(100%)

Source: Based on records kept at Lusitu Township Branch Office, Veterinary Departr
Ministry of Agriculture. Note that livestock grazed in Jamba have been recorded in the
book for the Changa area of Sinadambwe chiefdom since 1963. Since 1977, Ibwe Mun
livestock have been recorded in Mazabuka records.

like to go to stores frequented by Valley Tonga. This estimated dollar volume therefore refers to the Goba population only.

Estimated Dollar Volume of Beer Halls

Five stores in Namainga specialized in the sale of commercially produced African-style beer, known as *chibuku*. The beer is delivered fresh to the store every two to four days in 50-gallon drums from the brewery in Kafue Township on the northern plateau and emptied into a large plastic drum that stands upright in a corner of the store. Measuring lines on the drum show the customers how much beer remains. The wholesale cost per British gallon is $0.34, and it retails for $0.44 a gallon, selling briskly. A study of cash receipts from the brewery suggests that in an average month each store has an intake of about 868 gallons at a delivered cost of $281.33, gross sales of $374.94, and a profit of $93.61, less wages paid to the counterman. At a sales rate of $375.00 a month the store is running at the capacity allowed by government regulation, and the beer seldom has time to sour. The annual gross income works out to $4,500.00.

Three beer halls were operating at this level in Namainga by late 1968. Mweemba's beer hall served the large population in Njami District and attracted customers from Nabanda and Jamba in the west. Munsanje's beer hall on the southeast side of Njami Hill also served the Goba of the populous Njami District, together with groups of Valley Tonga men from the adjacent resettlement area, though there was still very little mixing of these ethnic groups at the beer hall in early 1969. Chinyama's beer hall was another popular spot, though many of the pockets it drained belonged to policemen and other nonlocal people working for wages in Chirundu Township or the Catholic mission nearby. In addition, the cooperative beer hall at Lusitu Township operated at only about half the capacity of Mweemba's and Munsanje's beer halls, apparently because of management problems, though the clientele was mainly Goba. Two smaller stores selling either *chibuku* or bottled European beer (Lion's and Castle's) also did about half as much business. The total volume of money drawn from Goba pockets by the beer halls and bottle stores amounted to an estimated $1,312 a month, or about $15,750 a year.

Livestock Holdings

Finally we consider the aggregate stock with cash value within the chiefdom in more permanent form. It lies principally in livestock holdings and small cash hoards. Livestock represents a fairly fixed form of saving. The cash hoard is tapped for minor current expenses and for unexpected contingencies.

Table 16 gives some figures for livestock holdings in Namainga. When allowance is made for irregularity in rough field counts, it appears that the total numbers of cattle kept in the chiefdom has been fairly stable, ranging from 600 head in 1963 to 436 head in

1967, when the most recent tally was made. In earlier years comparable totals were about the same, showing 538 in 1956, 435 in 1959, and 602 in 1962 (Colson 1971, p. 142; Scudder 1962, p. 170). In addition to death from tsetse-borne trypanosomiasis and other diseases, cattle die from snakebite and attacks by leopards and hyenas, and the mortality rate is high. The reproductive rate is low for a number of reasons. Grazing areas produce green food grasses on only a seasonal basis, causing animals to lose in the dry months almost all the weight gained in wet months. Inadequate food reduces the rate of reproduction, results in a late calving season, and contributes to the high mortality rates. Many herds have an excess number of bulls and overage animals, further reducing the rate of natural increase (see table 16 for age-sex breakdowns of cattle holdings). Individually owned cattle herds have experienced an uncertain rate of growth, which has been a serious drawback to economic development, inasmuch as investment in cattle has commonly been the best bet for capital growth (Dumont 1968). In a strict sense this "investment" opportunity has been a low-grade speculation. No Goba families that I know have become wealthy in this way, and some have become poorer, though all upland families try to funnel some savings into livestock.

The figures in table 16 do not reflect the total number of cattle owned by the Banamainga. Residents of all districts keep cattle outside the chiefdom in safer areas and those numbers are not included in the counts shown in the table. This practice dates from precolonial times, when the chief's herds were kept on the highlands above the Zambian escarpment. Today many are grazed in Nalauama chiefdom of Mazabuka District. Mazabuka, the main cattle area in southern Zambia, lies immediately west of Ibwe Munyama (Kay 1967, p. 54). Cattle have also been kept in the Changa area of Sinadambwe chiefdom, on the valley floor just west of Jamba. Protection from tsetse flies is the main reason for dispersal to less seriously infested regions, though the lending out of cattle is also an established way of spreading political alliances and hiding one's wealth from creditors (Colson 1951). Therefore, while the total number of cattle kept in the home chiefdom shows a roughly flat trend for ecological reasons, the practice of lending out cattle to friends in other areas means that the people probably own substantially more cattle than the figures indicate. Moreover, holdings in some districts are recorded in other stock books (table 16). To arrive at a realistic estimate of total cattle holdings, the numbers in table 16 should be at least doubled.

The figures for small stock shown in Table 16 can probably be accepted as accurate. Sheep and goats are less susceptible than cattle to tsetse flies, and they are kept under a watchful eye at home in the village. They have the further advantage in being better able to digest the thick cellulose feed provided by trees and scrub in this seasonally arid region. The increasing numbers shown for sheep and goats are thus likely to be a truer reflection of the growth of the local cash economy than the roughly flat trend in cattle, especially since cattle owners grazing herds outside the chiefdom eventually tend to follow their wealth in person.

The figures for pigs, fowl (mainly chickens), and hunting dogs are negligible and can be disregarded in the present context. The fowl are especially vulnerable to Newcastle's disease, as shown in the sharp decline in 1967. The Goba exchange small stock as gifts and use them for food on special occasions, but they are not considered a serious investment. Wives make pin money from chickens in good years, however, when traders provide a small market.

The purchase or sale of cattle is relatively rare, though several changed hands in 1967–69 at prices ranging from $69 to $72. Asking prices ranged from $105 to $110. Healthy heifers brought roughly the same price as adult cows because only their future reproductive potential is considered. They are never consumed for food. Since cows give milk for only a short time in the rainy season, milk production is not a consideration. Any small amount of milk that is taken is cooked with the staple porridge. Most families prefer to let the calves drink the milk. Oxen to be used for plowing brought $43 to $48 during 1967–69, while young tollies and calves sold for $31 to $36. The premium price for cows and heifers reflects their reproductive potential. Most oxen are untrained to pull plows, sledges, or carts, but an easier-handling animal may bring as much as $55, the same price a stud bull may bring.

There was a much larger turnover in sheep and goats than cattle in the late 1960s. Because they are cheaper and more numerous, they are bartered and sold, and the goats are consumed on a more casual basis. Prices for sheep and goats also fluctuated a good deal more than did those for cattle. Meat consumption from family herds is limited to very special occasions, such as a succession ceremony, a ritual work party at the chief's, or an elaborate (and fairly rare) coming-of-age ceremony for a young woman. On such situations a goat or chicken is consumed, along with beer. Sheep are rarely eaten, and cattle are never killed for food. They eat only those that die of natural causes. While the Goba crave meat, especially tasty fat sheep tails, they dislike the strong meat of old goats and wisely confine their meat consumptions to game animals.

In the late 1960s sheep prices ranged from $4.20 to $8.40 for a large, fat male castrate. Goat prices ranged from $1.20 for a sinewy older animal to $4.50, depending on age, sex (young females are preferred), fatness, and the hunger of the buyers. The standard price for a small sheep was $6.00, and for a large one $6.60. The standard price quoted for an average goat was $3.60. The average prices used for calculating the cash value of stock holdings is shown in table 16. Relatives lend animals to each other for use in plowing and training to the plow or for help in starting a herd. A herdboy is usually allowed to keep one goat from the herd when he grows up and moves on to other work, though that custom is not followed with sheep or cattle. There is no evidence that kinsmen quote lower prices for livestock to each other.

Government-supervised cattle sales have been planned for a number of years, and encouragement on this point has been part of the lecture series given by agricultural officers stationed in the Lusitu Resettlement Area. The objectives are to improve beef supplies to towns, increase participation in the cash economy, encourage beef consumption as game decreases with population growth, extend agriculture into presently unsettled areas, and cut down on the serious overgrazing practiced among the resettled Valley Tonga. Despite these efforts local agricultural reports show that as of 1967–69 no supervised cattle sales had yet taken place. Local sources were unanimous that the trouble has been the government's policy of using a weight scale in determining the price to be paid for cattle. Men prefer to operate on the basis of standard prices for each species of livestock, making rough adjustments for age, sex, and condition and leaving room for a good deal of bargaining. They fear that once they accept the idea of selling on scales at fixed prices per pound their unsold inventories will be worth much less than they have calculated. These fears are probably justified, because most local animals are thin and scrawny. Many Goba and Tonga men living near Lusitu Township, where the proposed government sales were to take place, do in fact bring their cattle there for appraisal by government veterinarians. Sales are sometimes arranged at such gatherings, but so far the transactions have been private ones without the use of scales and within the indigenous price structure indicated above. Livestock sales are among the few examples of interaction between the Goba and the new Tonga.

The Value of Cash Hoards

During my field study the Zambian authorities changed from currency based on British monetary units to a metric national currency calibrated in terms of *kwacha* (equal to 10 old shillings) and *ngwee* (100 *ngwee* equaling one *kwacha*). The conversion was fortunate because it became necessary for the people to convert their old paper money, which made up most cash hoards, into new paper currency at the banks in town. Minor holdings in coin were not immediately affected, and the older holdings continued to circulate alongside the new, with the town banks gradually retiring them as they came into their hands. The process of converting paper money necessitated a long, inconvenient trip, and identity cards had to be produced. Since many people were afraid of being shortchanged and some oldsters lacked identity cards, we arranged several trips to Lusaka to enable villagers to convert their funds before the deadline. A number of people asked me to conduct this business for them. It was an unusual opportunity to collect reasonably accurate information on the size of cash reserves, though my sample is not very large. In the figures given below holdings in coin are also included.

A sample of four young men who had recently returned from town and seemed likely to have ceased their tours of migrant wage work, had an average cash hoard of $42.50 each. The largest holding was $80.00, the smallest $20.00. These hoards are usually buried under the floor of the sleeping hut. More cash is held by prime-age adult men who no longer work for wages but help their women in the fields and gardens, plow their *temwa* acreages at least periodically, sell tobacco, and are beginning to collect initial sums of money from their own sons-in-law. A sample of six men in this category had an average of $73.00 apiece, and holdings ranged from $50.00 to $150.00, the largest recorded. Older men forming grandparental mainstay households and receiving cash from their tobacco gardens and several sons-in-law had an average of $75.00. The sample holdings of six men in this category ranged from $30.00 to $138.00. My sample of seventeen married women of all ages had an average of $8.60 and a range of from $4.80 to $40.00. Five older widows living fairly independently held an average of $16.00 ranging from $10.00 to $20.00. Older women living with well-established married daughters in old mainstay households had no cash at all, and neither did unmarried daughters and sons too young to start their own voyages to the towns. These old women were no longer controlling their own granaries and earning pin money from head-load sales or beer brewing, and their sons-in-law were no longer remitting marriage prestations and gifts. The unmarried daughters and younger girls were similarly situated. Young men and boys not yet traveling to find wage jobs usually touched petty cash only when running errands to the local country store. Cash holdings are summarized in table 17.

The Namainga Cash Economy

Gross annual injections of cash into the Namainga economy (table 17) approximated $45,693 for the chiefdom as a whole in the good year 1967. Over three-quarters of this stemmed from tobacco sales, as it usually does, which makes the cash sector of the local economy highly vulnerable in years of poorer rainfall. In 1968 cash income from tobacco was negligible for the chiefdom as a whole, while purchases of food at the country stores increased to partly offset the near-total loss of the staple sorghum crop. Such years reduce cash reserves to the low totals estimated, and some households have to sell livestock.

Cotton cropping seems assured of substantial future growth, though much of this is likely to benefit the resettled Valley Tonga, as it has in the past. The Valley Tonga continue to receive most of the government's attention, while few villages of the indigenous inhabitants are visited by development workers. In 1967–69 even the names and locations of most Goba villages were unknown to the local development agents. In addition, alert Zambians from the plateau with access to capital and market information were already beginning to stake out and sow large cotton acreages.

The growth of the cash economy and the land shortages that are sure to follow as the Valley Tonga expand, the mission irrigation plan in Farao consumes more land, and cotton acreages grow may well hurt many of the Goba. There were no spokesmen to defend the Goba as an ethnic unit. The resettled Valley Tonga preferred to picture the Goba as alien intruders from Zimbabwe-Rhodesia and Mozambique, with no just claim to Zambia's wealth. All the development agents I encountered on the local scene shared this opinion and held the Goba in generally low esteem. The assistant district secretary admitted that the Goba would probably end up as landless agricultural wage laborers. Progressive Goba leaders in the cash economy were pursuing their own advantage, operating country stores and planting cotton, like the Tonga newcomers. As businessmen and politicians these Goba naturally tended to orient toward the resettle Tonga, who were planting more cotton, were wealthier than the Goba, and were centrally involved in new government development plans stemming from UNIP. These progressive men were identifying themselves as Tonga in their own right,

Table 17
Cash Economy of Namainga in 1967

Item	Sample Village of 90 People	Per Capita[a]	Per Adult[b]	Projected Namainga Total	Percent of Total
Gross Annual Injections of Cash					
Migrant labor	$ 144	$ 1.60	$ 3.13	$ 7,207	16
Tobacco sales	691	7.68	15.02	34,550[d]	76
Cotton cropping	79[c]	0.88	1.72	3,936	8
Totals	$ 914	$10.16	$19.87	$ 45,693	100
Gross Estimated Annual Leakages of Cash					
Stores	$ 320[c]	$ 3.56	$ 6.96	$ 16,000	50
Beer halls	315[c]	3.50	6.85	15,750	50
Totals	$ 635	$ 7.06	$13.81	$ 31,750	100
Estimated Internal Circulation and Reserves					
Money hoards	$1,238	$13.76	$26.91	$ 61,900[d]	42
Cattle	814[c]	9.04	17.70	40,716	28
Sheep and goats	389[c]	4.32	8.46	19,460	13
Sorghum trade	492[e]	5.47	10.70	24,600[d]	17
Totals	$2,933	$32.59	$63.77	$146,676	100

[a]Per capita figures are the total for the sample village represented by Table 15, divided by its total population of 90.
[b]Adults are taken to be those in the 15–19 age bracket and over, based on the ages when women marry and men begin seeking wage employment. In the sample village represented by Table 15, there were 46 adults (51 percent of the population) forming 26 households. For the Zambian population as a whole, those aged 15 or more average 53.4 percent of the native-born total in the 1963 census (Government of the Republic of Zambia 1964)
[c]Namainga total divided by 50
[d]Sample village total multiplied by 50.
[e]The internal trade in *chiwoomba*, drums of beer, and *bucketi*.

a claim justified by the historical factors reviewed earlier. More conservative villagers were continuing to orient toward cattle and the safer grazing areas in the west, in Sinadambwe chiefdom and Mazabuka District, where ethnic identity also changes to Tonga. Most of these men were also following the cotton situation closely and will probably turn to this source of income in the future, if present favorable trends continue.

As cotton cropping increases, migrant labor is expected to decline, perhaps in direct proportion. The tendency to give up migrant wage labor when a viable local cash-earning alternative is available was already noticeable in 1967–69, as exemplified by the small but growing number of mostly younger adult men who were turning to cotton. It is interesting that most men turning to cotton had already secured their marriages by terminating the long cycle of marital prestations and delivering bridewealth (pfuma). Migrant labor continued to be an important part of most men's youth and early married years, since it combined saving for marriage prestations with an escape from uxorilocal residence. Once bridewealth has been delivered and the escape from uxorilocality is no longer a prime factor, many men prefer growing cotton independently, rather than engaging in migrant wage work for others, especially if savings from town enable them to avoid taking a government loan for their cotton operations. The tendency to abandon wage labor for good economic reasons when local alternatives are available is common in Africa, as Long and Scudder have pointed out (Long 1968, p. 32; Scudder 1969, p. 32).

Since most local men with significant cash savings have a strong desire to open country stores, the successful spread of cash-cropping efforts will probably cause more men to experiment with stores and beer halls of their own. As men turn to cotton and country stores, however, they invariably abandon tobacco production, an art that younger men often consider old-fashioned. Only when their stores begin to fail and loans for cotton are denied do a few return to tobacco. Cotton involves a good deal of traveling to local government centers to obtain instruction, loan information, seed, woolpacks, and final weighing of the harvest. Since many men view this opportunity as a welcome substitute for the frustrations of migrant wage labor, with its high unemployment rate, poor working condtions, low wages, job insecurity, and protracted absences from home, they tend to take the leading role as cotton entrepreneurs, and many wives help them in the fields. Though in the past the largest tobacco growers have been men, women also help their husbands with the work. Older women with grown children to help them grow tobacco on their own, even widows or women whose men are in town. Women produced 195 of 768 cones (25 percent) of the tobacco produced by the growers in table 15. In addition, woman power was a significant factor in the production of 463 (64 percent) of the cones; only 80 (11 percent) of the tobacco cones were grown by men working entirely on their own.

Though tobacco production seems unlikely to expand as much as cotton is expected to, the native tobacco industry seems likely to persist as both men and women come to rely on the cash economy more heavily. In time tobacco, the sorghum trade, and perhaps chicken raising may become more firmly associated with female sex roles as development intensifies, though beer brewing at home is likely to succumb to the popular beer halls if present trends are allowed to continue. This outcome would be unfortunate for the women. Government efforts to improve markets for native tobacco, sorghum, and chickens would help the women and keep these agricultural mainstays from becoming the forgotten factor in development (Boserup 1970, 1975).

In 1967 total estimated inflows of cash to Namainga exceeded estimated leakages by some $13,943, or 44 percent. This situation was reversed in 1968, when the cash value of reserves may have decreased by six thousand dollars or more as people held off on luxury imports and used their money stocks, sheep, and goats to purchase sacks of mealie meal at country stores. Tobacco and cotton income was negligible in most parts of Namainga in 1968. While an unusually large number of men set out to seek wage work, including many who had passed the normal age for this activity, it is doubtful that net remittances increased a great deal, since the drought was nationwide, and competition for jobs was greater than ever.

Despite occasional setbacks, the local cash economy has grown markedly over the long term, as Colson and Scudder have noted. Colson made her first trip to the Zambezi Valley in 1949, and since 1956 she and Scudder have been frequent visitors. Their focus has been on upstream populations of Valley Tonga, but they have also concentrated on the Valley Tonga of the Lusitu Resettlement Area, and their general surveys and observations are certainly applicable to my own area of coverage in Namainga under Chief Sikaongo (called Sigongo by Colson and Scudder) and Chiava chiefdom east of the Kafue River (Colson 1971, pp. 9–14) We have already seen that cash wages have grown tremendously, from the $0.60 a month, plus food and clothing, recorded in the district notebook for the early years of this century to the levels of 1967–69, when migrant

Goba men were making $7.00 to $11.00 a month, plus allowances, as garden boys; about $17.00 a month as casual farm laborers; and $15.00 to $22.00 a month, plus allowances, as cooks and domestic help. Rising wages are expected to continue. In 1969 the government announced a series of minimum wage levels that work out to the following monthly wages: $26.60 in agriculture, $132.20 in mining, $66.60 in manufacturing, $50.00 in construction, $71.00 in commerce, and $31.60 in private domestic service. While only about 9 percent of the Zambian population was employed in the cash sector in 1969, pay hikes such as these should increase Namainga's gross cash income in the future, when warlike conditions with Zimbabwe-Rhodesia come to an end (*Zambia Mail*, February, 1969; Government of the Republic of Zambia 1969, p. 21). While local cash income from migrant labor had increased markedly from the time of Colson's first trip in 1949 and the first full-scale Kariba study in 1956–57, there were further sharp gains after that as a result of the Kariba Dam (Colson 1971, pp. 137–39). Not only did the new roads give easier access to wage centers on the highlands, but many local people earned money on local projects associated with construction of the dam itself. The Valley Tonga received compensation for resettlement, and many local men reaped large sums from the early success of the Kariba fishing industry.

The mainstay of the Goba cash economy has been tobacco, however, and unfortunately we lack earlier figures for both volume and prices. The average cone of processed tobacco produced in 1967–69 weighed 4 3/16 pounds and sold for $0.90, or an average of $0.21 a pound. It is estimated that the Namainga Goba produced about 38,400 cones—about 160,000 pounds—of tobacco in 1967 with a cash value of $34,550.00 (table 17). According to Kosmin (1974), the Shona-speaking Shangwe peoples in the valley south of Namainga received about sixpence (about $0.06 at 1967 rates of conversion) a pound for tobacco in 1906. The volume seems to have been substantial, but we have no way of knowing whether Namainga tobacco production has increased, decreased, or remained roughly the same. In the future it will probably decline as cotton expands, unless women continue to replace men as the principal growers.

According to the Goba, there have always been country stores in Namainga to tap local wealth. The precolonial trade depots (*aringa*) along the Zambezi were ringed by circles or rows of live *muvurumira* trees, whose trunks had originally been used to construct defensive palisades. Some of the trees were still to be seen in 1967–69. The combination of esteem and distrust in which precolonial traders were held is evident from oral traditions, and the fluctuating prestige of the present-day storekeeper is probably not so different. The last Portuguese traders left Namainga and Chiava chiefdoms around the turn of the century and were soon replaced by early country stores operated by white settlers from the south. There are no comprehensive records for this development, but the earliest entry in the district officer's notebook mentions an establishment run by a man named Venables in Nyamusaya neighborhood, which Namainga elders say included some kind of trade outlet. A man named J. E. Roos operated another early store in Jamba neighborhood, and it is noted that he handled between two and three thousand pounds of tobacco a year. Additional stores appeared in the late 1930s, when the Zambezi River Bridge near Chirundu Hill, on the south bank, was completed and a township developed. After Kariba in the late 1950s, another wave of stores appeared throughout the Tonga Resettlement Area. All the beer halls are post-Kariba developments.

The amount of money, or cash value, in local circulation has grown along with the expansion of migrant wage labor, rising wages, and higher tobacco prices. Colson notes that the sale of beer for cash was unknown in 1949 (1971, p. 137), and for most individuals the rise of cattle ownership as a store of value is also an entirely new phenomenon in Namainga, since the region was dominated by the tsetse fly in the latter half of the nineteenth century (Colson 1960, p. 21; Scudder 1962, pp. 167–69).

This growth in the local cash economy will doubtless serve to prepare Namainga people for a future existence likely to be marked by a much greater dependence on cash as land pressure and cash cropping increase. Per capita cash flow is still low by comparative standards, but if the figures in table 17 are roughly accurate, the 1967–69 internal cash flow and reserves of about $146,700.00, or $63.77 per adult, was undoubtedly high by past standards. Total estimated cash holdings of $61,900.00, or $26.91 per adult, represented a substantial cushion against crop failure, though money, like land, was still considered a relatively minor part of the family estate in 1967–69. A closer look at Goba inheritance practices provides a good insight into their current state of economic development.

Cash, the Family Estate, and Future Prospects

When a family estate is divided, two basic distinctions are made: that which goes to the main heir (*nhaka*) and that which is distrib-

uted to subsidiary heirs (*chirumu*). The main heir is the person
who has been selected to succeed to the social positions previously
occupied by the deceased. What is of paramount importance here
is always the bundle of *social positions* vacated by death. The
changes primarily involve the domestic household of spouse and
children, though the main heir's activities also influence the deceased's other surviving relatives, because the main heir is the social successor to all the deceased's ongoing relationships. These
include marital, affinal, and parental ties together with the deceased's positions as a member of descent groups and kinship networks. It also includes relationships established through cattle
loans and cash debts. If it is disadvantageous to discontinue any of
the deceased's relationships, the successor continues them. This
common pattern in the ethnographic record is known as *positional
succession* (Richards 1960).

Any material objects passed on to the main heir are designed to
enable the successor to fill the new roles successfully. These objects are considered to have been important parts of the dead persons's social personality and household. They are not alienated
from the personal names and kinship positions handed over to the
successor. They are usually household items or items kept in or
near the sleeping hut. For a female heir they commonly include
mortars, pestles, grindstones, working hoes, and baskets, pots,
and other containers. Sometimes they include livestock purchased
on her own or received as gifts. They also include paraphernalia
associated with status in religious cults, such as ceremonial hoes,
battleaxes, walking sticks, beads, costumes, dishes, and other objects dedicated to the deceased's spirit familiars. Stored grain is
included if the deceased had no agricultural help from her husband. Otherwise, he is given a share. For a male heir the objects
similarly include domestic items normally considered to be male
property or personal things typically purchased by men from their
wage work or tobacco sales: livestock, perhaps a radio, a bicycle or
bicycle parts, tools used to repair bicycles, a store, sewing ma-
chine, axes, hoes, spears, drums, plows and perhaps a metal bed
purchased from a store. Religious equipment is also included.

Despite the presence of material items, the crucial factor in determining whether there will *be* a main heir is always the presence
of living children. If any children survive their biological mother
or father, the deceased parent's social responsibilities are always
perpetuated by a succession ceremony, even though the children
may have been alienated by the earlier separation or death of one
of the parents. If there are children to be reabsorbed and cared for

by the living community of survivors, the name and structural position of the deceased parent are passed on to a main heir. For men
this is a full brother, a half-brother, a first parallel male cousin, or
another male kinsman resident in the village or nearby, in that
order of preference. Because he must be an acceptable male to the
widow, a genealogically distant kinman must sometimes be chosen.
If a mother has died, the marriage is dissolved, and the female heir
needs only to act as a surrogate mother rather than a wife as well.
This custom facilitates selection of an able, adult successor, who is
commonly a sister already burdened with domestic responsibilities. Even if there are many cattle and a widowed wife willing to
marry the brother of her dead husband, no main heir need be
chosen, unless there are surviving children. If there are none, the
marriage and household are not continued, and the name and social position of the deceased are not perpetuated. All material
items normally passed on to a main heir are then reclassified as
chirumu and distributed in small lots to a large number of people.
In any event, the dead person's sleeping hut is destroyed and lev-
eled if it stands in a densely populated settlement, or simply abandoned to nature if it is off by itself on the edge of the village.

Temwa fields were never discussed at any of the succession ceremonies and protracted discussions I attended, and the Banamainga
say that this has always been the case. It has been reported that
land has never been considered inheritable property in traditional
Shona societies (Garbett 1963, p. 188). The *temwa* field of the deceased is handled in the same manner as fields left idle by families
moving elsewhere: close kin of the deceased, especially those who
farmed the fields next door, are considered to have first claim if the
land is still desirable. Otherwise it is abandoned and taken up by
the first comer or left to fallow.

The treatment of *matoro* gardens has been more variable. In
pre-Kariba times, when extensive annual flooding of the Zambezi
and lower Kafue rivers made certain *matoro* sites more valuable,
large gardens in thickly settled areas were passed on to the main
heir or assigned to others when the user became too old to use
them. When the main heir lived far from the *matoro*, an especially
valuable river garden was given out as *chirumu* to a kinsman or
friend who could put it to use. In Chiava chiefdom east of the Kafue, some present-day elders say that this was never done, even
before Kariba, because the population was low and good unused
matoro sites could simply be pioneered. Today unused river-garden sites may be taken up on a first-come, first-served basis in both
chiefdoms during droughts, though there is some tendency for rare

low-lying gardens that still flood extensively to be handed down to relatives during life or assigned to main heirs and close allies at succession ceremonies.

It is important to stress that in later years, as in the past, the chief features of the family estate were not the usufruct rights to land, cattle, cash, or other material goods it might contain. The chief attractions were the social positions previously held by the deceased and those newly created by his or her death. These non-material factors were symbolized by formal investiture of spirit names (*matehwe midzimu*). They provided the main heir with valuable publicly recognized structural positions within the segmentary descent-group system. The successor to an important bundle of social-structural positions was identified at a major installation ceremony (*dihwe*) and given a goatskin wristlet to wear (*matehwe*). It is significant that rivals competed for these valuable positions by attempting to become owners of the same spirit names (*sazita midzimu*) through alternate means, such as spirit possession, divination, or simply the assertion of a forceful personality. Rivals commonly did this even though the *material* portions of the estate could not be alienated from the chosen heir.

The minor items of wealth (*chirumu*) handed out in small lots to a large circle of close kin, allies, and creditors, includes the deceased's cash holdings, clothes, shoes, and such things as hurricane lamps, suitcases, the personal store of tobacco, and other possessions. If there is no main heir and the household is being disbanded, the grain and all the other items typically given the successor are also distributed as *chirumu* in small lots. A man's muzzle-loader is usually given to a young namesake during life, and some of the cattle, sheep, and goats are also likely to be distributed before death.

The Goba cash economy is dominated by men. The women help the men grow most of the tobacco and all of the cotton. Men are also the labor migrants, going to distant locations to earn funds for their marriage prestations, which they later deliver to the older men at home in the villages. Village-bound mothers with no husbands or effective male descent-group elders find their young daughters difficult to control in the earlier stages of the marriage cycle and eager to escape to the excitement of the towns, while many daughters in this position eventually find themselves burdened with children and abandoned by their men. The older village men are freer to track down errant sons-in-law and exert the pressure necessary to maintain the brideservice system now that eloping youngsters in town are out of sight of their compound eld-

Matrilocal residence and the skill of Goba women as independent subsistence farmers gave Goba women high status, but male-dominated cash cropping and other developments are putting women in a marginal position, as illustrated here.

ers. Without this vital pressure, the long brideservice cycle would seldom be completed, and the system of matrilocal extended families forming female village cores would come to an end. The prestige-sphere exchanges that symbolize the proper steps in the marriage cycle are thus largely dependent on men for their proper execution though the residential system that results from the marriage system has traditionally given women a great deal of social, religious, and political importance in the villages. Under this system elite male behavior has traditionally been coordinated with that of their elite female counterparts, the ranking *vasamukadzi*. But prestige-sphere exchanges that symbolize the moral and legal dimensions of village life have gradually become monetized and merged with the growing operations of the cash economy dominated by men. The role of women is becoming less important.

All the basic sources of cash inflow—tobacco gardening, labor migration, and cash cropping—are controlled by men, and men also control most of the local cash reserves—the money hoards, cattle, goats, and sheep. New institutions—the country stores and beer halls—have begun tapping the growing male-oriented cash economy. In the process they form a new set of elite male facilities supporting and enhancing the prestige of male behavior. A similar male-oriented institution, the government-run court system, which, like the others, has been accessible to women in only limited ways, has had similar effects in increasing the male role in the local political economy (see Appendix).

These twentieth-century developments favor male viewpoints and preferences, and as yet there have been no comparable de velopments for women. The matrilocal residence pattern and village structure generated by the brideservice system probably still gives Goba women a greater role and a higher status than that of women in most descent-group systems based on variations of the bridewealth complex, under which children are filiated mainly to their father's descent group, though it would be difficult to measure this influence precisely. Ethnographic data suggest that coresident Goba women in locally dominant descent-group cores enjoy high status in village life. The ancestral cult embodies the basic philosophy and morality of descent-group life. While prestige-sphere exchanges symbolize important turning points in the life cycle, it is generally the ancestral cult so deeply influence by co-resident women that actually guides the life cycle through its strong mystical sanctions. Yet the role of women in the ancestral cult may very well change decisively in the not-so-distant future.

Women's role in today's cash economy is small compared with that of men. Female participation in the cash economy is essentially restricted to the sorghum trade, a minor business even in good years, in which annual volume is measured in head loads, small buckets of grain, and a few drums of beer. The sorghum trade represented only 17 percent of the estimated cash value of internal trade in 1967, and not even that was entirely in women's hands, since the husband shared in any cash proceeds from beer sales if he had helped produce the grain used. The practice of brewing beer for cash sale seems to have been unknown in 1949, when Colson first visited the valley. With the growth of consumption at the beer halls, even this small share of the cash economy is being taken out of women's hands.

On the basis of changes that had already become apparent by 1967–69, the greatest nearer-term impact to be expected in the future from the continuing growth of the cash economy lies in its increasing involvement with prestige-sphere behavior and marriage exchanges in particular. The rise of cash as an acceptable form of wealth has already led to the establishment of cash equivalences for the manual brideservice labor once performed in person in the wife's village. It has also led to development of a terminal cash bridewealth prestation in the standard marriage cycle. Since the development of terminal cash bridewealth, younger men have become increasingly dissatisfied with the expensive, time-consuming earlier stages of the marriage cycle. It is probably only a matter of time until most men will be able to curtail the marriage cycle by earning money for the earlier prestations more quickly. The growth of the local cash economy will probably seriously curtail or eliminate the customary uxorilocal period of postmarital residence. This likelihood is enhanced by other forces that are working in the same direction.

Now that the government court system has been placed in the hands of progressive younger men and removed at least a step from the influence of village women and the more conservative male elders, there is increased pressure for a single bridewealth prestation early in the cycle. That the system of government courts did not have this effect many decades earlier is probably due to the conservative influence of the chiefs in their former role as court presidents and judges. Another factor contributing to change is likely to be growth of local cattle holdings, as the westernmost Banamainga continue to orient to healthier upland cattle areas, while others orient toward areas cleared of tsetse for use by the resettled Valley Tonga. Population trends, cash needs, and government pressure to market cattle suggest that a cattle bridewealth complex is unlikely to develop, since per capita cattle holdings are unlikely to reach very high levels. But better conditions for cattle raising may be expected to increase local cash wealth available for use in marriage prestations. Finally, pressure for acceptance of bridewealth early in the marriage cycle also comes from outside social influences: both the Tonga in upland cattle areas and those in the Lusitu Resettlement Area marry that way themselves (Colson 1958, 1971). Since the Goba have long been upgrading their ethnic identity and much of Namainga has been officially classified as a Tonga area for many years, the desire to merge with other Tonga in neighboring areas should eventually lead to the adoption of similar systems of marriage and residence. Since Namainga is far from isolated today and the resettled Valley Tonga in the Lusitu area are expanding, these changes may not take a great deal of time.

The effect of this projected change to an earlier bridewealth prestation in line with the practices of neighboring populations would inevitably be to strengthen the rights of the husband-father. The largely virilocal residence pattern of the neighboring Tonga peoples does not necessarily create large coresident patrilineal descent groups, since virilocal residence does not automatically become viri-patrilocal residence, but the experience of these neighboring groups suggests that the coresident female village cores described in this study will probably disappear (Lancaster 1971). With this loss the social position of women is sure to decline.

11

Dual Descent in Cross-Cultural Perspective

When I was planning my research among the Goba, my intention was to explore the interface between economic life, sex roles, and social and political organization. In the late 1960s the basic subsistence resources were good land for fields and gardens and adequate rainfall and flooding along streams and rivers. Subsistence also depended to a more limited extent on gathering, local exchanges, the cash economy, animal husbandry, hunting, and fishing, roughly in that order. Land resources were still sufficient to preclude the need for private ownership and unnecessarily complicated methods of transfer. The technical knowledge necessary for subsistence was still common knowledge and, like land, did not enter directly into questions of marriage, residence, and descent-group formation. The predominance of one line of descent over another in social organization seems to have been a matter of local cultural adjustment and style, as expressed in marriage-exchange preferences affecting postmarital residence, the relative position of husband and wife, and the filiation of children (Richards 1950). But the growth of the local cash economy and its increasing involvement with marital prestations have been changing the social system. Because the system of dual descent lines observed in 1967–69, unusual in comparison with established regional ethnography, was changing it is helpful to summarize the situation briefly here in terms suitable for cross-cultural perspective. In chapter 12, I will then take a closer look at the changing relations between the sexes.

A Summary View of the Social System

We have seen that Goba society is based on localized matrilines in which common descent is the recognized basis for group member-

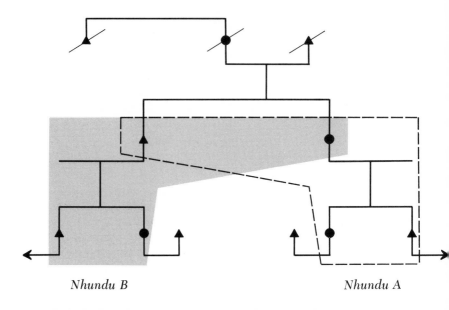

Nhundu B   *Nhundu A*

Figure 16. Matrilineal Descent-Group Segments

ship. A minimal matrilineal descent group (*nhundu* A in fig. 16) is formed by a mother and her co-resident married daughters under the prevailing system of uxorilocal marriage. Together with a linked coresident brother (or coresident mother's brother) to act as the mother's ritual assistant in the ancestral cult, this matrisegment can act as an independent unit in the social system. In weighty matters affecting other households, other household heads may have to be consulted. Similarly, with the assistance of his mother or sister, a coresident male and his coresident married daughters may form a similar unit in the localized descent group of his mother and sisters. This kind of unit is not distinguished by name or origin (*nhundu* B in fig. 16). It too is a segment of the larger group to which the brother and sister belong. When a group like *nhundu B* is formed, the brother has usually practiced local endogamy and married a matrilineally related kinswoman. Otherwise the brother marries out, lives elsewhere, and his children do not belong to his matrilineal descent group. Lineage segments of types *A* and *B* comprise all the larger units of Goba society, and it is important to stress that common matrilineal descent is recognized as the basis for membership in both. Men marrying endogamously and living among close matrikin form lineage segments when their married daughters stay at home under the uxorilocal system. The men who do this (or who manage to return to the village of their matrikin while they are still young) often succeed to the social position of their mother's brother and thus may manage to share ritual controls with their sisters (*vasamukadzi*), over the larger coresident *nhundu* aggregations formed by the addition of females cousins, as demonstrated earlier.

Here we seem to have a straightforward system of matrilineal descent groups. It is true that some older male descendants, who are neither leaders nor among those who have made endogamous marriages, also return to their mother's villages in their later years. *Their* children are also considered full group members. We have seen that affines and unrelated friends are numerically prominent in larger settlements. Because of this untidiness it might be supposed that Goba settlements represent some kind of voluntary association based on ego-centered friendship networks and the need to share village facilities and certain seasonal work loads. To a limited extent that is true. Choice soils and favored village sites from which to exploit them are limited. Cooperation in protecting crops from animal predators and bringing home harvests is found to be both useful and necessary. Futhermore, the matrilineal ties recognized and put to use at any one moment *are* often fictive and voluntary in the sense that closer genealogical ties to residents in other villages may be ignored. But some degree of heterogeneity is to be expected in any system of descent, and the use of fictive ties could perhaps be taken as an indication of the pervasiveness of the dominant matrilineal mode of kinship reckoning.

There can be no doubt that we are dealing with a system of *descent* because each lineage segment is ancestor-oriented and is literally an association of ancestral-cult members, while larger lineage aggregations are held together by the sanctions emanating from more remote common ancestors and the senior living descendants who act as their spokesmen. Goodenough (1951) showed that kinship groups ancestor-oriented in this way are descent groups, and Fortes (1961) showed that a focus on the ancestors is the very calculus of descent systems in general.

Goba matrilocal families combine to produce local descent-group cores predominantly comprised of matrilineally related females, and links through women pervade the kinship system.

While anthropologists sometimes suppose that matrilineal descent groups flounder where property is important, all evidence suggests that the matrilineal descent-group cores supporting established Goba villages are stable. The wealth around which the descent-group cores form is not a material, purely economic, or personal form of property such as Americans might value in their society. It consists of interpersonal rights and obligations in the behavior of the assembled members of the descent group itself, as mediated through the operations of the ancestral cult. Contrary to some views on women and "important" property, village women seem well able to manage this kind of localized descent-group wealth, aided by their husbands and one or two coresident brothers to help serve the ritual needs of the group and to travel for social and political reasons when the women are tied down with garden work and child care (Fox 1967; pp. 130–31). These social rights centered in the domestic sphere comprise a kind of property that men have not been able to monopolize under an uxorilocal system.

But Goba society is not based on simple matrilineal descent groups alone. Most Goba trace ancestry from the Zimbabwe culture south of the Zambezi. There the cattle complex, with bridewealth marriage, patrilocal extended families, and patrilineal descent has been preferred over the bride-service complex, with its matrilocal extended families and matrilineal organization considered fit only for domestic slaves. The Goba still retain something of this patrilineal ideology. It underlies the ideal of an aristocratic father line described by the succession of senior male ritual leaders (dundumuntuli) in large descent-group cores. Figure 16 can now be reinterpreted in a different light, as shown in figure 17.

The long-established practice of uxorilocal service marriage and life in what appears to be a reasonable facsimile of matrilineal descent groups, for most practical purposes, has had an impact on local kinship reckoning. Sister's sons commonly succeed their mother's brothers as dundumuntuli, as described in connection with figure 16, but patrilineal thinking also continues. Nhundu A and nhundu B are not differentiated by the Goba because the same man, father A or his successor, son B, can have equal rights in both. Uxorilocal marriage places female agnates (sisters and daughters) in the place of brothers and sons in local organization, and a father has potential lineage rights in his coresident female agnates as if they were men. Since male succession normally proceeds from father to son when the father has delivered bridewealth and is a descent-group leader as an independent householder,—as we shall pretend A was,—a Goba dundumuntuli such as son B is expected

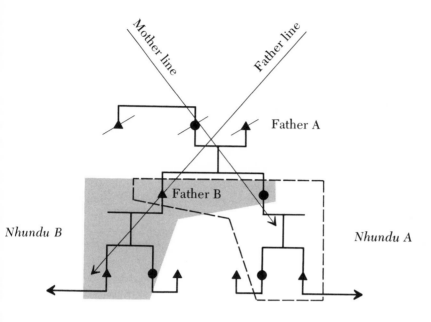

Figure 17. Dual Descent Lines

to have rights over both kinds of *nhundu* shown in figure 17. These
are the ones formed by the marriages of his coresident sisters,
nhundu A, plus those formed by his father's sisters, if they are
present and those formed by his own coresident daughters,
nhundu B.

In former times, when a service husband living among nonkin
could offer only a goat or two, some beads and reed mats, and one
or two ritual hoes as marriage prestations after many years of uxorilocal service, his in-laws might never permit him to remove his
wife from their compound. He might never become an independent householder like father *A*. In most cases he would remain a
dependent in his wife's *nhundu* under the legal and ritual guidance
of her matrikinsmen, though his own kin would see that he was
fairly treated. To the extent that this occurred to most of the men

most of the time, the system was truly matrilineal. His son, *B*, would be able to exercise rights as a male descent group leader in the ancestral cult of his *mother* only if he married a kinswoman of his mother and remained in her village. Son *B* might then act as *dundumuntuli* for the children of his coresident sisters. In that event *B*'s marriage to a "sister" would make his children members of his natal matrilineal descent group, though their own *dundumuntuli* would probably be their mother's mother's brother, mother's brother, or an in-marrying mother's brother's son. Their father, like their father's father, might remain a lineage dependent in his wife' *nbundu*.

Without having delivered proper bridewealth in his marriage, any chance that a son might have to exercise his latent patrilineal rights in the father line of *dundumuntulis* depended on matrilineal links in his father's marriage. If father *A* had married a "sister" and had lived as a co-resident member of her matrilineal descent-group core, then *B* would be both a son and a sister's son in the descent-group core. This has been considered the hallmark of aristocracy in large descent-group cores dominating prominent villages. In that event *B* would stand a very good chance of succeeding his father patrilineally and serving as *dundumuntuli* for *nhundus* *A* and *B*. In any event, father *A*'s wife and daughter would serve as *vasamukadzi* for the same units.

We are dealing with what is in effect a system of dual descent lines. Figure 17 shows how mother lines and father lines exist side by side. Women clearly have an advantage under this kind of system because all women automatically belong to matrilocal descent groups at birth and can trace a effective mother line made tangible by coresidence and daily interaction. All they need do is get along and remain together. On the other hand, a good deal of positive action involving endogamy, jockeying for popularity, and perhaps extra marriage prestations, is required to establish a comparable situation for males. Even then only a few males are likely to enjoy the benefits. A few men who marry into their mothers' matrilineal descent-group cores or who grow up there as a result of their fathers' earlier marriages to kinswomen, have a chance to form father lines centrally involved in the affairs of the group.

The father lines are a residual from a patrilineal past. The social system is now slowly changing back toward a more clearly patrilineal form. With the increasing use of cash money in the villages most fathers-in-law have been accepting marriage prestations in cash since the turn of the century. Since the 1920s one of these prestations has been accepted as the equivalent of the bridewealth (*pfuma* or *lobola*) long preferred on the Zimbabwe highlands. At first the conservative elders accepted this prestation only at the end of a very long "initial" brideservice sequence, however, and the legal and religious aspects of the matrilocal residential system were largely preserved. Some men have been able to make their bridewealth prestation after only a few years of migrant wage labor, and as this trend continues, the more prestigious bridewealth complex is expected to become dominant. When a father is finally able to deliver bridewealth in his marriage, the legal claims of this wife's people to the children are finally ended. When all fathers are able to do this early enough in life for patrilateral ties to become dominant in a legal, religious, and residential sense, the de facto matrilineality established centuries ago by domestic slavery and uxorilocal marriage in the tsetse-infested Zambezi Valley will have run its course and vanished. Cash will have replaced cattle in the bridewealth complex. The spatial distribution of patrilineal systems in this part of Africa will have changed according to newly relevant ecological correlates measured by access to cash. We are dealing with a system of kinship and marriage that, like many other systems, is in a state of transition. We will consider these changes more closely in chapter 12. Here the system will be described as it was in the late 1960s.

Goba Society in Cross-Cultural Perspective

As in *double descent* systems, a Goba male who practices "sister" marriage has rights and obligations in respect both to his own children, as would a father who produces children for his patrilineage, and to his sister's children, as would a brother in a matrilineage. Similarly a woman can produce children as if for her husband's patrilineage while still playing the role of sister as in a matrilineage. But in contrast to a true system of double descent, which recruits two kinds of unilineal descent group simultaneously, only one kind of descent group exists among the Goba. It is the de facto matrilineage of female agnates created by the necessity of brideservice marriage, which is then broadened into a *cognatic* descent group by the endogamy of sisters' sons or their return after their brideservice is completed. Unlike unilineal or double descent systems, which recruit groups on the basis of one sex or the other, both male and female group members reproduce the group, and in theory a member belongs to as many cognatic descent groups as he or she has recognized ancestors. In theory this process can create an unwieldy kin grid lacking any system of discrete, nonoverlapping groups. But in practice the system works well.

In the first place, it is rare, if not impractical cross-culturally, for members of cognatic descent groups to practice exogamy. Instead endogamy is often preferred so as to keep a core of close kinsmen together. Among the Goba endogamy is planned deliberately. An entire cognatic lineage cannot be kept together in any event, and so the usual strategy, cross-culturally, is to keep a core together, as Goba do, and to compete with other cores for peripheral and loosely attached members. Long-term endogamy among descent-group core members thus not only increases internal solidarity but also sharply reduces the number of ancestors who found splinter groups in a position to compete for a core's members, eliminating excess groups and giving some order to the social scene.

In addition, the number of viable descent groups generated by a cognatic system is limited by the comparatively small number of established village at any one time to house them. Village facilities, and the image each settlement projects as a good place to live, are important factors in social organization. The Goba like to live in villages famous enough to validate family status and large enough to provide a satisfactory number of companions for people of all ages and both sexes. These preferences limit the proliferation of groups, for new villages of satisfactory size and reputation are difficult to establish in a society where wealth is measured in terms of people, and residential allies are in great demand. Once large villages become established and the critical threshold for a rich social life has been surpassed, settlements tend to be long lived, despite the normal exodus of defectors leaving because of quarrels. The factor of size alone is usually sufficient to attract dissatisfied people from other settlements and offset the losses. The longer a village lasts, the greater becomes its attractive power as a cultural focal point in the chiefdom. Each village becomes an active factor in local politics. The potentially large number of small, competitive cognatic descent-group cores must then coalesce sufficiently to find accommodation within the established framework of a limited number of famous villages.

In addition, sets of closely related villages created by past fissioning or linked by old alliances tend to be on friendly terms and more or less hostile to other villages. While most individuals can readily trace real or classificatory ties to all the villages in their home chiefdom, as they can to the chiefly line, they would actually consider residing in only a few of them. The relative scarcity of

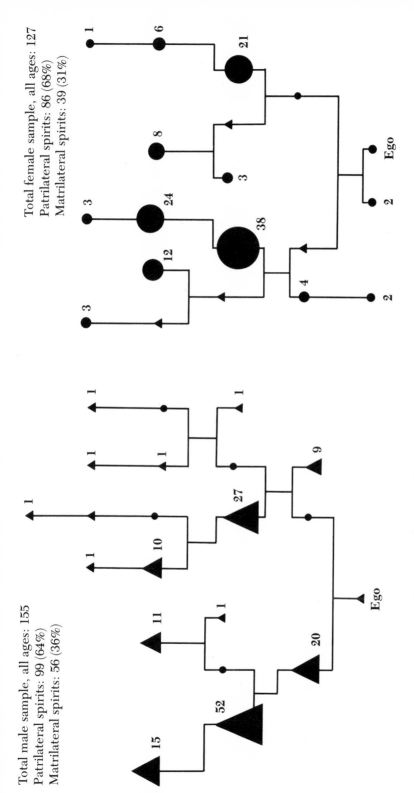

Total male sample, all ages: 155
Patrilateral spirits: 99 (64%)
Matrilateral spirits: 56 (36%)

Total female sample, all ages: 127
Patrilateral spirits: 86 (68%)
Matrilateral spirits: 39 (31%)

Figure 18. The Distribution of Ancestral Spirit Guardians, 1967–69
Source: Lancaster 1977, p. 238.

suitable residence sites means that the process of forming bounded, identifiable groups is not necessarily impeded, as perhaps might be expected by recognition of cognatic descent.

The Goba define their cognatic descent groups as being comprised of those who choose to live together and recognize mutual ties in the *nhundu* as they share a village and the land. This unit is the "effective" *nhundu*. To be technically correct, this is a *restricted* cognatic descent group, since recruitment of membership is skewed (Fox 1967; p. 152). To take an ego-centered point of view (as Goba often do), one's scattered kindred (*hama*) do not necessarily form themselves into regularized named groups with predictable locations, memberships, or relationships to ego. The kindred is seen as a fluid field of bilateral kin, who may or may not become associated with one's effective *nhundu*. The prevailing uxorilocal marriage pattern makes maternal ties dominant, but there is no a priori structural imperative forcing ego to recognize specific members of his kindred as member of discrete kin groups standing in a special relationship to him. This would happen in a system of matrilineal descent groups. In that event one's mother, mother's father, father's mother, and father's father would represent points of contact with matrilineal descent-group segments. Among the Goba a young adult would be *likely* to find that an elder standing as his great grandmother's brother or great grandmother's sister is in fact the head of, or a senior elder in, an allied cognatic descent group core, though that is more a function of group size and genealogical distance than an invariable feature precisely specified by the structure of the system.

Within an effective *nhundu* kin relations are expressed in primary terms. A great grandmother's brother is simply a maternal uncle, both in reference and in address. Elders laboriously work out their exact relationship to elders in separate descent-group cores when problems make it necessary to decide which *dundumuntuli* and *samukadzi* should be consulted. But in daily usage the related core will simply be known as the *nhundu* of Gasulamate, or of X male or Y female, who stands as maternal uncle or maternal aunt to the *nhundu* heads. The final criterion of core-group membership is always membership in the coresident ancestor cult (the local political alliance), rather than some specific kin relationship and sex, which are the characteristic criteria for membership in unilineal or double descent-group systems.

The localized effective *nhundu*, or restricted cognatic descent group, has a matrilineal bias among the Goba, primarily because of rules affecting uxorilocal marriage and matrifiliation of children.

Together with inherently human matrifocal tendencies, this bias gives rise to Goba mother lines. In common with restricted cognatic descent groups elsewhere in the world, where ambitious men compete for limited goods, limited status positions, or limited space on Pacific Islands or in prestigious Central African villages, the effective *nhundu* also has something of a patrilineal bias, as seen in the aristocratic father lines (see Fox 1967 for an excellent discussion of cognatic descent groups). In most societies many (though by no means all) men choose to complete for whatever system of rewards their world affords. What most ethnography has failed to point out is that women are the same as men in this respect. That does not necessarily mean that "successful" or "happy" men and women are aggressive or domineering, however, for life's rewards are social ones among the Goba, and unbridled aggressiveness and dominance are handicaps.

Among the Goba, life's richest rewards, in the human sense, are found in large aristocratic descent group cores where men and women identify with the dual matrilines and patrilines that are such important elements in Goba social organization. Of course, the father line also derives from cultural ideas common to Shona-speaking peoples generally. The gradual reinstitution of a bride-wealth complex measured in cash money rather than cattle is now giving the father line added strength. The mother line is now showing signs of becoming a father's mother-line for more and more women whose fathers have delivered bridewealth and thus filiated the children to the father's *nhundu*. The center of gravity in the kinship system is shifting in favor of paternal kin. That is reflected in the selection of personal ancestral guardian spirits, the ultimate indicator of kin-group orientation, as shown in figure 18. Of course, the mother line would always have been a father's mother line among "brother-sister"-marrying aristocrats.

12

From Mother Right to Father Right in Marriage, Polygyny, and Divorce

A man does not initiate a polygynous marriage until he has completed the prestations required to secure his current marriages. In the eyes of his in-laws a marriage is considered satisfactorily completed after he has presented his elopement damages (*mari ye murandu* or *mhoswa*) and betrothal prestation (*tsambo*). Elopement damages represent a large share of a suitor's remittances during his years of poorly paid migrant wage work and have come to be preferred by all concerned as a substitute for manual service labor in residence. Elopement damages now constitute the largest single prestation in the marriage cycle. Expressed in monetized terms, they average about $48 of a total of $96 transacted in the average bride-service sequence. That is roughly in line with the cash value of marriage prestations transacted by other peoples in this region, including patrilineal bridewealth-paying groups (Lancaster 1974*a*).

In precolonial times the total value of marriage prestations was generally lower in matrilineal societies. Prestations to mark transitions in the career of the marriage have always been required of the groom. But rights to bride removal and filiation of children (genetricial rights) remained vested in the wife's matrilineal descent group and could be transferred only by special prestations. For example, in the western portions of the central African matrilineal belt, among the Kongo, the Mayombe, and some groups in the Kwango and lower Kasai areas, men could deliver special payments for bride removal. Among the Kuba and Bolia of Zaire, and the Nyamwezi of Tanzania, special payments could be made for the patrifiliation of individual children. These payments were exceptions to the matrilineal rule, however. As a result, marriage payments were lower, even token, when compared with those in patrilineal societies needing to recruit fresh generations through rights of patrifiliation. With fewer rights being transferred to the husband's group in matrilineal-descent systems, the value of marriage presentations was correspondingly lower. There was also less compensation for adultery, and the marriage bond was generally weaker.

Since colonial times the growing use of cash as bridewealth has undermined matrilineal systems dependent on matrilocal residence of the bride and retention of rights to her offspring. Goba elders countered this threat to their social order by inflating cash demands associated with earlier phases of the bride-service cycle to discourage or delay bride removal. The result is a bride-service system that generates roughly as much cash as do the bridewealth systems of neighboring groups. With the growth of this cash substitute for local bride-service, manual labor for the in-laws is now generally restricted to token tasks, though some men make special remittances from the towns to enable their in-laws to hire help for specific tasks or come home to personally help a widowed mother-in-law or an aged father-in-law.

After elopement damages have been satisfied, the *tsambo* ("betrothal gift") permits a man to build a hut and take up regular residence as a dependent in his mother-in-law's compound. At this stage the in-laws are reasonably content with the situation. Much of the husband's bride payment will already have been delivered, and, except for the token *tsambo* prestation, they are not returnable. The in-laws still retain full legal rights to their daughter and grandchildren as against the husband-father and his heirs. The son-in-law may still be rejected and the daughter remarried in the event the husband abandons his family or severely mistreats them. The husband is no longer legally liable in the village and the government courts for having abducted the daughter. He has paid his damages, and his elopement "marriage by capture" has ended. Payment of damages also erases most of his service obligations, though a wise son-in-law will continue to curry favor in little ways. Now the wife and children have been returned to their proper home, which is with her parents at this stage, and delivery of *tsambo* gives the husband domestic rights of coresidence with his wife and children. He is also entitled to damages if he can prove that his wife has been seduced by another man, though the in-laws can elect to return his *tsambo* and reject him if the wife prefers her new lover. Should the husband suddenly be removed from the picture at this time through death or divorce, the wife and children would continue to belong to their maternal descent group as in a purely matrilineal system. The levirate would not apply in providing her with a successor husband, and the former husband's descent group would have no further claims to her and her children.[1]

The Push for Bridewealth to End Waiting

So far the marriage cycle has been viewed from the standpoint of the wife's parents. But since cash has been accepted as bridewealth (*pfuma* or *lobola*), a husband understandably does not consider his marriage secure or satisfactorily completed until he has delivered *pfuma* and ended his uxorilocal dependency altogether. This transaction filiates the children to his own descent group in addition to that of their mother and gives him the right to move his wife and children to a location of his own choosing, though it is considered polite to give additional tokens in celebrating the final move.

In earlier times, once *pfuma* had been accepted, the married couple and the wife's father went together to register the marriage at the tent of the district officer during his annual tour of the valley or at his permanent administrative headquarters (*boma*). Later the marriage was recorded at the government courthouse in or near the chief's settlement. The couple received a receipt (*muchato*), which was originally meant to serve as an official warranty that the husband's period of service was at an end. The British introduced *muchato* because they were interested in ending "slavery." They thus attempted to strike at the roots of the uxorilocal system by making a show of registering the marriages of "free" men (*muchetes*) who had either completed a long period of service or had paid a bridewealth equivalent. Here for once the interests of the British and the Goba husband coincided.

The district officer's notebook makes it clear that fathers-in-law were pressed and wife-seekers encouraged to sue for *muchato*. *Muchato* essentially meant "the end of the waiting" for the Goba husband, as was intended. Strictly speaking, there is no word for "husband" in the Goba language. A wife-seeker who had not terminated his uxorilocal period was referred to as a *mukwasha* ("wife-seeker") or *mugariri* ("one who waits"). During this traditional waiting period the man in debt for a wife was aptly compared with a slave (*muranda*). In European cultural terms he was best de-

---

[1]When the husband delivers unusually large claims for damages, it may be considered proper to allow his brother or sister's son to succeed him in case of death to continue the marriage cycle, if the wife is willing. This adjustment, which seems to be a fairly recent reaction to "price inflation," will be discussed later (see also Appendix).

scribed as a suitor rather than as a husband. Once *muchato* was in hand, he was simply known as a *murume* ("man"), which meant that he was married, was living in his own independent household in a settlement of his own choice. The district officer supported duly registered men wishing to end their uxorilocal "slavery." The idea was to put pressure on the dilatory tactics of in-laws seeking to preserve their social system by prolonging the uxorilocal period. The wife's influential mother, who had everything to gain by keeping her daughter at home, was not encouraged to attend the ceremony surrounding the *muchato* prestation. It seems clear that, while the district officers were intelligent, they had little knowledge of the marriage system they were trying to abolish and not much sympathy for the family that would have little compensation when a daughter was married by "capture" or taken away like a "slave" girl after only a few years of uxorilocal residence.

Because no records have come down to us, it is impossible to judge how many bride-service periods were in fact significantly abbreviated by the introduction of *muchato*. When I made inquiries in the course of my census work in 1967–69, almost every man over the age of forty included *muchato* when reciting his marriage prestations. Most older men dated their marriages as the years in which they had obtained *muchato*. But while *muchato* clearly became institutionalized in the early years of this century, I suspect that European ideas of justice did less for father right among the Goba than was perhaps true in Sierra Leone, Ghana, southern Nigeria, and parts of coastal Angola, where uxorilocal bride service, forms of domestic slavery, and matrilineality were also widespread in former times (Leacock 1972; pp. 34–43).

As mentioned earlier, unlike many other regions, the low-lying middle Zambezi around the Kafue confluence has been remote from outside influence. There was Swahili and Portuguese activity from at least the fifteenth century, but business was generally in indigenous hands, and until very recently there were no significant influences stemming from settled alien populations. Portuguese cultural influence was held to a minimum. There was usually a high rate of turnover among individual backcountrymen, and those who remained longer and established close local contacts were usually deeply Africanized to begin with. Although small populations were drawn to mines and trading settlements in the region, most immigrants were African, shared African values, and probably reacted to cultural and historical changes in ways similar to local response. Typical examples were the well-known trade centers of Zumbo-Feira, established about a hundred miles down the Zambezi at the Luangwa confluence in the mid-sixteenth century. A Catholic mission was recently established near the Kafue in Farao neighborhood. The missionaries were still devoting their efforts to building construction at the time of my arrival. Since the turn of the century the Goba have been in touch with the outside world mainly through the migrant-labor experiences of their men. This relatively minor, indirect contact has been channeled through the framework of the bride-service system and has served to preserve if not strengthen it. For all that it has been updated and mone-tized, the bride-service system still flourished in the late 1960s, and its impact on residence, filiation, and descent remained tilted in favor of maternal connections.

The Modern Bride-Service Cycle

The leisurely bride-service sequence consists of seven major pres-tations associated with phases in the development of a marriage: (1) a more or less casual engagement, signaled by an exchange of love tokens (nhumbi); (2) an elopement to town and a generally lengthy stay there, incorporating old elements of "bride capture" and ending with delivery of elopement damages (mari ye mhoswa); (3) a variable probationary period of sanctioned cohabitation in the girl's family compound, ushered in by the groom's delivery of the betrothal prestation (tsambo); (4) formal acceptance of the groom as a legally recognized husband and junior member of his wife's natal household, taking place when he delivers ritual hoes (badza re nyika) and other goods signifying his incorporation; (5) delivery of bridewealth (pfuma), marking the patrifiliation of children to complement their matrifiliation and establishing the conjugal family as a potentially independent household, though still coresi-dent with the wife's parents; (6) the muchato ceremony, ending the groom's formal obligation to render occasional service and to reside uxorilocally; (7) establishment of the groom's right to remove wife and children from their natal maternal compound, signaled by the delivery of mutsimutso or nhakura.

Valley Tonga living west of the Goba appear to follow a roughly similar sequence, though there is no rule among them that a couple should live uxorilocally after delivery of elopement dam-ages. Provided the groom proceeds satisfactorily with his damages and other prestations, he is free in his choice of residence and usu-ally lives with his father (Colson 1960, 1971). I mention this con-trast to underscore that the Goba have deliberately postponed the possibility of wife removal. Though perhaps influenced by their

Shona neighbors, the Valley Tonga have traditionally been known as dissidents in the Shona scheme of things, as measured by their claim of political independence from precolonial confederacies of Shona-speaking peoples. This independence has been part of their ethnic identity and distinguishes them from the Goba.

The Goba, as Valley Korekore, were thoroughly associated with the confederacies, and it is significant that kin marriage, the uxorilocal residence of young men at their wife-giver's compound, and their tributary service formerly provided much of the model of patron-client relations upon which Zimbabwe confederacies were built. In their roles as tributary treecutters, hunters, raiders, defending soldiers, bodyguards, traders, and messengers (*vanyai*), precolonial husbands represented their home settlements in Shona-speaking political hierarchies to such an extent that Goba populations were frequently known as BaNyai in a collective sense. Participation in the Zimbawe confederacies became an important part of the people's identity. While the matrilineal or "slave" aspects of the bride-service system have proved embarrassing at times, the Goba, like the *mwene mutapa* themselves, developed a pattern of "brother-sister" marriage and aristocratic father lines to offset the unfavorable implications of matrilineality. In this context brideservice has been a key element in a cultural tradition they have been unwilling to change and continue to value highly. Instead of using cash money to provide early bridewealth and a quick changeover to patrilocal extended families, Goba elders have preferred to retain the traditional stages of their service system, insisting on uxorilocal residence even *after* the elopement, and retaining the fourth stage, the husband's adoption into the wife's group, which clearly would have been given up had the elders been eager to change their social system.

The introduction of *muchato* failed to change the system. While "progressives" wishing to curry favor with the colonial administration may have been flattered by the idea of a "registered" marriage in what they supposed was the European manner (Posselt 1928; p. 72), *muchato* was simply tacked onto the end of the marriage sequence and served to prolong its consequences. Before undertaking the journey to see the district officer, the in-laws expected gifts, usually beer, cash, chickens, goats, or articles of European clothing. *Muchato* became one more hurdle for the wife-seeker though it seems to have fallen into general disuse by the late 1950s. Even after *muchato* a final closing prestation of goods or cash (*mutsimutso*) has been customary before the final act of removing the wife and children, and I am told that in-laws have been able to use

ancestral-cult sanctions to postpone acceptance of this final prestation for a year or more. Today the terminal significance of both
muchato and *mutsimutso* has been largely absorbed into the bridewealth prestation as it gradually assumes greater importance.

Polygyny, Succession, and High Status for Both Sexes

When contemplating polygyny, a man generally waits until bridewealth has been accepted in his earlier marriages and they have
been secured to his satisfaction. Prospective in-laws also approve,
for they know that then they will have first claim on the man's
assets and earning power. Otherwise, parents of earlier wives are
likely to inflate their demands when they discover that their son-
in-law considers himself wealthy enough to take another wife. The
need to satisfy the requirements of each union in serial fashion
keeps most men under forty from practicing polygyny unless they
have been unusually fortunate in the labor market or their in-laws
have for some reason accepted smaller prestations and an abbreviated cycle. Under these unfavorable circumstances, the 27.5 percent polygyny rate is rather high, especially since most polygynists
are over forty and nearing the end of the average life-span (see
table 18).

For many decades men who were able to become polygynists
were those who had left the villages and begun seeking wage work
when they were around fourteen or fifteen years old. They were
also successful savers, which is not easy in the expensive towns. A
few benefited from their fathers' cash-cropping efforts and helped
them in that work, especially growing cotton. This crop was still
too limited to have had much effect when I was in the field, though
it will probably contribute to earlier bridewealth and increased polygyny in the future. Today most polygynists have steady incomes,
holding local government positions as court clerks, judges, chief's
constables, or game- and tsetse-control guards, or earning cash
from successful occupations as fishermen, hunters, tobacco growers, or shopkeepers. Men in these categories are usually on the
lookout for favorable opportunities to add wives, mostly for reasons
of prestige and the ancestral-cult sanctions they will enjoy with the
added number of children. Because women prefer prominent
wealthy husbands, such men also "inherit" wives through positional succession after the death of real or classificatory brothers
and mothers' brothers. Major descent-group leaders (*dundumuntuli*) are also in this position because ancestor-cult controls over
marriageable daughters bring in cash and make them wealthier

Table 18
The Frequency of Polygyny, Death, and Divorce in Marriages

Item	Males Number	Males Percent of Total	Females Number	Females Percent of Total
Number of married persons in sample (all ages)	85		119	
Total number of marriages recorded for the sample*	153		167	
Marriages per capita*	1.8		1.4	
Number of polygynous marriages	42	27.5	NA	
Number of marriages caused by death of previous spouse	9	5.9	27	16.2
Number of divorces, using ratio A (Barnes 1949)*†	20	13.1	33	19.7
Divorces per capita*	0.24		0.28	
Percent of persons divorced at least once*	22.4		22.7	
Percent of marriages ended by death and divorce	18.9		35.9	

*Probably substantially understated for reasons discussed in the text.
†The sample used here is drawn only from individuals with well-known life histories. While too small to stratify into meaningful age cohorts, the sample is reasonably comparable with those used by other fieldworkers. Since few marriages, divorces or deaths are likely to be observed in the field, it has been customary to draw statistics from the cumulative life experiences of a selected sample (Barnes 1949).

than other men, while their more diversified kin links at the center of the group give them potential successional claims to a wider range of inheritable wives.

Almost all polygyny is accounted for by male positional succession. Positional-succession ceremonies (dihwe) are major events in the lives of both men and women. It is important to understand that there are actually two kinds of marriages today: elopement marriage followed by the modern, monetized bride-service cycle, and marriage through positional succession. Elopement marriage is unconnected with public ceremony or ritualized transactions until the groom returns the woman from town and begins to bargain for terms. Although elopement marriage is standard for young people, it is nonetheless legitimate to think of it as a relatively minor event in view of the tenuous nature and relative social unimportance of its early stages, when the young couple are living in town and their social position in the village scene is marginal. Experienced elders often emphasize this point.

Positional succession, on the other hand, involving a major public ceremony, is sometimes termed the "big marriage." It is discussed throughout the chiefdom and may last two weeks. Most women expect to elope in their youth (marriage for love, as the Goba call it) and to make an inherited marriage later (marriage for social position). The relative ages at which men and women begin their marital experiences dictates this, since men elope for the first time in their mid-to late twenties, and most girls elope at about sixteen to eighteen. If it appears that a woman's elopement will stabilize into her only marriage, it is common to perform a post facto marriage ceremony years later in the form of a belated coming-of-age ceremony for the woman (nkolola or chisungu). This rite is a variant of a widespread institution in Central Africa (Richards 1956). Its timing is usually said to be indicated by spiritual warnings received in dreams or illnesses. When the nkolola is not performed in this fashion, the woman is likely to become active in a spirit-possession cult instead. Most of my sources felt that the social recognition obtained through the belated nkolola and spirit-dancing activities of middle-aged women helps fill the vacuum left as children mature and take up their own activities. A few families belonging to large descent groups or made prominent through successful migrant labor celebrate coming-of-age cermonies for their daughters before elopement. This ceremony is likely to be the major event in the woman's social life until many years later, when, if her husband dies, she must choose a successor spouse or she becomes an adept in a spirit-dancing cult. In most cases, however, a woman first becomes an important social figure at the time she receives a successor husband.

The succession ceremony (*dihwe*), in which wife inheritance takes place, is designed to provide for the replacement of an elder. The manipulations involved in the transfer of the deceased's responsibilities as *dundumuntuli* or *samukadzi*, spouse, and parent, represent the descent group's efforts to reconstitute itself after a significant loss. The act of providing a widow with a replacement husband usually marks her entrance into senior elderhood as a key figure whose social placement and support is important to the community. For his part, a man strives to become an independent householder and junior elder through the toils of the protracted service marriage of his youth. Higher social position, if any, comes later, with the positional succession connected with his second marriage.

As noted, the standard first marriage for young people today is an elopement marriage.[2] There is a large element of romance and trial and error in elopement. Divorce is likely because of the many strains involved. Years of migrant labor, separations, careful saving, and marriage prestations still lie ahead when the couple return to the village scene and try to come to terms with village practices. Many attempted marriages are cut short at the elopement stage. Women may bear the children of several genitors before establishing a stable marriage, particularly when there is no male playing the role of coresident guardian father, brother, or mother's brother to force a lover to proceed with his bride-service sequence. Similarly, a man may be involved in several short-lived unions before finding a wife he can secure by working his way through the cycle.

Having advanced through the bridewealth stage, both husband and wife are junior elders and may then augment their personal

---

[2]In 1967–69, I encountered many younger men who were voluble about their dislike of migrant labor, town life, wage work in general, and European employers in particular. Some form of migrant wage work on farms, in rural locations, or in towns was nonetheless experienced, often between bouts of unemployment and "illness" in the wife's village. In view of the difficulty of obtaining wage paying jobs in 1967–69, such tactics sometimes succeeded in reducing the suitors' financial obligations to the in-laws; sometimes the result was that they were rejected as suitors by their women's parents. I met only one young man who had never been a labor migrant, preferring labor for his in-laws. Because his in-laws had other sons-in-law remitting cash, they were content with the situation. Rather than elope, the son-in-law agreed to remain a resident of his wife's compound indefinitely.

status by succeeding to key social positions as death takes its toll of more senior decent-group elders. That is especially likely for those living within their descent-group cores, at the center of their kin networks and in a position to support the group leader in times of stress. Because positional succession for males involves wife inheritance, polygyny is the hallmark of the high-status man. While table 18 expresses polygyny as a percentage of all the marriages entered into by the sample, polygyny does not occur at random within a population, nor is its rate of incidence expected to be even. Polygyny adheres to key kin positions and dynastic titles. Upon the death of each incumbent in an important line of *dundumuntuli*, the surviving wives and social responsibilities are redistributed to the successor and other key male descent-group elders.

For their part women find that polygyny can give them many advantages. Young village women look forward to the excitement of a relatively long elopement to town and to the store merchandise their man' earnings can bring them. They prefer a young husband in his late twenties or thirties who is already experienced in town ways, is still traveling to the towns and, preferably, is in his first marriage, when payments are generally higher and town life more prolonged. But many women who are less attracted to men, are perhaps burdened with children and less able to enjoy town life, or are divorced or widowed, find polygyny comfortable. Polygyny limits the attentions and demands of the husband while giving a woman the comforts, status, and relative freedom of an independent householder. Moreover, a woman who is unwilling to leave her descent-group core prefers an ambitious rotating polygynist to a man who will one day force her to leave the high status she enjoys among her assembled matrikin.[3]

While polygyny is a sign of high status for a man, it has generally been just as prestigious for the woman. Polygyny stemming from positional succession indicates that she is a key element in the so-

---

[3] I never encountered sororal polygyny involving coresident uterine sisters, probably because no one had much to gain from the practice. Coresident women in a descent group core usually can avoid friction with a sister cowife. Men marrying into their own descent group core also have nothing to gain by marrying more than one sister and obviously have much to lose if sororal jealousy should destroy the marriage. I have heard it said that a popular in-marrying kinsman might theoretically be offered another full uterine sister in marriage upon the death of his original sister wife, but I collected no evidence of the sororate. It is possible for a married man to inherit a wife who happens to be a classificatory sister of his wife.

cial system and that her new spouse is a key elder whose status has been elevated by the polygyny that must accompany successful male positional succession. Moreover, it must be remembered that the woman has the final word in the selection of a successor husband. The polygynous redistribution of widows allows women to play an important role in the selection of male leaders, as noted earlier, and the male elder's influence always depends on the continued cooperation of his female associates, including his wives. His role as *dundumuntuli* for the children of his wives and sisters depends upon the goodwill of these women. Should an inherited wife terminate their marriage, the advantages of positional succession are likely to be nullified. Polygyny therefore does not debase a woman or indicate subservience to male interests.

Divorce

Both mothers and fathers worry about the high divorce rate. They attribute it to the cash demands and time-consuming nature of the modern monetized bride-service system; the inconveniences of life in town, where the young couple are usually far from stabilizing parental influences, and the attractions of town life—some men come to prefer it and never return to the village. As the desire for modern town life has increased, urban and periurban settlements have mushroomed at the expense of rural farming areas like the Zambezi Valley, which have lost manpower (Kay 1967*a*, 1967*b*). Many young village women join their men in town for fear of losing them permanently but find it too expensive to purchase store food as their families grow. Eventually most women are forced to return to their villages, where they can work the land in company with older women, children too young for town adventures, and older men who have returned after failing to find viable lives in the towns. In some respects, then, village life has become a residual factor in the minds of the young—something to fall back on in case their life plans centering on the attractions of the towns fail to materialize (Bettison 1961).

The divorce rate is probably higher than that indicated by the figures in table 18, which range from 13 percent for men to 19 percent for women. Men marry much later than women do, die somewhat sooner, have shorter marital "careers" during which to divorce, and therefore have a lower divorce rate. A more accurate figure might come closer to the 30 to 50 percent range found in other matrilineal societies of Central Africa, where marriage has commonly been described as "brittle" (see table 19).

Table 19
Comparative Divorce Rates*

Group	Percent
Ndembu (southern Lunda)	52.7 matrilineal (Turner 1957, p. 62)
Chewa (Maravi)	43.5 matrilineal (Marwick 1965, p. 173)
Luvale	39.0 matrilineal (White 1960, p. 40)
Yao	34.6 matrilineal (Mitchell 1949, p. 298)
Bemba	33.2 matrilineal (Mitchell 1963)
Lamba	33.1 matrilineal (Mitchell and Barnes 1950, p. 47)
Plateau Tonga	29.8 matrilineal (Colson 1958, p. 181)
Fort Jameson Ngoni	28.5 cognatic (Barnes 1951, table xi)
Mambwe	19.8 patrilineal (Watson 1958, p. 114)
Goba	19.8 cognatic (Table 18, rate for women)
Valley Tonga (Chezia)	19.5 matrilineal (Colson 1960, p. 212)
Ambo (Nsenga)	18.9 matrilineal (Stefaniszyn 1964, p. 114)
Nuer	9.4 patrilineal (Evans-Pritchard 1945, pp. 31ff.)
Plateau Shona	9.4 patrilineal (Mitchell 1963)

*I have used Barnes's "ratio A" (Barnes 1949, 1967) throughout because I worked with live adults and my sample includes extant marriages:

$$\text{Ratio A} = \frac{\text{Marriages ended in divorce}}{\text{All marriages}} \times 100$$

It is difficult to obtain accurate figures on Goba divorces. If a young couple decide that their love is strong enough, they elope to a distant town. There they can break the routine of village life and live together openly without troubling with extended discussions with their elders about present and future obligations. Depending upon such variables as age, amount of town experience, cash resources, previous marital experience, and luck in finding a job and a place to stay, the length of this early trial stage is varied. Sometimes it is brief and ends quickly; the girl goes home, and the relationship lapses. When the anthropologist inquires about the "marriage" experiences of his census sample, this brief relationship is likely to be omitted, especially by older respondents remembering *muchato*. It is often only one of several marriage cycles an individual will have begun.

If the relationship survives the early elopement and lasts a few years, the girl eventually is forced to return to her mother's compound to care for her infants. The return can be postponed by leaving weaned youngsters with a grandmother, mother, or sister, but the time usually comes when it is too expensive for a village wife to live in town. Even if she is unburdened with children, she finds it impossible to get respectable work. She eventually has to return home and gamble on her husband's commitment to work, save, and await the day, perhaps some ten years distant, when he too may return home permanently with his marriage prestations behind him and a decent amount of cash put by for the future. Of course many men waver, because of the availability of town women, the difficulty of finding and keeping wage-paying jobs, and the problem of saving money, even when living alone. Most men under age forty or so are thus fairly permanent town residents. Some develop emotional ties with town women and may be alienated from their in-laws back home, if not their jealous wife, over arrears in their remittances for the original elopement damages at a time when the elopement is long since over, the girl is far away, and the marriage is likely to seem stale.

At this point some men will elect to stay in the towns and the surrounding rural areas if they can obtain the services of another wife more easily, perhaps by occasional visits to a town widow or divorcee (Schuster 1979). While the men are thus in effect polygynous during these years of migrant labor, some village wives are often more or less polyandrous, since they take lovers. It may then be an open question whether the incipient legal bond between the absent husband and his village wife will prevail over that of the wife and her local lover on the one hand and that of the husband and his town woman on the other. The incipient legal bond loses out fairly often. Many frustrated husbands return to the villages at this point and try to catch their wives in a compromising position so that they can win a verdict for adultery damages at the local court. Men are entitled to sue if they have delivered their betrothal gift (*tsambo*).

It is rare that a father in this position will be able to take the children upon dissolution of the marriage. Prestations for the patrifiliation of children come late in the cycle, when the marriage is likely to be more stable. Most failed marriages have ended well before that time. In any event it is rare for unmarried children to follow their father upon divorce to live with a stepmother interested in children of her own. Most people see to it that the youngsters remain with their own mother, who continues to grow their food, feed them, see to their petty cash needs at the local country store, and otherwise care for them, usually with the aid of her mother and sisters.

While a divorced father is deprived of his children's company, the Goba permit a man to make retroactive prestations (*pfuma*) for the patrifiliation of individual children reared in this way by divorced mothers. That usually occurs long after the divorce, when the children are grown and on the brink of marriage themselves. By then father is in a better position to make a large cash investment and coresidence with a possibly jealous stepmother is no longer a problem. In 1967–69 retroactive *pfuma* payments were made only for daughters, and for two reasons. First, the families of coresident married daughters were still the basis for village organization, despite the reinstitution and growing importance of bridewealth, and the size of these coresidential followings was still the prime measure of status for both a father and a wife. Second, the remittances of his coresident sons-in-law finally free a father from migrant labor and give the household a steady flow of cash.

It should be noted that retroactive bridewealth severely penalizes the mother and her matrikin by deflecting at the eleventh hour all the income generated by a daughter's marriage prestations into the hands of a father who may never have visited the girl in the long years of her youth or contributed to her support. There is no provision that the father must share with the mother or her kin any of the proceeds he receives in this way, and in fact he does not do so in instances where the parents have divorced.

This development, so favorable for fathers, can be credited to the male-dominated government court system. Before 1964 the chief was sole judge of civil cases that were not settled less formally in the villages. As senior *dundumuntuli* in the territory's most prestigious descent group, and as a leader sensitive to public opinion in the woman-centered villages, the chief was still sympathetic to the older matrilocal system dependent on bride service. The new court judges are civil servants not dependent on support from the old system. As local men who have tasted the frustrations of the old ways, they stand on the side of the bride-service husbands who want change (see Appendix).

While bridewealth in any tangible form is relatively new among the Goba, it represents principles of father right that the Goba have shared with their patrilineal Shona-speaking relatives south of the Zambezi. In the past father right was always exercised by free men fortunate enough to belong to numerically large descent group cores in which they could marry endogamously. In that event the child, mother, and father all belonged to the same descent-group, and no filiative prestations were necessary or made. In other Zambezi Valley groups, an exogamously marrying service husband was sometimes freed of his bride-service obligation when his own daughters married into their mother's descent group, thus canceling their father's debt for a woman (Chigumi 1923; Posselt 1926). This custom provided belated recognition of the free man's right to choose his own residence. Along the lower Zambezi in Portuguese East Africa, infant betrothal allows boys to perform their bride service earlier in life (Lacerda 1944; p. 82). Different groups have made their own adjustments to life in an area where bridewealth cattle have usually been too rare for regular use as tokens in the marriage system. Since the turn of the century the Goba have responded by introducing a cash bridewealth, gradually increasing its size and gradually making it effective as a release for the husband earlier in the cycle, as *muchato* and *mutsimutso* have fallen by the wayside. As this trend continues the formerly permanent bride-service requirements will probably be reduced to an initial brief period of uxorilocal residence, as it already is for some men, and society will develop along more patrilineal lines. This had not yet happened in 1967–69, and mother right was strongest in the early stages of a youthful elopement marriage, while father right developed only later in the cycle.

A final note on the divorce rate is in order here in view of Gluckman's seminal work in the subject (Gluckman 1950) and the continuing interest of other prominent Africanists (Barnes 1949, 1951; Epstein 1953; Mitchell 1957, 1961, 1963). The comparatively low divorce rate reported for the Goba in table 19 is not solely an artifact of inaccuracy in view of the high rate of failure in the early trial stages of love affairs and elopement marriages. My field experience convinced me that if better data were available the divorce rate clearly *would* be somewhat higher, but other factors are at work here as well. High divorce rates have been associated with matrilineal societies where the husband's position has been marginal in the early years of marriage and the wife's group retains genetricial rights in the children. Stable marriage has thus been linked to father right, and, as Mitchell noted (1961), one should expect higher divorce rates among matrilineal peoples where genetricial rights are never transferred to the husband's group. This applies to the Ndembu, the Chewa, the Luvale, the Yao, the Bemba, and the Lamba (table 19). These matrilineal peoples have the highest divorce rates reported for Central Africa, ranging from 33 to 53 percent. The matrilineal Plateau Tonga, who have the next-highest divorce rate (30 percent), do transfer genetricial rights, but this practice seems to be a postcolonial development, and it still comes late in the marriage cycle. The Plateau Tonga's divorce rate is therefore still fairly high and about in line with that of the modern Fort Jameson Ngoni (28 percent), who only rarely deliver bridewealth. The patrilineal Mambwe pay substantial bridewealth, as do modern Valley Tonga, and in both groups the divorce rate is considerably lower (20 and 19 percent, respectively). The Ambo appear to be a typical matrilineal people, and since they do not transfer genetricial rights, I suspect that Stefaniszyn's account of their marital stability has been idealized and that, like the Goba, whom they resemble in many ways, there is actually a high divorce rate in the more tenuous early years of courtship and marriage. Since modern Goba deliver bridewealth in the closing stages of the marriage cycle, when patrifiliative rights are shared and inherited within the husband's descent group, their comparatively low divorce rate (19 percent) does not come as a complete surprise. Even though the divorce rate may reflect inevitable inaccuracies in data collection, it can be taken as an indication of the extent to which father right has increased since the turn of the century. Further changes along these lines are expected in the future. Of course, the rate should be lower among a more thoroughly patrilineal people like the Nuer (9 percent), or highland Shona (9 percent) where patrifiliative rights are transferred to a wealthy suitor early in the marriage cycle.

13
Conclusion

How forms of social organization evolved and took shape was a prominent anthropological question in the latter part of the nineteenth century. Many would agree that an important step toward sound comparative analysis was laid by Sir Edward Tylor in his famous paper of 1889, "On a Method of Investigating the Development of Institutions; Applied to Laws of Marriage and Descent." Tylor proposed that statistical associations between forms of marriage and kin grouping in different parts of the world could reveal functional relationships and shed light on the development of social institutions.

After a long period (roughly 1915 to 1940) during which "conjectural history" and reconstruction were out of vogue, there was renewed interest in how forms of social organization fit together and develop. This interest has been furthered by two major trends in anthropological inquiry. The first, led by G. P. Murdock, has been the systematic building of comparative files of cross-cultural evidence collected by modern professional investigators. The second, pioneered by Leslie White and Julian Steward, has been a revival of interest in cultural evolution, which has gone hand in hand with a concern for ecology and subsistence economics. Armed with worldwide samples that show how various kinds of kin groups are statistically associated with subsistence modes and settlement patterns, anthropologists have continued to assess the relationship between social organization and ecology.

A cross-cultural association of agricultural subsistence, sedentary residence, a division of labor in which women are important, and matrilineal descent has seemed to be fairly clear. The ethnographic record shows that matrilineal descent tends to appear within a narrow adaptive range centering on various forms of low-density, long-fallow shifting cultivation, or horticulture, as it was

297

known in the earlier literature. Similarly, the dominant theory of how patrilineal descent groups arise finds that the crucial generative factors are, first, divisions of labor in which men play the major part, as in herding and more intensive agriculture, and, second, the development of property and more complex jural-political institutions predominantly associated with men. Male dominance in these matters (expressed as a high social evaluation of these male-linked activities) may make a pattern of virilocal residence adaptive. Similarly, the development of property and status hierarchies can make some kind of corporate exercise of title adaptive. These broad interpretations seem to be solidly supported by ethnographic evidence.

This interpretation of general tendencies in social-organization change has been articulated most clearly by Murdock (1949, 1959). In such an interpretation a shift in subsistence mode, technology, or environment can alter the division of labor so that sex roles change at the subsistence level. If this change makes existing patterns of postmarital residence seriously inconvenient or maladaptive, the statistical frequency of residence choices is likely to shift, irrespective of past norms. Eventually the ideological rules of residence are also likely to reflect the change. The altered residence pattern changes the composition of local groups, and in time that change too is recognized through establishment of a different rule of recruitment (for example, a new rule of descent) or through a changed conceptualization of local groups.

Yet in an examination of the ethnographic record case by case the many exceptions to the sequence postulated above make it clear that the effect of ecological or subsistence forces has often been conceived as operating too directly and mechanically on social organization and that social structure has often been viewed too concretely (for a review of the problem see Keesing 1975; pp. 132–43). Ecological adaptation is unquestionably important in kin-group organization, but it probably shapes and prunes indirectly rather than directly, neatly, and consistently. Ecological pressures operate on individuals rather than on formal systems and superstructures, and it is individuals pursuing goals who create, sustain, and change "systems." It is for this reason that social anthropology since the 1960s has been focusing on actual behavior, situational analysis, law and conflict resolution, informal networks, quasi-groups, action sets, and the ideologies, motives, and strategies that generate behavior (see Gluckman 1961; Gluckman and Eggan 1965; Barth 1966; Mitchell 1969; Bailey 1971).

A modern approach to social change recognizes the importance of ecology and subsistence on the one hand and the importance of individuals as purposive manipulators of rules and opportunities on the other. There is clearly a process of mutual, ongoing adjustment at play among environmental opportunities, subsistence needs, population pressure (however it may be generated), technology and work effort, division of labor, social organization, political power, ideologies, and control of the means of production. This means that the field anthropologist seriously interested in change and adaptation must trace the prevailing relations among ecology, subsistence, social organization, and power.

These crucial relations are most easily traced and appreciated in hierarchical systems where a clearly defined power structure exercises unequal control over vital material resources and productive processes. It has been much more difficult to trace the roots of change in decentralized low-density, low-energy societies where marked social classes are absent and producers control their own resources and subsist on the fruits of their own labor. In such societies a series of "battle lines" may still be drawn along which social changes may be advanced and which are constantly being refought and renegotiated. There a battle line may form between the sexes, between youths and elders, or between units in segmentary systems (Keesing 1975). Shifts in ecological balance may very well enhance the bargaining power of one group versus another. In this situation, however, where subsistence life is individualized at the domestic level and where a clearly defined, more or less centralized political economy does not exercise corporate control over vital materialist interests, changes in social rules are not simply produced by changes in ecology or subsistence (Lancaster 1979*b*). Instead, the relationship between social organization and environment is indirect, mediated by ideologies of a diverse nature and affected by the dynamics of negotiation over issues that may be totally unconnected with subsistence needs. As a result the mechanical one-hundred-year search for perfect correlations of what-goes-with-what-under-what-conditions may be doomed to failure. In the analysis of low-density societies abstract formal models of reified social structures frozen into "adaptive" equilibriums must give way to models based on the dynamics of social process and individual psychology.

This approach is applicable to the Goba. The chief features of the family estate have not been usufruct rights to labor, land, sorghum granaries, cattle, cash, or other material items. The chief attractions have been social positions. The local political economy, organized in the ancestor cult, has been concerned with the manner in which these positions have been filled and the rights they convey in other persons. Agreements regarding these important manners of behavior have shaped the organization of coresident family units, influenced ideas of proper behavior, determined the nature of local political units, and set the kinds of processes likely to be found. These multiplex concerns of a broadly social nature have, of course, operated within environmental and technological constraints. As we have seen, the latter have dictated the mode of subsistence and a life-style tied to the agricultural cycle. They have determined the settlement pattern and, within limits, have influenced settlement size and permanency. But the precise way in which domestic and descent groups have been conceived and organized, whether matrilocal or patrilocal, unilineal or cognatic, has depended upon situational variables essentially divorced from the subsistence base. At a different level of organization precolonial political activity focused on military force and a system of rewards based on rank and trade goods rather than on subsistence.

This situation has probably been paralleled in most kin-based societies in the middle range of relatively homogeneous precapitalistic societies, where technology is relatively simple. Here, as Fortes and others have remarked, corporate social groupings based on rights to durable, relatively scarce, and highly valued property are not found. Instead social forms are comparatively labile. As opposed to adaptive systems where sex-linked estates of scarce land or livestock form the material basis for both subsistence and the organization of corporate social structures, access to food and material goods is generally less problematic and less important in the family structure of the low-density cultivator (Fortes 1953; Goody 1976). Neither sex then gains the materalist and political advantages that males alone almost universally have acquired under conditions of heightened scarcity, when subsistence comes to be based on plow agriculture and other forms of work- and capital-intensive farming, nomadic pastoralism, or even hunting-gathering and low-density horticulture under conditions where male sex-role contributions may be considered especially important (Aberle 1961; Lancaster 1976). Kinship position then remains the principal basis of descent-group organization, and, because neither sex is likely to have a complete monopoly on ancestral-cult seniority the organization of social life is seldom tied rigidly to sex-linked characteristics. Same-sex, or unilineal, descent-group structuring is therefore generally less overpowering and less corporate among low-density cultivators than that reported among most landed fixed-farming peasants and nomadic pastoralists.

Among the Goba in precolonial times matrilocal extended families were produced by a preference for bride-service marriage. Matrilineal links were especially important, and women's status was probably relatively high, reinforced no doubt by their importance as subsistence cultivators, though women worked just as hard in neighboring patrilineal societies on the south, where they probably enjoyed slightly lower status. Men, on the other hand, made significant contributions to agriculture themselves and played important roles as hunters, warriors, traders, and political representatives. Endogamous marriage made it possible for men to trace patrilineal ties when important social titles were at stake, much as men did in neighboring Shona-speaking areas, where bridewealth marriage was common. The lives of men and women differed markedly, making direct comparison uncertain. But while free women enjoyed relatively high status, it is doubtful that free men were ever a suppressed class, despite the presence of female-centered agriculture, uxorilocal residence, and female village cores.

Basic changes in the twentieth century have altered relations between the sexes. One change has been the growth of the local cash economy, which has been dominated by men. Men provide most of the income through their activities in the indigenous tobacco industry. Added to this has been recent encouraging success in cotton cropping, introduced by government. While climate and plant diseases will continue to impose limits and setbacks, cotton sales will probably experience considerable long-term growth by past local standards. Men have also provided cash as migrant wage laborers, and they control most of the cash savings held at village level, as well as the livestock.

Another major trend has been the monetization of the bride-service system. Wife-seekers, who were once easily controlled as they toiled locally for their women or went raiding and hunting under the direction of elders, now scatter individually and in small groups as they seek distant wage-paying jobs. The money they remit is an important contribution to a local cash economy no one wants to do without. In recurrent drought years when the sorghum crop is stricken, they rely on the cash economy for subsistence. That dependence promises to intensify in coming decades as land pressure restricts hunting, gathering, and fishing. Young male wage earners have bargaining power, and so do the older men, who must police their remittances and see that they eventually return home. In earlier times the bride-service system gave localized senior women relatively high status in large descent-group villages, a status that was shared and coordinated with that of the senior resident men. But the monetization of the bride-service cycle is merging it with the male-dominated cash economy, and the women are clearly in danger of losing ground.

As the amount of money in local circulation has grown, male-oriented institutions have been making the cash economy more prominent and prestigious on the local scene. These new institutions are the beer halls and the increasing numbers of country stores. Both are frequented almost exclusively by men, and they quickly draw off cash that once circulated more widely and slowly within the villages. In the past women participated in the cash economy through their home-brewing activities and their small-scale local trade in sorghum. Since sorghum is well adapted to local agricultural conditions, and since expanding urban and periurban populations on the Zambian highlands subsist on this popular African food staple, stimulation of the sorghum trade might capitalize on women's skills and increase local exports. As it is, however, the stores and beer halls are competing with the women, and basically male-oriented cash crops, such as cotton, are being encouraged.

Finally, the last important development has been the movement of the local court system from its former place in the village arena, where the assembled women had an important voice, to a government courthouse in the chief's village. Many disputes continue to be aired in the villages, as before, and in times past some cases always were appealed at the village of the chief. But now the former chief's court is run by progressive salaried young men appointed by the government, and they are more effectively insulated than the chief from direct village-level sanctions and the influence of women. Because of its distance from most of the villages, the government court is too far away for most women to attend. Thus, like the stores and the beer halls, the court has become one more place where male views predominate (see Appendix). Of course, decisions made at the government court affect behavior in the villages.

All these important developments strengthen the male role in the local political economy and favor male viewpoints and preferences, often at the expense of the women. Over the long term these trends are expected to continue as the growing cash economy elevates male status and influences marriage prestations. Bride-service manual labor was only rarely practiced in the villages in the late 1960s. By that time cash remittances from town had long since become the preferred payment. A terminal bridewealth prestation had already been added to the once long sequence of marriage exchanges, and it had already begun to appear earlier in the cycle. The initial, once-perpetual period of bride-service obligations was clearly on its way out. There was strong male pressure from the young, the old, and the government court for an even earlier bridewealth prestation, to be followed by religious, social, legal, and economic independence for a securely dominant male household head. Together with having a moderately successful career as a cash-cropping farmer or perhaps a shopkeeper, this description represented the modern male ideal in 1967–69.

Most young women disliked the remittance system, which took the young men away to the towns. While they were unhappy that store beer was displacing village beer and that they could get so little for their sorghum, women of all ages looked forward to a day when all the perceived benefits of town life would filter out to the country where they felt they belonged, to enrich the life they loved and, especially, to enable their boys and men to stay home. The women of Namainga realized that bridewealth marriage and virilocal residence would eventually enable them to merge more successfully with their neighbors, the numerically dominant Tonga peoples of Zambia, and thus facilitate participation in this hoped-for government-sponsored new life. Like the men, they also suspected that membership in UNIP, the national political party in power, would facilitate attainment of their goals.

Unless new markets develop for their traditional crops, the rural sorghum-growing women with their relatively high status in female-centered decent-group villages seem headed for a future as the helpful wives of market-oriented peasant-farming male household heads. How that prediction works out in practice remains to be seen.

Appendix:
Goba Men and
Women in
Court

Among the Goba most marital problems are settled privately between the spouses. When the wife feels seriously aggrieved, a husband will appeal to his in-laws for support—and may find that she has already done so. Only the more serious difficulties reach the attention of the village, through quarrels and gossip that reach public proportions and finally may require public arbitration in the clearing in front of the in-law's sleeping quarters. Problems that cannot be settled by public opinion at the village *dare*, or moot court, go to the government court, where fines can be levied and noncomplying offenders can ultimately be sentenced to prison. Frequent attendance at the government court and a study of its records is useful. Because litigants and witnesses travel there from all the villages in the chiefdom, visits to the court can correct distortions arising from the anthropologist's necessarily intensive immersion and participation in the affairs of only a few settlements. Once the action gets under way at the government court, where the problems are often more serious, the fine generally higher, and the results final, the anthropologist's presence is less distracting than that of a relative stranger surveying a larger area more superficially. This is true even at the beginning of the fieldwork, when curiosity about the anthropologist runs highest.

The court building is a modern structure dating from the 1950s and similar to the courthouses and school buildings found elsewhere throughout Zambia. It has brick walls surfaced with a cement plaster, smooth concrete floors, metal door frames, open windows, and a high-pitched metal roof with wide gables for protection from sun and rain. Until Zambian independence in 1964 the local court officers could ask questions during a hearing, but the chief passed final judgment. Now the president and vice-president of the local court have replaced the chief, who is no longer associated with the court. The president, (who was thirty-nine years old when I arrived in 1967) is employed by the Ministry of Justice, as is the vice-president (aged thirty-seven in 1967). Both men were born and raised in the chiefdom, had held their present positions for a number of years, and showed no tendency to discard their village heritages. Though their income permitted them to dress unusually well, both lived in villages and observed local life styles. The president was one of the more famous Shamans in the chiefdom. Both were personable, popular, and nondirective and could pass down decisions without unduly antagonizing anyone. They listened to cases with patient, sympathetic expressions. As a solution began to make itself evident, they gradually worked themselves up to some degree of passionate conviction, as is the local style, and each in turn candidly discussed the principles of the matter with the plaintiff, defendant, witnesses, and perhaps members of the audience of onlookers. By the time a decision was reached, it was usually acceptable to everyone as being "the way we always do it," though a few were appealed, English was never spoken in court.

On a typical day the president might be dressed in light-colored slacks, a long-sleeved cotton shirt open at the neck, and desert boots. Like the other members of the court, his clothes were always in good condition, clean, and freshly ironed. The vice-president often wore white slacks, a black shirt with a light-gray tie, a dark tweed jacket in cooler months, red socks, and shiny black-leather shoes. At the immediate right of the officer's platform the court clerk (aged forty) was seated at a table with all his papers and receipt books. He often wore a well-tailored brown suit, a white shirt with thin brown stripes, a brown necktie, and polished brown shoes. The sergeant-at-Arms, also acting as court messenger, delivered the court summons, kept order, arrested offenders, and confiscated unpaid judgments and fines. He usually sat in front of the clerk as the latter recorded the particulars of each case in his record book. Sometimes the uniformed messenger's place was taken by the postman or the chief's orderly, who were both associated with the office of the president of Zambia, as was the chief.

All the men associated with the court were still fairly young, and all were polygynists. Their personal attitudes reflected local male norms, and their viewpoints toward women, sex, and marriage clearly had a significant effect on local cultural trends. When they were appointed by the Judicial Service Commission, the president and vice-president were tested on their knowledge of local customary law. The court officers consider it to be Korekore customary law and it therefore reflects the patrilineal ideals of the Shona-speaking peoples. Occasionally, if they disagreed on a decision, the judges would adjourn the court and talk it over. Sometimes they consulted important village elders, much as a magistrate might consult his lawbooks. Women apparently were never consulted.

Table 20 summarizes the kinds of marital problems dealt with at the chief's court during my field research. Marriage-related cases accounted for 62 to 69 percent of all cases heard in the calendar years 1966, 1967, and 1968, and a similar proportion of marriage cases appears to have been heard in the immediately preceding years. The subclassifications used in the table suggested themselves to me after I had consulted the records and heard about twenty-five cases. The clerk and sergeant-at-arms, who worked closely with me, suggested a similar classification on the basis of their own training and experience.

Elopement Damages

Since elopement, or abduction, as they often call it, is an important part of the marriage cycle, it is the issue in a significant number of court cases each year. The cases are usually brought to court by the girl's father sometime after the girl has returned and the son-in-law has clearly failed to deliver his prestation for compensation in lieu of service in residence (*mari ye murandu*, literally "money for the case"). The term used for this often much-begrudged prestation indicates that court action must frequently be resorted to. If the girl is reasonably satisfied with her marriage, most fathers-in-law allow a good deal of time to elapse before asserting their legal rights.

It must be noted that elopement damages have usually consisted of three separate prestations, and none of them returnable under any circumstances. The first (*vunzirakuno*) announces the elopement soon after it has occurred and is usually delivered by the groom himself. If accepted by the girl's guardians, this token prestation removes the possibility of later court charges of abduction or seduction. It may be omitted altogether if the girl's parents have had advance public notice that an elopement is planned. The second prestation (*mari ye kudzoresa mukadzi*) is more significant, as much as $36 in recent years, and it is seen as compensation for having removed the daughter from her parents' compound without permission, that is, without having advanced step by step through the entire marriage cycle. The third prestation, the largest of the entire marriage cycle, has in the past served to compensate for the lack of manual service in residence. Fathers-in-law like to think of

Table 20
Summary of Marriage-Related Civil Cases in the Local Government Court

	1966		1967		1968	
	No. of Cases	Percent of Total	No. of Cases	Percent of Total	No. of Cases	Percent of Total
Abduction of daughter	6	14	8	17	6	12
Adultery	7	16	15	32	14	29
Public insult related to marriage	2	5	1	2	3	6
Return of *tsambo* or *pfuma*	1	2	3	6	1	2
Divorce	18	42	5	11	13	27
Child custody	4	9	8	17	5	10
Miscellaneous marital disputes	4	9	6	13	7	14
Return of gifts	1	2	1	2	0	0
Total marriage-related cases	43	(100%)	47	(100%)	49	(100%)
Total all cases	67		76		71	
Marriage cases as percent of total	64		62		69	

Source: Compiled from the monthly return book, Namainga Court, Sikaongo chiefdom, with the aid of Court Clerk John Chadukwa and Sergeant-at-Arms Melek Katobola.
Note: The percentage figures are rounded off in this table.

these prestation as three separate matters, while younger men, including the president and vice-president of the court, have preferred to simplify matters, shorten the cycle, and reduce the groom's total financial liability by lumping them together into one large sum (see case 5 below). This trend seems to be gaining acceptance. A high of $108 had been accepted as more or less standard in the late 1960s, both in the villages and at the government court, for total consolidated elopement damages in situations where, while the marriage was not necessarily being discontinued, the groom had not endeared himself to the in-laws and the maximum amount was being extracted. In recent years damages have averaged about $48 for subsistence-farming villagers without wage-paying jobs, and higher for shopkeepers and government employees. Examples of typical cases follow.

Case Abstract 1: Abduction of Daughter

James, Limbembe Village, Father-in-Law and Plaintiff v. Jailos, Kanyenye Village, Son-in-Law

Plaintiff's position: In 1965, Jailos abducted my daughter from my home and took her to Mazabuka. I charged him $72.00 (U.S.) for the damages, and of this amount he has paid me only $12.00. I want the court to make him pay me my money now.

Defendant: I disagree that the total compensation was set at $72.00, even $60.00. The original agreement was that the damages should be $24.00.

Plaintiff: The original agreement was for $24.00, but I have raised the sum to $72.00 because he has delayed payment for some three years [it has been common practice to raise or lower the amounts due on any part of the marriage sequence as conditions and relationships change].

Judgment: Plaintiff's claim is upheld on Jailos's admission that he has not yet paid his damages. Both parties have told the court that they had agreed to a sum of $24.00; therefore the court orders Jailos to pay James $24.00 on August 24, 1968. Jailos must also pay the court fee of $1.20 [the losing party usually pays the court fee].

OBSERVER'S COMMENTS The officers of the court told me that they felt that the father's claim for $72.00 was a little unreasonable, probably only a talking point, and that no solution could ever be found by supporting him at that level. The sum of $24.00 was agreed upon by both parties with no discussion. The $12.00 already paid by the son-in-law was a sop to the father for the delay. Damages came to a total of $36.00, a little below average but a reasonably good amount to receive after only three years.

Case Abstract 2: Abduction of Daughter

Chinyama, Mutena Village, Father-in-Law and Plaintiff v. *Peter, Chiota Village, Son-in-Law:*

Plaintiff's position: Peter abducted my daughter Selina in 1964. Damages were set at $64.80. Peter still owes me $48.00 of this amount, and I want the money immediately.

Defendant's position: I agree that everything my father-in-law has said is correct, but I have no money. Because of this case I have tried for a job with the Zambian police but still have not found the money [The police are an elite group, and his application was not very realistic.]

Court: Are you able to pay the money now?

Defendant: Yes, I am prepared to pay it but have no money unless the court gives me time. I have already paid $16.80 and still owe $31.20, because the total charge was $48.00, not $64.80. [Both the court and the plaintiff quickly agreed to accept the lower figure in hopes of reaching a settlement.]

Judgment: The defendant is ordered to pay the balance of $31.20, plus $4.80 court fee, in equal installments due on September 30 and October 30. [The case was heard in July, 1968.]

Case Abstract 3: Elopement Damages and Wifely Sanctions

Chisaka, Ndangila Village, Father-in-Law and Plaintiff v. *David, Mangaba Village, Son-in-Law*

BACKGROUND David eloped with Chisaka's daughter early in 1967 and took her to Lusaka. He kept her there six months and then returned her and gave Chisaka $26.40 for *mari ye kudzoresa mukadzi* ("taking the cow outside the gate"). Then David took her back to Lusaka for three more weeks. But she was tying her thighs together at night in bed, as unwilling women are wont to do, and she was going to bed with her clothes on too (both husband and wife usually sleep naked). David could not force her, even though he tried hard and even beat her. David came back with her to his in-laws and complained. David suggested that perhaps someone else had proposed to her. In that event he might be entitled to an adultery fee and have an excuse to end the marriage. Everyone agreed that the in-laws advised the girl to behave herself "since he had not yet paid the elopement damages of $36.00." She told her father that David had not been caring for her properly and that he had not bought her dresses and other things she needed from the stores, but she agreed to go off with David again. Before they left, he delivered the $36.00 in elopement damages.

Defendant: A month or two later she began the same system again. I brought her back and took back my $36.00 from my father-in-law. [He pushed the old man around roughly, threatened to beat him, and took the money by force.]

Plaintiff: I asked him why he was beating me and taking my money. He said it was because my daughter slept with her clothes on and tied her thighs together. Then I asked him who had witnessed that. Then he took the cash and left, and I came here for a summons. [It turned out that David in his rage also took the wife's clothes and cooking pots, which he had paid for, leaving her only with the clothes on her back. This was an insult second only to stripping her in public, and the court did not hide its displeasure.]

Judgment: The father-in-law has that money for elopement damages. Had it been for *pfuma* (Bridewealth), you would be entitled to its return. [The court advised the return of the $36.00. Otherwise the son-in-law would be committing an additional offense. The son-in-law agreed to return the money. In a long discussion afterward, the father-in-law said that David must try to persuade the woman himself if he wanted her back. "It is not for me to do. He must make her happy." As the plaintiff seeking court action, the father-in-law had paid $0.24 for the summons. That was returned to him by the clerk. The defendant then had to pay the $0.24 for the summons plus a hearing fee of $2.40.]

Case Abstract 4: Elopement Damages and Divorce

Zefa, Naloba Village, Wife v. Nelison, Jila Village, Chief Mwenda, Husband

Plaintiff's position: He has been my husband since 1963, and I have had two children with him, but he will not make any payments to my parents. He always beats me every time he comes home from a beer drink; therefore, I want to divorce him today.

Defendant: I agree that I assaulted her on May 30, 1968, when she refused to accompany me to my job at the Kafue Gorge. She first insulted me before I could say any nonsense words, and from then on she stopped sleeping with me in my own house and has been sleeping in her own house somewhere in her parents' village.

Court: Have you made any payments to her parents?

Defendant: No, I have not paid them anything but was told that I should deliver $43.20 for elopement damages.

Witness [the girl's aged father, Naloba, of Naloba Village]: He has not been properly married to my daughter and has only been friendly toward her, as he has never made any payment. I order him to pay me three head of cattle in order that his marriage to her might be confirmed, but he has refused to deliver anything, even though he has produced about two children with our daughter. [The defendant comes from the neighboring area of Plateau Tonga peoples under chief Mwenda, where cattle can be kept.]

Judgment: The claim for divorce is upheld. The court considers the marriage to have been a friendly marriage only, for he did not pay anything to her parents during her stay with him from 1963 to 1968. Therefore, the woman is ordered to pay the court fee of $2.40 and wins her divorce.

The children remain with the mother, of course. It is usually only in divorce cases where the plaintiff wife successfully wins her case that the winner, rather than the loser, must pay the court fees. The male members of the court say that they do this to discourage too many women from divorcing their husbands.

Case Abstract 5: Elopement Damages

Timothy, Bagasa Village, Father-in-Law and Plaintiff v. *Griffis, from the Area of Chief Namuyamba, Mongu District, Baroteseland*

BACKGROUND   The defendant, a stranger to the area, works as a district messenger at Siavonga, a small administrative center about forty miles west of the court in the Zambezi Valley. His job is a very prestigious one in village eyes, and he earns $69.00 a month, a very large sum by local standards. Two years before the defendant ran off with the plaintiff's daughter without giving any advance notice. That act coupled with the fact that he was considered a rich stranger, naturally exposed the defendant to heavy charges. The defendant took the girl home to Barotseland, kept her for about two months, and then returned with her to Siavonga, where he and the girl have lived ever since. As soon as the defendant returned to Siavonga, he gave his father-in-law $28.80. At the same time he and his father-in-law agreed on a sum of $84.00 for damages. The defendant's position has been that the $28.80 was the first installment on these damages, leaving an unpaid balance of $55.20. The plaintiff felt that the $28.80 was only for having eloped without permission.

Shortly after their meeting the son-in-law sent the plaintiff a letter with $12.00 enclosed. The letter specified that he would pay what he still owed in monthly installments of $12.00. The plaintiff sent it back and said that he wanted the $84.00 paid at once in a lump sum. The son-in-law made no reply and waited to be brought to court.

The son-in-law attended the hearing in a light bush jacket, dark slacks, and polished shoes and gave the impression of being "modern" and successful. Like most other village men, the father-in-law was barefooted and wore worn khaki pants and an old khaki shirt.

THE COURT'S POSITION   The president spoke long and earnestly with the plaintiff about the question of damages. He said that the fine for taking the girl without notice and the fine for the elopement itself should be one and the same thing, and never referred to its traditional function as a bride-service equivalent. He argued that when they agreed on the $84.00 that was the total amount and not $84.00 plus $28.80. Clearly it was not simply a matter of a judge handing down a decision. He argued warmly with the plaintiff, trying to persuade him to change his attitude.

Defendant: I now have two wives and many children to support. Some of them are going to school, and I cannot pay the damages in one lump sum.

JUDGMENT   After both parties have spoken and everyone in the courtroom had a chance to ask questions, everyone was asked to leave except the two judges, the clerk, and the sergeant-at-arms. The judges conferred together for about two minutes, and everyone was called back. The president announced the decision. The son-in-law owed $84.00 minus the $28.80 already paid. He was to pay the money in three monthly installments. He also paid the court fees. The plaintiff rose and smiled triumphantly at his friends in the audience. The son-in-law was poker-faced, though he must have been pleased. Both men took seats to hear the other cases scheduled for that day.

Adultery

Men charged with elopement damages in the early stages of their marriage cycle are usually many miles away from their wives and families, working in towns, in administrative centers, or on commercial farms. This pattern of wage labor interspersed with longer or shorter visits home continues for many years as the men try to pay their way through the long marriage cycle and earn additional funds for the establishment of their households, the education of their children, and, whenever possible, the establishment of a family business. Opening a small retail dry-goods store is a cherished ambition for most families seeking the best possible modern life in rural areas, but in practice most must be content with a small subsistence farm. Even after their marriages are secured, men continue their tours of migrant labor to save for a plow, a cart, draft oxen, and a small herd of cattle or, in most valley areas, small stock as a store of value against the future. A man is unlikely to acquire such possessions via positional succession until he has successfully secured his own marriage and subsistence farm, and there is little alternative to migrant labor for most men, unless they are willing to live in the villages and grow cash crops of tobacco or cotton. While few families achieve all their goals, the effort to do so by means of migrant labor keeps most men away from their wives and families for a long time and leads to a substantial number of adultery cases, as shown in table 20.

These court actions are usually brought by absent "cheated" husbands. If he is found guilty, the fine the adulterous lover must pay is rarely less than $72.00 and has been as much as $120.00 in recent years, the maximum the court allows. Court action for adultery commonly provides a way for the absent husband to get something back out of an insecure marriage before the final divorce and is thus tantamount to divorce in many instances, because all the man need do next is remove his things from his hut in his wife's village. If he has been living in town, as in case 6, even that is not necessary. The following cases are examples of those involving adultery.

Case Abstract 6: Adultery

Jackson, Bwenangoma Village, Husband and Plaintiff v. *Lameck, Mazabuka District, Defendant*

BACKGROUND   The plaintiff has not resided in the valley for many years, although he is still counted as a resident of his parents' village because he was unmarried when he left for town as a boy in his early teens. He comes to court looking very prosperous, dressed in a bush jacket and slacks with a fedora hat and briefcase. His town woman is with him in court, sitting quietly by his side as they wait for the hearing. She causes something of a stir. She wears makeup, a form-fitting short city dress, shoes, and stockings, and she is crocheting, a very prestigious activity for a woman. Jackson and his town friends did not visit his parents in their village when he came down into the valley for this case. He is thirty-six years old.

The defendant, aged thirty-eight, works as a tsetse-fly picket for about $29.00 a month at a fly gate near the Bagasa Village. He is a thin, hesitant man, dressed in a heavily starched, uncomfortable paramilitary uniform. He is a stranger, from the area of Chief Mwemba, Mazabuka District, on the plateau west of the valley.

COMPLAINT   It is now March, 1968. In 1966, while Jackson was away on migrant labor, the defendant abducted Jackson's wife, Saria, who had been living with her two children at Simamasindi Village, near the fly gate.

THE HEARING   The case begins with Jackson giving his side of the story and asking for the full compensation allowed by law, $120.00. The president then asks Saria to come forward and sit between the two men on the bench. She is young and nice-looking but obviously very "rural" compared with the other woman. She is barefoot and dusty from her long walk to reach the court. Like most other village women she wears an old baggy dress reaching down to her ankles, and she has a baby about a year old on her back. Lameck is the father. She stares at her knees throughout the proceedings. It is the vice-president's turn to take the lead in the questioning. Lameck is questioned about what happened, and he says that Saria told him that she had already divorced her husband when he met her. He says that it was not until after they had been living together and he sent an opening gift (nhumbi) of $2.40 to her father and asked to marry her that he found that "she was under Jackson." The judges find this very amusing. The vice-president laughs and tells him that he has been cheated. The president asks Saria if she still loves her husband. She says she loves Lameck. Jackson then says that he still loves Saria and wants her back.

JUDGMENT AND CONCLUSION   After a brief recess the judges announce that Lameck is to pay the plaintiff $120.00 in ten monthly installments. In view of this major victory, the plaintiff pays the fees for the hearing and the summons. The judges point out that Saria is still married to Jackson and should return home with him. If she wishes to divorce her husband, she must pay for a summons and give the reasons why she wishes to reject him. If Lameck misses a payment, he will be fined $24.00 for every payment missed. Lameck immediately hands over $9.60 of his first payment. I watch through the window as they leave. Lameck goes first, walking his bicycle. Saria follows him about ten feet behind with her head down. About ten minutes later Jackson, his town wife, and another well-dressed young city man break away from a crowd of admirers and walk off three abreast, talking and laughing. They go back to town.

OBSERVER'S COMMENTS   One man says that many men who do
not love their wives go off to town to work and never come back to
visit. They are just waiting for something like this to happen so
that they can go to court. If the woman had been sophisticated,
she would have rejected Jackson a long time ago, and then she
would not have brought so much trouble to Lameck. Now he will
never forgive her for cheating him.

Another influential man, a wealthy storekeeper, who had
dropped in to hear the next case, said aloud in court that the
woman should pay a fine too. "All the women are cheating us men."
But the diligent clerk said very seriously that there was not any law
about that, and everyone but the clerk laughed very heartily.

Outside a moment later another man comments to a group that
adultery cases always occur because a married woman goes off with
another man. You cannot have it the other way, he says, because,
if a man wants two women, he just takes another wife or goes off to
town and finds one there. So a woman cannot be damaged if her
husband wants two women, but a man can be damaged if his wife
wants two men.

LATER DEVELOPMENTS   A month later Lameck has come to
court, after the cases are over for the day, to pay his monthly installment of $12.00 adultery with Jackson's wife. He feels that the
monthly payment should sanction some current pleasures with
Jackson's wife. He places $9.60 in the vice-president's hand, prom-
ises to pay the rest later, and finally fishes the final $2.40 out of his
pocket. After paying the money, he says that his woman has been
taken back by her father now that Jackson has gone back to town.
"I have not got her anymore. Why should I go on paying?" The
court responds that the $120.00 fine was for his *past* offense of
living with another man's wife.

Lameck has one child by Jackson's wife, and he asks about that.
He complains that the girl's father has taken the child too. "Why?
I keep paying and have not even the child!" The court replies:
"Because the woman and child are not yours at all. You just slept
with her for adultery. The child is still sucking, and so it travels
with the mother. And you have not put *pfuma* [Bridewealth]." Lameck asks, "What if my child should die there?" The court is angry
at this implied accusation of witchcraft and shoots back that it
would only be an accident. "There is nothing to set straight. The
child is not yours. Since Jackson does not want to admit that the
child is his, the daughter will go to you when she matures, if you
put *pfuma*. Jackson has his $120, and rights to the *pfuma*, instead

of the person. If he had admitted the child was his, he might not have gotten the money for the adultery. Meanwhile, if the child dies at its mother's village, there is nothing to do, and you cannot claim a case."

Another elderly bystander then summed it up: "The child is Jackson's because the mother is Jackson's real wife. Jackson has finished all his marriage payments. You can sneak food from another man's granary; it happens, all right. But the owner of the granary eats more than you. If you want the child you must pay bridewealth for it, to Jackson." [Both the granary and the food it contains are symbolically linked with the wife who grows the grain contained in it, prepares the food, and often works in its shadow. The layout of most settlements is such that adult men are rarely seen near the granaries. They are sometimes decorated wtih large female breasts modeled in clay, and in discussions about adultery, the woman is often referred to as a granary.]

Case Abstract 7: Adultery

Dobi, Kademaunga Village, husband and plaintiff v. *Kachimba, Siamasanga Village, defendant*

COMPLAINT   Adultery with Dobi's wife.

BACKGROUND AND SETTING   At this point the frustrated husband just wants a face-saving hearing in court, and he hopes against hope, and the better judgment of the court clerk who advised him, that his estranged wife, Midia, will support him and deny the charges convincingly, even though everyone knows that they are true, and she has not been cooperative in planning how they will handle the case. The court records show that many wives who are firmly attached to their husband will agree to present a united front against a former lover in order to obtain large windfall damages for adultery, but after first seeming to agree to this Dobi's wife has finally refused. She has publicly accused Dobi of sterility before the hearing begins, the worst thing she can do to the man, and has decided to seek a divorce. By this time Dobi has already paid the hearing fee, and he stubbornly goes ahead with the case. Unlike many cases of this kind where the plaintiff has more confidence in his position, the amount of the compensation sought is left unspecified.

The president has started the first hearing of the day, and it is the vice-president's turn to preside and take the lead in questioning. The pretty woman is made to sit between the two men on the front bench before the judges; originally she was sitting next to the seducer. Someone in the audience next to me murmurs that by now she is afraid of her sulking husband.

Dobi begins his story, and the court listens closely and sympathetically. When he finally finishes, there is a long, unnatural silence while the court clerk catches up in his record book. When he has stopped writing, the vice-president consoles Dobi gently.

THE COURT'S VIEW   During a short recess the clerk comes over and brings me up to date on the court's position on this case. The case is considered an attempted frame-up by Dobi. He neglected his wife for a long time and left her alone. She is young and naturally needed someone, and she and the defendant were planning to marry. To bolster their legal position, they deny any sex. Dobi is just trying to salvage what he can before his wife divorces him, and it is known that he had hoped to win substantial adultery damages with his wife's cooperation. He had known of the love affair all along and had done nothing about his poor relationship with his wife.

TESTIMONY   Dobi relates that at Nyamoumba fishing camp in Nanyanga neighborhood where he lives, he met a friend who told him that his wife was sleeping with another man. This put suspicion in his mind, but he just kept it in mind (that is, he did not beat his wife). Dobi is a hunter for the Game and Tsetse Department and is away from home quite a bit. When he finally went home again (the village is only a few miles from the fishing camp) he asked his wife, "Do you live well here?" Then he tells her what he had heard. She denies it. Now he reveals that the friend who had told him the story was Kachimba himself, the defendant.

In her own testimony the wife claims that she sleeps with no one but that she does know Kachimba. This does not mean that she sleeps with him. She says that he came twice to propose but was refused. (there is a strong local tradition that the third time never fails).

Dobi interjects in injured tones to ask how much money she received. She says none, and Dobi answers that she should at least make some money out of it the next time she sleeps with him. Here the testimony and allegory of the exchange between husband and wife is such that it is left purposely unclear whether or not she slept with the defendant, and the question is immaterial in the eyes of the court unless she openly admits it or a witness is willing to come forward. The issue is left hanging.

The wife continues with her testimony, to the effect that Isaac never did show up the third time, at least not that Dobi ever found out. (Thus if the hearing was to be a trap against the defendant, as Dobi originally planned, it never sprung for Dobi's benefit.)

When it is clear that the wife will not admit anything, Dobi finally says that he just got tired of waiting for clear-cut evidence admissible in court and that his mind was not at rest because he was suspecting them all the time. The village elders could not settle down the angry Dobi and advised him to buy a summons at the government court. He did so.

The defendant, in his turn, denies even propositioning the woman. The wife, Midia, repeats that he did so twice. Dobi says, "How can you propose if you know she is under me?"

JUDGMENT   "Since there is no evidence that he ever slept with the girl," the vice-president says, "no to adultery." No witness steps forward. Dobi then wants Kachimba to pay just for having propositioned the woman, as Midia has admitted. This is interpreted by everyone later as a desperate gesture, for they believe that she agreed to come through in court and admit that they slept together. The court feels that it is perfectly natural for men to proposition women, and the president keeps repeating, "Get a witness before you get a summons."

Dobi gets worked up at this point: "If a man has a granary and I want sorghum, I cannot go there if I know the man refuses to sell. So my wife has a granary (meaning her body, which she can give or sell), and Kachimba has been around her though she has denied it here in court. She has killed me. I lose my case, and she has successfully betrayed me both in bed and again in court."

Dobi has to pay $3.60 for the long hearing. With a flourish the court clerk stamps the receipt loudly in the quiet room and hands it to the "convinced" party, Dobi. The hearing has lasted about an hour and a half, and by now Dobi seems to be taking it all right.

Before they leave, the vice-president says that it is always better to marry a girl of the same age. A woman in the audience waiting for a word with the court then claps and trills enthusiastically. The vice-president swells a bit and goes on: "Marry your own size, for she will want to go to dances, pleasure, play, but if you are bigger [older] you will only want to be respected in the house." Dobi was too old for the girl, in spirit if not in years, and he allowed his work and cronies to keep him away too long from a young and very beautiful girl. And he was too quick to go for a summons.

CONCLUSION   Dobi leaves—no one speaks to him—and wanders slowly down the path leading out of the village. Midia holds back near Kachimba as he remains seated and talks to some people. Then, as Kachimba studiously avoids even looking in her direction and walks out quickly, she wanders after the "big man," and at last, when Dobi reaches the road a mile or so away, she is beside him in silence, and they go off together.

Public Insult Related to Marriage

As illustrated in cases 1 through 5, fathers-in-law usually seek court action for elopement damages. Once these damages have been paid and the groom has delivered his *tsambo* bethrothal gift and won rights of cohabitation in the girl's village, the groom has the right to sue for adultery, as illustrated in case abstracts 6 and 7. A third kind of case may come later in the cycle, after *tsambo* and perhaps even after *pfuma* (bridewealth) have been delivered. This kind of case stems from jealousy and competition between women involved with the same man. It usually involves a woman whose marriage is legally secure and her husband's lover. In this situation the husband usually stays out of the picture if he can, preferring to retain both wife and lover. The wife usually seeks public redress for her injured pride and some financial compensation if she can find a willing witness to help her. Sometimes she may also be laying the basis for divorce action later. Most of these cases are aired fairly discreetly in the villages rather than the government court, and one rather blatant case that reached the court should suffice as an example.

Case Abstract 8: Public Insult

Zefa, Wife of the Court Vice-President, Siamwanja Village, Plaintiff, age Thirty-five, v. Katema, Siamuinga Village, Defendant, Age Twenty-nine

COMPLAINT   On April 15, 1968, at 7:00 P.M. at a beer party at the Lusitu Agricultural Camp, Katema insulted Zefa publicly. Compensation has been requested.

The President hears this case by himself, for the vice-president has taken his baby from his wife and is walking around with him outside. First the judge tries to determine why the women were fighting.

Plaintiff: Zefa tells her story first. She had been at a beer party at the agricultural camp most of the day, and at one point she found herself alone with Katema. Katema said to her, "You are a nice woman, but your husband will make you die." When Zefa asked why, Katema said, "One day when it was raining your husband came into my house to stay dry. He was talking against you and said that someday he would kill you." The two women then began arguing and cursing each other so loudly that Zefa's husband, Frank, came to them in the bushes and asked what was the matter. The women replied that it was a private matter, and he went away. A few minutes later he sent his sister, Saria, to call his wife back to the crowd. Saria returned and told them that the women were cursing each other. Frank then returned to them, and Zefa claims that she told him the whole story.

Defendant: Katema denies that she ever said those words about Frank.

Witness: Frank is then called back into the courtroom, and he denies that he ever went to Katema's house or said any words against his wife there.

Court: The president decides that the case cannot be settled until Saria can be brought to testify about what she overheard when the women were fighting. The case is adjourned.

The case has lasted from 10:45 to 11:30, and the court clerk later explains that such cases between two women over public insults are common. It is the only reason he can think of that one woman is likely to bring another woman to court.

The case is reconvened in May, 1968, and the long session can be summarized as follows: When the two women found themselves alone at the beer party, Katema, who is strikingly pretty, began making small talk to the baby on Zefa's back. Zefa snapped at Katema and asked her not to speak to the baby because "you are the one who sleeps with my husband. You slept with him during the rains one night, and that is why he came home late." Katema: "Now you have started this again, and last year we also quarreled about this." As their quarrel became noisy, Zefa's husband, Frank, came out to them and asked Zefa to come home with him for the beer was all gone. They would not tell him what the quarrel was about, and Zefa then drank from the pot of beer Frank was taking home. This was a nice show of her wifely rights because it would have seemed scandalous under these circumstances for the defendant to help herself from Frank's beerpot in that way. Frank says that he was bewildered. He then went back to the beer party, for the hosts had suddenly "discovered" another pot of beer, which they had been holding back for another time. Later he sent his sister, Saria, to fetch Zefa after their quarrel had started up again. By this time the women were ripping and tearing each other's clothes.

Everyone agrees that Saria did nothing to break up the fight, but Zefa noticed Saria watching them and asked her to get her husband in order to confront him with Katema's charges. Frank came back but left again as soon as the women tried to involve him in the quarrel. At this point both women admit that they were drunk.

Frank is pleased with himself as he tells how he took the baby from Zefa's back so that he would not be hurt. He then left to let them fight it out. "You fight now, and let us see who shall be the one who is beaten." He was eager to clear the air of this long-standing quarrel. Katema was a kinswoman and her brother was a leading male elder in Frank's village.

But Frank and the two women agree that the quarrel was not settled, and all three of them blame Saria for not doing anything to help break up the fight. The president praises Frank for sending his sister. Saria then admits her blame for having incited the women and helping Zefa to involve Frank.

JUDGMENT AND CONCLUSION   Zefa has to pay $1.80 hearing fee, since she was at fault for bringing the case with no proper witness. Zefa also has to pay $0.24 for the summons.

Zefa is most unhappy at this decision, and she harangues the court for a long time, standing and waving her arms as she recapitulates the whole story before she leaves. Saria, she claims, had seen Frank in the defendant's house and had promised to testify. The president wears a long-suffering expression and listens politely until she finally gives up.

Then the president says: "It is all right. No one pays any damages, and this is good. Otherwise there would be permanently hard feelings." Zefa goes on talking heatedly, while beautiful Katema sits very erect and poised. In all this she has said little, but her fingers are shaking as she occasionally sweeps her face. Both women are covered with flies from their long trek to the courthouse.

Zefa says: "Yes, no hard feelings. Katema is my friend; we live in the same village and both of us are women, but she does not talk to me. She only jokes with my husband. What do you make of that?"

Afterward I chat outside with the president, the clerk, the sergeant-at-arms and several elders, including Katema's brother.

They all agree that Katema is a beautiful woman, and they are in sympathy with her. Frank joins us momentarily and beams his agreement on that point. After he leaves, they all point out how very attractive he is to the women, very personable, "and strong in all things."

"Sure he is, why not?"

"Katema is unmarried, and she likes him."

"Ah, but there was no witness in court."

"Saria tricked Zefa after promising to help."

Otherwise they agree that Frank would have had to pay large damages to his wife and possibly to Katema's brother, who just grins and then says: "Oh, well, she is alone and what do you expect? Frank is a man."

A little later when I am alone with Frank, he shrugs and says, "I don't want two wives, so what can I do? Zefa is hard to handle. How could I live with both of them as cowives? Never any peace."

All of the men think that Zefa is a bit mean and cruel not to let the showy Frank play a little with such a lovely woman. One of the men sums it up this way:

She was too hasty. She should have been cannier with her witness and then she would have won. If a marriage partner wants to play and hide it, then it is wise to pretend that you do not know it. But if you duly find proof and proceed in a seemly way (none of this was seemly) it is all right to act as an injured party. This happens all the time. Yet if you are hasty, yell, beat, then all are against you, and none will stand up for you.

The man who spoke had been in court as an adulterer the week before.

Divorce

The next step for a woman in Zefa's position is to seek a divorce. Some typical divorces are illustrated in case abstracts 9 through 12 below.

Case Abstract 9: Divorce

Marita, Sialiyabwanda Village, Plaintiff and Wife v. *Siamungo, Kaliangile Village, Husband and Defendant*

COMPLAINT Marita wants a divorce because her husband does not treat her properly.

BACKGROUND   The plaintiff, Marita, is around forty. The defendant, Siamungo, is about fifty-two. Marita was married to the defendant's brother, and when he died, Siamungo succeeded to his brother's position. That was in 1959. Since that time two more children have been born to Marita. All marriage payments have long since been completed and are not at issue here.

TESTIMONY   The woman is asked to speak first, since it she who has sought action. She accompanies her story with continuous full-arm gesticulations. She speaks forcefully but sits turned at a ninety-degree angle away from her husband, never once looking at him.

She complains that her husband does not dress her or help her prepare her field. He does all this for his other wife, but not for her. She is wearing a faded dress and a shawl made from mealie-meal sacking. It is an uncommon sight, undoubtedly for the court's benefit. She says that her husband never comes to sleep with her but always goes to his other wife. At this everyone in the court laughs out loud, though inattention such as this is common grounds for divorce if it can be substantiated.

The husband answers that if he has not been the one to prepare her fields and buy her dresses all these years then he does not know who is the one who has done it. It was only this year that he did not do these things for her, and that was after he heard that she was going to divorce him. He says that whenever he comes to her house at night she runs away.

The woman denies this and says that last year she took her husband to task before the village council for the same reason. The husband interjects that it was for a different reason, because he had been cursing at her in the fields. One of the judges asks her if she has been cheating this man and only wants a divorce because she has found another man. The woman denies it.

The court tells the woman that she should have a witness for complaints. The wife responds that she has no one. The husband concludes by saying that he still wants to keep his wife.

At this point the judges call a recess to talk over their decision. The court clerk and some others sitting near me think that the judges will simply tell the woman to go home with her husband, saying that if he does these things again she can have a divorce then.

WITNESS   When the court reconvenes, Manchisi, the woman's brother, rises and asks to speak before the judges hand down their decision. He is a well-known elder with a good reputation. He says that his sister has come to him three times complaining that her husband does not dress her, help her cultivate, or sleep in her house. Manchisi says that he did not go personally to see how she was living because he did not want to make trouble. The judges speak together briefly. Manchisi turns his back on them and stuffs a handful of parched corn into his mouth.

JUDGMENT   The judges come to their decision quickly after the witness has spoken. The president says, "The woman is given the divorce because she went to her brother three times to ask for help."

The woman then says that if her husband tries to see her again, even though they are divorced, she will have to hang herself.

The woman pays $2.40 in court fees and $0.30 for the summons. The hearing has lasted from 9:45 to 10:35. The brother, Manchisi, walks out after the verdict but before the fees are paid. He stops and chats briefly with a friend on the way out, laughing loudly. He does not wait for his sister.

Case Abstract 10: Divorce

Jessica, ZhingaZhinga Village, Plaintiff and Wife, Age Twenty-three v. Philemon, ZhingaZhinga Village, Husband, Age Twenty-seven

COMPLAINT   The wife complains that her husband has not supported her or written her letters since he went to seek work in Lusaka. She wants a divorce.

The Woman's Story: Jessica has come to court with her father, who also lives in ZhingaZhinga Village. He pays the court fees for her and speaks up on her behalf several times during the hearing. Attractive younger women often have support of this kind when they come to court, especially if they live with their parents or other close relatives, while older women with poor reputations usually do not, as in cases 8 and 9. The couple were married in 1960. They have had four children; only one, a daughter, has survived. Jessica is very attractive.

She says that in 1967 she went to Lusaka with her husband when he went for work. One day he found her in the bush with another man. He sued the other man for adultery and collected damages. When they left the court, he told her that she could stay in town with him but she replied that she would rather go home to her village. He gave her money to ride the bus back to the Valley. After that he did not send her any money to take care of herself. Jessica says that he does not want to help her because of the adultery.

The Husband's Story: Philemon says that he gave Jessica an address to write to in case she needed anything but that she never wrote. He says that he still loves his wife and wants to keep her. He denies having treated her badly.

Witness: Johnny, Philemon's older brother, then testifies. He says that both the man and the woman are wrong. He points out that there has been trouble for a long time and reminds the court that Jessica's father told him that he wanted to reject Philemon several years ago. Jessica, for her part, has been seen at stores with various men from the neighboring villages and behaves very badly. They danced, smoked cigarettes, and drank beer or a soft drink. He asks the court to grant the divorce because otherwise Philemon might be moved to kill any man he finds with his wife.

CONCLUSION The court grants the divorce, and the woman pays the court fees. Since all the payments in the marriage are finished, Philemon will keep the surviving child, who happens to be a daughter and thus a source of future wealth. Johnny remarks that it is only fair that the father-in-law should keep the marriage payments because he has always been nice to Philemon. "It is only the woman who is bad." Johnny tells me privately later that they did not seek a return of the marriage payments because four children were born. Because Philemon has no other wife to care for his surviving daughter, the girl will be adopted by Johnny and cared for by one of his several wives.

Case Abstract 11: Divorce

Elina, Farao Village, wife and plaintiff v. *Mishek, Farao Village, Husband and Defendant*

Wife: He has been my husband since about 1953, and we have had five children together, and two of them died. In the last four years I have found that he has changed completely toward me and he has been ill-treating me badly in the house, beating me several times. I want a divorce.

Husband: I agree with all that she has been telling the court about me, and I have beaten her every now and then. This has been due to the fact that she has been very jealous of me and watches all my movements. She was very suspicious that I might be running up and down the towns with some common town prostitute instead of depending upon her. These suspicions were completely unfounded, but when the suspicions began she ran away from me in town, and she has been with her parents ever since.

Court [to the husband]: Do you want to continue your marriage to her?

Husband: Yes, I love my wife very much and do not want to divorce.

Wife [in answer to the same question]: No. I favor discontinuation of the marriage because he might kill me.

Wife's Father: As far as I can see he has been very cruel to his wife all these years and has beaten her many times. I am supporting her intention of ending this marriage. He paid me $36.00 *pfuma*, which I am willing to pay back if he should claim it. I am willing to do that to save my daughter.

JUDGMENT   Claim for the divorce is upheld on the defendant's admission to the facts of the case. He admitted to having beaten her and pulled off her dresses in public, and her parents have also supported her. He is ordered to pay $2.40 in court fees and also for the summons.

Case Abstract 12: Divorce

Elizabeth, Siambezyo Village, Wife and Plaintiff v. Simeon, Police Constable, Chirundu Township

Wife: He has been my husband since 1959 and has produced two children with me. But in 1964 he began neglecting me when he married another wife. He has not been feeding or clothing me and my children. Therefore I want to divorce him today.

Husband: I have nothing to tell the court, because my wife has asked for a divorce, which indicates that she does not love me. So for this reason I too agree that the marriage should be dissolved today provided that she keeps my children well. My bridewealth (*pfuma*) should not be returned to me, and all my clothes which I gave her should remain with her.

JUDGMENT AND CONCLUSION   The divorce is granted. The wife pays the court fees. This is a straightforward, typical case. Four to five years have been the conventional waiting time for a woman whose husband in the towns has not been heard from. A similar period has been accepted in cases where neglect is charged. In this case the husband is looking to his future claims to the marriage payments of his daughters and is making the divorce as agreeable as possible. Men attaining such elite jobs as police constable or any other permanent wage-paying job typically give up their village wives in favor of others more suitable to their new, higher status.

Child Custody

Case Abstract 13: Custody of Child

Eric, Chimowa Village, father of the child and plaintiff v. *Siamboko, storekeeper, Katwehele Village, guardian of the child and defendant*

BACKGROUND   The aged defendant is a wealthy storekeeper with many coresident kinsmen at his store but little influence at the court. Fifteen or sixteen years ago the plaintiff abducted the defendant's granddaughter, or "wombed her without my permission," as the local people usually put it. As the girl's guardian (*dundumuntuli*), the defendant took charge of the matter and the plaintiff was required to pay $96 in elopement damages. This was a notoriously large payment for an ordinary young villager in those days.

The defendant claims that at that point the plaintiff refused to continue with marriage cycle. In any event the couple separated. The plaintiff left the immediate area and had no further relations with the pregnant girl, who later gave birth to a daughter.

Many years later when the daughter was fifteen or sixteen and approaching the age of marriage, the plaintiff came to the defendant's store and bought some clothing and things for "his daughter," thus attempting to reestablish relations and make a claim to her forthcoming marriage payments. The defendant had the presents returned, saying: "Too late. You have never supported her, and so I will not let you start a claim now."

CONCLUSION   The defendant has taken care of his little great-grandchild all these years and has gotten used to her. He wants to keep her with him in his old age and see her marry uxorilocally at the store where her mother is.

But the court insists that he must accept some reasonable compensatory payment and give up custody of the child, at least in principle. The court wisely leaves it to the plaintiff and defendant to work out the details. The plaintiff pays the court fees.

The court's grounds for taking this position are interesting. In the village social system a *dundumuntuli* has rights and privileges over two classes of children: his own children (*vana*) and his *vazuk-uru*, his grandchildren or his sisters' children. Advancing age generally makes it impractical to wield much influence over great-grandchildren (*vazukuru chibvi*, literally "youngsters you bounce on your knee"). The court points out that the child in question is a *muzukuru chibvi* (singular), and thus the defendant has no traditional legal rights over her, especially since her "real father" in this case, the plaintiff or genitor, is willing to make an appropriate prestation to provide for the child's patrifiliation and mollify the defendant.

Because the plaintiff had paid a very substantial amount ($96) in damages, the court also felt that the great-grandchild's long childhood years had not been entirely unsupported by her father, as the defendant had claimed. In reinterpreting the significance of elopement damages in this way—as child support rather than a substitute for brideservice, the court was clearly reinforcing new trends toward the elimination of the bride-service custom altogether. A lower payment for damages would probably have softened the court's position, according to the court clerk.

No one connected with the court asked the girl's mother how she felt about this battle for custody of her child, and in fact that is never done in court cases of this kind. Custom provides for a mother's feelings through the rule that a child cannot be taken from its mother without her permission until it has reached puberty, around the age of fourteen or fifteen. Marriage for a girl usually comes a year or two later. Then if the child is a daughter she may be able to persuade her spouse to live with her mother in cases like this, if he can manage his financial obligations to the girl's father. That sometimes happens, and the father is usually content enough, having received part of the marriage prestations and established his rightful claims to the remainder.

Divorced fathers apparently never make retroactive marriage prestations to filiate their sons. In the Goba system of dual descent that is not considered strictly necessary for sons any more than it is for daughters, though in the case of a daughter payment of *pfuma* establishes the father's formal claim to her marriage payments. Fathers may help sons with their token *tsambo* betrothal payments in cases where an emotional tie exists, however.

To sum up, the position of the court is that a divorced father who has paid elopement damages (originally levied in lieu of service in residence) has established the right to reappear years later when the children have reached puberty to make a retroactive prestation for the formal patrifiliation of individual females to receive their marriage payments. This practice mitigates the harsh effects of the bride-service cycle on young men. Once he has delivered elopement damages and has been driven away, as happened in this case, the father is not considered responsible for his child's support. The child is attached to its mother during the prepuberty years in any event, and, like the mother, the child subsists from the mother's labor, which would be necessary in any event. That is often accomplished with little help from the father. Then when father reappears years later, his elopement damages have already been paid, and a *pfuma* prestation allows him to complete his interrupted marriage cycle and claim the proceeds from his daughter's marriage. There are strong spiritual sanctions favoring the husband in this respect, for, in local thinking, only a slave can be deprived of his rights in his children. In this case it is rights to a girl's marriage prestations that the man is primarily interested in.

Because the marriage cycle is usually long and a man's full rights in his wife and children develop slowly through a period of many years, in contrast to a mother's rights, which are full blown at birth, in cases involving child custody there is much debate over whether the genitor of a daughter really has the right to receive her marriage prestations. He may never have lived with the daughter's mother in legal sense, or not for a long time; he may not have contributed anything to her daughter's support, including school fees, which are gradually becoming necessary in local thinking, even for girls. Yet the nature of the bride-service system is such that fathers are often driven away from their children in the early stages of the cycle, when their rights are minimally developed. The Goba recognize that separation may be unjust and that it does not necessarily mean that a man's rights should be forgotten. Under their system of dual descent the Goba automatically think of the genitor as a potential social father (pater), whose rights should eventually parallel and complement those of the mother, unless he has clearly been at fault in his family relations.

In connection with this it appears that a man who has paid a substantial sum for elopement damages gains some "extralegal" consideration. Technically, and traditionally, the damages have been meant to compensate the group that controls the young woman's sexuality. In precolonial times and in the early years of the twentieth century, this group was usually her mother's group. While it was always held, ideally, that it should also be her father's group, as long as brideservice was a lifetime affair that was in fact the case only when endogamy or adoptive slavery made the father's group coincide with the mother's group or when an unusually influential father was able to abbreviate his bride-service commitments and gain a full measure of father right. In that event rights in the woman would be shared by both groups. Today the acceptance of cash in marriage prestations places most men in a position to terminate the cycle in their lifetime, and the old system based largely on mother right, is under pressure. Now it is commonly the father's group that controls the woman's sexuality and receives her marriage prestations. Now the mother's rights in her daughter's marriage wealth are permanently salvageable only by endogamy or by divorce before elopement damages have been accepted. As a result there is considerable strain between the sexes, as perhaps there has always been, and a high rate of both endogamy and divorce in the early trial stages of marriage.

Elopement damages have been meant to compensate whichever group controls the woman's sexuality. A surprise elopement removes the right to control whom, when, and under what circumstances she will marry. Because elopements often continue while the groom saves to pay his damages, the woman's group generally loses her company and his for a number of years and also loses any services they might have provided. Damages have been intended to make up for this. Since they come early in the marriage cycle, they have obviously favored the mother's group.

The new "extralegal" aspects of damages are illustrated in case abstract 13. They pertain to the later stages of the cycle and favor the father. If a young man has paid large damages and done nothing else, perhaps even vanishing for a number of years, he may nonetheless return as his daughters approach a wealth-producing age and successfully claim the right to deliver *pfuma* and receive their marriage prestations. Payment of a large claim for damages is thus being taken as an indication of some good faith on a lover's part. It is true that he often *would* have gone further had he not been discouraged by his wife's guardians, as happened in case 13. As a corollary, it indicates what the government court thinks of elders who make very large claims for damages. The judges clearly take the side of the young men, being themselves relatively young and progressive. Case 8, in which the court vice-president was the central male figure, illustrates the court's attitude toward relations between the sexes. Case 13 also indicates that Goba men are considered to have inherent rights to the children, despite the attempted controls of the elders.

Wives may win a divorce in court, but here too the tendency is to favor the men. Even when the court rules in favor of the wife in a divorce proceeding, she normally is required to pay the court fees. Since she has only a small cash income of her own, this decision by an all-male institution increases her dependence on other males. It is unusual for a winner in court to pay the fees. Fees usually are paid by the losing party, as in cases 1, 2, 3, 5, 7, 8, and 13. In case 11 the woman won her divorce, but an exception was made, and her husband had to pay the fees because the court felt that he was very deeply at fault. In all the other successful divorce cases brought and won by women that have been cited here to illustrate general practice (cases 4, 9, 10, and 12), the woman has paid the fees because the court felt that it is basically wrong for women to divorce their husbands. Case 6 is instructive in this regard, for the winner also had to pay the court fees. It was a case in which the winner won a major $120 award for adultery, which the judges privately felt was unjust to the male defendant and really the fault of the woman.

Bibliography

Aberle, David F.
1961   Matrilineal descent in cross-cultural perspective. In *Matrilineal kinship*, ed. D. M. Schneider and K. Gough. Berkeley: University of California Press.
Abraham, Donald P.
1962   The early political history of the kingdom of Mwana Mutapa. In *Historians in tropical Africa*. Salisbury: International African Institute.
1964   Ethno-history of the empire of Mutapa. In *The historian in tropical Africa*, ed. J. Vansina et al. London: International African Institute.
1966   The roles of "Chaminuka" and the Mhondoro cults in Shona political history. In *The Zambesian past*, ed. E. Stokes and R. Brown. Manchester: Institute for Social Research, University of Zambia.
Allan, William
1965   *The African husbandmen*. New York: Barnes and Noble.
———; Gluckman, M.; Peters, D. U.; and Trapnell, C. G.
1948   *Land holding and land usage among the Plateau Tonga of Mazabuka District*. Rhodes-Livingstone Paper no. 14.
Alpers, E. A.
1970   Dynasties of the Mutapa-Rozwi Complex. *Journal of African History* 11:203–20.
Alvord, E. D.
1929   Agricultural life of Rhodesian natives. *Southern Rhodesia Native Affairs Department Annual* 7:9–16.
Andrade, Antonio Alberto de
1955   *Relacoes de Mocambique setecentista*. Lisboa: Ministerio de Ultramar.
Axelson, Eric
1960   *Portuguese in south-east Africa, 1600–1700*. Johannesburg: Witwatersrand University Press.

1967   *Portugal and the scramble for Africa, 1875–1891.* Johannesburg: Witwatersrand University Press.
Bailey, F. G.
    1971   *Gifts and poison.* Oxford: Blackwell.
Bainbridge, W. R., and Edmonds, A. C. R.
    n.d.   "Northern Rhodesia Forest Department management book for Gwembe, South Choma, and South Mazabuka districts" (manuscript).
Barnes, John A.
    1949   Measures of divorce frequency in simple societies. *Journal of the Royal Anthropological Institute* 79:37–62.
    1951   *Marriage in a changing society: a study in structural change among the Fort Jameson Ngoni.* Rhodes-Livingstone Paper no. 20.
    1967   The frequency of divorce. In *The craft of social anthropology,* ed. A. L. Epstein. Manchester: Manchester University Press.
Barreto, M.
    1667   *Report upon the state and conquest of the rivers of Cuama.* Translation reprinted in *Records of south-eastern Africa,* G. Mc. Theal, ed. 3:436–95. Cape Town: 1899.
Barros, J. de
    1552   *Decadas da Asia.* Translated extracts reprinted in *Records of south-eastern Africa,* ed. G. Mc. Theal, 6:1–306. Cape Town: 1900.
Barth, F.
    1966   *Models of social organization.* Royal Anthropological Institute of Great Britain and Ireland Occasional Paper no. 23.
Bettison, David G.
    1961   Changes in the composition and status of kin groups in Nyasaland and Northern Rhodesia. In *Social change in modern Africa,* ed. A. Southall. London: International African Institute.
Bocarro, A.
    1876   *Livro do estado da India.* Translated extracts reprinted in *Records of south-eastern Africa,* G. Mc. Theal. 3:254–435. Cape Town: 1899.
Bond, G., and Clark, J. Desmond
    1954   The quaternary sequence in the middle Zambezi Valley. *South African Archeological Bulletin* 9:115–30.
Boserup, Ester
    1970   *Women's role in economic development.* London: Allan and Unwin.
    1975   *Integration of women in development.* New York: United Nations.
Bott, Elizabeth
    1957   *Family and social network.* London: Tavistock.

Bourdillon, M. F. C.
1972 The manipulation of myth in a Tavara chiefdom. *Africa* 42:112–21.

Brush, S. B.
1975 The concept of carrying capacity for systems of shifting cultivation. *American Anthropologist* 77:799–811.

Bullock, C.
1928. *The Mashona*. Cape Town: Juta.

Cabral, A. A. P.
1925 *Racas, usos e costumes dos indigenas*. Lourenzo Marques: Imprensa Nacional.

Carlson, Lucille
1967 *Africa's lands and nations*. New York: McGraw-Hill.

Chaplin, James H.
1960 A preliminary account of Iron Age burials with gold in the Gwembe Valley, Northern Rhodesia. *Proceedings of the First Federal Scientific Congress, 1960*, p. 397–406.

Chigumi
1923 "Kugarira" or "Uguriri." *Southern Rhodesia Native Affairs Department Annual* 1:79–81.

Chock, P. P.
1967 Kinship and culture: some problems in Ndembu kinship. *Southwestern Journal of Anthropology* 23:74–89.

Clark, J. Desmond
1950 A note on the pre-Bantu inhabitants of Northern Rhodesia and Nyasaland. *Northern Rhodesia Journal* 2:45–52.

Clements, Frank
1959 *Kariba*. London: Methuen.

Coale, A. J., and Demeny, P.
1966 *Regional model life tables and stable populations*. New Jersey: Princeton University Press.

Colson, Elizabeth
1948 Rain-shrines and the Plateau Tonga of Northern Rhodesia. *Africa* 18:272–83.
1951 The role of cattle among the Plateau Tonga of Mazabuka District. *Rhodes-Livingstone Journal* 11:10–46.
1958 *Marriage and the family among the Plateau Tonga of Northern Rhodesia*. Manchester: Rhodes-Livingstone Institute.
1960 *Social organization of the Gwembe Tonga*. Manchester: Rhodes-Livingstone Institute.
1962 *The Plateau Tonga of Northern Rhodesia*. Manchester: Rhodes-Livingstone Institute.
1967 The intensive study of small sample communities. In *The Craft of Social Anthropology*, A. L. Epstein. Manchester: Manchester University Press.
1969 African Society at the time of the scramble. In *Colonialism in Africa 1870–1960*, ed. L. Gann and P. Duignan. Cambridge:

Cambridge University Press.
1971 *The social consequences of resettlement: the impact of the Kariba resettlement upon the Gwembe Tonga.* Manchester: Institute for African Studies, University of Zambia.
—— and Scudder, Thayer
1975 New economic relationships between the Gwembe Valley and the line of rail. In *Town and Country in Zambia*, ed. D. Parkin. Pp. 190–210. Oxford: International African Institute.

Conceicao, Frei Antonio da
1696 Tratados dos rios de Cuama. Original reprinted in *O Chronista de Tissuary Periodico*, ed. J. H. da Cunha Rivara. 2:39–45, 63–69, 84–92, 105–11. Nova Goa: 1867.

Conklin, H. C.
1957 *Hanunoo agriculture.* Rome: Food and Agriculture Organization, United Nations.

Davies, D. H.
1972 *Zambia in maps.* New York: Africana.

Dotson, F., and Dotson, L.
1968 *The Indian minority of Zambia, Rhodesia, and Malawi.* New Haven: Yale University Press.

Dumont, Rene
1968 *False start in Africa.* London: Sphere.

Epstein, A. L.
1953 The role of African courts in the urban communities of the Northern Rhodesian Copperbelt. *Rhodes-Livingstone Journal* 13:1–17.

Evans-Pritchard, E. E.
1940 *The Nuer.* Oxford: Clarendon Press.
1945 *Some aspects of marriage and the family among the Nuer.* Rhodes-Livingstone Paper no. 11.

Fagan, Brian M.
1965 *Southern Africa.* London: Thames and Hudson.
1969 Excavations at Ingombe Ilede, 1960–62. In *Iron Age cultures in Zambia*, eds. B. M. Fagan, D. W. Phillipson & S. G. H. Daniels. Vol. 2. London: Chatto & Windus.
1972 *Ingombe Ilede: early trade in south central Africa.* Addison-Wesley Modular Publications no. 19.

Fanshawe, D. G.
1962 *Fifty common trees of Northern Rhodesia.* Lusaka: Government Printer.

Faria y Sousa, M. de
1674 *Asia Portuguesa.* Vol. 2. Translated extracts reprinted in *Records of South-Eastern Africa*, ed. G. Mc. Theal. 1:18–31. Cape Town, 1889.

Federation of Rhodesia and Nyasaland
1962 *Report of the commission of inquiry into the sugar industry.* Salisbury: Government Printer.

Floyd, Barry N.
1959 *Changing patterns of African land use in Southern Rhodesia*. Lusaka: Rhodes-Livingstone Institute.

Fortes, Meyer
1953 The structure of unilineal descent groups. *American Anthropologist* 55:17–41.
1961 Pietas in ancestor worship. *Journal of the Royal Anthropological Institute* 91:166–91.
1969 *Kinship and the social order*. Chicago: Aldine.

Foskett, R., ed.
1965 *The Zambesi journal and letters of Dr. John Kirk, 1858–1863*. Vol. 1. London: Oliver and Boyd.

Fox, Robin
1967 Kinship and marriage. Baltimore: Penquin.

Gann, L. H.
1958 *The birth of a plural society: the development of Northern Rhodesia under the British South Africa Company, 1894–1914*. Manchester: Rhodes-Livingstone Institute.

Garbett, G. K.
1963 The land husbandry act of Southern Rhodesia. In *African agrarian systems*, ed. D. Biebuyck. London: Oxford University Press.
1966 Religious aspects of political succession among the Valley Korekore (N. Shona). In *The Zambesian Past*, ed. E. Stokes and R. Brown. Manchester: Institute for Social Research, University of Zambia.
1967 Prestige, status, and power in a modern Valley Korekore chiefdom, Rhodesia. *Africa* 37:307–26.
1969 Spirit mediums as mediators in Korekore society. In *Spirit mediumship and society in Africa*, eds. J. Beattie and J. Middleton. New York: Africana.

Garlake, Peter S.
1973 *Great Zimbabwe*. London: Thames and Hudson.

Gibbons, A. St. Hill
1904 *Africa from south to north through Marotseland*. 2 vols. London: John Lane.

Gluckman, Max
1950 Kinship and marriage among the Lozi of Northern Rhodesia and the Zulu of Natal. In *African systems of kinship and marriage*, eds. A. R. Radcliffe-Brown and C. D. Forde. London: International African Institute.
1956 Social anthropology in Central Africa. *Rhodes-Livingstone Journal* 20:1–27.
1961 Ethnographic data in British social anthropology. *Sociological Review* 9:5–17.

Gluckman, M., and Eggan, F.
1965 Introduction. In *The relevance of models for social anthro-*

pology, eds. M. Gluckman and Eggan. London: Tavistock.

————; Barnes, J. A.; and Mitchell, J. Clyde
   1949   The village headman in British Central Africa. *Africa* 19:89–104.

Gomes, Antonio
   1644   Viagem que fez o Padre Ant. o Gomes, da Comp. a de Jesus, ao Imperio de le [sic] Manomotapa; e assistencia que fez nas ditas terras d. e Alg'us Annos, ed. E. Axelson. *Studia* 3(1959):155–242.

Goodenough, Ward
   1951   *Property, kin, and community on Truk*. New Haven: Yale University Press.

Goody, John R.
   1961   The classification of double descent systems. *Current Anthropology* 2:3–25.
   1973   Bridewealth and dowry in Africa and Eurasia. In *Bridewealth and dowry*, eds. J. Goody and S. Tambiah. Cambridge: Cambridge University Press.
   1976   *Production and reproduction*. Cambridge: Cambridge University Press.

Government of the Republic of Zambia
   1964   *Second report of the May/June, 1963, census of Africans*.
   1966   *Review of the operations of the Agricultural Marketing Commission during the year ended 30th June, 1966*. Lusaka: Government Printer.
   1969   *The Zambian industrial directory*. Lusaka: Government Printer.

Guerreiro, J. de Alcantara
   1944.   As minas de prata da Chicoa em um relatorio do seculo XVII *Mozambique* 39:7–91.

Harding, C.
   1905   *In remotest Barotseland*. London: Hurst and Blackett.

Harlan, J. R.; DeWet, J.; and Stemler, A., eds.
   1976   *Origins of African plant domestication*. The Hague: Mouton.

Hiernaux, Jean
   1974   *The people of Africa*. New York: Scribners.

Holleman, J. F.
   1951   Some "Shona" tribes of Southern Rhodesia. In *Seven tribes of British Central Africa*, ed. E. Colson and M. Gluckman. Manchester: Rhodes-Livingstone Institute.
   1952   *Shona customary law*. London: Oxford University Press.

Holub, Emile
   1975   *Emile Holub's travels north of the Zambezi, 1885–86*, ed. L. Holy. Manchester: Institute for Social Research, University of Zambia.

Howarth, D.
   1961   *The Shadow of the dam*. New York: Macmillan.

Huffman, T. N.
  1970 The Early Iron Age and the spread of the Bantu. *South African Archaeological Bulletin* 25:3–21.
  1971 A guide to the Iron Age of Mashonaland. *Occasional Papers of the National Museum of Rhodesia* 4:20–44.
Jackson, P. B. N.
  1961 *Ichthyology: The fish of the middle Zambezi*. Manchester: Manchester University Press.
Jordan, E. Knowles
  1959 Feira in 1919–20. *Northern Rhodesia Journal* 4:63–71.
Kay, George
  1967a *A social geography of Zambia*. London: University of London Press.
  1967b Maps of the distribution and density of African population in Zambia. University of Zambia Institute for Social Research Communication no. 2.
Keesing, R. M.
  1975 *Kin groups and social structure*. New York: Holt, Rinehart and Winston.
Keigwin, John
  1935 The Cambridge expedition to the Zambezi Valley, Southern Rhodesia, in 1934. *Geographical Journal* 86:252–62.
Kosmin, Barry A.
  1974 The Inyoka tobacco industry of the Shangwe. *African Social Research* 17:554–77.
Kuper, Adam
  1975 The social structure of the Sotho-speaking peoples of southern Africa, Part 2, *Africa* 45:139–49.
Kuper, Hilda
  1954 *The Shona*. London: International African Institute.
Lacerda, F. D. de
  1944 *Os Cafres*. Lisboa: Livraria Rodrigues.
Lacerda, Jose de
  1867 *Exame das viagens do Doutor Livingstone*. Lisboa: Imprensa Nacional.
Lancaster, C. S.
  1971 The economics of social organization in an ethnic border zone: The Goba (Northern Shona) of the Zambezi Valley. *Ethnology* 10:445–65.
  1974a Brideservice, residence, and authority among the Goba (N. Shona) of the Zambezi Valley. *Africa* 44:46–64.
  1974b Ethnic identity, history, and "tribe" in the middle Zambezi Valley. *American Ethnologist* 1:707–30.
  1976 Women, horticulture, and society in sub-Saharan Africa. *American Anthropologist* 78:539–64.
  1977 The Zambezi Goba ancestral cult. *Africa* 47:229–41.
——, and Pohorilenko, Anatole

1977   Ingombe Ilede and the Zimbabwe culture. *International Journal of African Historical Studies* 10:1–30.

1979*a* The Portuguese frontier in western Mozambique, 1890: a translation of the report of the governor of the district of Zumbo. *Papers in Anthropology* 20:63–91.

1979*b* The influence of extensive agriculture on the study of sociopolitical organization and the interpretation of history. *American Ethnologist* 6:329–48.

Leacock, Eleanor B.
1972   Introduction. In *The origin of the family, private property, and the state*, ed. F. Engels. New York: International.

Lee, Richard B.
1969   !Kung Bushman subsistence. In *Environment and culture*, ed. A. P. Vayda. Garden City, N.Y.: Natural History Press.

Lewis, I. M.
1959   The classification of African political systems. *Rhodes-Livingstone Journal* 25:59–69.

Livingstone, David
1858   *Missionary travels and researches in south Africa*. New York: Harper and Brothers.

———, and Livingstone, Charles
1865   *Narrative of an expedition to the Zambesi and its tributaries*. London: John Murray.

Lobato, Alexandre
1962   *Colonizacao senhorial da Zambezia e outros estudos*. Lisboa: Junta de Investigacoes do Ultramar.

Long, Norman
1968   *Social change and the individual*. Manchester: Institute for Social Research.

Lopes, M. M.
1907   Usages and customs of the natives of Sena. *Journal of the African Society* 6:350–66.

Mair, Lucy A.
1969   *African marriage and social change*. London: Frank Cass.

Marwick, Max
1965   *Sorcery in its social setting: A study of the Northern Rhodesian Cewa*. Manchester: Manchester University Press.

Maxey, Kees
1975   *The fight for Zimbabwe*. New York: Africana.

Middleton, John and Tait, David, eds.
1958   *Tribes without rulers*. London: Routledge.

Mitchell, J. Clyde
1949   An estimate of fertility in some Yao hamlets in Liwonde District of southern Nyasaland. *Africa* 19:293–308.

1956   *The Yao village*. Manchester: Rhodes-Livingstone Institute.

1957   Aspects of African marriage on the Copperbelt of Northern

Rhodesia. *Rhodes-Livingstone Journal* 22:1–30.

1961 Social change and the stability of African marriage in Northern Rhodesia. In *Social Change in Modern Africa*, ed. A. Southall. London: International African Institute.

1963 Marriage stability and social structure in Bantu Africa. In *Proceedings of the International Union for the Study of Population*. Vol. 2. London.

1967 On quantification in Social Anthropology. In *The Craft of Social Anthropology*, ed. A. L. Epstein. Manchester: Manchester University Press.

1969 The concept and use of social networks. In *Social networks in urban situations*. Manchester: Manchester University Press.

————, and Barnes, John A.

1950 *The Lamba village*. Communications from the School of African Studies, no. 24. Cape Town.

Montgomery, E.; Bennett, J. W.; and Scudder, T.

1973 The impact of human activities on the physical and social environments. *Annual Review of Anthropology* 2:27–61.

Murdock, George Peter

1949 Social structure. New York: Macmillan.

1959a Evolution in social organization. In *Evolution and anthropology*, ed. B. J. Meggers. Washington, D.C.: Anthropological Society of Washington.

1959b *Africa*. New York: McGraw-Hill.

Netting, Robert Mc.

1968 *Hill farmers of Nigeria*. Seattle: University of Washington Press.

Northern Rhodesia Government Reports

1951–56 *Annual Report, Department of Agriculture*. Lusaka: Government Printer.

nd The Gwembe District Notebook

Oliver, Roland

1966 The problem of the Bantu expansion. *Journal of African History* 2:1–13.

————, and Fagan, Brian M.

1975 *Africa in the Iron Age, c. 500 B.C. to A.D. 1400*. Cambridge: Cambridge University Press.

Phillips, John F. V.

1959 *Agriculture and ecology in Africa*. New York: Praeger.

Phillipson, David W.

1968 The early Iron Age in Zambia. *Journal of African History* 9:191–211.

1969 Later Iron Age sites in the Ingombe Ilede region. In *Iron Age cultures in Zambia*, ed. B. Fagan, D. Phillipson, and S. Daniels. Vol. 2. London: Chatto and Windus.

1972 Kasoko, a Portuguese entrepot in the middle Zambezi Valley.

Zambia Museums Journal 3:35–48.

1974 Iron Age history and archaeology in Zambia. *Journal of African History* 15:1–26.

1975 The chronology of the Iron Age in Bantu Africa. *Journal of African History* 16:32–42.

1978 *The Later prehistory of eastern and southern Africa.* London: Heinemann.

Radcliffe-Brown, A. R.

1935 Patrilineal and matrilineal succession. In *Structure and function in primitive society.* London: Cohen and West.

1950 Introduction. In *African systems of kinship and marriage,* ed. A. R. Radcliffe-Brown and C. D. Forde. London: International African Institute.

1951 Murngin social organization. *American Anthropologist* 53:37–55.

Read, J. Gordon

1932 *Report on famine relief: Gwembe, 1931–32.* Livingstone: Government Printer.

Reynolds, Barrie

1968 *The material culture of the peoples of the Gwembe Valley.* Manchester: National Museums of Zambia.

Ribeiro, Manuel F.

1879 *As conferencias e o itinerario do viajante Serpa Pinto atravez das terras da Africa austral nos limites das provincias de Angola e Mocambique—bie a Soshong.* Lisboa: Minerva.

Richards, Audrey I.

1932 *Hunger and work in a savage tribe.* London: Routledge.

1934 Mother-right among the Central Bantu. In *Essays presented to C. G. Seligman,* ed. E. E. Evans-Pritchard et al. London: Kegan Paul, Trench, Trubner.

1939 *Land, labour, and diet in Northern Rhodesia.* London: International African Institute.

1950 Some types of family structure amongst the Central Bantu. In *African systems of kinship and marriage,* eds. A. R. Radcliffe-Brown and C. D. Forde. London: International African Institute.

1956 *Chisungu.* New York: Grove Press.

1960 Social mechanisms for the transfer of political rights in some African tribes. *Journal of the Royal Anthropological Institute,* 90:175–90.

1963 Multi-tribalism in African urban areas. In *Urbanization in African social change.* Proceedings of the Inaugural Seminar held at the Center of African Studies, University of Edinburgh.

Robbins, Eric, and Legge, Ronald

1959 *Animal Dunkirk: The story of Kariba Dam.* New York: Taplinger.

Santos, Frei Joao dos
   1609   *Eastern Ethiopia.* Translated extracts reprinted in *Records of South-Eastern Africa,* ed. G. Mc. Theal. 7:1–370. Cape Town, 1901.
Schapera, Isaac
   1929   Matrilocal marriage in Southern Rhodesia. *Man* 29:113–17.
   1937   *The Bantu-speaking tribes of south Africa,* ed. I. Schapera. London: Routledge and Kegan Paul.
Schlegel, Alice
   1972   *Male dominance and female autonomy: domestic authority in matrilineal societies.* New Haven: Human Relations Area Files Press.
Schneider, David M.
   1962   The distinctive features of matrilineal descent groups. In *Matrilineal kinship,* eds. D. Schneider and K. Gough. Berkeley: University of California Press.
Scudder, Thayer
   1960*a*   Environment and a culture. *Natural History* 69:6–17.
   1960*b*   Fishermen of the Zambezi. *Human Problems in British Central Africa* 27:41–49.
   1962   *The ecology of the Gwembe Tonga.* Manchester: Rhodes-Livingstone Institute.
   1969   Relocation, agricultural intensification and anthropological research. In *The anthropology of development in sub-Saharan Africa,* eds. D. Brokensha and M. Pearsall. Monographs of the Society for Applied Anthropology no. 10.
   1971   *Gathering among African woodland savannah cultivators: a case study of the Gwembe Tonga.* Zambian Papers no. 5.
   ———, and Colson, Elizabeth
   1972   The Kariba Dam project: resettlement and local initiative. In *Technology and social change,* ed. H. Bernard and P. Pelto. Pp. 40–69. New York: Macmillan.
Shamuyarira, Nathan
   1967   *Crisis in Rhodesia.* Nairobi: East Africa Publishing House.
Schuster, I. M. G.
   1979   *New women of Lusaka.* Palo Alto: Mayfield.
Skelton, R. A.
   1958   *Explorer's maps.* London: Routledge and Kegan Paul.
Smith, Edwin W.
   1949   Addendum to the "Ila-speaking peoples of Northern Rhodesia." *African Studies* 8:1–9, 53–61.
   ———, and Dale, A. M.
   1920   *The Ila-speaking peoples of Northern Rhodesia.* London: Macmillan.
Smith, Raymond T.
   1973   The matrifocal family. In *The character of kinship,* ed. J. Goody. London: Cambridge University Press.

Smithers, R. H. N.
  1966 *The mammals of Rhodesia, Zambia, and Malawi*. London: Collins.
Soper, R.
  1971 A general review of the early Iron Age in the southern half of Africa. *Azania* 6:5–37.
Stanner, W. E. H.
  1961 Comments on Goody: the classification of double descent systems. *Current Anthropology* 2:20–21.
Stefaniszyn, Bronislaw
  1964 *Social and ritual life of the Ambo of Northern Rhodesia*. London: International African Institute.
Summers, R.
  1969 *Ancient mining in Rhodesia*. Bulawayo: National Museums of Rhodesia.
Sutton, J. E. G.
  1972 New radiocarbon dates for eastern and southern Africa. *Journal of African History* 13:1–24.
Tabler, E. C.
  1963 *The Zambezi papers of Richard Thornton: geologist to Livingstone's Zambezi expedition*. Vol. 1. London: Chatto and Windus.
Theal, George McCall
  1898– *Records of south-eastern Africa*. vols. 1–9. Reprint
  1903   ed. Cape Town: Struik, 1964.
Thomson, James
  1934 *Memorandum on the native tribes and tribal areas of Northern Rhodesia*. Livingstone: Government Printer.
Trapnell, Colin G., and Clothier, J. N.
  1937 *The soils, vegetation, and agricultural systems of northwestern Rhodesia: report of the ecological survey*. Lusaka: Government Printer.
Turnbull, Colin M.
  1968 The importance of flux in two hunting societies. In *Man the Hunter*, eds. R. Lee and I. DeVore. Chicago: Aldine.
Turner, Victor W.
  1957 *Schism and continuity in an African society*. Manchester: Rhodes-Livingstone Institute.
Tylor, Edward
  1889 On a method of investigating the development of institutions; applied to laws of marriage and descent. *Journal of the Royal Anthropological Institute* 18:245–69.
Van Onselen, C.
  1974 The 1912 Wankie Colliery strike. *Journal of African History* 15:275–90.

Vansina, Jan
  1966 *Kingdoms of the savanna*. Madison: University of Wisconsin Press.
Watson, William
  1958 *Tribal cohesion in a money economy*. Manchester: Rhodes-Livingstone Institute.
Weeks, J. H.
  1975 Employment and the growth of towns. In *The population factor in African studies*, eds. R. P. Moss and R. Rathbone. London: University of London Press.
Weinrich, A. K. H.
  1975 *African farmers in Rhodesia*. London: International African Institute.
White, F.
  1962 *Forest flora of Northern Rhodesia*. Oxford: Oxford University Press.
White, J. D.
  1970 Oral traditions in Urungwe. *South African Archaeological Bulletin 25:40–41*.
  1971 *Some notes on the history and customs of the Urungwe District. Southern Rhodesia Native Affairs Department Annual* 10:33–72.
Wilson, Monica, and Thompson, Leonard, eds.
  1969 *The Oxford history of South Africa*. Vol. 1. Oxford: Clarendon Press.
Wittwer, S. H.
  1975 Food production. *Science* 188:579–84.
Yanagisako, S. J.
  1977 Women-centered kin networks in urban bilateral kinship. *American Ethnologist* 4:207–26.
Yudelman, Montague
  1964 *Africans on the land*. Cambridge: Harvard University Press.

Index